PARLIAMENTARISM AND ENCYCLOPAEDISM

This book explores a specific aspect of modern parliamentarism: its ability to produce and organise political knowledge.

The book argues that the very meaning of modern parliamentarism cannot properly be understood without considering the cognitive value that is inherent in the representative function discharged by parliaments, vis-a-vis the political community. It does so by studying the 'encyclopaedic patterns' underlying modern parliamentarism. Exploring the concept from ancient times to modernity, it addresses the fundamental question of the relationship between knowledge and democratic decision-making.

This is a truly innovative book; challenging, provocative and asking crucial questions of how parliaments work and legislate.

Volume 9 in the series Parliamentary Democracy in Europe

Parliamentary Democracy in Europe

The European Union is founded on the idea of 'representative democracy'. Its citizens are directly represented in the European Parliament, but Union democracy is equally based on indirect forms of representation especially through the European Council and the Council – two Union institutions whose members will be democratically accountable to their national parliaments. The good functioning of the Union democracy assumes, therefore, the good functioning of the democratic institutions of each Member State.

What is the role and relationship between the European and the national parliaments in the democratic functioning of the Union? Do they exercise distinct or complementary functions? Has the European Parliament adopted a structure similar to national parliaments; and how do national parliaments assume their 'European' functions? These questions have gained particular relevance in recent years. Not only has the Lisbon Treaty conferred new functions upon national parliaments, especially concerning the scrutiny on the compliance with the subsidiarity principle (the so called 'Early Warning System'), the coordination of fiscal and economic policies at the European level has led to significant restrictions of national parliamentary powers.

The new Hart Series on 'Parliamentary Democracy in Europe', encompassing both monographs and edited collections, aims to answer some of these questions. The series offers new insights into rules and conventions shaping parliaments and parliamentary democracy in Europe. Its aim is to provide a better understanding of the role parliaments are playing in European constitutional law and its idea of 'representative democracy'.

Series Editors

Nicola Lupo
Robert Schütze

Interparliamentary Cooperation in the Composite European Constitution
Edited by Nicola Lupo and Cristina Fasone

The Italian Parliament in the European Union
Edited by Nicola Lupo and Giovanni Piccirilli

The Principle of Subsidiarity and its Enforcement in the EU Legal Order: The Role of National Parliaments in the Early Warning System
Katarzyna Granat

Parliamentary Oversight of the Executives: Tools and Procedure in Europe
Elena Griglio

The Internationalisation of Constitutional Law: A View from the Venice Commission
Sergio Bartole

Executive-legislative (Im)balance in the European Union: (Im)balance in the European Union
Edited by Diane Fromage and Anna Herranz-Surrallés

Germany's Dual Constitution: Parliamentary Democracy in the Federal Republic
Florian Meinel

The European Parliament and Delegated Legislation: An Institutional Balance Perspective
Merijn Chamon

Parliamentarism and Encyclopaedism: Parliamentary Democracy in an Age of Fragmentation
Giovanni Rizzoni

Parliamentarism and Encyclopaedism

Parliamentary Democracy in an Age of Fragmentation

Giovanni Rizzoni

•HART•
OXFORD • LONDON • NEW YORK • NEW DELHI • SYDNEY

HART PUBLISHING

Bloomsbury Publishing Plc

Kemp House, Chawley Park, Cumnor Hill, Oxford, OX2 9PH, UK

1385 Broadway, New York, NY 10018, USA

29 Earlsfort Terrace, Dublin 2, Ireland

First published in Great Britain 2024

A catalogue record for this book is available from the British Library.

A catalogue record for this book is available from the Library of Congress.

Library of Congress Control Number: 2023947945

ISBN: HB: 978-1-50996-391-1
ePDF: 978-1-50996-393-5
ePub: 978-1-50996-392-8

Typeset by Compuscript Ltd, Shannon

PREFACE

I started reflecting on the relationship between parliamentarism and encyclopaedism on the occasion of the IFLA General Conference, held in Boston in May 2001, where I presented a short paper entitled: 'Essential information for post-encyclopaedic parliaments: The Italian case' (still available on the web). In the paper, I focused primarily on the work of the Research Service of the Italian Chamber of Deputies, advocating for the need to replace the 'closed' encyclopaedic model on which traditional parliamentarism was based. Since then, I have frequently returned to the topic during my lessons on Comparative Public Law at the Political Science Department of LUISS University in Rome. Thanks to the keen comments and suggestions of the LUISS students, I had the opportunity to consider in greater depth many aspects of the complex relationship between parliaments and knowledge. I became convinced that the models through which parliaments gather, organise and produce knowledge constitute a matter of critical importance for the purpose of understanding some of the basic features of parliamentary representation. This idea was confirmed by my work within the Chamber of Deputies Research Service, where I have spent most of my professional life: there I have been confronted daily with the challenge of conveying useful information to contribute to parliamentary decision-making. In this inspiring environment, I had the opportunity, together with my colleagues, to address the practical and theoretical questions raised by this very demanding task. I also had the opportunity to engage in very beneficial exchanges with colleagues from other European parliaments within the European Centre for Parliamentary Research and Documentation (ECPRD).

The decisive incentive to further develop my research on a scholarly basis came from Nicola Lupo, Director of the Centre for Parliamentary Studies at LUISS, and from Olivier Rozenberg (Science Po, Paris), who encouraged me to devote a fully-fledged monograph to the relationship between parliamentarism and encyclopaedism. To both of them, I express my deepest gratitude, including for their comments and suggestions on some of the draft versions of this book. The idea of verifying the enduring validity of the parliamentary encyclopedia in an 'age of fragmentation' came from Gino Roncaglia's book, *L'età della frammentazione. Cultura del libro e scuola digitale* (Bari, Laterza, 2018): I had some very interesting discussions with Gino (università Roma Tre) regarding the challenges posed by the use of complex information in the digital sphere.

I extend my warm thanks for reading some versions of the book to Massimo Luciani (Università La Sapienza, Rome), Peter Leyland (SOAS – University of London), Pasquale Pasquino (New York University), Enrico Brissa (German Bundestag), Cristina Fasone (LUISS University) and Evanthis Hatzivassiliou (Foundation of the Hellenic Parliament): their comments greatly assisted me in refining my thinking and avoiding errors. The responsibility for any remaining shortcomings of the book is obviously entirely mine.

I also want to thank Robert Schütze (Durham, University and LUISS) – co-editor with Nicola Lupo of the series 'Parliamentary Democracy in Europe' – for having accepted my book into this prestigious series. I have also greatly benefited from the insightful comments provided by the two anonymous reviewers of my book proposal.

Sasha Jawed, my thoughtful and patient editor at Hart Publishing, kindly tolerated several postponements in the final delivery of the manuscript. Breony Allen carefully and professionally supported the linguistic revision of the text.

My special gratitude to the librarians of the Library of the Chamber of Deputies, who generously helped me to exploit the enormous bibliographic resources of the Library, an authentic hub of encyclopaedic knowledge serving the Italian Parliament. I am also indebted to them for permitting me to borrow from other libraries, which was invaluable to my research.

This book is dedicated to my wife Gloria and my daughters Francesca and Emanuela.

CONTENTS

Preface v

Introduction: Political Representation and Knowledge 1

1. Origins and Features of Modern Encyclopaedism 10
    - I. The Encyclopaedia as an Invention of Modernity 10
    - II. Pre-Modern Encyclopaedism 11
    - III. From Chambers' *Cyclopaedia* to Diderot and D'Alambert's *Encyclopédie* 16
        - A. Chambers' *Cyclopaedia* 16
        - B. Diderot and D'Alambert's *Encyclopédie* 18
    - IV. The National Encyclopaedias of the Nineteenth Century 21
    - V. The Nineteenth-Century Encyclopaedism between Philosophy, Pedagogy and Literature 24
    - VI. Encyclopaedism and Parliamentarism and their Parallel Transformations 27

2. Encyclopaedic Parliamentarism in the Nineteenth Century 30
    - I. Parliaments and Political Representation in the Nineteenth Century 30
    - II. Parliaments and the Bourgeois Public Sphere 32
    - III. The Birth of Modern Parliamentary Representation between Publicness and Separateness 37
    - IV. Parliaments as Political Theatres of the Nation 44
    - V. Parliaments as Cognitive Maps of Politics 48
    - VI. Parliamentary Time between Cyclicity and Syncronicity 53
    - VII. The Era of Generalist Politicians: The Centrality of Parliamentary Oratory 55
    - VIII. Parliamentary Libraries 58
    - IX. The Great Treaties on Parliamentary Procedures 61
    - X. Parliamentary Encyclopaedism and the Rationality of the Legislator 66
    - XI. The Crisis of the Nineteenth-Century Encyclopaedic Parliament 69

3. Encyclopaedic Parliamentarism in the Twentieth Century 73
    - I. Major Transformations in Twentieth-Century Parliaments 73
    - II. Party Parliaments 75
        - A. Germany 75
        - B. France 77
        - C. Italy 80
        - D. United Kingdom 82
        - E. Political Groups in the European Parliament 85

III. Parliamentary Committees and the Professionalisation of Politics 88
A. United States 90
B. Germany 91
C. France 93
D. Italy 94
E. United Kingdom 96
F. The European Parliament 97
IV. Bicameralism as a Resource for the Parliamentary Encyclopaedia 99
V. The New Knowledge Systems Supporting Parliaments 101
VI. Legislative Rationality in the Twentieth Century 105
VII. The Basic Structure of the Twentieth-Century Parliamentary Encyclopaedia 106

4. Crisis and Transformation of the Encyclopaedic Model 110
I. Encyclopaedias in the Twentieth Century between Crisis and Innovation 110
A. Philosophical Visions 110
B. Encyclopaedias in the Twentieth Century 111
C. The 'Wikipedian' Model 113
II. Deconstruction of the Parliamentary Encyclopaedia 116
A. Crisis of Institutional Representation 117
B. Transformations of the Public Sphere 119
C. The New Formats of Public Policies 121
D. The Crisis of Legislative Rationality 125
III. 'Resistance' (and Resilience) of the Parliamentary Encyclopaedia 126
A. Parliamentary Representation between Conservation and Innovation 126
B. Public Engagement: A Panacea for Delegitimisation? 128
i. E-Petitions 129
ii. Consultative and Deliberative Procedures 132
iii. Parliaments between Digitalisation and Physical Presence 134
C. New Forms of Relationship with the Public Sphere 135
D. Parliaments and the New Public Policies 137
E. Parliaments and the Challenges of Multilevel Governance 139

Conclusions: The New Parliamentary Encyclopaedia: Combining Specialised Knowledge with Common Sense 143
I. Old and New Encyclopaedism 143
II. Building 'Wikipedian Parliaments' 146
III. Developing the 'Federalising Capacity' of Parliaments 147
IV. Opening an Instituent Perspective in the Parliamentary Encyclopaedia 148
V. Memory, Reason and Imagination for the New Parliamentary Encyclopaedia 149

Bibliography *152*
Index *169*

Non può nessuno vantarsi di essere perfetto in nessuna umana disciplina, s'egli non è anche perfetto in tutte le possibili discipline e cognizioni umane. Tanta è la forza e l'importanza dei rapporti che esistono fra le cose le più disparate, non conoscendo i quali, nessuna cosa si conosce perfettamente. Ora, poiché ciò che ho detto è impossibile all'individuo, perciò lo spirito umano non fa quegl'immensi progressi che potrebbe fare. È però certo che se non perfettamente, almeno quanto è possibile, è realmente necessario di esser uomo enciclopedico, non per darsi a tutte le discipline e non perfezionarsi e distinguersi in nessuna, ma per esser quanto è possibile perfetto in una sola. In ciò l'opinione del tempo è ragionevole. Chi almeno nella superficie non è uomo enciclopedico, non può veramente considerarsi (e oggi non si considera) come gran letterato o insigne in veruna disciplina intellettuale.

Nobody can claim to be perfect in any human discipline, if he is not perfect in all possible disciplines included in human knowledge. So great is the strength and importance of the relationships among the most disparate things, that, if you don't know them, you can't say to know anything perfectly. Since what I have said is impossible to achieve by any individual, the human spirit does not make the great progress that could be done. But it is certain that, if not perfectly, at least as much as possible, it is really necessary to be an encyclopaedic man not in order to cultivate all disciplines, with the result of reaching the perfection in none, but in order to be as perfect as possible in just one. The common opinion of our time is therefore reasonable on this. Who at least on the surface is not an encyclopaedic man, he cannot really be considered (and today we do not consider) a true knowledgeable man in any intellectual discipline.

Giacomo Leopardi, *Zibaldone di pensieri*, n 1922 (15 October 1821)

Introduction: Political Representation and Knowledge

This book aims to explore a specific aspect of modern parliamentarism: its ability to produce and organise political knowledge. The central thesis of the volume is that the very meaning of modern parliamentarism cannot properly be understood without considering the cognitive value which is inherent in the representative function discharged by parliaments vis-a-vis the political community.

I start my argument by focusing on the relationship between institutions and knowledge. Starting from the distinction between 'information' and 'knowledge',[1] I make reference to some seminal works[2] that have emphasised the responsibility ordinarily borne by human institutions for not only processing already available knowledge, but also for *generating new knowledge*. From this perspective, institutions can aptly be described as 'machines for thinking',[3] in the sense that they help produce knowledge for the benefit of the community and individuals.[4] Institutions can thus be seen as examples of 'artificial intelligence' as they provide constraints and opportunities to shape humans' comprehension of the world.[5] Representative institutions, in particular, play a crucial role in supporting the community's

[1] 'Borrowing a famous metaphor from … Claude Lévi-Strauss, it may be useful to think about information as something "raw", while knowledge has been "cooked". Of course, information is only relatively raw, since the "data" are not "objectively" given at all, but perceived by human minds that are full of assumptions and prejudices. However, knowledge is "cooked" in the sense of being processed. The processes … include verification, criticism, measurement, comparison and systematization': P Burke, *A Social History of Knowledge: From the Encyclopédie to Wikipedia* (Cambridge, Polity Press, 2012) 5.

[2] On the relationship between institutions and knowledge, a crucial theoretical contribution can be found in the works of Emile Durkheim (1858–1917) and Ludwik Fleck (1896–1961). For an analysis of the theories of these two scholars, see M Douglas, *How Institutions Think* (Syracuse, NY, Syracuse University Press, 1986) 9–19. For an influential application of these theories to the history of science, see T Kuhn, *The Structure of Scientific Revolutions* (Chicago, IL, University of Chicago Press, 1962).

[3] Douglas (n 2) 111.

[4] Widespread interest in the topic of knowledge management arose as recently as the mid-1990s with respect to the private sector: this 'knowledge turn' asserted that we have moved into an Information Age wherein knowledge has become the organisation's principal asset. For a synthesis, see D Hislop, *Knowledge Management in Organizations: A Critical Introduction* (Oxford, Oxford University Press, 2009). See also M Koenig, 'Knowledge Management: Where is it Going?' in S McCallum, L Bultrini, J Sempéré and W Newman (eds), *Knowledge Management in Libraries and Organizations* (Berlin, De Gruyter, 2016). For an interesting study of a great international organisation from this point of view, see N Svenson, *The United Nations as a Knowledge System* (London, Routledge, 2016).

[5] C Donolo, *L'intelligenza delle istituzioni* (Milano, Feltrinelli, 1997) 55. For a very interesting study of the Athenian democratic institutions from a cognitive perspective, see J Ober, *Democracy and Knowledge: Innovation and Learning in Classical Athens* (Princeton, NJ, Princeton University Press, 2008). According to Ober, 'Cleisthenes created institutions that employed the principles of incentives for knowledge sharing, lowering communications costs, and context-sensitive information sorting' (at 139). On the latest developments on artificial intelligence and their applications to parliaments, see ch 4.

reflexive knowledge of itself.[6] It has correctly been observed that the capacity to enhance political knowledge is central to the success of representative democracy.[7]

In my volume, I apply this theoretical framework to parliaments.[8] Knowledge is vital to the discharge of most parliamentary functions.[9] In contemporary democracies, in order to legislate or to exercise their oversight function with respect to the executives, parliaments need to process a huge amount of information. In doing so, parliaments not only incorporate knowledge from outside, but also produce 'raw' data[10] and new knowledge for other institutions and citizens at large. The patterns underpinning this activity have the capacity to strongly influence not only the inner functioning of parliaments, but also their role within the constitutional system, and, more generally, the democratic quality of a society.[11]

[6] On the reflexive nature of democratic representation, see N Urbinati, *Representative Democracy: Principles and Genealogy* (Chicago, IL, University of Chicago Press, 2006) 102–05. Urbinati maintains that the Kantian doctrine of judgment can offer an adequate basis for the theoretical foundation of representative democracy: 'It is *autonomy of judgment* that makes indirectness legitimate, the fact that the ruler and the ruled can make an "as if" judgment and imagine themselves in the place of the other. *Acting in the place of* is a transitive mode of action that is predicative of a normative relationship of reciprocity; it designates that the law, not the will, is the site of power (and sovereignty)' (103, italics in the original text).

[7] WP Jaeger, J Lyons and J Wolak, 'Political Knowledge and Policy Representation in the States' (2017) 45 *American Politics Research* 907.

[8] In my book I use the term 'parliaments' to indicate parliamentary assemblies in general, even if I am aware of the proposals made to distinguish among different types of assemblies, with regard to their position in the institutional system or to the actual functions exerted. Among recent examples of classifications, see K Palonen, 'A comparison between three ideal types of parliamentary politics: representation, legislation and deliberation' (2018) 1 *Parliaments, Estates & Representation* 6; A Kreppel, 'Legislatures' in D Caramani (ed), *Comparative Politics* (Oxford, Oxford University Press, 2020). Less recent, but classical identifications of different types of parliaments, can be found in M Weber, '*Parliament and Government in Germany under a New Political Order*' in M Weber, *Political Writings* (1st edn 1918) (Cambridge, Cambridge University Press, 1994); KC Wheare, *Legislatures* (Oxford, Oxford University Press, 1968); G Loewenberg and SC Patterson, *Comparing Legislatures* (Lanham, MD, University Press of America, 1979); NW Polsby, 'Legislatures' in F Greenstein and NW Polsby, *Handbook of Political Science*, Vol 5 (Reading, MA, Addison-Wesley 1975). For more recent, excellent contributions on the methods to compare parliamentary assemblies, see O Rozenberg, 'Comparer les parlements' in Y Doloye and JM Waele (eds), *Politique Comparée* (Brussels, Bruylant 2018); N Lupo, 'Parliaments' in R Masterman and R Schuetze (eds), *The Cambridge Companion to Comparative Constitutional Law* (Cambridge, Cambridge University Press, 2019); C Fasone, 'Parliaments in comparative and political analyses' in C Benoît and O Rozenberg (eds), *Parliamentary Studies: Interdisciplinary Approaches to Legislatures* (Cheltenham, Edward Elgar, 2020).

[9] J Krueper, 'Das Wissen des Parlament' in M Morlok, U Schliesky and D Wiefelspuetz (eds), *Parlamentsrecht: Praxishandbuch* (Baden Baden, Nomos, 2016) 1141. For the application of an informational perspective to the study of the organisation of the US Congress, see K Krehbiel, *Information and Legislative Organization* (Ann Arbor, MI, University of Michigan Press, 1991). According to this theory, a well-designed legislature is a producer, consumer and repository for policy expertise, where 'expertise' is the reduction of uncertainty associated with legislative policies. The cognitive added value deriving from the parliamentary form of government was already clearly identified by the 19th-century theory on parliamentarism, according to which *information* was a crucial advantage in parliamentary deliberations: see W Selinger, *Parliamentarism: From Burke to Weber* (Cambridge, Cambridge University Press, 2019) 26.

[10] Parliaments have recently become providers of sizable sets of open data regarding their activity. Open data is defined as structured data that can be machine-readable, freely shared, used and built upon without restrictions.

[11] Quite recently, K Palonen, *Parliamentary Thinking: Procedure, Rhetoric and Time* (Cham, Palgrave Macmillan, 2019) has explored the features of what he defines as 'thinking politics parliamentarily'. For him, 'parliamentary thinking' consists of 'political judgements formed in dissensus and debate' (at 3). Palonen connects parliamentarism not to a specific political regime (centred on the confidence relationship between the assembly and the government), but rather to a procedural and rhetorical form of doing politics, that of speaking *pro et contra* on any subject submitted to parliamentary debate (at 7).

This book will focus on one of these patterns that I consider particularly crucial: the 'encyclopaedic pattern'. I employ this term to mean the tendency for parliaments to produce and organise knowledge according to comprehensive circular structures. Via these structures, the representative assemblies were able to offer a space for debate in which a kind of epistemic division of labour emerged among the MPs.[12] This feature can be traced back to the origins of modern parliamentarism[13] and can be studied, together with the parallel emergence of the great national encyclopaedias, as one of the predominant intellectual enterprises of modern Europe.[14] I maintain that the encyclopaedic pattern remains relevant to understanding the operation of parliaments in contemporary democracies, although due consideration must be given to the 'paradigm shifts' undergone by parliamentary representation from the eighteenth century to the modern age.

I focus on the relationship between parliamentarism and encyclopaedism as, in my view, this topic engages with a fundamental aspect of contemporary democracies: the question regarding the relationship between knowledge and political decision-making. This is particularly the case when scientific knowledge is at stake, as this cognitive sphere is controlled by strict and highly specialised verification rules. More than a century ago, Max Weber[15] identified the scientist and the politician as two opposing figures, led by two missions inspired by radically different values and targeting inevitably divergent purposes. Later, Hannah Arendt[16] reiterated the idea of an irremediable opposition between science and politics, granting the former the task of acting as a 'constitutional limit' vis-a-vis the destabilising freedom of the latter. She was of the view that such freedom could even come into conflict with the factual data established in the scientific arena.

By contrast with these theories, modernity has reaffirmed the need for maintenance of a continuous relationship between knowledge and political decision-making.[17] The recent dramatic experience of the pandemic[18] has confirmed that the failure to build effective bridges between these two spheres can produce widespread reactions in which anti-scientific

[12] G Conti, *Parliament the Mirror of the Nation: Representation, Deliberation and Democracy in Victorian Britain* (Cambridge, Cambridge University Press, 2019) 112–18.

[13] I use this term to encompass a very broad concept, regarding a form of government that had and still has a wide range of variants over time and across different countries. For a general definition from the point of view of constitutional theory, see AW Bradley and C Pinelli, 'Parliamentarism' in M Rosenfeld and A Sajo (eds), *The Oxford Handbook of Comparative Constitutional Law* (Oxford, Oxford University Press, 2012) 651: 'The essence of parliamentarism in modern constitutions is that the executive power is exercised by the Prime Ministers and other ministers, who have the confidence of the legislature'. See also, G Amato and F Clementi, *Forme di stato e forme di governo* (Bologna, il Mulino, 2012).

[14] J Loveland, *The European Encyclopaedia, From 1650 to the Twenty-First Century* (Cambridge, Cambridge University Press, 2019) 4: [encyclopaedism is] 'an originally and markedly European phenomenon that lasted around 300 years'.

[15] M Weber, *The Vocation Lectures: Science As a Vocation, Politics As a Vocation* (1st edn 1919) (Indianapolis, IN, Hackett Publishing, 2004).

[16] H Arendt, 'Truth and Politics' in *Between Past and Future* (1st edn 1968) (London, Penguin, 2006).

[17] R Pielke, *The Honest Broker: Making Sense of Science in Policy and Politics* (Cambridge, Cambridge University Press, 2007) 12.

[18] The pandemic emerged as a major stress test for political systems, institutions, decision-making processes and public policies all over the world. For a review of the existing literature on how politics has dealt with the Covid-19 challenge see L Barberia, T Plümper and GD Whitten, 'The political science of Covid-19: An introduction' (2021) 102 *Social Science Quarterly* 2045. See also, SL Greer, EJ King, EM da Fonseca and A Peralta-Santos, 'The Comparative Politics of COVID-19: The Need to Understand Government Responses' (2020) 15 *Global Public Health* 1413.

attitudes go hand-in-hand with anti-democratic compulsions.[19] The crisis has revealed once more how the sustainability of our democratic regimes depends upon the cognitive preconditions underpinning these systems. The key question is whether democratic institutions today are still able to offer sufficiently shared 'explanations of the world' that can serve as a common reference for all members of the polity. This is a horizon that today appears to be threatened by a number of different phenomena, including the fragmentation of specialist knowledge, the 'noise' resulting from the explosion of the communication sphere,[20] the dissemination of disinformation, and the implementation of post-truth strategies by forces which are openly hostile to liberal democratic systems.[21] I argue that parliaments – as the site of *government by explanation* – can represent a decisive counterweight to these trends, offering the possibility of a re-composition of the public sphere which seems indispensable for the development of any democratic polity.

I am aware that this thesis may appear counterintuitive, especially if we compare parliaments with other democratic institutions, like executives and heads of state. The representative functions of the latter are normally strongly oriented towards the paradigm of unification, since they ordinarily represent such values as the interests of the state, the consistency of executive policies, and the unity of the state. By contrast, in modern democracies, parliaments represent political pluralism, as they are physiologically divided between the majority and the opposition, and they are expected to protect the freedom of political action pursued by political parties and individual parliamentarians. Against this backdrop, it is clear that parliaments' crucial role is not to represent unity, but, rather, political conflict. This role may be differently discharged depending on the composition of a set of legal or cultural variables (including the entry thresholds imposed by the electoral laws, the prevalence of consensual or competitive patterns in the political culture of the country in question, etc). However, the very need to represent conflict and pluralism obliges parliaments to offer a common space for debate and confrontation to all those who engage in politics in the parliamentary arena. From this point of view, parliaments represent a powerful unifying platform which makes it possible to democratically address political conflict, without neutralising it. Moreover, parliamentary assemblies are wholly committed to the values of openness and transparency, as basic principles inherently connected with the constitutional role of representative assemblies and their historical link with the rise of a 'public sphere'.[22] From this perspective, parliaments are not limited to offering a neutral playground to the political forces. They do much more. They devise procedures to deal with political conflict, define safeguards to ensure that the public understands these procedures, and develop the categories aimed at

[19] W Jennings, G Stoker, V Valgarðsson, D Devine and J Gaskell, 'How Trust, Mistrust and Distrust Shape the Governance of the COVID-19 Crisis' (2021) 28 *Journal of European Public Policy* 1174; T Plümper, E Neumayer and KG Pfaff, 'The Strategy of Protest against Covid-19 Containment Policies in Germany' (2021) 102 *Social Science Quarterly* 2236.

[20] On the possible actions to reduce 'noise' in a wide set of decision-making contexts (from medicine to forensic science), see D Kahneman, O Sibony and CR Sunstein, *Noise: A Flaw in Human Judgment* (New York, Little, Brown Spark, 2021).

[21] See R Keyes, *The Post-Truth Era: Dishonesty and Deception in Contemporary Life* (New York, St Martin's Press, 2004).

[22] I assume – as does Habermas – that a modern 'public sphere' first emerged and assumed its functions in the 18th century as a part of the bourgeois 'civil society', even if notions of what is 'public' and what is not can be traced much further back in time. See J Habermas, *The Structural Transformation of the Public Sphere: An Inquiry into a Category of Bourgeois Society* (1st edn 1962) (Cambridge, Polity, 1992) 14 ff.

selecting, classifying and making politically manageable the issues that need to be discussed and decided upon. In so doing, they offer an indispensable cognitive basis for democratic debate, that, as such, appears to be the only viable alternative to the opposing threats of populistic rejection of expertise[23] and of 'epistocracy'.[24]

This is what I mean when I assign an intrinsic 'encyclopaedic' nature to modern parliamentarism. My intention is to explore in detail this aspect of parliamentarism and its relationship with encyclopaedism at large, as a peculiar form of institutional organisation of knowledge that emerged in Europe in parallel with the development of modern parliaments. Above all, my aim is to check whether this powerful paradigm supporting modern parliamentarism is still valid today, when the encyclopaedic model seems radically challenged by new cognitive paradigms.

In order to support my thesis, I focus on three major moments in the history of parliamentarism: the nineteenth century, as a golden era of liberal parliamentarism; the twentieth century, dominated by party parliaments; and the current era, characterised by the crisis of parties and the fragmentation of the public sphere. Each of these periods is distinguished by parliaments adopting specific forms of organisation of knowledge.

This interpretation of the history of modern parliamentarism adopts a methodological perspective that views institutions not just as mechanisms for aggregating individual preferences, but also as powerful sources of new collective knowledge and political identities. This approach was revived in the early 1990s of the last century from seminal works such as those of March and Olsen,[25] and has now been embraced in important reflections such as that conducted by the Italian philosopher Roberto Esposito.[26]

Economists, sociologists and political scientists have accumulated a considerable amount of scholarship discussing the learning processes occurring within the institutions. These scholars have pointed out that the knowledge produced by political institutions does not relate to scientific knowledge, but rather to a kind of 'useful knowledge' that is developed not only by experts, but by every individual who encounters the practical problems faced by the institution within which he or she operates. The scholarship concerning knowledge management has emphasised the importance of the processes that allow the implicit knowledge present in any given organisation to emerge. More recently, the peculiarity

[23] T Nichols, *The Death of Expertise: The Campaign Against Established Knowledge and Why It Matters* (Oxford, Oxford University Press, 2017).

[24] A Esmark, 'The technocratic take-over of democracy: connectivity, reflexivity and accountability', paper prepared for ICPP 2017, Singapore, available at: www.ippapublicpolicy.org/file/paper/594bba371f736.pdf. On the accountability of experts in public decision-making, see C Holst and A Molander, 'Public Deliberation and the Fact of Expertise: Making Experts Accountable' (2017) 31 *Social Epistemology* 235. See also fn 52. On the different version of the technocratic challenge to democracy, see PP Portinaro, *Tecnocrazia* in *Enciclopedia Treccani delle Scienze Sociali* (1998), available at: www.treccani.it/enciclopedia/tecnocrazia_%28Enciclopedia-delle-scienze-sociali%29/. See also the classical pages of M Duverger, *Janus: Les deux faces de l'Occident* (Paris, Fayard, 1979).

[25] J March and J Olsen, *Rediscovering Institutions: The Organizational Basis of Politics* (New York, The Free Press, 1989). For an account of the first and the second phases of institutionalism, see BG Peters, *Institutional Theory in Political Science: The 'New Institutionalism'* (London, Continuum, 2005). For an overview of the core concepts of the new and old institutionalism, see V Lowndes and M Roberts, *Why Institutions Matter: The New Institutionalism in Political Science* (London, Palgrave Macmillan, 2013).

[26] R Esposito, *Living Thought: The Origins and Actuality of Italian Philosophy* (Stanford, CA, Stanford University Press, 2012); R Esposito, *Pensiero istituente: Tre paradigmi di ontologia politica* (Torino, Einaudi, 2020); R Esposito, *Istituzione* (Bologna, il Mulino, 2021).

of democratic institutions has been identified in their special (by comparison with non-democratic systems) capacity to aggregate useful knowledge (not merely preferences or interests).[27]

As regards parliaments in particular, extensive literature highlights the importance of knowledge for the performance of primary parliamentary functions.[28] Parliaments could not legislate or exercise control over the government and other institutions without having adequate information bases. From this point of view, scholars have emphasised the importance of parliamentary procedures specifically dedicated to the collection of information, such as those concerning the inspection functions or the committees of inquiry. There is also quite extensive literature on administrative structures that support the fact-finding work of parliaments, such as parliamentary libraries, research services or agencies for the assessment of financial costs or the technological implications of legislative choices. How parliaments digest the available information (deriving from different sources: the government, political groups, individual MPs, experts, representatives of vested interests) and produce new knowledge has been the subject of far less exploration. The lack of sufficient investigation regarding these crucial aspects has led, in my view, to obvious limitations in understanding the meaning of some key structures and modes of operation of parliaments.

Having regard to this general methodological approach, the book develops its analysis primarily through the use of analytical tools deriving from three different disciplinary areas: theory and history of political representation; comparative constitutional law; and knowledge history.

This multidisciplinary approach is necessitated by the main purpose of my research, which focuses on studying parliaments as institutions capable of producing political knowledge for the benefit of the entire political community. The multidisciplinary consideration of modern parliaments as 'encyclopaedic' institutions adheres to a methodological approach currently characterising the field of 'parliamentary studies', which has already been adopted by a number of recent pieces of research devoted to this topic.[29]

This approach leads primarily to the central role played by parliaments in shaping the structures of democratic representation in the modern age. From this point of view, parliaments have been and still are essential for the pluralistic representation of complex societies. In particular today, parliaments are confronted with the difficult task of mediating between the traditional unifying function of political representation and the trend towards increasing fragmentation and disintermediation of social demands. The thesis of the book is that,

[27] Ober (n 5).

[28] 'The fact that legislative assemblies need information to fulfil their constitutional functions is 'an old and common insight of constitutional theory': E Griglio, *Parliamentary Oversight of the Executives: Tools and Procedures in Europe* (Oxford, Hart Publishing, 2020) 76.

[29] 'In an age of extreme specialisation in social science, the gathering of a great diversity of contributions constitutes a leap of faith in the universality of knowledge that is intimately connected with a special consideration of legislatures. Encyclopaedism and parliamentarianism share the same destiny': C Benoit and O Rozenberg, 'Introduction' in *Handbook of Parliamentary Studies: Interdisciplinary Approaches to Legislatures* (Cheltenham, Edward Elgar, 2020) 12–13.

in order to fulfil this fundamental function, it is still critical for parliaments to put in place a type of *cognitive representation* alongside their responsive representation.[30]

This means that they are representative not only because they reflect the will of the electors, *but because they offer the possibility of a viable political understanding of the social complexity*. It is precisely the cognitive value of parliamentary representation that highlights the integrative rather than aggregative nature of these institutions. In fact, they are flexible platforms for unifying and transforming social pluralism, rather than merely a political arena reflecting the balance of power between the majority and the minority.

Of course, parliaments do not perform this function in isolation, but in a continuous relationship with other institutions, first and foremost with the executives, albeit in different ways in the parliamentary and presidential systems. It is consequently necessary to interpret the developments under consideration via the analytical tools offered by comparative constitutional law. Through these instruments, the book seeks to highlight the constitutional changes that have taken place over the period covered by the study (from the eighteenth century to the present day). These changes are studied from the point of view of the production and distribution of knowledge resources. This cognitive perspective provides a very effective description of the evolution of power relations between the different institutions, contributing to the comprehension of a crucial aspect of the actual constitutional arrangements in any given system.

Finally, my research draws on studies carried out regarding the history of knowledge and its sources. These studies have primarily been developed in the Anglo-Saxon area and have focused on forms of institutionalisation of knowledge in different historical contexts.[31] Today, these studies focus, in particular, on the transformations in the organisation of our knowledge caused by the digital 'infosphere' and the new communication environment offered by the web. One aspect of these disciplines that is particularly important for my research is the approach offered by the current scholarship on digital humanities.

The book is structured in four chapters.

The first chapter offers an overview of the origins of modern encyclopaedism in eighteenth- century and nineteenth-century Europe. I analyse the meaning of the epistemological shift marked by Diderot and D'Alambert's *Encyclopédie* (1751–72). The French

[30] As is well known, the cognitive nature of the democratic process has been extensively elaborated in the work of J Habermas, *Theorie des kommunikativen Handelns* (Frankfurt am Main, Suhrkamp, 1981); *Faktizität und Geltung: Beiträge zur Diskurstheorie des Rechts und des demokratischen Rechtsstaates* (Frankfurt am Main, Suhrkamp, 1992). More recently, the theory on the epistemology of democracy emphasised the need to exploit the common knowledge of the citizens and their representatives as a condition to countering both the 'populistic' trends (ie, the temptation to oversimplify the issues implied in democratic decision-making) and the 'epistocratic' shift (ie, the transfer of decisions to the 'experts') in contemporary democracies. These theories view democracy as an institution for pooling widely distributed information about problems and policies of public interest by engaging the participation of epistemically diverse knowledge-holders (E Anderson, 'The Epistemology of Democracy' (2006) 3(1–2) *Episteme* 8). Parliaments can be viewed as one of the crucial institutions performing this task. From this point of view, they embody a cognitive form of representation as opposed to a merely responsive one.

[31] On the contemporary meaning of the history of knowledge, see P Burke, *What is the History of Knowledge?* (Cambridge, Polity Press, 2015); P Sarasin, 'Was ist Wissensgeschichte?' (2011) 36(1) *Internationales Archiv für Sozialgeschichte der deutschen Literatur* 159; P Sarasin, 'More Than Just Another Specialty: On the Prospects for the History of Knowledge' (2020) 1 *Journal for the History of Knowledge* 1.

encyclopaedists rejected the '*esprit de système*' of the tradition which preceded them, in order to carry out a work which refrained from providing a comprehensive and harmonious picture of human knowledge in its entirety. Rather, the *Encyclopédie* assumes that human knowledge is limited, while being subject to continuous expansion and correction, according to the progressive outlook typical of the Enlightenment. The publication of the French encyclopaedia paved the way for subsequent large national encyclopaedias. The characteristics of these works differed significantly from the French example, but shared some basic preconditions with it. Underpinning the great success of the encyclopaedic model in the nineteenth century was the need to provide an intellectual response to two contradictory needs: on the one hand, the necessity of accepting the growing specialisation of knowledge, and on the other, the will to preserve the cultural unity of the *Bildung* reserved to the ruling class.

In the second chapter, I explore how modern parliaments emerged between the eighteenth and nineteenth centuries as the political encyclopaedias of the nascent liberal bourgeoisie. I discuss how the basic principles of parliamentarism (free mandate and national representation) were functional in shaping a new kind of representative institution in strong connection with the birth of the bourgeois public sphere. Even with respect to their physical form (the French hemicycle), continental parliaments offered new cognitive maps of politics. From this point of view, parliaments were expected to be an effective 'mirror of the Nation', a true 'epitome' of the diverse civil body of the Nation. As contemporary national encyclopaedias, they played a crucial role in the nation-building process of most European countries in the liberal age. The chapter discusses this parallel development with special reference to some European countries, like Great Britain, France and Italy.

In the third chapter I discuss the transition from the liberal parliaments (composed of both notables and 'genaralist' politicians) to the new parliaments of the twentieth century, whose structure is dominated by the presence of political parties. This crucial shift was directly connected with other major transformations, like the professionalisation of politics and the emergence, vis-a-vis the parliamentary assemblies, of big bureaucratic apparatuses supporting the executives. This chapter illustrates how these phenomena deeply affected the parliamentary encyclopaedia, the cognitive matrix through which the assemblies digest and organise their political knowledge. The grid deriving from the intersection between the political groups and the system of permanent sectoral committees constituted an integrated and 'circular' environment capable of dealing with any subject of legislation. This development led to the emergence of 'expert parliaments', supported by a set of specialist technical bodies, like research services, budget offices and units for the evaluation of technological choices.

The fourth chapter analyses the challenges posed to the parliamentary encyclopaedia of the twentieth century by the radical changes under way in the public sphere. The new communicative environment seems to reject any attempt at encyclopaedic synthesis and offers the alternative perspective of the web as an open and potentially infinite horizon of limitless connections. I discuss how parliaments have reacted thus far to this 'great transformation' with a mixed strategy comprising conservativism (in the structures of the political groups and sectoral committees) and innovation (in their use of the contemporary communicative tools, with a new interactive approach towards citizens).

In the final chapter, I draw some problematic conclusions from my research. I emphasise the risks and the opportunities for parliaments when facing some of the great phenomena of our age (fragmentation of knowledge, the crisis of some shared values of citizenship, and the growing complexity of the public sphere). These developments demand a radical change to parliaments' traditional structure and operational procedures. I maintain, however, that the role of parliaments remains crucial today, in order to propose forms of unitary reconstruction of contemporary social complexity. The very possibility for parliamentary representation to survive in the current context depends crucially on parliaments' effective ability to build a new 'parliamentary encyclopaedia' capable of meeting the cognitive needs of contemporary democracy.

1

Origins and Features of Modern Encyclopaedism

I. The Encyclopaedia as an Invention of Modernity

Encyclopaedias as we know them today are an invention of modernity. By encyclopaedia, we mean a reference work organised according to alphabetically ordered articles, which can either be general in scope or devoted to a particular discipline (eg, law, medicine, history). In this form, encyclopaedias became established in Europe during the eighteenth century: the first encyclopaedic work in a modern sense is generally considered to be the *Cyclopedia* by Ephraim Chambers, the first edition of which was published in 1728. *Cyclopedia* was a great success, with several editions being published over the century and the text being translated into Italian and Spanish. Diderot's *Encyclopédie* itself was originally conceived as a French translation of Chambers' work.

In the following section, we will analyse the particular characteristics of *Cyclopedia* and the reasons for its success. The importance of encyclopaedias for the culture of modern Europe, however, could not properly be understood without considering how these works were connected with the broader phenomenon of *encyclopaedism*, as the ensemble of 'the ways in which a series of authors (primarily located within Western European culture) made use of a range of shared rhetorical and compilatory techniques to create knowledge-ordering works of different kinds, works that often claimed some kind of comprehensive and definite status'.[1] In this chapter my intent is to trace some of the roots of the modern encyclopaedias within this broader cultural tradition, starting from the obvious premise that no single model of encyclopaedism is suitable for all periods.[2] The intellectual precedents of the modern encyclopaedia are in any case of great interest for the purpose of understanding some enduring features of this cultural enterprise. These characteristics are also of significance in framing the parallelism between encyclopaedism and the emergence of modern parliamentarism.

[1] J König and G Woolf, 'Introduction' in J König and G Woolf (eds), *Encyclopaedism from Antiquity to the Renaissance* (Cambridge, Cambridge University Press, 2013) 1.

[2] ibid, 6.

II. Pre-Modern Encyclopaedism

The word encyclopaedia appeared for the first time in Europe in the fifteenth century.[3] As a single word, it was a completely new term, produced by the union of two distinct words which, in the culture of Greek and Latin classicism, formed the expression *enkuklios paideia*. In this context, this term did not refer to a particular type of written text, but rather to the idea of 'general culture', a comprehensive course of study capable of covering all the disciplines necessary for the training of a cultivated citizen.[4] The first work to be explicitly entitled 'Encyclopaedia' was Paul Scalich's *Encyclopaedia; seu, Orbis disciplinarum, tam sacrarum quam prophanarum epistemon* published in Basel in 1559.[5] However, the use of the expression *enkuklios paideia* in a work fundamental to the foundation of Western encyclopaedic tradition, such as the *Naturalis Historia* of Pliny the Elder (AD 23/24–79),[6] helped to associate the two terms with intellectual enterprises similar to Pliny's work, which were united by the ambition of collecting and systematising the available knowledge on a particular subject or even the entire breadth of human knowledge.[7] From this point of view, the Aristotelian corpus can be regarded as the most influential *avant la lettre* encyclopaedia of antiquity,[8] composed in such a way as to ensure that all types of disciplines were addressed, from the most abstract, such as logic, to the most practical, such as morals and politics, without neglecting physics, astronomy or biology. Moreover, the Aristotelian corpus had a strong pedagogical imprint, both because most of the philosopher's works actually reflected the lessons given by the philosopher to his students, and because of Aristotle's reputation as a tutor of the young Alexander the Great.

Another form acquired by the encyclopaedic ideal in antiquity was the library. From this point of view, the most renowned example is offered by the library established in Alexandria in Egypt, probably during the reign of Ptolemy II Philadelphus (308–246 BC). The library was part of a larger research institution called the Mouseion, and included a collection estimated between 40,000 and 400,000 papyrus scrolls. This example was replicated by the Romans in Rome and in some of the most important cities of the Empire.[9] The library as universal encyclopaedia represents an enduring model, that was revived in modernity by some great institutions like the Library of Congress in Washington DC and other parliamentary libraries, as we shall see in more detail in the following chapter.

[3] R Fowler, 'Encyclopaedias: Definitions and Theoretical Problems' in P Binkley (ed), *Pre-Modern Encyclopaedic Texts* (Leiden, Brill, 1997) 27–29.

[4] W E Preece and RL Collison, 'Encyclopaedia' in *Encyclopaedia Britannica*, available at: www.britannica.com/topic/encyclopaedia.

[5] ibid.

[6] See Pliny, *Natural History*, Vol I, Loeb Classical Library (Cambridge, MA, Harvard University Press, 1938) Preface, 14.

[7] R Collison, *Encyclopaedias: Their History throughout the Ages* (New York, Hafner, 1966) 25.

[8] 'By far the most significant philosophical predecessor to the later ideas of encyclopedic compilation was surely Aristotle': J König and G Woolf, 'Encyclopaedism in the Roman Empire' in J König and G Woolf (eds), *Encyclopaedism from Antiquity to the Renaissance* (Cambridge, Cambridge University Press, 2013) 25.

[9] P Nelles, 'Libraries' in A Grafton, GW Most and S Settis (eds), *The Classical Tradition* (Cambridge, MA, The Belknap Press of Harvard University Press, 2010) 532–36; U Eco, 'Dall'albero al labirinto' in U Eco, *Dall'albero al labirinto. Studi storici sul segno e l'interpretazione* (Milano, La Nave di Teseo, 2017) 40.

During the Middle Ages, the encyclopaedic tradition developed mainly through the production of treatises and compendiums intended to summarise the fundamental elements of human knowledge organised on the basis of the disciplines of *trivium* and *quadrivium*. It is significant that some of the most important encyclopaedic works produced during this period made reference in their titles to the image of the mirror.[10] These works sought to present themselves as faithful representations of the state of knowledge available at the time of their publication. This knowledge was considered to be immutable because it was acquired once and for all via divine revelation or from the authority of tradition.[11] The notion of the immutability and permanence of human knowledge was rapidly abandoned by modernity. However, even during the subsequent centuries, encyclopaedias continued to claim to serve as a *speculum*, as a systematic representation of the reality surrounding them.[12] This 'representative' claim of encyclopaedias is certainly of significance since it marks a long-term characteristic of the encyclopaedic undertaking, which would be confirmed in the modern age. This is clearly a very important feature for the purpose of understanding the links between the encyclopaedic enterprise and the emergence of parliamentarism as one of the political forms of modernity.

As we have seen, the word 'encyclopaedia' is a neologism coined in fifteenth-century European humanistic circles. What was the meaning of 'encyclopaedia' in the first modernity and how does it differ both from medieval encyclopaedias and from subsequent developments in encyclopaedism?

One element of continuity with the medieval tradition is the fact that the humanistic encyclopaedia also aspired to represent a body of knowledge deemed to be acquired once and for all, mainly derived from the study of classical texts. As in the Middle Ages, the purpose of the encyclopaedic enterprise in humanistic times also remained essentially educational: the encyclopaedia summarised the course of study considered most suitable for human learning. This ideal of immutability, however, began to be called into question during the fifteenth and sixteenth centuries. The recovery of new classical texts, made possible by the arrival of several manuscripts from the Byzantine world, destabilised the canon formed in the Middle Ages. Later, the introduction of the printing press led to a rapid and soon overwhelming increase in the number of available written texts, both sacred and profane. The explosion in the number and accessibility of printed texts that had already begun in the sixteenth century gradually led to a radical change in the meaning of the encyclopaedic enterprise: encyclopaedias were now expected to serve as a guide to a body of potential sources of knowledge that was constantly expanding. Geographical discoveries and religious schisms contributed to opening new perspectives which were incompatible

[10] See, eg, the *Speculum Majus* (*The Greater Mirror*; completed 1244), one of the most important of the medieval encyclopaedias, produced by French scholar Vincent of Beauvais: Vincent de Bouvais, *Opus Preclarum Speculum Maius intitulatum in Speculum Naturale, Speculum Doctrinale, Speculum Morale et Speculum Historiale Quadripartitum Vincentii Presulis Inchoat numine felici* (Venezia, Liecthenstein, 1494). See Preece and Collison (n 4).

[11] 'The medieval encyclopaedia is a 'common ideal space' that was conceived as 'a round *speculum* or *theatrum* whose shape echoed that of the world and seemed also to encompass everuthing within it': WN West, *Theatres and Encyclopedias in Early Western Europe* (Cambridge, Cambridge University Press, 2002) 17.

[12] 'Encyclopaedias have often reflected fairly accurately the civilisation in which they appeared; that this was deliberate is shown by the frequency with which the earlier compilers included such words as *speculum* ("mirror"), *imago* ("image"), and so forth in their titles': Preece and Collison (n 4).

with traditional cognitive frames. However, as Ann Blair has observed,[13] the Renaissance 'information explosion' was accompanied, more decisively than any other new discovery, by the emergence of a new cultural attitude of seeking out and stockpiling information (a kind of 'info-lust', or information obsession), which became a central ingredient of the encyclopaedic ambition of the age.

In parallel with these new attitudes, critical views were also emerging regarding the possibility of ensuring a comprehensive synthesis of all available knowledge. One of the first works in which the term encyclopaedia appears – the Rabelais' *Gargantua* – seems to express a somewhat ambivalent position as to the actual nature of the encyclopaedic undertaking: it defines encyclopaedia as both a 'well', that is, a source of knowledge, and an 'abyss', a place of perdition and confusion.[14]

Another particularly interesting aspect of encyclopaedism in early modernity is the reference to the idea of theatre. By humanistic times, the above-mentioned medieval concept of the encyclopaedia as a *speculum*, that is, as a faithful representation of reality, was reworked in theatrical terms:

> [T]he culture of early modern Europe was a theatre culture, fascinated by ostentation, performance, pretence and pretentiousness of all kinds. But it was also … an encyclopedia culture, obsessed with collecting and sorting information, diligently reducing knowledge to the possession of discrete facts, driven by the desire to map the world's order and to construct a universal theory of everything.[15]

Even before real theatres began to be built in Europe, many authors of the fifteenth and sixteenth centuries expressed the view that encyclopaedias needed to adapt to the shape of a theatre. The theatre was considered to be the most appropriate form to reflect the ideal of a knowledge circuit, in which all parts of the knowledge were properly represented. The author of the most advanced and comprehensive interpretation of this theory was the Italian philosopher and rhetorician, Giulio Camillo Delminio (1485–1544).[16] In his *L'Idea del Teatro*, Delminio describes an amphitheatre (which seems to have actually been built as a wooden structure) designed as a machine for learning and memory. In this theatre, a series of paintings or statues were arranged in a semi-circle in order to organise different topics borrowed from Cicero's works: the purpose of this positioning was to allow the spectator to quickly locate the different topics according to the humanistic ideals of separation, distance, absolute vision and instant intelligibility.[17] Concurrently with this form of intellectual theatre, the real theatre, as a physical place dedicated to the scenic representation of dramatic events, began to emerge in Italy and England in the seventeenth century. Clearly, the real theatre could not be based on a static system of symbols and images to be

[13] AM Blair, *Too Much to Know: Managing Scholarly Information before the Modern Age* (New Haven, CT, Yale University Press, 2010) 21.

[14] With reference to a travelling English scholar, Pantagruel says (with the intent of signifying praise or derision) that 'I can ensure you that he has opened for me the true well (*puys*) and abyss of the encyclopedia': see F Rabelais, *Complete Works* (Berkeley, CA, Berkeley University Press, 1991) ch 20, 298, quoted by West (n 11) 14.

[15] West (n 11) 1.

[16] On Delminio, see G Stabile, 'Camillo, Giulio, detto Delminio' in *Dizionario Biografico degli Italiani*, Vol 17 (Roma, Istituto dell'Enciclopedia italiana, 1974). Other important encyclopaedic works inspired by the theatrical form following Delminio's ideals were the *Universae Naturae Theatrum* of Jean Bodin (1595) and the *Theatrum Vitae Humanae* of Theodor Swinger.

[17] West (n 11) 56.

offered for the viewer's pure contemplation. On the contrary, in clear contrast with the form of intellectual theatre theorised by some humanistic encyclopaedists, the real theatre had to be a place of action and drama requiring the emotional involvement of the audience. It should be noted, however, that although the theatre of that extraordinary era was of a different nature, it also had at its very heart an encyclopaedic intent inspired by the ambition to bring the whole of humanity and the different historical times to the stage. It is no coincidence that the London theatre in which the works of Shakespeare and Johnson were performed was called 'The Globe', confirming the aspiration for an almost cosmological interpretation of this space.[18] In addition, as William West observed, 'the circular space of the public theatre, like the imagined circle of the encyclopedia, requires the creation of a neutral place, a segment of the world set apart from the rest of the world. Independent from the world, yet supposedly mirroring it exactly'.[19] A 'theatre – aquarium', in short, which defines an intellectual *Gestalt* very important for its re-evaluation, two centuries later, by the theory underlying the construction of the parliamentary public space. Here again, as we shall see, we encounter a 'theatre' space that is exposed to the public while being protected from any form of direct interaction with it.

The final stage of the encyclopaedic programme's revitalisation in early modernity was heralded by Francis Bacon. Bacon's work is of particular importance as it supports the ideal of a unifying encyclopaedic organisation of knowledge according to an inductively built *arbor scientiae*. However, Bacon rejected the pansophic utopia of the Lullian tradition, admitting the limits of human knowledge, but remaining convinced that it would be possible to identify cognitive keys to be used as criteria for the purpose of discovering new knowledge.[20] According to the author of *De Augmentis scientiarum* and *Instauratio Magna*, the *ars inveniendi* must be assisted by the *ars reminiscendi*. Bacon emphasised the link between the organisation of the encyclopaedia and the articulation of human faculties, which are divided into three main elements: memory, reason and imagination. This approach would be adopted by Diderot and D'Alambert's *Encyclopédie*, more than a century later.

After Bacon, other major encyclopaedic enterprises followed in the seventeenth century.[21] Of these, some resumed the Renaissance programme of a systematic presentation of knowledge, as was attempted by Johan Heinrich Alsted (1588–1638) who, in his *Encyclopedia septem tomis distincta* (1630),[22] intended to methodically organise all the sciences, reflecting the order and harmony of nature in an atlas. Other works – like for example Furetière's *Dictionnaire universel* in 1690[23] – adopted the approach of alphabetical organisation in articles. Accordingly, the encyclopaedia as an alphabetical book of knowledge took shape during this century. The alphabetical order, on the one hand, had the advantage of providing rapid and easy access to information, but, on the other hand, contradicted the search for a systematic presentation of knowledge. In the background

[18] F Yates, *Theatre of the World* (London, Routledge & Kegan Paul, 1966).

[19] West (n 11) 50.

[20] W Tega, 'L'unità del sapere e l'ideale enciclopedico nel pensiero moderno' in W Tega (ed), *L'unità del sapere e l'ideale enciclopedico nel pensiero moderno: Antologia* (Bologna, il Mulino, 1983) 13 ff.

[21] C Vasoli, *L'enciclopedismo del seicento* (Napoli, Bibliopolis, 1978).

[22] JH Alsted, *Encyclopedia septem tomis distincta* (Herborn, 1630).

[23] A Furetière and H Basnage de Beuval, *Dictionnaire universel contenant généralement tous les mots françois tant vieux que modernes, et les termes des sciences et des arts* (Leers, The Hague, 1701).

of the alphabetical arrangement loomed an egalitarian idea suggesting the reduction of all subjects to the same level: a solution that 'allows indefinite additions without the pressure to insert these into a pre-established system, to display connections or renegotiate categories'.[24] Clearly, not only practical considerations, but also different epistemological and even political visions underpinned the choice between a systematic arrangement and a mere alphabetical ordering of subjects. As we shall see, later encyclopaedias tried to reach a compromise between these two conflicting options. In any case, the systematic approach was not completely abandoned: even in the nineteenth century some great encyclopaedic works – like Coleridge's *Encyclopaedia metropolitana*[25] or the *Encyclopédie Methodique*[26] – adopted this option as the preferred approach to a simple alphabetical arrangement.

Among the encyclopaedic works produced in the seventeenth century, special mention should be made of Pierre Bayle's *Dictionnaire historique et critique* (1697).[27] The significance of this work lies in the critical approach taken to many of the topics addressed in the *Dictionnaire*. Above all, through the rich apparatus of notes, Bayle attacked some alleged truths of tradition and official religion. Bayle also intended to publicly identify the mistakes made in previous compilations, such as Luis Moréri's *Grand Dictionnaire Historique* (1674). The philosopher wanted to address his work to the 'Republic of Letters', the expression used to describe the community of cultivated and critical members of the public, which comprised the first core of a European 'public opinion'. Bayle was in constant contact with this audience via a series of periodical publications such as the *Nouvelles de la République des Lettres*, which he published in Rotterdam from 1684 to 1687. For these reasons, his work had a huge influence in the following century: Bayle was responsible for starting a trend of 'critical encyclopaedism' which culminated in Diderot and D'Alambert's *Encyclopédie*.

For the following three centuries, printed encyclopaedias were an important element of European culture and of people's lives, initially just among Europe's educated elites, but later also among the lower classes. Encyclopaedias emerged in modern Europe 'not as works claiming to register everything that actually exists, but what people traditionally think exists – and therefore everything that a cultivated person should learn, not only to know the world, but also to understand the speeches about the world'.[28] Within this broad encyclopaedic production, Jeff Loveland distinguishes three main genres: the dictionary

[24] R Yeo, *Encyclopaedic Visions: Scientific Dictionaries and Enlightenment Culture* (Cambridge, Cambridge University Press, 2010) 25.

[25] *Encyclopaedia Metropolitana*, 20 vols (London, Fellowes et al, 1817–45).

[26] *Encyclopédie Methodique*, 200 vols (Paris, 1782–1832).

[27] P Bayle, *Dictionnaire historique et critique* (Rotterdam, P Leers, 1697). On Bayle's *Dictionnaire* see the famous pages written by Paul Hazard in his *La crise de la conscience européenne*: 'ce Dictionnaire historique et critique, reste le réquisitoire le plus accablant qu'on ait jamais dressé pour la honte et pour la confusion des hommes. Presque à chaque nom surgit le souvenir d'une illusion, d'une erreur, d'une fourberie ou même d'un crime. Tous ces rois qui ont fait le malheur de leurs sujets; tous ces papes qui ont abaissé le Catholicisme au niveau de leurs ambitions, de leurs passions; tous ces philosophes qui ont bâti des systèmes absurdes; tous ces noms de villes, de pays qui rappellent des guerres, des spoliations, des massacres': P Hazard, *La crise de la conscience européenne* (1st edn 1935) (Paris, Le livre de Poche, 1994) 75.

[28] Eco (n 9) 43. Eco makes a clear-cut distinction between dictionaries (works intended to define the essential conceptual elements associated with each term) and encyclopaedias (works aimed at making available the knowledge of the world as it actually exists).

of arts and sciences; the universal dictionary; and the historical dictionary.[29] Each of these contributed to shaping the modern encyclopaedia.

III. From Chambers' *Cyclopaedia* to Diderot and D'Alambert's *Encyclopédie*

A. Chambers' *Cyclopaedia*

Ephraim Chambers is an unfamiliar figure to non-specialists and certainly much less famous than the editors of, and many of the contributors to, the French *Encyclopédie*. However, his *Cyclopaedia*,[30] the first edition of which was published, as noted earlier, in 1728, exerted a huge influence on European encyclopaedism. In many ways, this work represented the first real modern encyclopaedia, setting standards that helped to stabilise some of the characteristics of this type of work.

Chambers' *Cyclopaedia* was the third and most successful of the new genre of dictionaries of arts and sciences, inaugurated by Furetière's *Dictionnaire Universel* of 1701[31] and continued by John Harris' *Lexicon Technicum* of 1704–20.[32] Chambers' work did not, therefore, cover historical events or biographies; rather, it was intended to provide concise information on subjects relating to the most diverse disciplines of human knowledge, from science, to the arts, to law. The various entries were presented in alphabetical order, contributing to rendering this option predominant within European encyclopaedism. The great success of Chambers' work is largely due to its ability to anticipate the needs of a new audience of readers. As Rolf Engelsing pointed out,[33] during the eighteenth century the reading style of the 'bourgeois reader' underwent a profound change, from intensive reading, as required by the major treatises of the seventeenth century, to 'expansive' reading aimed at accessing a much larger number of books. It was an age marked by the proliferation and the consequent desacralisation of books that triggered a 'reading revolution' 'in the sense of a shift toward the practices of skimming, browsing and chapter-hopping in the course of consulting books for information on a particular topic'.[34] Hence, the public requested concise and reliable information on the most diverse range of disciplines. *Cyclopaedia* thus sought, following on from Bayle's previous attempt in the *Dictionnaire*, to replace the direct reading of a large part of the scientific literature which continued to be published on a wide range of subjects. According to Chambers, his *Cyclopaedia* 'would answer all the Purposes of a Library, except

[29] J Loveland, *The European Encyclopedia: From 1650 to the Twenty-First Century* (Cambridge, Cambridge University Press, 2019) 15.

[30] E Chambers, *Cyclopædia: or, An Universal Dictionary of Arts and Sciences*, 1st edn (London, James & John Knapton; John Darby; and others, 1728).

[31] Furetière and Basnage de Beauval (n 23).

[32] J Harris, *Lexicon Technicum; Or an Universal English Dictionary of Arts and Sciences*, 2 vols (London, Brown et al, 1704–10).

[33] R Engelsing, *Der Buerger als Leser: Lesergeschichte in Deutschland 1500–1800* (Stuttgart, JB Metzlersche and AE Poeschel, 1974).

[34] A Briggs and P Burke, *A Social History of the Media from Gutenberg to the Internet* (Cambridge, Polity Press, 2009) 53.

Parade and Incumbrance; and contribute more to the propagating of useful Knowledge thro' the Body of a People, than any, I had almost said all, the Books extant'.[35]

From this point of view, Chambers' work supplied a viable solution to the information overload for both scholars and novices.[36] Again following Bayle's approach, the sources of the *Cyclopaedia* came from the vast production of magazines and periodicals that satisfied the need for constant adjournment of the 'Republic of Letters'. Chambers himself, following the publication of the *Cyclopaedia*, was the editor, between 1735 and 1736, of a periodical entitled *The Literary Magazine: or, the History of the Works of the Learned*. The magazine's subtitle described it as 'containing an account of the most valuable books publish'd both at home and abroad, in most languages in Europe, and in all arts and sciences'.[37]

The programme proclaimed by Chambers' magazine confirms the nature of *Cyclopaedia*, which defined itself as a 'universal dictionary of arts and sciences'. The subtitle indicated not only that the work targeted all types of readers and included any piece of information relevant to the vast field covered by the encyclopaedia, but it also made reference to a certain cosmopolitan openness of the work. This character was consistent with the orientation of a large part of eighteenth-century encyclopaedism, which tended to target audiences across national borders, within the European context. Translations of the *Cyclopaedia* into other languages corroborated the actual success of this approach. The strong connection of Chambers' text with its audience is also confirmed by the fact that a considerable number of readers interested in his undertaking subscribed to purchase his work before it had even been published. Chambers was among the first publishers to adopt this method, which clearly had the advantage of significantly reducing the financial risks associated with the publication of a large work. Beyond the economic aspects, the subscription system, together with the serialisation of many encyclopaedias – that is, their publication staggered over time – ended up bringing these works closer to periodical publications and magazines, contributing to the expansion and consolidation of the works' readership. *Cyclopaedia* is a remarkable intellectual achievement, not least because it was the result of the work of Chambers alone, who was not supported by a team of collaborators or experts. The author managed to summarise the content of an enormous number of books and publications he personally consulted, with very impressive results, demonstrated by the huge number of the entries, including on specialised topics. See, for example, the article 'Parliament', which provides very detailed information regarding specific aspects, such as the legislative process followed at that time by the English House of Commons. Since *Cyclopaedia* was designed as a summary and compendium of other works, it had to cope with English copyright law, which, under an Act of the Parliament passed in 1710, had protected the right of authors and publishers to publish their works on an exclusive basis for a period of 14 years. In response to the possible objections connected with the will to protect those rights, Chambers replied that works such as his own had to be regarded as exempt from strict compliance with the obligations laid down by law,

[35] Chambers (n 30) *Preface*.

[36] R Yeo, 'A Solution to the Multitude of Books: Ephraim Chambers's Cyclopaedia (1728) as "the Best Book in the Universe"' (2003) 1 *Journal of the History of Ideas* 61.

[37] Yeo, *Encyclopaedic Visions* (n 24) 45.

insofar as they were intended to fulfil a public service function relating to the dissemination of knowledge. This is certainly one of the common aims of the eighteenth-century encyclopaedia: dissemination of knowledge aimed at the enlargement of an increasingly broad and informed public. It remains to be assessed how much Chambers' *Cyclopaedia* referred to some type of systematic organisation of knowledge. As we have seen, the alphabetical arrangement by articles made it possible to consult the entries on an ad hoc basis, without having to follow any particular reading order. However, Chambers wanted to prevent his work from becoming a mere warehouse of disparate information, without any connection between the several articles. This function of connecting the entries of the encyclopaedia was fulfilled through a dense network of mutual cross-references, a solution which Chambers was the first to use systematically. Thanks to this solution, the reader was led to access further information following on from the first entry article. On the basis of this systematic framework Chambers claimed that his dictionary, compared with that of 'former lexicographers', who had not attempted 'anything like Structure in their Works', was in some measure capable of the 'advantages of a continued discourse'.[38] The *Cyclopaedia* therefore also had the ambition of being adopted as a study text by universities, as happened in Cambridge. The cross-referencing system was completed by a table intended to offer a comprehensive 'View of knowledge', through which Chambers offered a classification of the different disciplines, starting from the major partition between 'natural and scientific knowledge' and 'artificial and technical knowledge'. The 'View of knowledge' was included for the purpose of showing 'the origin and derivation of the several parts, and the relation in which they stand to their common stock and to each other'. The form adopted for this systematisation was again that of a tree: this structure, and its ramifications, suggested an open model of knowledge, subject to continuous expansion. With its rich content on a wide range of subjects, *Cyclopaedia* presented itself as a useful work for the education of gentlemen, based on a notion of a circle of learning which, although complex, could still be regarded as accessible to an individual reader.

B. Diderot and D'Alambert's *Encyclopédie*

Compared with the rich encyclopaedic production of the eighteenth century, Diderot and D'Alambert's *Encyclopédie* (1751–72) was certainly a great novelty.[39] Despite its inception as a simple translation of Chambers' *Cyclopaedia* into French, the final outcome of the project was an entirely different type of work, which marked a radical break with the established notions of knowledge, implying that traditional learning amounted to nothing but prejudice and superstition.[40] In doing so, the *Encyclopédie* 'operated an epistemological shift that transformed the topography of everything known by man'.[41] Diderot and D'Alambert

[38] Chambers (n 30) *Preface*.

[39] The literature on the *Encyclopédie* is immense: see, for instance: R Venturi, *Le origini dell'Enciclopedia* (Roma, Edizioni U, 1946); J Proust, *Diderot et l'Encyclopédie* (Paris, Albin Michel, 1962); R Darnton, *The Business of Enlightenment: A Publishing History of the Encyclopédie, 1775–1800* (Cambridge, MA, Harvard University Press, 1979); L Delia, *Droit et philosophie à la lumière de l'Encyclopédie* (Oxford, Voltaire Foundation, 2015).

[40] Darnton (n 39) 7.

[41] ibid.

abandoned the pansophic projects that had been the basis of many encyclopaedic works between the Renaissance and the seventeenth century.[42] The French encyclopaedists rejected the '*esprit de système*' of the tradition which preceded them, in order to produce a work which refrained from providing a comprehensive and harmonious picture of the entire human knowledge. Rather, the *Encyclopédie* assumed that human knowledge, though limited, is subject to continuous expansion and correction, according to the progressive outlook typical of the Enlightenment.[43] This is achieved through the rejection of the principle of authority and the adoption of a spirit of critical research. In this context, discovering errors – in Bayle's style – is almost as important as the acquisition of new knowledge. The falsification of the presumed truths and the admission of ignorance are fundamental components of the vision of encyclopaedists.[44]

Furthermore, Diderot and his fellows accepted a certain degree of relativism: if the encyclopaedia is a map to navigate the maze of knowledge, they acknowledged that this map can offer very different representations of the land depending on the vantage points chosen for its description.[45]

In this new approach to knowledge, a significant role is played by the recognition of 'implicit knowledge' as a precondition for the exercise of arts and trades. Professions and crafts have a very important place in the *Encyclopédie*: their valorisation was tantamount

[42] Tega (n 20) 77.

[43] It can be interesting to note how the 'virtue of auto-correction' is identified by the *Encyclopédie* (in the entry 'Parlement d'Angleterre' written by Louis de Jaucourt) as the main feature of the English parliamentary institutions: 'La chambre des pairs & celle des communes sont les arbitres de la nation, & le roi est le surarbitre. Cette balance manquoit aux Romains; les grands & le peuple étoient toujours en division, sans qu'il y eut une puissance mitoyenne pour les accorder. Le gouvernement d'Angleterre est plus sage, parce qu'il y a un corps qui l'examine continuellement; & qui s'examine continuellement lui-même; telles sont ses erreurs qu'elles ne sont jamais longues; & que par l'esprit d'attention qu'elles donnent à la nation, elles sont souvent utiles. Un état libre, c'est-à-dire, toujours agité, ne saurait se maintenir, s'il n'est par ses propres lois, capable de correction; & tel est l'avantage du corps législatif qui s'assemble de tems en tems pour établir ou révoquer des lois': *Encyclopédie; ou Dictionnaire raisonné des sciences, des arts et des métiers*, 28 vols (eds D Diderot and J le Rond D'Alambert) (Paris, Briasson et al, 1751–72) Vol XII (1765) 40.

[44] 'Arrêtons – nous un moment ici, & jetons les yeux sur l'espace que nous venons de parcourir. Nous y remarquerons deux limites où se trouvent, pour ainsi dire, concentrées presque toutes les connaissances certaines accordées à nos lumières naturelles. L'une de ces limites, celle d'où nous sommes partis, est l'idée de nous – mêmes, qui conduit à celle de l'Etre tout – puissant, & de nos principaux devoirs. L'autre est cette partie des Mathématiques qui a pour objet les propriétés générales des corps, de l'étendue & de la grandeur. Entre ces deux termes est un intervalle immense, où l'Intelligence suprême semble avoir voulu se joüer de la curiosité humaine, tant par les nuages qu'elle y a répandus sans nombre, que par quelques traits de lumière qui semblent s'échapper de distance en distance pour nous attirer. On pourrait comparer l'Univers à certains ouvrages d'une obscurité sublime, dont les Auteurs en s'abaissant quelquefois à la portée de celui qui les lit, cherchent à lui persuader qu'il entend tout à – peu – près. Heureux donc, si nous nous engageons dans ce labyrinthe, de ne point quitter la véritable route; autrement les éclairs destinés à nous y conduire, ne serviraient souvent qu'à nous en écarter davantage': JB D'Alambert, 'Discours Préliminaire' in D Diderot and J le Rond D'Alambert (eds), *Encyclopédie; ou Dictionnaire raisonné des sciences, des arts et des métiers*, 28 vols (Paris, Briasson et al, 1751–72) Vol 1 (1751) vii.

[45] 'Mais comme dans les cartes générales du globe que nous habitons, les objets sont plus ou moins rapprochés, & présentent un coup d'œil différent selon le point de vûe où l'œil est placé par le Géographe qui construit la carte, de même la forme de l'arbre encyclopédique dépendra du point de vûe où l'on se mettra pour envisager l'univers littéraire. On peut donc imaginer autant de systèmes différents de la connoissance humaine, que de Mappemondes de différentes projections; & chacun de ces systèmes pourra même avoir, à l'exclusion des autres, quelque avantage particulier': D'Alambert, 'Discours Préliminaire' (n 44) xv. On the importance of cartography and its 'visual grammar' as a cognitive form of Western thought, see G Monsaingeon, *Mappamundi: Art et Cartographie* (Marseille, Editions Parenthèses, 2013).

to the discovery of an area of knowledge hitherto ignored by official science and the academy.

The space devoted to mechanical arts in the text of the *Encyclopédie* was complemented by the presence of a great number of illustrations: more than half of the plates included in the work displayed the operations of book-binding, sugar refining, tanning, and so on.[46] More generally, the use of illustrations played a prominent role in Diderot and D'Alambert's work: the 17 volumes of the text are accompanied by 11 volumes of plates. The separation of the text from the images invites the reader to turn a critical eye to what he or she reads and what he or she can see more concretely.[47] The extensive use of illustrations also established a precedent for later encyclopaedic works in the nineteenth and twentieth centuries.[48] From this point of view, encyclopaedias made a significant contribution to the visualisation of knowledge even before the advent of modern mass media. In so doing, they offered new paths for the dissemination and popularisation of cultural content in the modern age.

Compared with the models of the past, another original aspect of Diderot and D'Alambert's work was the inclusion of contributions from a very large number of personalities from culture, science and philosophy.[49] The work resulting from this cooperation was an intellectual undertaking characterised by a remarkable pluralism in approaches. It was the vivid confirmation of the existence of a 'Republic of Letters' claiming broad autonomy and freedom vis-a-vis the establishment. The purely alphabetical ordering of the articles also helped to underline this spirit of intellectual freedom and the refusal of a hierarchical organisation of knowledge. The rejection of the *esprit de système*, however, did not mean that encyclopaedists refused any systematic approach to knowledge. On the contrary, they were focused on carrying out a work based on a precise organisation of knowledge, inspired by the model of the Baconian *arbor scientiarum*.[50] The *Encyclopédie* was not, therefore, intended to be a mere repertoire of juxtaposed dictionary entries without any relationship with each other. Rather, it proposed a specific plan for the organisation of knowledge. The knowledge tree was divided, following Bacon's approach, into three broad faculties: memory, reason and imagination.

In this tri-partition, I would like to stress the importance of memory. A work such as the *Encyclopédie*, based on a progressive ideal of knowledge, nevertheless reserved a key role for memory and historical sciences in the development of new knowledge.

[46] Loveland (n 29) 230.

[47] M Delon, 'L'Encyclopedie de Diderot et d'Alambert, totalisation et inachèvement' in *Enciclopedismo antico e moderno* (Bari, Fondazione Gianfranco Dioguardi, 2020) 5.

[48] W Hupka, *Wort und Bild: Die Illustrationen in Wörterbüchern und Enzyklopädien* (Tübingen, Max Niemeyer Verlag, 1989) 96–98. The *Encyclopédie* represents, however, only one example of the wide use of illustrations in encyclopaedic works during the course of the eighteenth century: the 10 volumes of Gianfrancesco Pivati's *Nuovo dizionario scientifico e curioso sacro-profano* (Venice, Milocco, 1746–51) included almost 600 copperplates. Among later encylopaedias, the *Enciclopedia italiana* is recognised as the work of its genre that achieved the highest results in terms of the number and quality of its illustrations (Loveland (n 29) 217).

[49] 'C'est à l'exécution de ce projet étendu, non seulement aux différents objets de nos académies, mais à toutes les branches de la connoissance humaine, qu'une *Encyclopédie* doit suppléer; Ouvrage qui ne s'exécutera que par une sociéte de gens de lettres & d'artistes, épars, occupés chacun de sa partie, & liés seulement par l'intérêt général du genre humain, & par un sentiment de bienveillance réciproque': D Diderot, 'Encyclopedie (Philosophie)' in D Diderot and J le Rond D'Alambert (eds), *Encyclopédie; ou Dictionnaire raisonné des sciences, des arts et des métiers*, 28 vols (Paris, Briasson et al, 1751–72) Vol VII (1755) 636.

[50] Tega (n 20) 94–97.

In addition to the reference to the Baconian tree, what gave unity and circularity to Diderot and D'Alambert's work was the dense system of internal cross-references among the almost 72,000 articles of the work.[51] It has been said that this system – borrowed from Chambers' *Cyclopaedia* – makes the *Encyclopédie* the ancestor of the hypertext.[52] Diderot considered these links to not only serve as a mere reference tool, but also as a means of representing the circularity of human knowledge as a continuum. It is thanks to this internal architecture that his work acquired its proper encyclopaedic character.[53]

The publication of the French encyclopaedia paved the way for subsequent large, national encyclopaedias.[54] These works had characteristics which differed significantly from the French example but shared some basic preconditions with it. Underpinning the great success of the encyclopaedic model in the nineteenth century was the will to provide an intellectual response to two contradictory needs: on the one hand, the need to accept the growing specialisation of knowledge, and on the other, the desire to preserve the cultural unity of the *Bildung* reserved to the ruling class. The somewhat paradoxical character of this cultural programme was acutely noted by some intellectuals of the age.[55] It is precisely those preconditions that provide the basis for drawing a parallel between the emergence of parliamentarism and modern encyclopaedias.

IV. The National Encyclopaedias of the Nineteenth Century

The *Encyclopédie* addressed the citizens of a 'Republic of Letters', ideally transcending national borders. Diderot and D'Alambert's work was fully inspired by the ideals of cosmopolitism

[51] 'Ainsi trois choses forment l'ordre encyclopédique; le nom de la Science à laquelle l'article appartient; le rang de cette Science dans l'Arbre; la liaison de l'article avec d'autres dans la même Science ou dans une Science différente; liaison indiquée par les renvois, ou facile à sentir au moyen des termes techniques expliqués suivant leur ordre alphabétique': D'Alambert, 'Discours Préliminaire' (n 44) xviii–xix.

[52] E Brian, 'L'ancêtre de l'hypertexte' (1998) 47 *Les Cahiers de Science et Vie* 28.

[53] G Blanchard and M Olsen, 'Le système de renvois dans l'Encyclopédie: Une cartographie des structures de connaissances au XVIIIe siècle' (2002) 31–32 *Recherches sur Diderot et sur l'Encyclopédie* 45.

[54] On some of these works which succeeded the *Encyclopédie*, see F Kafker, *Notable Encyclopedias of the Late Eighteenth Century: Eleven Successors of the Encyclopédie* (Oxford, Voltaire Foundation at the Taylor Institution, 1994).

[55] G Leopardi, *Zibaldone di pensieri*, n 1922 (15 October 1821) in *Opere Complete*, Vol II (Firenze, Sansoni, 1969) 521: 'Non può nessuno vantarsi di essere perfetto in nessuna umana disciplina, s'egli non è anche perfetto in tutte le possibili discipline e cognizioni umane. Tanta è la forza e l'importanza dei rapporti che esistono fra le cose le più disparate, non conoscendo i quali, nessuna cosa si conosce perfettamente. Ora, poiché ciò che ho detto è impossibile all'individuo, perciò lo spirito umano non fa quegl'immensi progressi che potrebbe fare. È però certo che se non perfettamente, almeno quanto è possibile, è realmente necessario di esser uomo enciclopedico, non per darsi a tutte le discipline e non perfezionarsi e distinguersi in nessuna, ma per esser quanto è possibile perfetto in una sola. In ciò l'opinione del tempo è ragionevole. Chi almeno nella superficie non è uomo enciclopedico, non può veramente considerarsi (e oggi non si considera) come gran letterato o insigne in veruna disciplina intellettuale': 'Nobody can claim to be perfect in any human discipline, if he is not perfect in all possible disciplines included in human knowledge. So great is the strength and importance of the relationships among the most disparate things, that, if you don't know them, you can't say to know anything perfectly. Since what I have said is impossible to achieve by any individual, the human spirit does not make the great progress that could be done. But it is certain that, if not perfectly, at least as much as possible, it is really necessary to be an encyclopaedic man not in order to cultivate all disciplines, with the result of reaching the perfection in none, but in order to be as perfect as possible in just one. The common opinion of our time is therefore reasonable on this. Who at least on the surface is not an encyclopaedic man, he cannot really be considered (and today we do not consider) a true knowledgeable man in any intellectual discipline'.

and universality central to the vision of the eighteenth century Enlightenment. Despite these characteristics, all around Europe, contemporaries noted in the work the strong footprint of the French national spirit: this perception was even stronger when, after 1789, the *Encyclopédie* was viewed as the ideological forerunner of the French Revolution. In response to the soft power exercised by France through the *Encyclopédie*, other major European nations reacted by launching their encyclopaedic enterprises, often distinguished by very different characteristics from the French archetype.[56] Almost all the great encyclopaedic enterprises between the eighteenth and nineteenth centuries shared the ambition of reflecting a national identity that was already established or was still in the making.[57] In a long-standing progression that peaked in the middle of the twentieth century, 'the fact of producing a national encyclopaedia such as those of Germany, Britain and France came to be seen as a sign of the country's strength and modernity'.[58] In practice, encyclopaedias in many countries were a major feature of national unification from a cultural point of view: their realisation was thus directly linked to the nation-building process, as was the case, for example, in Norway.[59] In other countries, especially where national unification was still in progress, as in Germany, this link was more indirect, but was clearly felt by their contemporaries.

Germany was one of the most important centres of production of encyclopaedias in the nineteenth century. The most popular genre was the *Konversations-Lexicon*, the first examples of which appeared in the early eighteenth century.[60] The *Konversations-Lexicon* was intended primarily as a tool to facilitate conversation and as a support for the reading of periodicals and newspapers. It therefore represented an alternative model by comparison with the gigantic encyclopaedic enterprises that flourished in the nineteenth century, such as the French *Encyclopédie Méthodique* (1782–1832)[61] and the German *Allgemeine Encyclopädie der Wissenschaften und Künste* (1818–89).[62] In keeping with this function, the first editions of these works were distinguished by a clear liberal orientation and included several essay-like articles, thus confirming their closeness to the world of journalism.

[56] 'The keen intent of Germany, Italy, Spain, and Switzerland to produce encyclopaedias of their own in the eighteenth century clearly manifests itself as a function of national interest, similar to the race to organise national language academies and dictionaries that was characteristic of the seventeenth century': C Donato, 'Eighteenth-century Encyclopedias and National Identity' (1993) 4–6 *History of European Ideas* 959.

[57] 'Each nation has its own particular encyclopedia because each nation has its own language, has its own ideas, has its own maxims, has its own arts … has its own prejudices … a European Encyclopedia is impossible': G Abbattista, 'La "Folie de la raison par alphabet": le origini settecentesche dell'Encyclopaedia Britannica (1768–1701)' in G Abbattista (ed), *L'enciclopedismo in Italia nel XVIII secolo* (Napoli, Bibliopolis, 1996) 397, quoted by Loveland (n 29) 3.

[58] Loveland (n 29) 87.

[59] E Bolstad and SA Pettersen, 'How to Build an Encyclopedia for the 21st Century: Lessons Learned from *The Great Norwegian Encyclopedia*' (2019) 13 *Studia lexicographica* 153, 154.

[60] The first example of a *Konversation-Lexicon* was published in 1708 with the title *Reales Staats- und Zeitungs- und Conversations- Lexicon:* this work had more than 40 editions by the early nineteenth century. The work was later imitated, but with the introduction of significant innovations, by the *Conversations lexicon mit vorzueglicher Ruecksicht auf die gegenwaertigen Zeiten*, published in Leipzig in six volumes by Renatus Gotthelf Loebel and Christian Wilhelm Franke between 1796 and 1808 and later acquired by Friedrich Brockhaus: this encyclopaedia was commonly known as 'the Brockhaus' and was published in several editions throughout the nineteenth century. For the history of the *Konversations-Lexica* in Germany, see Loveland (n 29) 36–43.

[61] J-M Roland de la Platière et al (eds), *Encyclopédie méthodique: Manufactures, arts et métiers* (Paris, 1785–1828).

[62] *Allgemeine Encyclopädie der Wissenschaften und Künste* (Leipzig, Gleditisch and Brockhaus, 1818–89).

The *Konversation-Lexica* made reference to an 'imagined public sphere of sociability among equals',[63] naturally associated with liberalism and freedom.[64] In some cases, the editors of the *Lexica* were directly involved in the political events of the Vormärz and the 1848 revolution: this was the case for Joseph Mayer, the editor of the popular homonymous *Konversationlexicon*, who was a supporter of radical stances when sitting as a member in the second chamber of the Saxon Landtag.[65] By the mid-nineteenth century, however, even these kinds of encyclopaedic works had become more scholarly and objective.

In Great Britain too, the *Encyclopaedia Britannica* was conceived to provide Britain with a work for the specific needs of the national public. Compared with the *Encyclopédie*, what is particularly striking in this work is the absence of any anti-establishment sentiment: the main purpose of *Britannica* was to provide an authoritative and easily accessible reference work for the benefit of the new middle-class public.[66]

The first edition of the *Britannica* was published in Scotland in 100 weekly instalments between 1768 and 1771. Like the *Cyclopaedia* before it, the *Britannica* was the work of a single man, William Smellie, who was responsible for compiling all the entries of the three volumes comprising the encyclopaedia. Through its several editions, the *Britannica* rapidly became a symbol of the prestige and power of the imperial Great Britain on the world stage. From the publication of its first edition, the work adopted an organisational style that was explicitly in opposition to the French *Encyclopédie*. Any attempt to offer a systematic arrangement of knowledge was rejected. Instead, the *Britannica* declared the intent to contrast the fragmentation of knowledge via the illustration of the main sciences in separate treatises, each of which was accompanied by some short satellite articles redirecting the reader to the main entries. In the later nineteenth-century editions of the encyclopaedia, several articles were compiled by the most renowned specialists of the age,[67] with the intent of offering not only the established knowledge, but also the perception of the scholarly debate about the most controversial subjects of scientific research. Inevitably, this approach had the effect of increasing the complexity of the texts, thereby limiting the readership to the most cultured public.

Over the course of the nineteenth century, and later, the *Britannica* shared with the other great encyclopaedias the need to strike a difficult balance between the growing specialisation of knowledge and the desire to remain relevant to the general public. In some countries, the growth of the public potentially interested in encyclopaedias suggested the publication of works which were explicitly aimed at the lower classes: this was the case, for example, in Great Britain of the *Penny Cyclopaedia* (1833–43),[68] in France of

[63] Loveland (n 29) 41.

[64] For an interesting comparison between the popular encyclopaedias in Germany and Great Britain in the XIX century, see U Spree, *Das Streben nach Wissen: Eine vergleichende Gattungsgeschichte der populären Enzyklopädie in Deutschland und Großbritannien im 19 Jahrhundert* (Berlin, De Gruyter, 2009). The author emphasises a significant shift in the major German encyclopaedias from a liberal stance prevailing at the origin of these works to a more nationalistic approach after 1870.

[65] ibid, 251.

[66] On the Encyclopaedia Britannica, see H Kogan, *The Great EB: The Story of the Encyclopaedia Britannica* (Chicago, IL, University of Chicago Press, 1958); and Collison (n 7) 137–55.

[67] For instance, in the ninth edition (1875), the article 'Evolution' was authored by TH Huxley, while JC Maxwell wrote the article 'Physical sciences'.

[68] *Penny Cyclopaedia of the Society for the Diffusion of Useful Knowledge*, 27 vols (London, Knight, 1833–43).

the *Encyclopédie nouvelle* (1834–42),[69] and in Germany of the *Kleineres Brockhaus'sches Conversations-Lexicon* (1854).[70] Ordinarily, these works were published on a serial basis and were sold at a very low cost for each instalment. The spread of these kinds of publications marked an evident trend towards the democratisation of encyclopaedias in Europe, paving the way for later publications aimed at the mass market, such as the *Larousse* in France.

In our short review of the major national encyclopaedias, we must mention two late examples of encyclopaedias initiated and completed in the first half of the twentieth century: the *Enciclopedia universal ilustrada europeo-americana* (also called the *Enciclopedia Espasa*, or *Enciclopedia Espasa-Calpe*) and the *Enciclopedia italiana*.

The *Espasa*[71] was a gigantic encyclopaedia published in 72 volumes between 1908 and 1930, with the addition of an appendix of 10 further volumes published between 1930 and 1933. The work was one of the amplest of its genre, dealing with every kind of subject, and very richly illustrated.[72]

The *Enciclopedia italiana* (1929–37)[73] has been defined as 'the supreme example of an encyclopaedia that set out to present the best possible image of its people and the wealth and stature of their culture'.[74] Responsibility for the design and the scientific direction of the *Enciclopedia* was assigned to the philosopher Giovanni Gentile, one of the ideologues of the Fascist regime. Undoubtedly, one of the main purposes of this work was the celebration of fascism also as a cultural power (the article 'Fascism' was signed by Mussolini himself). It must be said, however, that the respected specialists invited to contribute to the *Enciclopedia* were permitted a considerable degree of freedom in dealing with their subjects. In fact, the *Enciclopedia* represented the first example in Italy of a large-scale collective intellectual enterprise.[75] The result was a remarkable work, of reliable scientific quality, that was continued after the end of Fascism thanks to the support of the Istituto dell'Enciclopedia italiana.

V. The Nineteenth-Century Encyclopaedism between Philosophy, Pedagogy and Literature

As we have seen, nineteenth-century encyclopaedism as a cultural phenomenon inspired a vast production of encyclopaedias and dictionaries aimed at an ever-increasing public of readers. In parallel, some of the leading philosophers of the age, from Hegel, to Humboldt and Comte, put the encyclopaedic reform of all available knowledge at the centre of their thought.

[69] *Encyclopédie Nouvelle*, 8 vols (Paris, 1834–42).

[70] *Kleineres Brockhaus'sches Conversations-Lexicon*, 4 vols (Leipzig, Brockhaus, 1854).

[71] [Espasa] *Enciclopedia Universal ilustrada Europeo-americana*, 72 vols (Madrid, Espasa et al, 1908–30).

[72] Collison (n 7) 201.

[73] *Enciclopedia italiana*, 35 vols (Rome, Treccani, 1929–37).

[74] Preece and Collison (n 4). On the history of the *Enciclopedia italiana*, see G Turi, *Il fascismo e il consenso degli intellettuali* (Bologna, il Mulino, 1980) 22 ff.

[75] M Bray, 'Dall'Enciclopedia Italiana alla Enciclopedia Einaudiana' in *Enciclopedismo antico e moderno* (Bari, Fondazione Gianfranco Dioguardi, 2020) 36.

Hegel published the first edition of his *Enzyklopädie der philosophischen Wissenschaften im Grundrisse* in 1817. In this book, the philosopher outlined a radical criticism of Diderot and D'Alambert's *Encyclopédie* due to its lack of any real systematic approach to knowledge that reduced the work to a collection of empirical findings.[76] Hegel maintained that the true, philosophical encyclopaedia had to be systematic. Philosophy as a system can provide the scientific, that is, the conceptual, foundation of all the particular sciences: from this perspective, in Hegel's view, philosophy and encyclopaedia coincide.[77] The Hegelian philosophical encyclopaedia is divided into three parts: the science of logic; the philosophy of nature; and the philosophy of spirit, corresponding to the three developmental stages of the spirit. The image that best expresses the essence of this encyclopaedic vision is the circle of circles, in which every circle is a necessary element of a system that manifests itself in all its components.[78]

Hegel's views were translated into an actual education programme thanks to the work of Wilhelm von Humboldt. As Under Secretary of State of the Prussian monarchy, Humboldt suggested the foundation in 1810 of a new state university in Berlin inspired by the principles of German idealism. As stated in a famous speech of 1810,[79] the new university was based on the principle of the unity of research and teaching, and on a holistic approach to knowledge in which philosophy as '*Mutter aller Wissenschaften*' had a prominent role in securing the unity of all sciences.[80] The other cornerstone of this intellectual programme was the external and internal autonomy of higher education in the pursuit of qualified knowledge. These principles had to be protected in the state's own 'enlightened' interest, with the intent of forming the *Bildung* of the nascent national elite. The Humboldtian model enjoyed widespread success and was imitated and replicated in Europe as well as in the United States. As Robert Anderson put it:

> The Humboldtian university can be seen as the characteristic form of the university idea until the growth of mass higher education in the late twentieth century. It had a number of interlocking features, some new, some inherited from the past, and was inevitably marked by the deep forces of the age, including nationalism, secularisation, the growth of the modern state, and the shift of social power from aristocracies to the middle classes, on the basis of merit, intellectual expertise, and professionalism.[81]

The Humboldtian reform was completed with the creation of the *gymnasium*, conceived as a preparatory school from which students could proceed to access higher degrees of education. Humanities, like philosophy and history, had a central place in the new academic encyclopaedia, although Wilhelm's brother, Alexander von Humboldt, a naturalist

[76] GWF Hegel, *Encyclopedia of the Philosophical Sciences in Basic Outline* (1st edn 1817) (Cambridge, Cambridge University Press, 2010) § 16.

[77] Tega (n 20) 100.

[78] Hegel (n 76) § 15.

[79] W von Humboldt, 'Über die innere und äussere Organisation der höheren wissenschaftlichen Anstalten' in *Werke in fünf Bänden*, Bd 4 (1st edn 1810) (Darmstadt, Wissenschaftliche Buchgesellschaft, 2010).

[80] T Nybom, 'The Humboldt Legacy: Reflections on the Past, Present, and Future of the European University' (2003) 16 *Higher Education Policy* 141, 144.

[81] R Anderson, 'The "Idea of a University" Today' (2010) History and Policy. Policy Papers, available at: www.historyandpolicy.org/policy-papers/papers/the-idea-of-a-university-today.

and explorer,[82] played a significant role in also promoting the study of scientific disciplines, a field in which the Berlin university acquired an undisputed leadership in Europe. In the second part of the century, however, the generalist and humanistic model promoted by the Humboldtian university was confronted with the challenge of the increasing specialisation in scholarship. The genesis of the much-envied German *Technische Hochschulen* was a sign of this development, although these schools too had to establish chairs in philosophy and history in order to secure their scientific quality.[83]

An evident pedagogical intent is also at the core of another nineteenth-century philosophical encyclopaedia: that promoted by Auguste Comte. The first volume of Compte's *Cours de philosophie positive* appeared in 1830, the same year as the third edition of Hegel's *Enzyklopädie*. The French philosopher pleaded for a new encyclopaedic systematisation of knowledge based not on abstractions, but on the actual nature of the objects submitted to classification. The new encyclopaedia coincided with a general plan of education conceived of as the only truly scientific and rational access to knowledge. Compte emphasised the need to make this knowledge open to all:

> Le problème général de l'éducation intellectuelle consiste à faire parvenir, en peu d'années, un seul entendement, le plus souvent médiocre, au même point de développement qui a été atteint, dans une longue suite de siècles, par un grand nombre de génies supérieurs appliquant successivement, pendant leur vie entière, toutes leurs forces à l'étude d'un même sujet.[84]

In order to be properly understood, the new encyclopaedic system should go from the most abstract sciences (like mathematics and astronomy) to the more complex ones (like the study of social phenomena). The whole plan was described by Comte via a synoptical table that preceded the text of his lessons. The enormous influence exerted by Comte during this era represented another channel for the propagation of the encyclopaedic ideals in nineteenth-century Europe.

Furthermore, some great masterpieces of European and American literature can be viewed as encyclopaedic interpretations of the culture of their time. As Edward Mendelson observed, encyclopaedic narrative occupies a central importance in Western literature: works like Goethe's *Faust*, Melville's *Moby Dick* and Tolstoy's *War and Peace* 'attempt to render the full range of knowledge and beliefs of a national culture, while identifying the ideological perspective from which that culture shapes end interprets its knowledge'.[85] Franco Moretti views these works as a form of modern epic: a sort of super-genre that has provided many of the 'sacred texts' of Western literary culture.[86] In some way or another, these works replicate in modernity the encyclopaedic pattern of

[82] Alexander von Humboldt was an encyclopaedist himself: he was the author of *Kosmos*, a monumental work in six volumes (*Kosmos – Entwurf einer physischen Weltbeschreibung* (Stuttgart, Cotta, 1845–62), in which he outlined the findings of his research on science and nature. The work had an enthusiastic reception especially in Britain and the United States.

[83] Nybom (n 80) 146.

[84] A Compte, *Cours de Philosophie Positive* (Paris, Bachelier, 1830) T 1, Leçon 2, 79.

[85] E Mendelson, 'Encyclopedic Narrative: From Dante to Pynchon' (1976) 91(6) *Modern Language Notes* 1267, 1269.

[86] F Moretti, *Modern Epic: The World System from Goethe to García Márquez* (New York, Verso 2010).

Western culture's 'sacred book', the Bible, which is itself an encyclopaedic collection of different books (*ta biblia*).[87]

The work that in nineteenth-century Europe perhaps most profoundly expressed an encyclopaedic ambition was Honoré de Balzac's *Comédie humaine*. The *Comédie* can indeed be seen as an encyclopaedic accumulation of knowledge, facts, ideas and heterogeneous narratives referring back to one another:[88] as Roland Barthes put it, Balzac's masterpiece is a kind of 'Livre-Somme ..., encyclopédie transcendée par un sens qu'on donne au monde'.[89]

VI. Encyclopaedism and Parliamentarism and their Parallel Transformations

Encyclopaedias between the eighteenth and nineteenth centuries played an important role in structuring the new public sphere. They responded to the request for a synthesis of knowledge in a cultural context that was becoming increasingly complex and fragmented into specialist disciplines. European encyclopaedias had the ambition of being reliable 'mirrors' of their age, in continuity with the Renaissance tradition that compared these works to theatres, sites representative of the diversity of the world. They made a significant contribution to the formation of a new intellectual citizenship by creating a common foundation of sociability and knowledge sharing. While, especially in the eighteenth century, the natural recipient of encyclopaedic works was the citizen of an ideal 'Republic of Letters', conceived of as cosmopolitan and indifferent to national borders, this reference changed markedly during the following century. Encyclopaedias increasingly became explicit expressions of the culture of nation states which were already established or were still in the making. In this new context, encyclopaedias were part of a communicative ecosystem together with other media, such as periodicals and magazines.

Encyclopaedism embraced different patterns in the two centuries. The eighteenth-century encyclopaedias still referred to the ancient concept of *enkuklios paideia*, intended as a circular learning programme aimed at developing the general knowledge of the amateur gentleman.[90] Following this model, works such as Chambers' *Cyclopaedia* could still be proposed as texts which were potentially readable as a 'continuous discourse' as they were aimed at educating the ruling class of their time. These works, like Diderot and D'Alambert's *Encyclopédie* later, while adopting a structure based on alphabetically ordered articles, did not refrain from providing a systematic framework for linking the various disciplines: this was done through the dense network of cross-references between the different articles. Moreover, the underlying connecting structure was offered by 'knowledge trees', more or less directly linked to the Baconian model.

[87] On the encyclopaedic influence exerted by the Bible on Western literature, see N Frye, *The Great code: the Bible and literature* (New York, Harcourt Brace Jovanovich, 1982).
[88] T Conrad, 'Balzac, l'épique et l'encyclopédique' (2016) 2 *Romantisme* 35, 36.
[89] R Barthes, *La Préparation du roman* (Paris, Seuil, 2003) 248 quoted by Conrad, ibid, 36.
[90] Yeo, *Encyclopaedic Visions* (n 24) 250.

During the nineteenth century, however, most of the great national encyclopaedias abandoned the Baconian classifications, but did not give up a systematic arrangement of knowledge, such as the one implied by the monographic treatises included in the *Britannica*. Compared with the past, these new encyclopaedias, which were sometimes enormous in size, aspired to reach an even greater degree of comprehensiveness, seeking to deal with any and every object of human learning. By developing this programme, encyclopaedias made a decisive contribution to shaping the epistemological environment of their age. They were one of the constitutive elements of national cultures, extending their influence well beyond the nineteenth century. However, even in its heyday, the encyclopaedic ambition to comprehensively represent all the available knowledge encountered some serious challenges. On the one hand, scientific, geographical and historical knowledge kept expanding at an accelerated pace, forcing encyclopaedias to frequently update their content. On the other hand, the increasing specialisation of knowledge made it difficult to strike a balance between the accessibility to common readers and the inclusion of highly technical contents. These difficulties led to an increasing diversification of encyclopaedic works in relation to their target audiences. In particular, from the second half of the century, some encyclopaedias were explicitly aimed at lower classes, with the intent of offering a much more accessible product in terms of both content and purchase prices. The popularity of encyclopaedias continued for much of the twentieth century, in the context of an expanding market for these kinds of works. Their relative importance as a cultural medium, however, was increasingly challenged by the new electronic media like radio and television. Moreover, the advent, at the turn of the century, of the internet confronted traditional encyclopaedias with a radical paradigm shift that I will analyse in chapter four.

The emergence and establishment of parliaments as central institutions of the new representative regimes presents direct connections with the development of encyclopaedism as one of the leading cultural phenomena of modernity. I believe that the analysis of these common elements may be useful for the purpose of highlighting certain features of parliamentarism which have not been sufficiently examined thus far and which I consider to be important also for understanding some aspects of contemporary parliaments and their possible future. Modern parliaments can be studied as 'political encyclopaedias' of their age. In carrying out their representative role, parliaments have decisively contributed to shaping political communities by making an otherwise evasive entity such as 'national politics' visible and intelligible within the public sphere. Like encyclopaedias, they have played a crucial role in making the political debate accessible to the public. In order to connect with the public sphere, parliaments abandoned the traditional practice of keeping their proceedings secret[91] with a major shift that ultimately led to the full publicity of parliamentary deliberations.[92] By integrating into the nation-building processes of their age, parliaments were expected to perform a 'teaching function' vis-a-vis the nation.[93] However, the connection between parliamentarism and encyclopaedism not only arises due to their common social preconditions, but also, primarily, due to their epistemic foundations. They both referred to an open model of knowledge, submitted to relentless correction and expansion.

[91] J Habermas, *The Structural Transformation of the Public Sphere: An Inquiry into a Category of Bourgeois Society* (1st edn 1962) (Cambridge, Polity, 1992) 60–61.

[92] ibid, 63. For more details about this development, see ch 2, section II.

[93] W Bagehot, *The English Constitution* (1st edn 1867) (Oxford, Oxford University Press, 2009) 100–01.

Moreover, like contemporary encyclopaedias, modern parliamentary representation assumed a generalist character, not only in the sense of representing a supposed general interest, but also by reason of its ability to deal with any political subject, with the aim of finding a rational compromise between conflicting interests. This process developed over three centuries, during which parliamentary representation has undergone radical structural transformations. In the next chapter, we shall see the main features of the encyclopaedic parliaments between the eighteenth and nineteenth centuries. In the third chapter I shall analyse the structural transformations brought to these institutions in the course of the twentieth century.

2

Encyclopaedic Parliamentarism in the Nineteenth Century

I. Parliaments and Political Representation in the Nineteenth Century

Modern parliaments emerged between the eighteenth and nineteenth centuries as the political encyclopaedias of the nascent liberal bourgeoisie.[1] They were based on the dual paradigm of parliamentarians' free mandate and national representation:[2] two principles which distinguished these institutions from pre-modern parliamentary assemblies. The latter were composed in order to reflect the basic composition of society according its different ranks (*Stände*). Modern parliaments, by contrast, asserted their separation from the society they sought to represent. Their peculiar representative claim[3] was based on a status of autonomy which rendered legislative assemblies circular and self-sufficient institutions.

On the basis of these assumptions, legislative assemblies in the liberal era played a fundamental role in the nation-making process in many European countries, such as France, Belgium and Italy. Pascal Ory has recently emphasised the plural historical paths leading to the consolidation of the political idea of nationhood.[4] This concept is rather recent and came to be defined in a period between the French Revolution and the era characterised by the full affirmation of liberalism[5] when the crucial factor for the identification of a nation was not ethnicity, language, or other substantial elements (as would be the case at the end of the nineteenth century with the rise of nationalistic movements). Rather, what characterised the nation was the fact that it represented a collective commitment to common interests as opposed to particular interests.[6] This interpretation was not only typical of the revolutionary period, but was shared by many thinkers of the liberal era. Walter Bagehot, for example, in recognising nation-making as one of the essential features of nineteenth-century politics, believed that the essence of the nation consisted not primarily of its ethnical features, but

[1] On representative government as a peculiar form of the political organisation of the European bourgeoisie, see EJ Hobsbawm, *The Age of Capital* (London, Weidenfeld & Nicolson, 1975) 55.

[2] HF Pitkin, *The Concept of Representation* (Berkeley, CA, University of California Press, 1967) 170.

[3] M Saward, *The Representative Claim* (Oxford, Oxford University Press, 2010).

[4] P Ory, *Qu'est-ce qu'une nation? Une histoire mondiale* (Paris, Gallimard, 2020).

[5] EJ Hobsbawm, *Nations and Nationalism Since 1780: Programme, Myth, Reality*, 2nd edn (Cambridge, Cambridge University Press, 1990) 17.

[6] ibid, 21.

of a gradual process of convergence of opinions on some common values, a development promoted by the influence of political or religious leaders.[7]

At a time when many European monarchies were still engaged in a gradual process of nationalisation,[8] legislative assemblies represented the most advanced political institutions for the concrete representation of the concept of nationhood. They played a significant role in the construction of the nation as an 'imagined community', that is, as a political community built on solidarity and simultaneity.[9] The self-proclamation of the Third Estate as 'National Assembly' (17 June 1789) marks a watershed from this point of view.[10] Parliaments were consequently crucial institutions for enabling the bourgeoisie to become 'the first class in world history to achieve a sense of solidarity on the basis of essentially imagined foundations'.[11] This development, however, was far from beeing linear, especially if we consider

> the self-perception of the ruling class. In some countries, like Italy, the liberal elite proved to be very reluctant in recognizing parliamentarism as a positive factor in the nation-building process: … in the second part of the century, some prominent Italian political leaders overtly accused the Parliament – with its fragmentation and particularism – of working against the political unity of the nation.[12]

In this chapter I will analyse the different components underlying the emergence of parliaments as great encyclopaedias of nineteenth-century politics. I will focus, initially, on the link between parliamentarism and the bourgeois public sphere, and on the symbiosis between parliaments and the new communication dimension represented by print media. I will then focus on the particular relationship that was established between the notion of parliaments' autonomy from society and the principle upholding the public nature of parliamentary work. I will therefore analyse the multiple meanings of the emergence of the theatre as the leading form for nineteenth-century parliaments. I will subsequently examine the characteristics

[7] W Bagehot, *Physics and Politics* (London, Henry S King & Co, 1872) ch III: 'The problem of "nation-making" that is, the explanation of the origin of nations such as we now see them, and such as in historical times they have always been – cannot, as it seems to me, be solved without separating it into two: one, the making of broadly-marked races, such as the negro, or the red man, or the European; and the second, that of making the minor distinctions, such as the distinction between Spartan and Athenian, or between Scotchman and Englishman. Nations, as we see them, are (if my arguments prove true) the produce of two great forces: one the race-making force which, whatever it was, acted in antiquity, and has now wholly, or almost, given over acting; and the other the nation-making force, properly so called, which is acting now as much as it ever acted, and creating as much as it ever created'. In contemporary nation-making processes, Bagehot therefore considers the influence exercised by political and religious leaders to be crucial in setting 'the tone which others take, and the fashion which others use'. For him 'this unconscious imitation and encouragement of appreciated character, and this equally unconscious shrinking from and persecution of disliked character, is the main force which moulds and fashions men in society as we now see it'.

[8] Rituals such as royal funerals played an important role in this process of the nationalisation of monarchies during the nineteenth century: see C De Spiegeleer, 'The nationalization and mediatization of European monarchies in times of sorrow: Royal deaths and funerals in the second half of the nineteenth century' in E Woodacre, LHS Dean, C Jones et al (eds), *The Routledge History of Monarchy* (London, Routledge, 2019).

[9] B Anderson, *Imagined Communities. Reflections on the Origin and Spread of Nationalism*, 2nd edn (London, Verso, 1991) 36.

[10] Ory (n 4) 66.

[11] ibid, 76.

[12] F Cammarano, 'Nazionalizzazione della politica e politicizzazione della nazione. I dilemmi della classe dirigente nell'Italia liberale' in M Meriggi and P Schiera (eds), *Dalla città alla nazione. Borghesie ottocentesche in Italia e in Germania* (Bologna, il Mulino, 1993) 142–43.

of the liberal parliamentary class and its connection with an encyclopaedic conception of culture. In this regard, I will devote a section to the rise of the great parliamentary libraries, as 'institutions within institutions', focused on providing an encyclopaedic knowledge-base for the work of deputies. These libraries were also the places where the great ninenetenth-century parliamentary treatises, such as the 1844 Erskine May *Treatise*, were conceived: I briefly decribe some of these remarkable encyclopaedic collections of parliamentary precedents and usages. I will then consider the links between parliamentary encyclopaedism and the idea of legislative rationality in the nineteenth century. Finally, I will discuss the causes of the crisis regarding the nineteenth century's encyclopaedic parliamentarism and the emergence of alternative models of political representation.

II. Parliaments and the Bourgeois Public Sphere

In his 1962 seminal work on the structural transformation of the public sphere, Jürgen Habermas highlighted the close connection between parliamentarism and the emergence of the modern public sphere.[13] The work of representative assemblies presupposes the existence of a critical and informed public capable of appreciating the political relevance of parliamentary debates. In turn, parliamentary debate, through the mediation provided by the press and political associations, played a key role in shaping a modern, politically oriented public opinion. A discursive public opinion emerged in which parliamentary and social communication spaces were interconnected.[14]

These developments were first evident in Great Britain,[15] as a consequence of a series of events affecting the economic, the social and the political spheres. Between the eighteenth and nineteenth centuries Great Britain was home to the first industrial revolution in human history. Far from being the result of a political economy of mere *laissez-faire*, this disrupting, multifaceted phenomenon had strong relationships with institutional change. As SR Epstein put it:

> The establishment of capitalist markets and individual property rights required the centralization of political sovereignity and the abolition of decentralized rent-seeking based on social class and privilege: in other words, the establishment of clear state property rights. Contrary to theories of natural rights and natural markets, the main precondition for both modern individualism based on self-autonomy and self-ownership … was the rise of the modern state: the rise, that is, of a state with a division between legislative, executive and judicial powers, in which the jurisdictional boundaries between different centres of institutional power are strictly defined, and in which the possession of full and legitimate sovereignity empowers it to enforce collective agreements. These crucial institutional changes were achieved in England from the latter half of the seventeenth century and elsewhere in Europe in the course of the eighteenth and nineteenth century.[16]

[13] J Habermas, *The Structural Transformation of the Public Sphere: An Inquiry into a Category of Bourgeois Society* (1st edn 1962) (Cambridge, Polity, 1992) 57–88.

[14] A Schulz and A Wirsching, 'Introduction' in A Schulz and A Wirsching (eds), *Parlamentarische Kulturen in Europa. Das Parlament als Kommunikationsraum* (Duesseldorf, Droste Verlag, 2012) 15.

[15] Habermas (n 13) 57.

[16] SR Epstein, *Freedom and Growth* (London, Routledge, 2000) 173, quoted by L Magnusson, *Nation, State and the Industrial Revolution: The Visible Hand* (London, Routledge, 2009) 10–11. About the social and economic preconditions that triggered the Industrial Revolution in Britain, see RC Allen, *The British Industrial Revolution in Global Perspective* (Cambridge, Cambridge University Press, 2009).

The rise of the parliamentary form of government played a crucial role in this development. During the eighteenth century, the British Parliament progressively strengthened its constitutional privileges. The balance of power between the Parliament and the king shifted decisively in favour of the former. With the Hannover monarchs, the principle of the Cabinet's political accountability to the House of Commons definitively imposed itself, with the resulting convention requiring the king to appoint a prime minister capable of obtaining the support of the elected chamber.[17] On the other hand, in the House of Commons, a fundamental division emerged between the members supporting the king's government and those opposing it. Thanks to the principle of the freedom of speech and other immunities granted to parliamentarians, the opposition could freely express its criticism of the government's actions, without fear of violent repression.[18]

For the first time, conditions were emerging which supported a peaceful rotation between the groups vying for power, without recourse to civil war. Two parties were formed in the Parliament, namely the Whigs and the Tories, alternately coming to power throughout the eighteenth century: while the majority supported the Prime Minister and the other members of the Cabinet, the minority group remained loyal to the Crown,[19] thus realising the institutional incorporation of the opposition into the English political system.

Meanwhile, having regard to the social dimension, the elimination of all forms of preventive censorship in the press[20] encouraged the publication of a number of newspapers and periodicals whose content was explicitly political, including criticism of the government's actions. This development was linked to the emergence of clubs and associations, which in turn opened up spaces for debate and discussion on the major political issues of the day. Also as a result of this development, the existence and autonomy of civil society became the subject of explicit philosophical reflection.[21] For its part, for much of the eighteenth century, the British Parliament sought to defend the ancient privilege of the confidentiality of its work, prohibiting the dissemination of parliamentary debates. Nevertheless, it eventually had to yield to growing pressure from the public: in the early nineteenth century, journalists were admitted to House of Commons sittings, although dedicated press stands were only established following the reconstruction of the building after the 1834 fire, 'two years after the first reform Bill had transformed Parliaments, for a long time the target of critical comment by public opinion, into the very organ of this opinion'.[22]

[17] D Baranger, *Parlamentarisme des origines: Essai sur les conditions de formations d'un exécutif responsable en Angleterre (des années 1740 au début de l'âge victorien)* (Paris, PUF, 1999) 117–63.

[18] On these developments, see the classical book of AS Foord, *His Majesty's Opposition 1714–1830* (Oxford, Clarendon Press, 1964).

[19] The definition of the parliamentary opposition as 'His Majesty's Loyal Opposition' was coined in the first half of the 19th century: it appears in a speech held by Sir John Cam Hobhouse at the House of Commons in 1826 (N Johnson, 'Opposition in the British Political System' (1997) 32 *Government and Opposition* 489).

[20] Censorship came to an end with the adoption of the Licensing Act 1695, although the press continued to be subject to the strict Law of Libel and to the restrictions connected with the numerous privileges of the Crown and Parliament (Habermas (n 13) 59).

[21] As is well known, the idea of civil society was at the centre of the reflection of the Scottish Enlightenment with the work of Adam Ferguson, *An Essay on the History of Civil Society* (Dublin, Boulter Grierson, 1767). For a brief overview of the history of the concept, see J Ehrenberg, 'The History of Civil Society Ideas' in M Edwards (ed), *The Oxford Handbook of Civil Society* (Oxford, Oxford University Press, 2011).

[22] Habermas (n 13) 62.

Both politically and socially, these processes had their social basis in the emergence of the leading economic role of the capitalistic bourgeoisie.[23] This development was, however, far from resembling a linear process. On the one hand, the English nobility proved capable of playing an active and positive role in the construction of the British Empire, assuming important political and military leadership roles. On the other hand, the strict class division was tempered by the potential for the affluent bourgeoisie to be associated with aristocracy through the acquisition of noble titles.[24] It should also be emphasised that the emergence of the middle class as the dominant social component in the liberal era was for a long time more a political programme than a social reality.[25] At the beginning of the nineteenth century, English society was still very diverse, with evident differences, for example, between urban and rural areas. Moreover, the middle class was undoubtedly internally divided according to multiple social cleavages, as confirmed by the perception of contemporaries which distinguished, for example, between *Besitzbürgertum* and *Bildungsbürgentum* in Germany or between *grande, bonne* and *petite bourgeoisie* in France.[26] Despite all these differences, in the nineteenth century the bourgeoisie was widely identified, both by its detractors and by its apologists, as a unitary social class that was at the heart of the political system, as claimed, for example, by one of the most influential liberal thinkers, James Mill:

> It is to be observed, that the class which is universally described, as both the most wise, and the most virtuous part of every community, the middle rank, are wholly included in that part of the community which is not the aristocratical. It is also not disputed, that in Great Britain the middle rank are numerous, and form a large proportion of the whole body of the people … There can be no doubt whatever that the middle rank, which gives their most distinguished ornaments to science, to art, and to legislation itself, to every thing which exalts and refines human nature, is that part of the community of which, if the basis of representation were now so far extended, the opinion would ultimately decide. Of the people beneath them, a vast majority would be sure to be guided by their advice and example.[27]

Similar statements were made on the other side of the Channel by another champion of liberal thought – Benjamin Constant: 'La pauvreté a trop peu à perdre, mais la richesse peut trop risquer. Dans la médiocrité, dans la classe intermédiaire, est éminemment l'intérêt de la conservation et, par-là même, de l'ordre'.[28]

[23] I use the terms 'middle class' and 'bourgeoisie' indifferently, even if I am aware of the different historical origins of the words, with the former, for example, far more extensively used in 19th-century Britain: see F Moretti, *The Bourgeois: Between History and Literature* (London, Verso, 2013) 8–12.

[24] L Stone and J Fawtier, *An Open Elite? England 1540–1880* (London, Oxford University Press, 1986): according to the authors, this partial osmosis between social classes explains one of the reasons why England was one of the countries with the strongest class consciousness and, at the same time, with a low degree of violence and a high level of social deference.

[25] This is the central thesis of D Wahrman, *Imagining the Middle Class: The Political Representation of Class in Britain c 1780–1840* (Cambridge, Cambridge University Press, 1995).

[26] J Kocka, 'Bürgertum und bürgerliche Gesellschaft im 19 Jahrhundert: europäische Entwicklungen und deutsche Eigenarten' in J Kocka (ed), *Bürgertum im 19 Jahrhundert: Deutschland im europäischen Vergleich*, Band 1 (München, Deutscher Taschenbuch Verlag, 1988).

[27] J Mill, 'On Government' in *Essays on Government, Jurisprudence, Liberty of the Press, Prisons and Prison Discipline, Colonies, Law of Nations, Education* (London, Innes, 1823) 32. It is worth mentioning that the Essay was originally written by Mill for the supplement of the fifth edition of the *Encyclopaedia Britannica*.

[28] B Constant, *Cours de politique constitutionelle*, 3rd edn (Brussels, 1819) 403–04.

Constant completely agreed with the opinions expressed on this point by another key figure among the ranks of the so-called *doctrinaires* – Pierre-Paul Royer-Collard. In a debate held at the French Chamber of Deputies about the different interpretations of the 1814 Charter, Royer-Collard remarked:

> C'est, en effet, évidemment dans la classe moyenne que tous les intérêts pouvaient trouver leur représentation naturelle; au dessus est un certain besoin de la domination contre lequel il faut se tenir en garde; au dessous, l'ignorance, l'habitude et le besoin de l'indépendance, et par conséquent inaptitude complète aux fonctions dont il s'agit.[29]

These arguments were used as a basis for specific political programmes, such as those aimed at enlarging suffrage. From our point of view, however, what is most relevant in these positions is the claim of the role of the bourgeoisie as a 'general class', as a component that is better able to express the interests of society as a whole. It was a vision that fitted perfectly with the model of parliamentarism in the liberal age. In Parliament, the bourgeoisie could, on the one hand, reaffirm its loyalty to the established order and, on the other, discuss the political issues of the day by freely expressing its internal divisions. As Peter Gay put it:

> The historian attempting to understand the nineteenth-century bourgeoisie must come to terms with pervasive conflicts among those who defined themselves as 'middle class' as much as with the qualities that made them kin; … Not unexpectedly, conflicts within the middling orders were more pronounced than peaceful cooperation; … Economic self-interests, religious agendas, intellectual convictions, social competition, the proper place of women became political issues where bourgeois battled bourgeois.[30]

Of course, national political conditions significantly differentiated the political role of the middle class. In France, for instance, the situation for most of the eighteenth century was very different. The centralisation of power in the hands of the king left even the nobility without any real political or military functions. All public functions were held by the sovereign, and the bourgeoisie was de facto excluded from possessing any political role. Moreover, the presence of a strict censorship kept the activity of the press under control. In this unfavourable context, the Paris salons played a very important role in the establishment of an initial form of public opinion. It was here that the 'civilisation of the conversation', as it was described by Benedetta Craveri, emerged.[31] The salons, governed by the great *dames* of the French nobility, provided an opportunity for an exchange between members of the aristocracy (but also with the frequent involvement of representatives of the bourgeoisie) on a wide variety of topical issues. Although this sphere did not yet have a direct political impact, it undoubtedly produced a new dimension of social life: that of *opinion*, which was increasingly difficult to ignore. In this context, the voices directly critical of power were confined to printing clandestine publications; the market of prohibited books and magazines published abroad, mainly in the Netherlands, was also flourishing.[32] Only after the second half of the

[29] Quoted by Wahrman (n 25) 275.
[30] P Gay, *Schnitzler's Century: The Making of Middle-Class Culture, 1815–1914* (New York, Norton, 2002) 5.
[31] B Craveri, *La civiltà della conversazione* (Milano, Adelphi, 2001).
[32] On the underground book market in 18th-century France, see R Darnton, *The Forbidden Best-Sellers of Pre-Revolutionary France* (New York, Norton, 1996).

eighteenth century was an increasingly explicit critical role played by a group of intellectuals who managed to assume a powerful position in public opinion.

As we have seen in the previous chapter, the publication of the *Enyclopédie* was a real turning point in the mobilisation of a public which was consciously critical of the established power. The occurrence of the revolutionary events of 1789, with the opening of the Constituent Assembly, produced a major acceleration in relation to the emergence of a politically oriented public sphere. 'The revolution in France created overnight what in Great Britain had taken more than a century of steady evolution: the institutions … for critical debate on political matters'.[33] As we will see in more detail in the following sections, the debates of the Revolutionary Assemblies, including through the publication of the minutes of their work, immediately had resonance with public opinion in the country. The articulation of assemblies into informal groups of deputies with distinct political orientations was also crucial in making the political fight understandable outside the parliamentary sphere. As we will see shortly, the parliamentary geography, centred on the right–left orientation, played a fundamental role in this respect, making parliaments the 'encyclopaedias of politics' for much of the nineteenth century.

The medium that allowed parliaments to perform this function at a national level was the press. The rise of parliamentarism was naturally linked to the introduction of a set of technological innovations that represented a real revolution in the communications system of the nineteenth century. The main modernisations included steam machinery, railways and the introduction of new print reproduction systems. From this point of view, the terms 'industrial revolution', 'transportation revolution' and 'communication revolution' can be considered as part of the same complex.[34]

Parliaments entered in a symbiosis with this new public sphere, paving the way for a journalism specialising in parliamentary reporting.[35] Not only in England, an important part of major newspapers was now devoted to reporting parliamentary debates. Parliamentary politics gained resonance with the public only through the mediation of newspapers. The most authoritative newspapers gained so much prestige that some of them, such as *The Times*, came to be thought of as a 'fourth Estate'. The ninettenth century can be rigtly defined as 'the age of the newspapers'.[36] As Benjamin Disraeli put into the mouth of one of the characters in his novel *Coningsby*, 'Opinion is now supreme and opinion speaks in print'.[37] This trend reached its peak in the Victorian age:

> Systematically and, for the most part, unabashedly, newspapers were used on an unprecedented scale to formulate party programmes, to implement political strategies, and to serve personal ambitions. This collaboration, pursued with varying enthusiasm and success, helped to determine

[33] Habermas (n 13) 70.

[34] A Briggs and P Burke, *A Social History of the Media from Gutenberg to the Internet* (Cambridge, Polity Press, 2009) 98.

[35] On the story of parliamentary journalism in Britain, see A Sparrow, *Obscure Scribblers: A History of Parliamentary Reporting* (London, Politico's Publishing Ltd, 2003); see also I Harris, 'What Was Parliamentary Reporting? A Study of Aims and Results in the London Daily Newspapers, 1780–96' (2020) 39 *Parliamentary History* 255.

[36] A Pettegree, *The Invention of News: How the World Came to Know Itself* (New Haven, CT, Yale University Press, 2014) 367.

[37] Quoted by Briggs and Burke (n 34) 187.

> alignments in Parliament, allegiances in constituencies, and, to a decreasing extent as time wore on, general patterns of electoral behaviour. Fitful but steady, this development drew its primary impetus from the concurrent growth of broadly based party organizations to which journalists, like politicians themselves, became affiliated for various motives of self-interest and ideological commitment.[38]
>
> The very concept of a political press rests on a particular interpretation of political culture [that assumes] the Parliament as the supreme political and social institution of the realm'. 'Momentous events might inconveniently occur in distant places, but their impact was fully registered only when they were debated in Parliament and appraised by the leader-writers of the London press. Newspapers exemplified the elective and deliberative process for which 'parliamentary' seems the only name.[39]

It is therefore true that the parliamentary assemblies of the nineteenth century were – as we shall see in further detail later – the great theatres of politics, the place par excellence of parliamentary oratory. However, the format of orality was only relevant in the limited sphere of the parliamentary chambers. The content of parliamentary speeches was intended to be transposed immediately into the written text, both in the parliamentary reports and in the newspapers. Unsurprisingly, literacy was among the qualifications required for franchise in many European countries during the decades of liberalism. The encyclopaedic parliaments of the nineteenth century were assemblies intrinsically linked to the dimension of the written word, disseminated through the medium of the press.

The connection with nation-building processes therefore found its privileged expression, for both parliaments and encyclopaedias, in their relationship with the emerging bourgeois public sphere. The voters of the eighteenth-century parliaments were also the readers of the contemporary encyclopaedias. They became the core of emerging public opinion. This class expressed a new need: the ability to rapidly obtain reliable information on the issues underlying the political debate via different channels which were more easily accessible than those offered by specialist and academic scholarship.

In the following sections, I will review the main components of this peculiar phase of encyclopaedic parliamentarism.

III. The Birth of Modern Parliamentary Representation between Publicness and Separateness

A crucial moment for the birth of modern political representation can be traced back to a decision made by the deputies of the Third Estate in the Estates General convened by Luis XVI in May 1789. Disrupting the traditional scheme of representation based on the 'Estates', the Third Estate declared itself to be the national assembly. A few days later, by contrast with the attempts of the king to restore the existence of three different assemblies corresponding to the states, the Third Estate took the 'Tennis Court Oath', agreeing 'not to separate and to reassemble wherever necessary until the Constitution of the kingdom is established'.

[38] S Koss, *The Rise and Fall of the Political Press in Britain* (Chapel Hill, NC, University of North Carolina Press, 1981) 1.

[39] ibid, 23.

In accordance with this vote, the Assembly renamed itself the National Assembly. The main inspiration for this historical decision came from Emmanuel-Joseph Sieyès, who sat in the Estates General as a representative of the Third Estate. According to him, France needed a new constitution, based on the representative principle.

Sieyès viewed the national representation as comprising the king and the National Assembly. He conceived of representative institutions as the only political voice of the nation: the will of the people should be expressed by a unitary national assembly.[40] Representation was not viewed by him as a mere substitute for the real presence of the people, but as an option to be considered better than direct democracy. This system, on the one hand, organises the process of shaping political will (with the division of labour, which is the structural principle of bourgeois society) and, on the other hand, guarantees greater individual freedom.[41] Representative government, in Sieyes's view, should therefore be considered as a solution perfectly functional to the actual condition of modern society.[42] From this point of view, Sieyes expressed a 'pan-representative' view:

> Tout est représentation dans l'Etat social. Elle se trouve partout dans l'ordre privé comme dans l'ordre public; elle est la mère de l'industrie productive et commerciale, comme des progrès libéraux et politiques. Je dis plus, elle se confond avec l'essence même de la vie sociale.[43]

The members of the assembly, since they are the sole depositories of the general will, have no need to consult the citizens (as their '*commettants*') on dissent that does not in fact exist. Sieyès was therefore a staunch supporter of the freedom of mandate for the nation's representatives. This position had some remarkable precedents in French political theory. In his *Esprit des Lois*, Montesquieu observed that, in the English constitution, the Parliament could effectively counterbalance the power of the king only because the representatives had the possibility of deliberating without continuously consulting with their constituencies.[44] More problematic was the position expressed by D'Holbach in his article 'Répresentans' of the *Encyclopédie*. For Holbach, a well-governed state cannot be conceived of without a representative system:

> Nul homme, quelles que soient ses lumières, n'est capable sans conseils, sans secours, de gouverner une nation entière; nul ordre dans l'état ne peut avoir la capacité ou la volonté de connoître les besoins des autres; ainsi le souverain impartial doit écouter les voix de tous ses sujets, il est également intéressé à les entendre & à remédier à leurs maux; mais pour que les sujets s'expliquent sans tumulte, il convient qu'ils aient des *représentans*, c'est-à-dire des citoyens plus éclairés que les autres, plus intéressés à la chose, que leurs possessions attachent à la patrie, que leur position mette à portée de sentir les besoins de l'état, les abus qui s'introduisent, & les remèdes qu'il convient d'y porter.[45]

[40] N Urbinati, *Representative Democracy: Principles and Genealogy* (Chicago, IL, University of Chicago Press, 2006) 153.

[41] H Hofmann, *Repreaesentation: Studien zur Wort-und Begriffsgeschichte von der Antike bis ins 19 Jahrhundert*, 4 Aufl (Berlin, Duncker & Humblot, 2003) 348.

[42] P Pasquino, *Sieyès et l'invention de la Constitution en France* (Paris, Odile Jacob, 1998) 39–40.

[43] Discours du 2 thermidor an III, in P Bastid, *Les Discours de Sieyès, dans les débats constitutionnels de l'an III (2 et 18 thermidor)*, thèse complémentaire pour le doctorat ès lettres (Paris, 1939) 16, quoted by Pasquino, ibid, 38.

[44] C-L Montesquieu, 'Esprit des lois' in *Œuvres Complétes*, vol II (Paris, Gallimard, 1951) Lib X, cap VI.

[45] PH D'Holbach, 'Rèpresentans' in D Diderot and J le Rond D'Alambert (eds), *Encyclopédie; ou Dictionnaire raisonné des sciences, des arts et des métiers* (Paris, Briasson et al, 1751–72) Vol XIV (1765) 143.

D'Holbach identifies these 'more enlightened' citizens as representatives of nobility, clergy, the merchant class and landowners. Representative assemblies should therefore be:

> de ceux que leurs possessions rendent citoyens, & que leur état & leurs lumières mettent à portée de connoître les intérêts de la nation & les besoins des peuples; en un mot c'est la propriété qui fait le citoyen; tout homme qui possède dans l'état, est intéressé au bien de l'état, & quel que soit le rang que des conventions particulières lui assignent, c'est toujours comme propriétaire, c'est en raison de ses possessions qu'il doit parler, ou qu'il acquiert le droit de se faire représenter.[46]

These views paved the way for a theory and practice of political representation, which sees property as its main source of legitimacy. This theory had its precedents in the work of the seventeenth-century English thinkers who viewed the individual 'as essentially the proprietor of his own person or capacities, owing nothing to society for them'.[47] However, in spite of the substantial coincidence between represented and representatives, D'Holbach considers that there is a need for instruments enabling the former to exercise close control over the latter, although he accepts that the best way to limit the power of representatives is to hold elections at regular intervals.[48]

Sieyès developed these theories on the basis of a more radical approach that identified the Third Estate with the Nation and attributed full freedom of mandate to its representatives.[49] This idea of representation had its social basis in the narrow suffrage allowing direct contact between elected representatives and voters in a context of substantial social homogeneity. This paradigm was also, due to its nature, hostile to the role of parties and factions in political representation. These formations were seen as an impediment to the political elite sharing a set of common values. Voters did not have to divide themselves on the basis of ideological positions, but had to choose their representatives by looking at their personal qualities.

In France, Sieyès's theories were reflected by the 1791 Constitution that proclaimed the principles of the free mandate and of the national representation of deputies.[50]

[46] ibid, 145.

[47] CB Macpherson, *The Political Theory of Possessive Individualism: Hobbes to Locke* (Oxford, Clarendon Press, 1962) 3.

[48] 'Les *représentans* supposent des constituans de qui leur pouvoir est émané, auxquels ils sont par conséquent subordonnés & dont ils ne sont que les organes. Quels que soient les usages ou les abus que le tems a pu introduire dans les gouvernemens libres & tempérés, un *représentant* ne peut s'arroger le droit de faire parler à ses constituans un langage opposé à leurs intérêts; les droits des constituans sont les droits de la nation, ils sont imprescriptibles & inaliénables; pour peu que l'on consulte la raison, elle prouvera que les constituans peuvent en tout tems démentir, désavouer & révoquer les *représentans* qui les trahissent, qui abusent de leurs pleins pouvoirs contre eux-mêmes, ou qui renoncent pour eux à des droits inhérens à leur essence; en un mot, les *représentans* d'un peuple libre ne peuvent point lui imposer un joug qui détruiroit sa félicité; nul homme n'acquiert le droit d'en représenter un autre malgré lui. Nul ordre de citoyens ne doit jouir pour toujours du droit de représenter la nation, il faut que de nouvelles élections rappellent aux *représentans* que c'est d'elle qu'ils tiennent leur pouvoir. Un corps dont les membres jouiroient sans interruption du droit de représenter l'état, en deviendroit bientôt le maître ou le tyran' (D'Holbach (n 45) 146).

[49] Pasquino (n 42) 14.

[50] See Title III, s 1, arts 2 and 3 of the Constitution: '2. The nation, from which alone all powers emanate, may exercise such powers only by delegation. The French Constitution is representative; the representatives are the legislative body and the King. 3. The legislative power is delegated to a National Assembly, composed of temporary representatives freely elected by the people, to be exercised by it, with the sanction of the King, in the manner hereinafter determined'. According to art 7 of s 3 of the same Title, 'The representatives elected in the departments shall not be representatives of a particular department, but of the entire nation, and no mandate may be given them'.

The Constitution thus provided for the abandonment of the Estates system and created a homogenous assembly that competed with the king in the representation of the nation, that is, in incarnating the people as *persona moralis* and ideal subject.[51]

As is well known, on the other side of the Channel, the idea of a revolutionary change of regime in the pursuit of an abstract programme of political freedom and protection of human rights was fiercely opposed by Edmund Burke. Burke rejected any parallelism between the events of the French Revolution and the English 'Glorious Revolution'. In his view, the latter was to be interpreted as a successful attempt to restore the ancient English constitution, provided that the constitution was not the outcome of a single constituent act of a particular moment, but rather the result of a long and deliberate political development.[52] Burke, however, shared Sieyès's opinion on the inherent necessity of a representative government for a well-ordered polity. For him, only a selected elite could transform the changing opinions of the people into well-balanced decisions in the interests of the whole community. In order to discharge this difficult task, representatives should be independent from binding mandates. This idea is brilliantly illustrated by Burke in his often-quoted speech to the electors of Bristol (3 November 1774):

> Certainly, gentlemen, it ought to be the happiness and glory of a representative to live in the strictest union, the closest correspondence, and the most unreserved communication with his constituents. Their wishes ought to have great weight with him; their opinion, high respect; their business, unremitted attention. It is his duty to sacrifice his repose, his pleasures, his satisfactions, to theirs; and above all, ever, and in all cases, to prefer their interest to his own. But his unbiassed opinion, his mature judgment, his enlightened conscience, he ought not to sacrifice to you, to any man, or to any set of men living. These he does not derive from your pleasure; no, nor from the law and the constitution. They are a trust from Providence, for the abuse of which he is deeply answerable. Your representative owes you, not his industry only, but his judgment; and he betrays, instead of serving you, if he sacrifices it to your opinion.
>
> My worthy colleague says, his will ought to be subservient to yours. If that be all, the thing is innocent. If government were a matter of will upon any side, yours, without question, ought to be superior. But government and legislation are matters of reason and judgment, and not of inclination; and what sort of reason is that, in which the determination precedes the discussion; in which one set of men deliberate, and another decide; and where those who form the conclusion are perhaps three hundred miles distant from those who hear the arguments?
>
> To deliver an opinion, is the right of all men; that of constituents is a weighty and respectable opinion, which a representative ought always to rejoice to hear; and which he ought always most seriously to consider. But *authoritative* instructions; *mandates* issued, which the member is bound blindly and implicitly to obey, to vote, and to argue for, though contrary to the clearest conviction of his judgment and conscience, – these are things utterly unknown to the laws of this land, and which arise from a fundamental mistake of the whole order and tenor of our constitution.
>
> Parliament is not a *congress* of ambassadors from different and hostile interests; which interests each must maintain, as an agent and advocate, against other agents and advocates; but parliament is a *deliberative* assembly of *one* nation, with *one* interest, that of the whole; where, not local purposes, not local prejudices, ought to guide, but the general good, resulting from the general

[51] Hofmann (n 41) 346.

[52] P Chiantera-Stutte, 'Fiducia, interesse e consenso: riflessioni sulla rappresentanza in Edmund Burke' (2015) 29(I) *Giornale di storia costituzionale* 119.

> reason of the whole. You choose a member indeed; but when you have chosen him, he is not member of Bristol, but he is a member of *parliament*. If the local constituent should have an interest, or should form an hasty opinion, evidently opposite to the real good of the rest of the community, the member for that place ought to be as far, as any other, from any endeavour to give it effect.[53]

In Burke's view, representatives should be superior men of wisdom and ability, a 'natural aristocracy' with a special capacity for practical reasoning, 'for Burke conceives of their function as essentially ratiocinative'.[54] For him, representation was not a matter of responsiveness to the electorate, but rather a function that Parliament performs for the nation as a whole. Parliament is conceived of by Burke as a 'deliberative machine' that, 'through deliberation and wise judgment reaches conclusions which the society could arrive at only indirectly and more slowly'.[55] The representatives must have the capacity to understand the complexity of the interests to be considered when the government of a great empire is at stake:

> To be a good member of parliament, is, let me tell you, no easy task; especially at this time, when there is so strong a disposition to run into the perilous extremes of servile compliance, or wild popularity. To unite circumspection with vigour, is absolutely necessary; but it is extremely difficult. We are now members for a rich commercial city; this city, however, is but a part of a rich commercial nation, the interests of which are various, multiform, and intricate. We are members for that great nation, which however is itself but part of a great empire, extended by our virtue and our fortune to the farthest limits of the east and of the west. All these wide-spread interests must be considered; must be compared; must be reconciled if possible. We are members for a free country; and surely we all know, that the machine of a free constitution is no simple thing; but as intricate and as delicate, as it is valuable. We are members in a great and ancient monarchy; and we must preserve religiously, the true legal rights of the sovereign, which form the key-stone that binds together the noble and well-constructed arch of our empire and our constitution. A constitution made up of balanced powers must ever be a critical thing.[56]

As is also evident in this last passage, Burke supported the notion of a British constitution in which the representative function is shared between the monarch and Parliament. This view was vehemently opposed by those, such as Thomas Paine, who were in favour of a monist approach that concentrated the whole representative function in the National Assembly. Paine was convinced – by contrast with Montesquieu – that democracy was a form of government also suited to large-scale polities. The precondition for adapting democracy to a vast nation was representation: a solution which had not been available in the Athenian 'simple democracy'. Paine terms 'simple democracy' the direct democracy of the ancient Greeks, in which society governed itself 'without the aid of secondary means'. According to him, 'by engrafting representation upon democracy, we arrive at a system of government capable of embracing and confederating all the various interests and every extent of territory and population'.[57] Paine had, of course, the example of the nascent American republic in mind: 'what Athens was in miniature, America will be in magnitude'. The representative system

[53] E Burke, 'Speech to the Electors of Bristol' in *The Works of the Right Honourable Edmund Burke* Volume 1 (London, Rivington, 1826) 18–20.
[54] Pitkin (n 2) 169.
[55] ibid, 181.
[56] Burke (n 53) 21.
[57] T Paine, *The Rights of Man* (1st edn 1791) (Mineola, NY, Dover Publications, 1999) 121.

'concentrates the knowledge necessary to the interests of the parts, and of the whole … It admits not of a separation between knowledge and power'.[58]

To further illustrate this concept, Paine uses a geometric metaphor:

> A nation is not a body, the figure of which is to be represented by the human body; but is like a body contained within a circle, having a common center, in which every radius meets; and that center is formed by representation. To connect representation with what is called monarchy, is eccentric government.[59]

Jeremy Bentham did not take sides in the controversy between Burke and Paine, but in his *Essay on Political Tactics* (1791) he defended the idea that a parliamentary assembly had to keep constantly in touch with its electors. For him publicity was the only way to secure the necessary two-way communication between Parliament and the people:

> In an assembly elected by the people, and renewed from time to time, publicity is absolutely necessary to enable the electors to act from knowledge … Another reason in favour of publicity: – To provide the assembly with the means of profiting by the information of the public. A nation too numerous to act for itself, is doubtless obliged to entrust its powers to its deputies. But will they possess in concentration all the national intelligence? Is it even possible that the elected shall be in every respect the most enlightened, the most capable, the wisest persons in the nation? – that they will possess, among themselves alone, all the general and local knowledge which the function of governing requires? This prodigy of election is a chimera.[60]

Paine's vision of representation was shared by some of the framers of the American Constitution. Even if the founding fathers were deeply divided about the nature of political representation, they agreed on the need to build a constitutional system capable of affirming the civic virtues of the governing elites against the force of the masses.[61] The majority supported the Burkean principle of the representatives' 'natural aristocracy': the aim of every political constitution

> is or ought to be first to obtain for rulers, men who possess most wisdom to discern, and most virtue to pursue the common good of the society; and in the next place, to take the most effectual precautions for keeping them virtuous, whilst they continue to hold their public trust. The elective mode of obtaining rulers is the characteristic policy of republican government. The means relied on in this form of government for preventing their degeneracy are numerous and various. The most effectual one is such a limitation of the term of appointments, as will maintain a proper responsibility to the people.[62]

On the basis of these theories, the introduction of representative government in America – as well as in France and in Britain – promoted a system of rules designed to give elected representatives a higher status than other citizens. This is what has been called the 'principle of difference'.[63] Especially in the United States, however, the effect of this principle has been

[58] ibid.
[59] ibid.
[60] J Bentham, *Essay on Political Tactics* (1st edn 1791) (Oxford, Clarendon Press, 1999) 33.
[61] L Cedroni, *La rappresentanza politica: Teorie e modelli* (Milano, Franco Angeli, 2004) 79–106.
[62] James Madison, 'Federalist, no 57' in *The Founders' Constitution* (University of Chicago Press), available at: press-pubs.uchicago.edu/founders/documents/v1ch4s26.html.
[63] Cedroni (n 61) 101.

moderated by the concern about ensuring that parliamentarians are constantly in touch with the actual feelings of the electors: the frequency of elections was deemed the best solution to achieve this goal.[64]

As we have seen in our short overview, between the eighteenth and the nineteenth centuries, the 'founding fathers' of representative government in Europe and in the newborn American Republic were inspired by very different – and sometimes opposing – constitutional theories. Despite these obvious differences, however, they shared a number of beliefs on the paradigm of political representation that were dominant for much of the nineteenth century. According to this paradigm, political representation defined itself as an autonomous sphere, separated and independent from the rest of the political community. If the deputies must be 'independent', then so should their electors. This parallelism explains the introduction of different types of qualifications (census, property, literacy) that limited the suffrage during the liberal age. Only these conditions were considered capable of proving the real political capacity of the citizens:

> [I]n this kind of system, the founding principle of individualism in political citizenship expresses itself through a set of different cultural values and legal norms which stress, above all, the importance of granting 'independence' to both the elector and the elected.[65]

Within this ideological setting, the sphere of political representation was marked by a superior ideal value connected with the unity of the political community. The meaning of representation consisted in its function of making this value possible and visible: 'in brief, only representation makes possible the formation of the will of the people as a political community'.[66] This idea of 'absolute representation' was justified by the attribution to the deputies of a distinctive political competence based on moral and intellectual virtues. These qualities were supposed to make politicians competent leaders fit for governing the country. It should be noted, however, that this 'competence' was very different from the 'technocratic' approach later prevailing – as we shall see in the next chapter – among the twentieth-century politicians: 'when Montesquieu, Madison, Sieyès and Burke referred to "competence" they meant a kind of honourable dedication to the good of their society in the form of a competent service, something a gentleman was educated to do since his early youth'.[67]

This ideal was reaffirmed in France after the revolutionary period by the political thought of the *doctrinaires*. According to Guizot:

> Dans toute société il existe une certaine somme d'idées justes et de volontés légitimes sur les droits réciproques des hommes, sur les relations sociales et leurs résultats. Cette somme d'idées justes

[64] See Alexander Hamilton or James Madison, 'Federalist no 52': 'As it is essential to liberty that the government in general should have a common interest with the people, so it is particularly essential that the branch of it under consideration should have an immediate dependence on, and an intimate sympathy with, the people. Frequent elections are unquestionably the only policy by which this dependence and sympathy can be effectively secured' *The Founders' Constitution* (University of Chicago Press), available at: press-pubs.uchicago.edu/founders/documents/a1_2_1s14.html.

[65] R Romanelli, 'Electoral Systems and Social Structures: A Comparative Perspective' in R Romanelli (ed), *How Did They Become Voters? The History of Franchise in Modern European Representation* (The Hague, Kluwer Law International, 1998) 11.

[66] G Leibholz, *Das Wesen der Repräsentation unter besonderer Berücksichtung der Repräsentativsystems: Ein Beitrag zur allgemeinen Staats- und Verfassungslehre* (Berlin, Walter de Gruyter, 1929) 58.

[67] Urbinati (n 40) 161.

> et des volontés légitimes est dispersée dans les individus qui composent la société, et inégalement repartie entre eux, en raison des causes infinies qui influent sur le développement intellectuel et moral des hommes.[68]

The function of representative goverment is therefore 'de recueillir partout les fragments épars et incomplets de ce pouvoir, de les concentrer et de les constituer en gouvernement'.[69]

Along the same lines, the Duke of Broglie observed:

> Le propre du gouvernement représentatif est d'extraire du milieu de la nation l'élite de ses hommes les plus éclaires, de les réunir au sommet de l'édifice social, dans une enceinte sacrée, inaccessible aux passions de la multitude, et là, de les faire délibérer à haute voix sur les intérêts de l'Etat.[70]

The views of these authors converge in their support of an 'encyclopaedic interpretation' of parliamentary representation as a forum for gathering and concentrating political wisdom by a narrow elite entrusted with the task of illuminating and educating the entire nation. As is well known, this belief was also shared by Bagehot, who identified the 'teaching function' as one of the core tasks of the House of Commons:

> A great and open council of considerable men cannot be placed in the middle of a society without altering that society. It ought to alter it for the better. It ought to teach the nation what it does not know.[71]

What is most striking in the views of the theorists of nineteenth-century parliamentary representation is their insistence on the *cognitive added value of representation* and its ability to provide the nation with a higher form of reflexive political knowledge. It is a kind of knowledge that serves an eminently political purpose: contributing to building the nation's self-awareness. Political representation was therefore part of a nation building process that invested many European states during the nineteenth century, involving military events (such as the independence wars), but also, of course, economic, cultural and artistic factors.

IV. Parliaments as Political Theatres of the Nation

The relationship between parliaments and theatres has a long historical tradition, since the early stages of modern parliamentarism:

> John Hooker drew attention to the physical resemblance between Parliament and the theater in 1572 when he remarked that the interior structure of the Lower House was 'like a theater'. With the advent of the public, political debate and exchange, Parliament became the preeminent institution of the 'public sphere' and as it did so, its intrinsically theatrical dynamics, vividly illustrated in the 1620s, came to comport more fully with the theater than any other early modern venue,

[68] F Guizot, *Histoire des origines du gouvernement représentatif* (Cours de 1820–1822) (Paris, 1856) t II, 149, quoted by P Rosanvallon, *La démocratie inachevée: Histoire de la souveraineté du peuple en France* (Paris, Gallimard, 2000) 121.

[69] ibid, 150.

[70] V de Broglie, *Ecrits et discours* (Paris, 1863) 51, quoted by P Rosanvallon, *La démocratie inachevée: Histoire de la souveraineté du peuple en France* (Paris, Gallimard, 2000) 121.

[71] W Bagehot, *The English Constitution* (1st edn 1867) (Oxford, Oxford University Press, 2009) 101.

> institution, or practice. As a place of staged rhetorical performance in an auditorium as vigorous and dynamic as any playhouse, Parliament was understood by its members and by early moderns more generally to be an institution whose structures and practices were closely analogous to those of the theatre.[72]

As remarked by Hooker, this relationship was fostered by the architectural structure of parliaments. 'Parliamentary architecture can perpetuate, manifest, and shape political culture':[73] the physical form of parliaments bears a great importance for our study of parliamentary encyclopaedism between the eighteenth and nineteenth centuries. In line with this assumption, the role played by the architecture of parliaments and more specifically of their plenary halls goes well beyond the aesthetics and functionality of parliamentary premises. The articulation of the parliamentary space has deep consequences for the inner life of the assemblies and for their relationship with that which remains external to them.

With respect to the form of parliaments, the definition of the relationship between the parliamentary sphere and the public space plays a preliminary role. Once again, in continental Europe, the moment of transition between the Estates general and the French National Assembly has a special significance from this point of view. While, during the sessions of the Estates General, a large number of curious visitors were admitted to the Assembly's premises,[74] the meetings of the National Assembly were characterised by a clear separation of the space reserved for members from that which was accessible to the public. The actual parliamentary space was built so as to contrast that of the agora, the public square.[75] This solution was consistent with the paradigm of the separateness of the political representation from civil society, which we discussed in the previous section.

However, this separation was not complete: the public was permitted to attend the sessions of the Assembly in special spaces. Moreover, this public presence was considered to be essential in order to allow citizens to control the work of the Assembly. The open nature of the Assembly's proceedings was also ensured by the decision to publish the minutes of its sittings. This move marked a clear break from the English parliamentary tradition, which – as we have seen – until much of the eighteenth century had remained anchored in the principle of the confidentiality of parliamentary proceedings. By offering a critical and curious audience the opportunity to read the minutes of its debates, the National Assembly made an important contribution to the construction of a bourgeois public sphere, which would have been an essential feature of the communicative environment of nineteenth-century parliamentarism.

[72] CR Kyle, *Theater of State: Parliament and Political Culture in Early Stuart England* (Stanford, CA, Stanford University Press, 2012) 1–2.

[73] CT Goodsell, 'The Architecture of Parliaments: Legislative Houses and Political Culture' (1988) 18 *British Journal of Political Science* 287, 301; see also, C Macintyre, 'Parliamentary Architecture and Political Culture', paper presented as a lecture in the Senate Occasional Lecture Series at Parliament House, Canberra, 9 May 2008, available at: www.aph.gov.au/~/~/~/link.aspx?_id=3AB8830A90D34C71AB5337BF650579F9#_ftn25.

[74] 'La sale était continuellement inondée de visiteurs, de curieux, qui se promenaient partout, et se plaçaient dans l'enceinte destinée aux députés, sans aucune jalousie de la part de ceux-ci, sans aucune réclamation de leur privilège': E Dumont, *Souvenirs sur Mirabeau et sur les deux premières assemblées législatives* (Paris, PUF, 1932) 44, quoted by J-P Heurtin, *L'espace public parlementaire: Essai sur les raisons du législateur* (Paris, PUF, 1999) 28.

[75] Heurtin, *L'espace public parlementaire* (n 74) 29.

The form chosen for the physical arrangement of the deputies' benches also had significant consequences for the subsequent developments in parliamentarism, at least in continental Europe. Instead of other proposed solutions (eg, a circular format), the hemicycle arrangement was preferred. This form – reminiscent of the ancient Greek theatres – was considered to be the most suitable for ensuring the Assembly's openness to the public, which, as we have seen, was viewed as a fundamental requirement of the new Assembly. In France, the semi-circular shape was first introduced thanks to the work of the French architect Jacques-Pierre Gisors, who built the meeting hall of the National Convention from premises previously occupied by the Tuileries theatre. The option of the hemicycle finally materialised with the construction between 1828 and 1832 of the new plenary hall in Palais Bourbon, which had been the site of the French Parliamentary Assemblies since 1798. The French *constituents* adopted the semi-elliptic form, to hold peaceful political meetings where speakers could be seen and heard by all, a solution that was adopted in keeping with their revolutionary goals.[76] As Marcel Detienne has observed, the circle as 'microconfiguration of politics' is a shape that most suits 'societies aiming to be equalitarian'.[77]

The break from the English tradition, characterised by the provision of two sets of opposing benches occupied by majority and opposition members respectively, was evident. The French solution also distinguished itself by the location of the Speaker's podium in the lower centre of the hemicycle. At the same time, the Assembly's Rules of Procedure imposed the requirement to speak from the rostrum. This constraint created a particular dynamic for the verbal exchange within the Assembly, encouraging a declamatory style of parliamentary speech.[78] The parliamentary assemblies of the golden age of bourgeois parliamentarism were peculiar theatres in which the actors and audience coincided, for those who watched the play were always ready to reply to those who performed it, thus becoming *dramatis personae* themselves. Parliamentary representation consequently took on a theatrical format, albeit with the particular and rather paradoxical feature of being directed internally rather than externally, a seat of a self-referential elite working towards the construction of national identity. As Nicolas Rousselier put it:

> The parliaments of the 19th century were keen to present the face of an aristocratic academy of reason: a meeting of enlightened rather than mandated personalities, selected rather than elected. The decision that the discussion should be a true public deliberation – the right to discuss and the power to decide by the exercise of this right – had the effect of changing the nature of the power. The art of exchanging arguments was no longer a technique or a virtue, but the representation of modern political power.[79]

[76] M Holbraad and M Lamrani 'Revolutionary circles. A morphology of radical politics' (2021) 91 *Focaal–Journal of Global and Historical Anthropology* 1, 5–6.

[77] M Detienne, 'From Assembly Practices to Forms of Politics: A Comparative Approach' in M Detienne, *Comparing the Incomparable* (Stanford, CA, Stanford University Press, 2008) 86.

[78] On oratory as one of the central features of 19th-century French parliamentarism, especially during the Third Republic, see JP Rioux, 'Le Palais-Bourbon' in P Nora (ed), *Le lieux de la mémoire*, II, *La Nation*, Vol 3 (Paris, Gallimard, 1986).

[79] N Rousselier, *Le Parlement de l'éloquence: La souveraineté de la délibération au lendemain de la Grande Guerre* (Paris, Presses de Sciences Po, 1997) 11 (author's translation).

These features encouraged the theatralisation of parliamentary proceedings,[80] making the Assembly the great political theatre of the nation. Perhaps the greatest example of this format was achieved at the beginning of the twentieth century in Rome with the new plenary hall designed for the Italian Chamber of Deputies by the great Sicilian architect Ernesto Basile, who had worked with his father Giovanni Battista in the design of the Teatro Massimo in Palermo.[81]

It should be emphasised that the theatrical form of the nineteenth-century parliaments was not only conducive to the full expression of parliamentary oratory. Rather, parliaments as theatres acquired another of the key functions assigned to modern encyclopaedias, since Diderot and D'Alambert's work: that of representing the living memory of the national political identity. Parliamentary premises also became 'theatres of memory' in the sense of presenting themselves as institutions symbolising the memory of the nation, particularly in countries where the nation state was still in the making.[82] In many European countries, the new parliamentary premises built after the French Revolution were modelled after the idea of Parliament as a Monument, a building that, with its very structure, expresses the values and the history of the national civic traditions. According to this tradition, 'preservation' is among the typical functions of modern parliamentary architecture.[83] This function is exemplified by the building's occupancy of sacred sites, its symbolisation of new constitutional orders, its celebration of nationhood, and its expression of the stability of the state and the continuity of legislative traditions. 'By providing a tangible symbol of a new political system, the edifice helps to "jell" fluid constitutional situations and thereby helps to preserve the incipient order'.[84]

A very significant example of this monumental use of Parliament is the construction of the new Reichstag building in Berlin between 1883 and 1893. The new building was intended, in the aftermath of the triumphant war against France, as a symbol of victory over France and testimony of the completion of German national unity.[85] It embodied an ideological programme which, however, contrasted with the limited powers recognised to the German parliamentary assembly vis-a-vis the government. Moreover, in German political history, the highly symbolic value of the building was tragically confirmed by the fire of 1933, an event that assumed a central significance in the tragic series of events that led to the seizure of power by the Nazi regime. The end of that regime was later certified in the eyes of the world by the iconic photo of the Russian soldier caught in the moment of hoisting the

[80] On the 'theatralisation' of the parliamentary assemblies during the French Revolution, see Heurtin, *L'espace public parlementaire* (n 74) 108–59; see also, G Rizzoni, 'Political Architecture and the Seduction of Space: The Form of Parliaments and European Identity' in L Rorato and A Saunders (eds), *The Essence and the Margin: National Identities and Collective Memories in Contemporary European Culture* (Amsterdam, Rodopi, 2009).

[81] See the contributions included in the volume *The New Plenary Hall of the Chamber of Deputies on the 1918–2018 Centenary* (Soveria Mannelli, Rubettino, 2018).

[82] H Trapp, 'Orte der Versammlung' in Oesterreichische Gesellschaft fuer Architektur (ed), *Umbau 27 – Plenum. Orte der Macht. Sonderausgabe Biennale Venedig 2014* (Basel, Birkhaeuser, 2014). See also, Goodsell (n 73) 301.

[83] Goodsell (n 73) 299.

[84] ibid, 289. On the different aspects of the visualisation of parliamentary democracy in the nineteenth century, see A Biefang, 'Visualisierungen des Parlamentarismus im 19 Jahrundert. Ein Problemaufriss in europaeischer Perspektive' in A Schulz and A Wirsching (eds), *Parlamentarische Kulturen in Europa. Das Parlament als Kommunikationsraum* (Duesseldorf, Droste Verlag, 2012).

[85] H Wefing, *Parlamentsarchitektur. Zur Selbstdarstellung der Demokratie in ihren Bauwerken. Eine Untersuchung am Beispiel des Bonner Bundeshauses* (Berlin, Duncker & Humblot, 1995) 157.

Soviet flag at the top of the destroyed Reichstag. These particular historical precedents were the basis, following the reunification of Germany in 1989 and the transfer of the federal capital to Berlin, of the decision to proceed with a radical reconstruction project to allow the site to house the German Lower Chamber. The project was carried out by architects Norman Foster and Stephan Braunfels and went far beyond the restoration of the venerable monument. The architects aimed to preserve the memory of the historical events that had invested the building: for instance, they decided to keep the Cyrillic graffiti left on many of the walls by the Soviet soldiers during the occupation of the city. It is also worth mentioning here the truly extraordinary event that took place before the commencement of Foster's project. After a heated debate, the Bundestag Assembly granted two world-renowned artists (the Bulgarian Christo and the French American Jeanne-Claude) permission to wrap the monument in giant sheets of white fabric. This gesture was highly symbolic: the wrapping of the building evoked the notion of maternal protection of a precious piece of heritage, befitting of the parliamentary institutions whose intrinsic fragility had been so tragically demonstrated by history; moreover, its temporary concealment represented the possibility of both experiencing a sense of loss and undergoing a process of mourning before the inception of the building restoration.[86]

V. Parliaments as Cognitive Maps of Politics

Parliaments were not only theatres in the sense that they were the scenes of parliamentary politics or the living sites of a burgeoning national identity. They were also theatres in that they represented a tool for the systematisation and synthesis of the political knowledge of the age: they were instruments for acquiring knowledge of contemporary politics, like the renaissance 'Theatres of memory', which had the role of both representing and memorising universal knowledge.[87] The semi-circular form of parliamentary chambers evokes the idea of a political sphere which is circular and all-embracing. Their shape was instrumental in providing *a cognitive map of politics*:

> The circle, by its convexity, creates a closure toward its exterior. There is an autonomy, a self-sufficiency of the circle. This leads to the question of the status of the circle of the National Assembly in regard to the location of sovereignty .... The public parliamentary space is indeed this space of closeness and togetherness .... This is an essential moment: it is in this very operation that the nation keeps its distance from itself and by which, in the same distance, it achieves self-awareness and it is constituted reflexively as a 'complete nation'.[88]

From this point of view, the comparison between the English and French parliamentary plenary halls presents us with two different cognitive patterns. As mentioned above, the House of Commons is rectangular in shape and is occupied by two sets of opposing benches divided at one end by the Speaker's chair. As is well known, this structure stems from the shape of the St Stephen chapel in Westminster, which was used as a meeting venue for the

[86] Rizzoni (n 80) 189.
[87] F Yates, *The Art of Memory* (London, Routledge, 1966).
[88] J-P Heurtin, 'The Circle of Discussion and the Semicircle of Criticism' in B Latour and P Weibel (eds), *Making Things Public: Atmospheres of Democracy* (Cambridge, MA, ZKM Karlsruhe, Mit Press, 2005) 764.

House of Commons from 1548 to 1834, when the Parliament's building was largely destroyed by a disastrous fire. Although it preceded the existence of the two-party English system, this shape is perfectly suited to representing the 'adversarial' relationship between majority and opposition, seated at directly opposing desks, with the majority occupying the desks to the right of the Speaker. The plenary also expresses another fundamental principle of the British form of government: the *fusion of powers* between government and Parliament.[89] Members of the government do not occupy separate positions from those of parliamentarians, but sit on the first row of the benches reserved for the majority, with the Prime Minister directly facing the head of the opposition sitting in the centre of the opposition row. The head of the opposition is in turn surrounded by members of the Shadow Cabinet. With the exception of these majority and opposition parliamentarians who, according to their position, are referred to as 'frontbenchers', the other MPs do not have fixed seats. It is also well known that the chamber has a much smaller number of seats than the number of members: this tradition was also preserved after the reconstruction of the House following the German bombing in 1941, thanks to a memorable intervention at the session of 28 October 1943 by Prime Minister Winston Churchill. In that speech, Churchill explained in very clear terms the institutional reasons for maintaining the traditional form of the English parliamentary chamber instead of the hemicycle prevailing within continental parliaments:

> There are two main characteristics of the House of Commons which will command the approval and the support of reflective and experienced members. They will, I have no doubt, sound odd to foreign ears. The first is that its shape should be oblong and not semi-circular. Here is a very potent factor in our political life. The semi-circular assembly, which appeals to political theorists, enables every individual or every group to move round the centre, adopting various shades of pink according to the weather changes. I am a convinced supporter of the party system in preference to the group system. I have seen many earnest and ardent parliaments destroyed by the group system. The party system is much favoured by the oblong form of chamber. It is easy for an individual to move through those insensible gradations from Left to Right but the act of 'crossing the floor' is one which requires serious consideration. I am well informed on this matter, for I have accomplished that difficult process, not only once but twice. Logic is a poor guide compared with custom. Logic which has created in so many countries semi-circular assemblies which have buildings which give to every member, not only a seat to sit in but often a desk to write at, with a lid to bang, has proved fatal to parliamentary government as we know it here in its home and in the land of its birth.
>
> The second characteristic of a chamber formed on the lines of the House of Commons is that it should not be big enough to contain all its members at once without over-crowding and that there should be no question of every member having a separate seat reserved for him. The reason for this has long been a puzzle to uninstructed outsiders and has frequently excited the curiosity and even the criticism of new members. Yet it is not so difficult to understand if you look at it from a practical point of view. If the House is big enough to contain all its members, nine-tenths of its debates will be conducted in the depressing atmosphere of an almost empty or half-empty chamber. The essence of good House of Commons speaking is the conversational style, the facility for quick, informal interruptions and interchanges. Harangues from a rostrum would be a bad substitute for the conversational style in which so much of our business is done. But the conversational

[89] On the concept of 'fusion of powers', see P Leyland, *The Constitution of the United Kingdom: A Contextual Analysis* (Oxford, Hart Publishing, 2021) 71–73.

> style requires a fairly small space, and there should be on great occasions a sense of crowd and urgency. There should be a sense of the importance of much that is said and a sense that great matters are being decided, there and then, by the House.
>
> We attach immense importance to the survival of parliamentary democracy. In this country this is one of our war aims. We wish to see our Parliament a strong, easy, flexible instrument of free debate. For this purpose a small chamber and a sense of intimacy are indispensable.[90]

In his speech, Churchill directly connects the structure of the House of Commons with the British form of government. For Churchill, one of the essential elements of this system is the clear division between majority and opposition, represented by the arrangement of benches in the House. The structural solution adopted at Westminster encourages the division of the political system on the basis of a clear political alternative, rather than the deployment of a multiplicity of political positions from the Right to the Left. For Churchill, the 'party system' remains at the core of parliamentary government: the set up of autonomous parliamentary groups would be fatal to this structure. It is also interesting that the British statesman attaches great importance to the small size of the House, which, in his view, allows the 'conversational style' of the British Parliament, which makes it 'a strong, easy, flexible instrument of free debate'. We will see in the next chapter how these features continued to mark the identity of the British parliamentarism in the twentieth century. Here, it should be observed that the cognitive map of the House of Commons offers two essential pieces of information: the first, concerning the power ratio between majority and opposition; and the second, relating to the hierarchical distinction between the leading group and the remaining members of both the majority and the opposition.

In continental Europe, the origins of the MPs' seating arrangements according to the Right–Left orientation are traditionally traced back to a vote taken by the French National Assembly on 28 August 1789 regarding the royal veto. The deputies who supported the introduction of an absolute veto gathered to the right of the President, whereas those in favour of a 'suspensive' veto gathered to his left.[91] Despite this important precedent, the distinction between the Right and the Left was only gradually entrenched in French parliamentary topography.[92] Even in the revolutionary assemblies, this distinction failed to take hold as a fixed criterion of differentiation between groups of deputies characterised by different ideological visions. The widespread revolutionary aversion to 'parties' as permanent aggregations of the elected countered this evolution, which was viewed as a threat to the freedom of deputies and as a possible form of diversion from the pursuit of

[90] HC Deb 28 October 1943, vol 393, cols 403–10.

[91] 'Tous les partisans du veto allérent s'asseoir à droite du président; tous les antagonistes se groupèrent dans la partie opposée. Cette séparation rendait plus facile le calcul des voix dans le vote par assis et levé, qui avoie té conservé. Depuis long-temps déjà, et avant la réunion des ordres, l'extrême gauche et l'extrême droite étaient devenues le point de réunion des députés les plus ardents dans les opinions alors opposées, Chaque groupe avait été en augmentant en nombre, au fur et à mesure que les discussions devenaient plus irritantes': BJ Buchex and PC Roux, *Histoire parlementaire de la révolution française, ou journal des assemblées nationales, depuis 1789 jusqu'en 1815* (Paris, Paulin Libraire, 1834) T 2, 350.

[92] M Gauchet, 'La droite et la gauche' in P Nora (ed), *Les lieux de mémoire*, tome 3, *Les France. 1. Conflits et partages* (Paris, Gallimard, 1992) 395.

the general interest. This explains the recurring proposals to prevent deputies from being given a fixed seat in the Assembly, and the preference for the allocation of seats by lot. From this point of view, we can agree with Marcel Gauchet that 'if the French Revolution has in fact introduced the Right–Left distinction into political language, it has done so in spite of itself'.[93]

In French parliamentary topography, the Right–Left distinction reappeared in the Chamber of Deputies during the Restoration period. It is during this same period that maps of the parliamentary plenary halls designed to indicate the orientation of members from Right to Left started to appear.[94] It should be acknowledged, however, that in the French parliamentary tradition, the distinction between the Right and the Left never became a principle of net division, such as the British cleavage between majority and opposition. Rather, it was simply used as a general criterion to indicate the political orientation of members, within a very wide range of nuances.

The Right–Left distinction presupposes the existence of a centre, to which the majority of MPs often belonged during the period of the Restoration and the Orleanist constitutional monarchy. The main advantage for the cognitive strength of the Right–Left criterion was, moreover, to make the idea of radical antagonism compatible with the concept of a wide range of political nuances.[95] This 'open' pattern made it possible to better describe the parliamentary life and behaviour of individual members, including their changes with regard to the political spectrum as a whole. For these reasons, the Right–Left pair was ultimately more successful and enduring than other oppositions, such as that between the 'Whites' and the 'Reds', which was prevalent in the context of the 1848 Revolution. The distinction between 'Whites' and 'Reds' referred to a cleavage of a 'substantial' nature determined by the political positions towards the trauma resulting from the French Revolution.[96] Precisely for this reason, this opposition related to a rigid ideological criterion, which the Right–Left pair avoided in favour of a paradigm capable of describing more fluid political contexts affected by multiple types of conflict.

In a situation in which political parties were still largely active only in Parliament, and were subject to highly fluid transformation processes, the distinction between the Right and the Left therefore emerged predominantly within the parliamentary context. In France, this opposition became a true marker of an ideological cleavage only towards the end of the nineteenth century.[97] From this point of view, the events linked to the 'Affaire Dreyfus' undoubtedly had the effect of polarising French political life. However, it was only with the full emergence of mass parties that the distinction between the Right and the Left materialised in French political culture as a stable contrasting element beyond the parliamentary institution too. The fact remains that, for most of the nineteenth century, French

[93] ibid, 401.

[94] Gauchet mentions the 'Plan figuratif de la Chambre des députés indiquant avec exactitude la place qu'occupe chacun des membres'. The document was published in 1819.

[95] Gauchet, 'La droite et la gauche' (n 92) 410.

[96] J-L Ormières, 'Les rouges et les blancs' in P Nora (ed), *Les lieux de mémoire*, tome 3, *Les France. 1. Conflits et partages* (Paris, Gallimard, 1992).

[97] M Crapez, 'De quand date le clivage gauche/droite en France?' (1998) 48(1) *Revue française de science politique* 42, 70–72.

parliamentary chambers played a key role as an 'encyclopaedia of politics', providing a cognitive map, always in very rapid change, of the different orientations of the national political class.[98]

In Italy's constitutional monarchy too, the divide between the Left and the Right was mainly referred to in the parliamentary context, in connection with the different political positions represented in the elective chamber, the Chamber of Deputies. This distinction emerged somewhat paradoxically, however, since the rules of the Chamber did not provide for a fixed disposition of the seats.[99] The Right–Left divide was typically a distinction marking different factions within the same liberal ruling class on the basis of their different visions about some of the major political issues of the time, like loyalty to the monarchy or the means to achieve the country's political unity (especially with reference to the '*questione romana*', that is the debate regarding the temporal power of the popes as rulers of a part of the Italian territory including the city of Rome). In any event, the Right–Left divide was never a clear-cut barrier. Rather, on the contrary, it allowed the existence of infinite nuances and the frequent passage of individual politicians from one side to the other. Cavour's appointment as Prime Minister in 1852 was made possible by an alliance (the so-called '*connubio*') with the factions of the Left led by Urbano Rattazzi (who was elected President of the Chamber of Deputies). Later, the 'parliamentary revolution' of 1876 brought to power the left-wing government led by Agostino De Pretis on the basis of the support secured by some of the parliamentarians belonging to the Right. This fluidity of parliamentary divisions was defined by the political observers of the time as evidence of the 'transformism' of the Italian political class.[100] This phenomenon was judged differently in historical and political terms. For Benedetto Croce, for example, transformism was a positive and inevitable expression of the elasticity of liberal leadership in response to varying political balances and situations (such as the loss of importance of the '*Questione romana*').[101] For others, such as Carducci[102] and Salvemini,[103] this attitude was in fact one of the causes of corruption and the inherent weakness of the national ruling class.[104]

[98] XML, *Parliament* (Amsterdam, XML, 2016): the book provides a worldwide comparison of the architectural structure of the plenary halls of 193 parliaments.

[99] 'Each Member may choose the place which he prefers, if available, for the entire duration of the parliamentary session. Old parliamentarians usually occupy the same place as long as they remain in Parliament. In any event, the fact of having an allocated seat does not prevent Members from sometimes occupying other posts': M Mancini and U Galeotti, *Norme ad usi del Parlamento italiano* (Roma, Tipografia della Camera dei deputati, 1887) 146.

[100] The term *trasformismo* was used for the first time in 1874 by a representative of the moderate right-wing ranks, Carlo Alfieri di Sostegno, in an open letter to Francesco De Sanctis. It later became popular, especially with the executives led by one of the representatives of the Italian 'historic left', Agostino De Pretis. De Pretis made frequent reference to the need for a 'transformation' of the Italian political system that he presented as a positive and necessary evolution of the old divisions.

[101] B Croce, *Storia d'Italia dal 1871 al 1915* (Bari, Laterza, 1929) 13–26.

[102] G Carducci, 'Candidature' in *Edizione nazionale delle opere di Giosuè Carducci*, Vol XXV, *Confessioni e battaglie*, Serie seconda (Bologna, Zanichelli, 1938).

[103] G Salvemini, *Il ministro della malavita e altri scritti sull'Italia giolittiana* (Milano, Feltrinelli, 1962).

[104] On the Italian Transformism in liberal Italy see also, S Rogari, *Alle origini del trasformismo: Partiti e Sistema politico nell'Italia liberale, 1861–1914* (Roma-Bari, Laterza, 1998); F Cammarano, *Storia politica dell'Italia liberale: L'età del liberalismo classico* (Roma-Bari, Laterza, 1999); G Sabbatucci, *Il trasformismo come sistema: Saggio sulla storia politica dell'Italia unita* (Roma-Bari, Laterza, 2003); L Musella, *Il trasformismo* (Bologna, il Mulino, 2003).

Beyond these different opinions, the importance of parliamentary alignements for defining the cognitive map of national politics remains fully evident in the case of liberal Italy.

VI. Parliamentary Time between Cyclicity and Syncronicity

The organisation of parliamentary working times is a typical feature of modern legislative assemblies. The pre-modern parliaments met sporadically, without a predetermined schedule. By contrast, the duration and working times of modern parliaments are determined on the basis of precise rules laid down by constitutions, parliamentary rules or long-established practices. The principle of the periodic renewal of elected assemblies is inherent in the concept of modern representative government.[105] Through regular elections, it is ensured that the composition of parliaments corresponds to the voters' will. This requirement is, for example, particularly strongly reflected in the US Constitution, providing that the term of office of members of the Chamber of Representatives is only two years, which corresponds to the six-year term of office of senators (one-third of whom are elected every two years). Even in countries whose constitutions provide for longer legislative terms, the power of dissolution, usually reserved for the monarch and the government, often reduces the length of the parliamentary mandate. In 1887, Mancini and Galeotti pointed out that the duration of a term of the Italian Chamber of Deputies had always been shorter than the five years laid down in the Albertino Statute, due to repeated dissolutions adopted over the years.[106]

The legislative term between two elections is in turn often divided into sessions, with varying rules applicable in each country. Within the sessions, prorogations and adjournments further organise parliamentary time.[107]

Having regard to these rules and practices, parliamentary time is characterised by two main features: *cyclicity* and *synchronicity*. Both elements reflect key aspects of the parliamentary encyclopaedia. Cyclicity is a typical quality of Parliament's time: the organisation of working time on the basis of regular and pre-established rhythms that mirrors the periodicity of the solar calendar expresses the continuity of the parliamentary institution, which in turn is one of the most important components of the continuity of the constitutional order itself.[108] This diachronic dimension connects each new parliament with its predecessors. The regularity of parliamentary work contributed to the shaping of 'public time' as a shared chronological frame capable of 'building trust, fostering a sense of community,

[105] B Manin, *The Principles of Representative Government* (Cambridge, Cambridge University Press, 1997) 79 ff.

[106] Mancini and Galeotti (n 99) 82.

[107] G Riescher, *Zeit und Politik: Zur institutionellen Bedeutung von Zeitstrukturen in parlamentarischen und praesidentiellen Regierungssystemen* (Baden Baden, Nomos, 1994).

[108] 'Le Parlement apparait, plus que tout autre institution démocratique, comme le produit du temps long qui marque son identité et par conséquent la manière dont il exerce ses fonctions et les activités qui s'y rattachent': E Cartier, 'Le Parlement et la durée' in G Toulemond and E Cartier (eds), *Le Parlement et le temps: Approche comparée* (Paris, Institut Universitaire Varenne, 2017) 33.

encouraging solidarity, but also imposing order and discipline'.[109] From this point of view, it can be said that the formation of the nation state coincides with the notion of public time.[110]

The pace of parliamentary work, protected by constitutional and parliamentary rules, is also instrumental in securing another fundamental aspect of the parliamentary regime in the liberal era: the minimum time needed for deliberation, based on the free exchange of views between parliamentarians.[111] For this reason, a parliamentary decision can never be immediate. Rather, it necessarily requires sufficient time for a genuine debate to take place between the various opinions present in the assembly. Without permitting this time, parliamentarism simply loses all its meaning.

Equally importantly, synchronicity is an essential element of parliamentary time.[112] Modern parliaments have a direct relationship with the events of their time. The symbiosis between legislative assemblies and the press, which I have analysed above, was a crucial aspect of this relationship. Legislative assemblies shared some key characteristics with periodical news: periodicity, regularity, contemporaneity, miscellany (presenting many different topics at the same time).[113] As a consequence, parliaments became major producers of political news. They in turn consumed news, which often triggered parliamentary initiatives. The synchronisation of parliamentary time was also made possible by other important innovations in the nineteenth century, such as modern rail transport, which allowed for continuous contact between parliamentarians and their electors and a much higher frequency of work in chambers. Acceleration, as a distinctive characteristic of time in modernity,[114] thus also affected parliamentary work. The parliamentary encyclopaedia was required to constantly keep up with the times.

The need for timeliness had also some important effects on the division of powers. Particularly in the second half of the century, the executives tried – with unequal success in the different countries[115] – to impose their rhythm on parliamentary work. The various government needs, first and foremost those relating to international policy, required parliamentary decisions to be taken within a set time frame. These were felt even more strongly in the following century, in relation to the need to swiftly implement increasingly complex and urgent intervention programmes. The executives will then act as disruptive agents vis-a-vis the need for weighted political debates in the parliamentary assemblies. The

[109] J Zielonka, *The Lost Future and How to Reclaim It* (London, Yale University Press, 2023) 33. Regarding the institutionalisation of time as a major defining element of democracies and a condition of their stability and legitimacy, see A Schäfer and W Merkel, 'The Temporal Constitution of Democracies' in KH Goetz (ed), *The Oxford Handbook of Time and Politics*, online edn (Oxford Academic, 4 April 2019), available at: academic.oup.com/edited-volume/35419.

[110] Zielonka, ibid, 33.

[111] On the importance of time in democratic deliberation, see C Fumagalli, 'Time and Democratic Deliberation' in KH Goetz (ed), *The Oxford Handbook of Time and Politics*, online edn (Oxford Academic, 4 April 2019), available at: academic.oup.com/edited-volume/35419.

[112] B Ridard, 'L'activité parlamentaire et l'instant' in G Toulemond and E Cartier (eds), *Le Parlement et le temps: Approche comparée* (Paris, Institut Universitaire Varenne, 2017) 77 ff.

[113] Pettegree (n 36) 364.

[114] H Rosa and J Trejo-Mathys, *Social Acceleration: A New Theory of Modernity* (New York, Columbia University Press, 2013).

[115] For a comparison of the procedural reforms in Britain, France, Sweden and Germany intended to rationalise parliamentary decision-making, see M Koß, *Parliaments in Time: The Evolution of Legislative Democracy in Western Europe, 1866–2015* (Oxford, Oxford University Press, 2018).

continuing state of emergency in the different areas of public policy will risk replacing the time of parliaments with the time of the executives, characterised by urgency and the need for an immediate reaction.[116]

VII. The Era of Generalist Politicians: The Centrality of Parliamentary Oratory

Nineteenth-century European parliaments shared some common features in terms of both their composition and their functioning. The liberal parliamentary class was typically composed of 'notables'.[117] Notables derived most of their legitimacy from the prestige and power positions they enjoyed at a local level. In view of the severe limitations on voting rights, parliamentarians in the liberal era were de facto elected on the basis of a self-selection process which began and ended within an extremely narrow social sphere. For most of them, political engagement was still a part-time activity compared with the rest of their social commitments. The classical Weberian definition of 'amateur politicians', however, only partially suits the nineteenth-century parlamentarians. On the one hand, their presence and work in the parliamentary sphere represented a first form of professionalisation of politics. Parliaments, with their peculiar procedures and rituals, were certainly important in encouraging the self-awareness of the ruling class about its leadership at the helm of the nation. Parliamentary assemblies therefore played a crucial, if often underestimated, role in the structuration of national political elites. On the other hand, the parlamentarians as 'notables', through their patronage activity and advocacy of local interests, were pivotal figures in the mediation between the state and civil society, responding to the multiple integration demands coming from the lower classes towards the emerging sphere of liberal modernity.[118]

[116] On the 'motorisation' of ordinary legislative activity promoted by the pressure exerted by twentieth-century executives, see W Scheuerman, *Liberal Democracy and the Social Acceleration of Time* (Baltimore, MD, Johns Hopkins University Press, 2004).

[117] On the 'notables', see the classical pages of M Weber, *Economy and Society* (1st edn 1922) (Cambridge, MA, Harvard University Press, 2019). Weber describes the progress from the parliamentary parties being controlled by the notables (*Honoratiorenparteien*) to the prevalence of 'party notables' with the advent of mass parties. In France, the golden age of the notables comprising the political leading class is usually identified as being the years from 1815 to 1848, when first the restoration of the Borbonic monarchy and then the Orleanist monarchy accepted the representative system, even with the well-known limitations of the franchise. The Third Republic witnessed a gradual transition to a new political leadership that was described by Robert de Jouvenel: R De Jouvenel, *La République des camarades* (Paris, Grasset, 1914) as the passage from the 'République des ducs' to the 'République des camarades', with the extension of the suffrage and the emergence of the mass parties: on these developments, see A Jardin and AJ Tudesq, *La France des notables*, 2 vols (Paris, Seuil, 1973). In Italy, the dependence of the parliamentary class on the local notables was vehemently criticised by Gaetano Mosca in his *Teorica dei governi e governo parlamentare* (1884) now in *Scritti politici*, vol I (Torino, UTET, 1982). According to Mosca, the notables were able to exercise an occult and negative influence on the country's political leadership, resulting in the prevalence of merely private interests over national politics. Mosca was one of the leading inspiring figures of the anti-parliamentary movement in Italian political thought (on this movement, see below (n 185)). On the notables in Italian politics, see: R Romanelli, *Il comando impossibile: Stato e società nell'Italia liberale* (Bologna, Il Mulino, 1988); P Farneti, *La classe politica italiana dal liberalismo alla democrazia* (Genova, ECIG, 1989); G Solia, 'Notabili' in *Enciclopedia Treccani delle scienze sociali* (Roma, Istituto dell'Enciclopedia italiana, 1996), available at: www.treccani.it/enciclopedia/notabili_%28Enciclopedia-delle-scienze-sociali%29/; A Mastropaolo, 'Notabili, clientelismo e trasformismo' in L Violante (ed), *Storia d'Italia. Il parlamento* (Torino, Einaudi, 1999).

[118] F Cammarano, 'Le notable à l'époque libérale' (2002) 114 *Mélanges de l'école française de Rome* 673.

From this perspective, the substantial presence of lawyers in nineteenth-century parliamentary chambers indicates the emergence of a first type of 'double face' professional, relying on the synergy between his legal expertise and his activity in the parliamentary sphere.[119]

As a rule, nineteenth-century parlamentarians were not specialists in specific sectors of public intervention, but they were able to address any political question in the context of the parliamentary debate. From this point of view, therefore, they could be better described as 'generalist' and 'encyclopaedic' rather than 'amateur' politicians. This definition also appears more appropriate if we consider the institutional environment offered by nineteenth-century parliaments.

From the point of view of their functioning, 'theatre parliaments' were parliaments in which debate in the assembly prevailed over work in committees. In this respect, the British model had a strong influence on continental parliaments for most of the nineteenth century. In these parliaments, committees did not constitute a specialised forum for examining legislative proposals. Rather, they simply represented a particular stage in the legislative process: their members were selected by drawing lots to set up temporary bodies responsible for the preliminary examination of bills. The establishment of a temporary committee was often an alternative to the option of referring a bill to the plenary, which met as a 'committee of the whole house'. In the UK Parliament, committees of a permanent nature were established primarily in order to carry out inquiries. However, the use of this kind of committee declined during the nineteenth century in favour of the creation of royal commissions: bodies set up on the initiative of the government with the presence, in addition to parliamentarians, of experts on the subjects being dealt with in each case. As pointed out by Joseph Redlich:

> Two great facts have prevented in England the birth of a strong committee system: the rise of the system of parliamentary party government and the establishment of the Cabinet as the chief organ of government, the cabinet acts as the 'joint committee' of the two Houses of Parliament: the pivot of modern English constitution, parliamentary cabinet government.[120]

The absence of stable committees with legislative competence was, in any event, one of the main causes of the weak professionalisation and specialisation of the nineteenth-century parliamentary class. Presence in Parliament required other types of skills, first and foremost oratory ability. The nineteenth century witnessed the golden era of parliamentary oratory. We have seen that nineteenth-century parliaments as theatres were primarily aimed at an internal audience, composed of the MPs themselves. When addressing his colleagues, the orator was supposed to speak with the aim of convincing his peers. This dynamic expressed the ideal view of the Parliament as a free forum of the nation, which we had already seen emerging with Burke, and which would be further developed by the great ideologists of liberalism in the nineteenth century:

> [T]he Parliament has an office not inferior even to this in importance; to be at once the nation's Committee of Grievances and its Congress of Opinions; an arena in which not only the general

[119] J Joana, 'L'invention du député: Réunions parlementaires et spécialisation de l'activité politique au XIXe siècle' (1996) 35 *Politix. Revue des sciences sociales du politique* 23.

[120] J Redlich, *The Procedure of the House of Commons: A Study of its History and Present Form* (1st edition 1905) Vol II (London, Constable, 1908) 211.

> opinion of the nation, but that of every section of it, and, as far as possible, of every eminent individual whom it contains, can produce itself in full light and challenge discussion; where every person in the country may count upon finding somebody who speaks his mind as well or better than he could speak it himself – not to friends and partisans exclusively, but in the face of opponents, to be tested by adverse controversy; where those whose opinion is overruled, feel satisfied that it is heard, and set aside not by a mere act of will, but for what are thought superior reasons, and commend themselves as such to the representatives of the majority of the nation; where every party or opinion in the country can muster its strength, and be cured of any illusion concerning the number or power of its adherents; where the opinion which prevails in the nation makes itself manifest as prevailing, and marshals its hosts in the presence of the government, which is thus enabled and compelled to give way to it on the mere manifestation, without the actual employment of its strength; where statesmen can assure themselves, far more certainly than by any other signs, what elements of opinion and power are growing and what declining, and are enabled to shape their measures with some regard not solely to present exigencies, but to tendencies in progress. Representative assemblies are often taunted by their enemies with being places of mere talk and bavardage. There has seldom been more misplaced derision. I know not how a representative assembly can more usefully employ itself than in talk, when the subject of talk is the great public interests of the country, and every sentence of it represents the opinion either of some important body of persons in the nation, or of an individual in whom some such body have reposed their confidence.[121]

In this deliberative context, the arts of rhetoric were undoubtedly of special significance. The great statesmen of the nineteenth century were also distinguished by the distinctive features of their oratory style.[122] In this regard, Kari Palonen[123] rightly stresses the importance of parliamentary rhetoric, which goes far beyond the mere style of parliamentary speech. As an expression of 'government by speaking' (Macaulay 1857) or of 'government by discussion' (Bagehot 1872), parliamentary rhetoric is linked to some of the founding values of parliamentarism, such as the freedom of speech and the egalitarian status of the members. According to Palonen, parliamentary procedure is the primary conceptual site of debating *pro et contra*, and it is the procedure that distinguishes parliaments from other political assemblies. Parliamentary procedure therefore acts as both a political type of ideal and as a substrate for the parliamentary version of deliberative rhetoric.[124]

One of the crucial components of parliamentary rhetoric is *dispositio*, as the function that gives order and hierarchy to the topics to be dealt with:

> The moment of dispositio, or the arrangement of items for debate, is a decisive aspect in distinguishing the role of parliamentary procedure from the practices of oratory. It includes the classification of issues into types of questions to be debated, the range of utterances into discrete speech acts, and the trajectory of items into an orderly journey of different stages on the agenda, with the vote being the final speech act. The transformation of issues into items on the

[121] JS Mill, 'Considerations on Representative Government' in JS Mill, *On Liberty and Other Essays* (1st edn 1861) (Oxford, Oxford University Press, 1998) 282–83.

[122] For an analysis of the argumentative style of some protagonists of the Italian parliamentary life (Cavour, d'Azeglio, Garibaldi, Giolitti), see F Giuliani, 'Il discorso parlamentare' in L Violante (ed), *Storia d'Italia. Il Parlamento* (Torino, Einaudi, 2001) 864–68.

[123] K Palonen, *The Politics of Parliamentary Procedure: The Formation of the Westminster Procedure as a Parliamentary Ideal Type* (Leverkusen-Opladen, Verlag Barbara Budrich, 2016).

[124] ibid, 12.

> parliamentary agenda has reference to the proceduralisation of politics, one that conditions and mediates the elocutio of rhetorical practice through and through.[125]

The nineteenth-century parliamentary rhetoric therefore has an intrinsically encyclopaedic scope, as it has the potential to deal with any kind of subject. At the same time, it is submitted to a set of rules and constraints that impose a clear order to the discussion of each topic. Its approach, of course, is not scientific, but rather eminently narrative and practical, based on a common reference to humanistic culture.[126] The reference of the nineteenth-century parliamentary class to a common humanistic culture transcends even political and ideological cleavages[127] and explains the generalist, and ultimately encyclopaedic cultural background of most of the prominent politicians of the liberal age.

VIII. Parliamentary Libraries

The pedagogic and encyclopaedic features of nineteenth-century parliamentarism are confirmed by the contemporary emergence of the great parliamentary libraries. These 'institutions within the institutions' offered extensive bibliographic collections which tended to cover every field of knowledge with the intent of ensuring an adequate information base for parliamentary work.

The most striking example is the Library of Congress, which gradually became a kind of universal collection of human cultural products of all kinds.[128] This encyclopaedic imprinting was given to the Library by its principal founder, Thomas Jefferson. In promoting the foundation of the Library, Jefferson was inspired by a 'doctrine of completeness and inclusiveness', which was further developed over the two centuries of history of this key congressional institution. The Library reflects the cultural background of many of the American Founding Fathers:

> We owe this monumental pile of facts to the work habits of the Founding Fathers. They were book oriented from the very first. Most of them were lawyers and shared their profession's traditional respect for the printed word in codes and precedents; most of the few who were not lawyers were philosophers and pamphleteers, nourished on the literature of the Enlightenment. For them, thinking meant first reading – and then, as a rule, writing more themselves.[129]

From its very beginning, the Library's holdings encompassed a full spectrum of factual and fictional writing. By 1812, the Library had over 900 titles whose content spanned from history, to biography, to natural history, with a significant collections of classical writers (from Machiavelli to Shakespeare). The most expensive titles in the collection were

[125] ibid, 24.
[126] R Bod, *A New History of the Humanities: The Search for Principles and Patterns from Antiquity to the Present* (Oxford, Oxford University Press, 2013) 184: Bod makes reference to the opinion of Cicero, according to whom the competent orator should know everything, on the condition that his knowledge has a practical use.
[127] J Joana, *Pratiques politiques des députés français au XIXe siècle: Du dilettante au spécialiste* (Paris, L'Harmattan, 1999) 47–48, who emphasises the *empire des humanités* in the formation of the French liberal politicians.
[128] On the Library of Congress and its history, see JY Cole and J Aikin, 'America's Library: A Brief History of the Library of the Congress' in JY Cole and J Aikin (eds), *Encyclopaedia of the Library of the Congress: For Congress, the Nation and the World* (Washington, DC, Library of the Congress, Bernan Press, 2004) 1–14.
[129] CA Goodrum and HW Dalrymple, *The Library of Congress* (Boulder, CO, Westview, 1982) 7.

the 33 volumes of the French *Encyclopédie*.[130] In 1814, the British army invaded the city of Washington and burned the Capitol, including over 3,000 volumes of the Library of Congress. In order to restore its collections, the Congress decided to purchase the Jefferson personal library, comprising over 6,000 volumes. Jefferson was a man of encyclopaedic interests and his library included works on architecture, music, history and geography. This acquisition contributed to expanding the scope of the Library far beyond the bounds of a legislative library.[131]

Over the years, and on the basis of further acquisitions, the Library of Congress become the de facto National Library of the United States, even if it never lost its original mission of serving the information needs of the Congress. Under US copyright law, the Library received items registered for copyright protection nationwide from 1846 until 1859, and the practice started again in 1865. The Copyright Law of 1870 stipulated that two copies of every book, pamphlet, map, print, photograph and piece of music registered for copyright be deposited in the Library. On the basis of this privilege, and due to other acquisitions, by the end of the century the Library had amassed an enormous collection comprising almost one million volumes. The emergence of the Library as an institution of national significance was solemnly marked by the inauguration in 1897 of the new library premises, a magnificent building (now called the Thomas Jefferson Building) that was immediately hailed as a national monument. Jefferson's concept of the Library's extended mandate was relaunched in the twentieth century, especially when the 1965 Higher Education Act directed the Library to acquire, insofar as possible, all current library materials of value to scholarship published all over the world and to provide cataloguing information for these materials.[132] Over the years the Library has affirmed itself as a key reference institution for all the libraries of the nation. Today the Library can been defined as 'the world's greatest Multi-Media encyclopedia' with a catalogue that includes 18 million records for books, serials, manuscripts, maps, music, recordings, images and electronic resources.[133]

Compared with the Library of Congress, the origins of the Library of the British House of Commons are more strictly linked to the institutional functions of the Parliament. A parliamentary library in Britain was first founded in 1818, with the appointment of the first House of Commons Librarian by the Speaker, Charles Manners-Sutton. The Library's main task was ensuring the collection of reports, statutes and other official papers which were previously attributed to the custody of the Clerk of the House. In 1834, the Speaker appointed the first Standing Committee on the House of Commons Library to assist him in guiding the direction of the Library. Among the members of the first Committee were some prominent MPs, including Robert Peel and the young William Gladstone. The Committee issued some strict guidelines about the nature of the collections: the Library should not

> contain the ancient or modern classics of any language; or in general, works of science, or books of theology, or any works which may render it a reading room for others than the Members, or for Members themselves in any pursuit distinct from those which belong to them in the immediate discharge of their parliamentary duties.[134]

[130] ibid, 12.
[131] Cole and Aikin (n 128) 3.
[132] ibid, 12.
[133] ibid, 14.
[134] D Menhennet, *The House of Commons Library: A History* (London, House of Commons Library, 2000) 9.

The contrast with the encyclopaedic and humanistic character of the Library of Congress is striking. This approach, however, changed dramatically after the disastrous fire in October 1834 that destroyed a significant part of the parliamentary premises and, with it, some of the most precious items of the historical library holdings. The new parliamentary premises built after the fire by Charles Barry and August Pugin, and inaugurated in 1852, reserved large and prestigious locations for the libraries of the House of Commons and of the House of Lords on the principal floor facing east across the river Thames. The sheer size of the new libraries suggested expansive purchasing policies. The acquisitions of new volumes was inspired by a generalist approach that changed the nature of the Library profoundly. On the basis of these developments, the House of Commons Library 'had come to resemble something between a very fine, large scale country gentlemen's library … and an aspiring national collection'.[135] The composition of the House of Commons had been significantly renovated after the 1832 Reform Act, however,

> despite two more reform Acts in 1867 and 1884 respectively, and the fact that major changes in the theory and practice of representation were already beginning to show, the full impact of such changes on individual members' background and attitudes had not yet happened. As a result, most members of the House of Commons were still relatively well-off, financially prosperous and independent. Many had private libraries of their own and employed assistants to gather information for them. In the House of Commons library they looked for and found a very good general library, offering on the one hand essential parliamentary and official literature, on the other, the cultural amenities associated with a first-class club or country gentleman's library.[136]

In France, the establishment of the first parliamentary library was determined during the Convention on the initiative of the Committee for Public Education in February 1794. The Library was able to immediately acquire significant collections thanks to the volumes coming from the *dépôts literaires*, and its funds were also bolstered by the libraries of convents and other suppressed institutions.[137] These events explain the generalist character of the first nucleus of the Library, which received books on the most diverse disciplines: from Greek and Latin classics, to history, geography, law and theology. There was also an important collection of geographical maps. This encyclopaedic orientation was also confirmed when the Library became the *Bibliothéque du Corps législatif* on the basis of the *Loi 14 ventose an IV* (4 March 1796) voted by the Council of Five Hundreds and the Council of Elders. The first librarian, Armand-Augustin Camus (1740–1804), played a fundamental role in consolidating the prestige and funds of the Library, even after its transfer to the Palais Bourbon. In addition to the books coming from the *dépôts literaires*, Camus undertook to obtain funding for new acquisitions, including of rare and precious works. The major renovations of the Palais Bourbon, started in 1831 under the direction of architect Jules de Joly, also involved the Library, which was earmarked for a much larger space in the new premises, in particularly prestigious rooms,[138] which are those still occupied by the Library today. Also

[135] ibid, 48.
[136] ibid, 55.
[137] ibid, 25–28.
[138] J de July described his works with these words: 'Nous avons cherché, en établissant la nouvelle Bibliothèque de la Chambre des députés, à luy donner un style grave et soutenu; nous avons voulu qu'elle réunit à une grande disposition toutes les ressources que la décoration permet d'y emploier avec succès' (quoted by J Marchand, *La Bibliothèque de l'Assemblèe Nationale* (Bordeaux, Societé des Bibliophiles de Guyenne, 1979) 146).

thanks to the funding provided by Thiers, then Minister of Commerce and Public Works, the young Eugène Delacroix was called upon to decorate the domes of the new Library. The artist decided to draw inspiration from the great disciplines represented in the collections of the Library. The frescoes of the five domes (which were only completed by Delacroix and his disciples in 1847) were dedicated, respectively, to the sciences, philosophy and history, legislation and eloquence, theology and poetry: the encyclopaedic inspiration of the parliamentary library thus found in this series of frescoes its most explicit and complete figurative representation.

In Italy too, the history of the Library of the Chamber of Deputies clearly demonstrates that the content of the Library's collections reflected not only the need to provide documentary support for legislative work, but also the desire to build a library of 'general culture', which tended to 'represent what Members represented',[139] that is, the whole nation. At the heart of the establishment of the Library of the Chamber of Deputies was a pedagogical programme built on the idea of the library as an open educational institution, even if it was not directly relevant to the work of the legislator. This inspiration was developed also during the twentieth century with the acquisition of new bibliographic funds that made the Library one of the greatest institutions of its genre. Since opening to the general public in 1989, the libraries of the Chamber of Deputies and of the Senate today play a prominent role in the cultural life of contemporary Rome, with the organisation of exhibitions and other events.

IX. The Great Treaties on Parliamentary Procedures

Over the course of the nineteenth century, and in parallel with the genesis of the parliamentary libraries, parliaments began to develop their own encyclopaedic works, that is, great syntheses and compendia about the practices and procedures governing parliamentary business.

Of the three classic encyclopaedic components (memory, reason and imagination), the first was undoubtedly privileged in the earliest parliamentary manuals. The case of the United Kingdom is illuminating from this point of view. Until the publication of Erskine May's *Treatise*, there was no reliable and systematic description of the rules of procedure in use by the 'mother of parliaments'. The very notion of confining the modes of parliamentary action within a determined set of rules was even viewed as incompatible with the principle of parliamentary sovereignty. According to Coke, the law of the parliaments is 'so transcendent and absolute, that it cannot be confined, either for causes or persons, within any bounds'.[140] Deference towards the antiquity of Parliament's rules was a well-established value within the British legal tradition, with the consequence of rendering very difficult the understanding of parliamentary procedures. This rather esoteric knowledge was available

[139] F Venturini, *Libri, lettori e biblioteche a Montecitorio: Storia della Biblioteca della Camera dei deputati* (Milano, Wolters Kluwer, 2019) 392.

[140] E Coke, *The first part of the Institutes of the lawes of England, or a commentarie upon Littleton, not the name of a lawyer only, but of the law it selfe* (London, 1629) fo 11v (bk 1, ch 1, s 3) quoted by P Evans, 'Introduction: The Growth of Many Centuries' in P Evans (ed), *Essays on the History of Parliamentary Procedure: In Honour of Thomas Erskine May* (Oxford, Hart Publishing, 2017) 2.

to only a very narrow circle of professionals (first and foremost the Clerks of the House), who relied primarily on their personal memories to offer advice on procedural matters. In principle, precedents were assumed to constitute the most important validating authority for procedure, but, in practice, the difficulty of identifying their exact content exposed the procedural decisions to the arbitrariness of the House majority. These difficulties reflected the actual state of parliamentary law in Britain: the proceedings of the House of Commons were regulated 'by ad hoc motions rather by any standing orders which could be consulted in advance and on which one might reasonably hope to predict the order and duration of the day's business'.[141] The consequence was that the House of Commons was 'not only politically, but also legislatively, chaotic and incoherent'.[142] During the eighteenth and nineteenth centuries, this situation prompted the publication of several works intended to serve as guides to parliamentary procedure. None of them, however, offered an effective and systematic description of the rules governing parliamentary business. Between 1776 and 1796 John Hatsell published a work in four volumes, *Precedents of Proceedings in the House of Commons with Observations*, which, despite comprising a remarkable collection of the usages of the British Parliament, did not attempt to operate any selection in the vast maze of parliamentary tradition. Interestingly, a more concise and effective description of the House of Commons procedures was offered in 1789 by Samuel Romilly's *Reglemens observés dans la Chambre des Communes pour débattre les matières et pour voter*. This work was composed by Romilly at the request of the Comte de Sarsfield, and was intended to serve as a guide to parliamentary procedures for use during the impending meeting of the Estates General in France.[143] Almost contemporary to Romilly's work was the already mentioned *Essay on Political Tactics* written by Jeremy Bentham, also with the intention of providing guidance to the meeting of the French Estates General.[144] This book offered a reasoned description of the main parliamentary procedures, based mainly on the usages of the British Parliament. It was full of brilliant and insightful comments regarding several aspects of parliamentary life, like attendance in sittings, the hours of business, and the manner of positioning the members in the Chamber. *Political Tactics* was in fact the first attempt to explain parliamentary procedures not by making reference to tradition, but rather to the practical purposes implied in the organisation of an assembly. The work became very popular in Europe: after its French translation in 1816, translations into German, Italian, Portuguese and Spanish appeared between 1817 and 1829.

In 1801, in Washington, Thomas Jefferson published *A Manual of Parliamentary Practice, for the Use of the Senate of the United States*. Jefferson had been Vice-President and thus presiding officer of the Senate from 1797 to 1801, before becoming President in 1801.

[141] Evans, ibid, 7.

[142] ibid.

[143] P Seaward, 'Parliamentary Law in the Eighteenth Century: From Commonplace to Treatise' in P Evans (ed), *Essays on the History of Parliamentary Procedure: In Honour of Thomas Erskine May* (Oxford, Hart Publishing, 2017) 109.

[144] *Essay on Political Tactics Containing Six of the Principal Rules proper to be observed by a Political assembly in the Process of Forming decisions: with the Reasons on which are Grounded and a Comparative Application of them to British and French Practice; Being a Fragment of a larger Work, a Sketch of which is Sub-joined* (London, T Payne, 1791). A full version of the *Essay* (with new parts from Bentham's manuscripts and the Réglement of the Geneva Assembly authored by Dumont) was published in French in 1816, edited by Etienne Dumont. On the history of the publication of this text, see the 'Editorial Introduction' in J Bentham, *Political Tactics* (1st edn 1791) (Oxford, Clarendon Press, 1999) xiii–xl.

He prepared the *Manual* for his own guidance of the Senate. For its compilation, the author relied upon personal notes and on the works of the most important English authors on parliamentary procedure, especially Hatsell's *Precedents*. Despite being prepared for the Senate, Jefferson's *Manual* also became a reference work for the House of Representatives. Even today, the House reprints an edition of the *Manual* bound together with the House's rules and a vast commentary.[145]

In Britain, a rather advanced attempt to provide a clear and comprehensive description of parliamentary procedures was made in 1825 by Anthony Hammond with his *Treatise on the Practice and Proceedings in Parliament; the passing of Public and Private Bills; and the Law of elections*. The very use of the word *treatise* signals the author's intention to draft a systematic guide to parliamentary law capable of recognising 'underlying principles, a basic logic to procedure, rather than a mass of particular responses to individual questions'.[146]

Two decades later, this idea was taken up by Erskine May for his *Treatise on the Law, Privileges, Proceedings and Usage of Parliament*. The first edition of this 'bible of British parliamentarism' was published when May was Assistant Librarian of the House of Commons. Most of May's work was based on his experience assisting with the preparation of the systematic indexes to House of Commons journals. At the *Treatise*'s core, there is therefore an 'encyclopaedic' endeavour connected with the activity of the House Library. What made the work a renowned authority in its field was the author's explicit intent to offer a systematic illustration of the main parliamentary procedures well beyond the mere collection of precedents. In so doing, May was sympathetic to the contemporary movements supporting some kind of codification of the common law.[147]

The break with the tradition of the old parliamentary manuals was very clear:

> The arrangement of the work has been designed with a view to advancing from the more general to the particular and distinct proceedings of parliament, to avoid repetition, and to prevent any confusion of separate classes of proceedings and each subject has been treated, by itself, so as to present, first, the rules or principles; secondly the authorities, if any be applicable; and thirdly the particular precedents in illustration of the practice.[148]

The author's ambition was clearly an encyclopaedic one, aimed at extracting, in systematic order, the rules or principles governing parliamentary business in the context of the English constitution. In line with this general purpose, the alphabetical index of subjects annexed to the *Treatise* was intended to offer a rapid and clear guide for the reader. In his lifetime, May published nine editions of his *Treatise* (1844, 1851, 1855, 1859, 1863, 1867, 1873, 1879 and 1883): in this time span the author became first Clerk Assistant (1856) and later Clerk of the House (1870). His work was widely recognised as the most authoritative source of parliamentary law in Britain and in the Commonwealth countries. Even after May's death, the publication of the *Treatise* was continued under his name, exactly as had occurred for

[145] D Natzler, D Bagnall, J-P Brochu and P Fowler, 'Controversy at the Antipodes (and Elsewhere). The International Cousins of the Treatise' in P Evans (ed), *Essays on the History of Parliamentary Procedure: In Honour of Thomas Erskine May* (Oxford, Hart Publishing, 2017) 133.

[146] ibid, 114.

[147] Evans, 'Introduction: The Growth of Many Centuries' (n 140) 8–9.

[148] T Erskine May, *Treatise on the Law, Privileges, Proceedings and Usage of Parliament* (London, Knight, 1844) vi.

some of the great European encyclopaedias. Today May's *Treatise* has reached its twenty-fifth edition, which has been made freely accessible to the public.

During May's lifetime, the nine editions of his *Treatise* accompanied the gradual consolidation of British parliamentary law into written rules. This development was the consequence of more general pressure to modernise the House of Commons in order to make this chamber fit for governing a global superpower, like the United Kingdom in the nineteenth century: a programme that was passionately supported by Erskine May. An important shift was made in this direction in 1852 when the Sessional and Standing Committee converted a whole series of resolutions and sessional orders into standing orders. Further reforms were introduced in the 1880s, also as a consequence of the Irish Party's obstructive campaigns. During this period

> the House procedure was drastically reformed, putting enormous power into the hands of the majority ... in 1888, with the conversion of a series of previous reforms into standing orders, the House had effectively created for the first time at least part of a written and formally promulgated parliamentary code.[149]

In France, the first systematic work on parliamentary procedures was published in 1878 with the *Traité pratique de droit parlementaire*. The two authors, Jules Poudra and Eugène Pierre, were at the time, respectively, Secretary General and Assistant to the Secretary General of the Chamber of Deputies.[150] In the following years, they published two supplements to the *Traité* (1879 and 1880). After Poudra's death in 1885, Pierre was appointed as the new Secretary General, a position that he maintained until his death in 1925. During the 40 years of his mandate, Pierre published seven new editions of his work (1893, 1902, 1906, 1910, 1914, 1919 and 1924). The *Traité* was much more than a guide for practitioners: it illustrated parliamentary law in the context of the constitutional system of the Third Republic. It had the ambition of extracting from parliamentary practice the principles governing the Chamber's prerogatives and its relations with the other institutions, first the executive:

> La plupart des matériaux que nous devions mettre en œuvre n'avaient pas encore été réunis; ils se trouvaient dispersés dans le Bulletin des lois, le Moniteur; les Archives et les Annales parlementaires. Il ne suffisait pas d'amasser des textes et des précédents; il fallait les distribuer dans un ordre logique, créer un plan simple et clair, qui offrît aux recherches les avantages du classement-alphabétique, sans détruire les vues d'ensemble, sans rompre l'enchaînement naturel des principes.[151]

This collection of precedents was therefore functional to an encycloapedic systematisation of parliamentary law and practice that became the reference work in this field in France.[152]

[149] Evans, 'Introduction: The Growth of Many Centuries' (n 140) 12.

[150] On the life and work of the two authors, see the section entitled 'Traité de droit politique, électoral et parlementaire d'Eugène Pierre' on the French National Assembly website, available at: www.assemblee-nationale.fr/connaissance/droit_eugene_pierre.asp.

[151] J Poudra and E Pierre, *Traité pratique de droit parlementaire* (Versailles, Cerf et fils; Paris, J Baudry, 1878) vi.

[152] Between 1984 and 2002, Jean Lyon (Secretary General of the National Assembly from 1971 to 1978) published three supplements to Pierre's *Traité* that cover the end of the Third Republic, the Fourth and the Fifth Republics.

In Italy, the first systematic illustration of parliamentary usages was offered in 1887 by Mario Mancini and Ugo Galeotti with their *Norme ed usi del Parlamento italiano: Trattato pratico di diritto e procedura parlamentare (Norms and Usages of the Italian Parliament: Practical Treatise of Parliamentary Law and Procedure)*. The work appeared after the translation into Italian of some of the most remarkable foreign manuals, like Bentham's *Tactics*, May's *Treatise* and Pierre's *Traitè*, and was intended to offer a practical guide to parliamentary procedure in the Italian Chamber of Deputies and the Senate. The second part of the volume, however, was devoted to the prerogatives of the Crown and of the executive. Even rejecting a theoretical approach to parliamentary law, Mancini and Galeotti discussed the procedural precedents, taking a systematic approach to the organisation and procedures of the Italian Parliament. This method is very clear, for example, when they discuss the role of the President of the Chamber as supreme authority guaranteeing the autonomy of the parliamentary assembly.[153] For this reason their Treatise anticipated other important works on parliamentary law, such as those published in Italy in the early twentieth century by Santi Romano[154] and Vittorio Miceli.[155]

In Germany, the interest in parliamentary procedures arose from the conversion of some of the German States, like Bayern and Baden-Württemberg, from absolutism to constitutional monarchies, with the consequent participation of the *Landtagen* in legislative decision-making. Models were offered by the experiences, predominantly, of France and the United Kingdom, elaborated upon to adapt to the needs of nascent German parliamentarism.[156] During the life of the Frankfurt National Assembly elected in 1848, Robert von Mohl made a significant contribution to this field. As a member of the Assembly, the great German jurist promoted the drafting of the new standing rules.[157] He also addressed specific aspects of parliamentary law in several of his scientific works, with a special focus on the peculiarities of English parliamentarism.[158]

In the German speaking world, the most important treatise on parliamentary government was, however, published by an Austrian scholar, Joseph Redlich, in 1905[159] and its subject was the procedure of the British House of Commons. Redlich intended 'to examine the law and practice of English parliamentary procedure as the expression of the historical and national characteristic of the English parliamentary system, both in its different stages of growth and in connection with the growth of the constitution'.[160] With his remarkable work, Redlich aimed to encourage a change in German constitutional culture towards parliamentarism, taking account of the fact that 'nowhere has the tendency to

[153] At 93–100.

[154] S Romano, 'Sulla natura dei Regolamenti delle Camere parlamentari' [1905] *Archivio giuridico* 75.

[155] V Miceli, *Principi di diritto parlamentare* (Milano, Società Editrice Libraria, 1910).

[156] B Mertens, *Gesetzgebungskunst im Zeitalter der Kodifikationen: Theorie und Praxis der Gesetzgebungstechnik aus historisch-vergleichender Sicht* (Tübingen, Mohr Siebeck, 2003) 170–71.

[157] ibid, 171.

[158] See, eg, R von Mohl, *Politik (Staatsrecht, Voelkerrecht und Politik: Monographien 2)*, 2 vols (Tübingen, 1862–69) Vol 1, para 558.

[159] J Redlich, *Recht und Technik des Englischen Parlamentarismus: die Geschaftsordnung of Commons in ihrer geschichtlichen Entwicklung und gegenwartigen Gestalt* (Leipzig, Duncker & Humblot, 1905). The work was soon translated into English as *The Procedure of the House of Commons: A Study of its History and Present Form* (n 120). The English translation was produced by Courtenay Ilbert, clerk of the House of Commons.

[160] Redlich, *The Procedure of the House of Commons*, Vol 11 (n 120) xv.

belittle parliaments been more marked than in countries where the German conception of the state has been adopted, both within and without the bounds of the present German Empire'.[161] A few years later, Max Weber expressed similar views, pointing out the negative role played by anti-parliamentarism in hindering the development of a modern system of government in Germany.[162]

X. Parliamentary Encyclopaedism and the Rationality of the Legislator

The encyclopaedic character of nineteenth-century parliamentarism is reflected in the typical product of the representative assemblies of the time: legislation. Despite the diversity of constitutional systems, during the nineteenth century the legislative function was generally attributed to the parliamentary assemblies. This was the case even if the formation of the law passed through different procedural phases, which required the intervention of other organs of the state with the adoption of acts of promulgation or sanction of differing values in monarchical or republican regimes.[163]

The concept of legislative function took shape in the eighteenth century with very different characteristics compared with the law-making activity of pre-modern regimes. Despite the diversity of national legal traditions, pre-modern legislation was devoid of typical formal characteristics and lent itself to serving very different purposes, including the regulation of local situations or individual statuses. Positive legislation also coexisted with a large body of customary law.

The Age of Enlightenment required legislation to perform very differently.

First, legislation is expected to introduce general and abstract rules into the legal system. These characteristics are considered to be the only ones compatible with the new concept of autonomy associated with the government of the political community. Parliamentary representation, as an expression of the general will, must in turn produce rules aimed at the generality of citizens, regardless of the actual conditions of individuals and social groups.[164]

Second, the provisions of the law are directed towards the future and are functional for a project of social transformation. As remarked by Denis Baranger, 'la loi ancienne était correctrice; la loi moderne devient constructive', as it is oriented towards a political project

[161] ibid, xxvi.

[162] As is well known, a strong Parliament and responsible parliamentary parties were, in Weber's view, the best balancing forces vis-a-vis the plebiscitary trends in modern democracies: see M Weber, *Parliament* and *Government in Germany under a New Political Order* in M Weber, *Political Writings* (1st edn 1918) (Cambridge, Cambridge University Press, 1994). On these aspects of Weber's views regarding parliamentarism, see K Palonen, 'Max Weber, Parliamentarism and the Rhetorical Culture of Politics' (2004) 2 *Max Weber Studies* 273.

[163] G Astuti, 'Legge (diritto intermedio)' in *Enciclopedia del diritto* (Milano, Giuffrè, 1973) Vol XXIII, 866.

[164] Art 6 of the Declaration of the Rights of Men and Citizens reads: 'La loi est l'expression de la volonté générale. Tous les citoyens ont droit de concourir personnellement, ou par leurs représentants, à sa formation. Elle doit être la même pour tous, soit qu'elle protège, soit qu'elle punisse'. The principles clearly reflect Rousseau's views on legislation. On the conception of the law as expression of the will of the people, see the classical work by R Carré de Malberg, *La Loi expression de la volonté générale: Etude sur le concept de la loi dans la Constitution de 1875* (Paris, Librairie du Recueil Sirey, 1931).

intended to improve the welfare of citizens.[165] Having regard to the potentially infinite character of the social needs to be dealt with, it can be said that modern legislators passed 'from a closed world to an infinite universe'.[166]

In order to face this new horizon, inherent in the very idea of legislation is the need for a systematic ordering of rules, which is transparent and rational to the highest degree. The principles of encyclopaedism – memory, reason and imagination – also apply to the legislative field, stimulating the emergence of a new science of legislation with great interpreters such as Cesare Beccaria and Gaetano Filangieri in Italy or Jeremy Bentham in Great Britain.

The need for rationality and systematicity is evident in the legislative codification efforts undertaken in many European countries between the end of the eighteenth century and the beginning of the nineteenth century, even if these projects were often promoted by enlightened monarchs and were conducted in overt opposition to the philosophical approach advocated by the theorists of the science of legislation. From this point of view, the position of Jean-Etienne-Marie Portalis is significant in its strong criticism of legislative reform projects based on an abstract rationality. For the most important architect of the *Code Napoléon*, the codification work should have been oriented towards absorbing, as much as possible, the rules of law most frequently used at a customary level, rather than setting completely new norms.[167] The success of the *Code* and the launching of similar projects by other European countries would confirm the opinions of the great French jurist.

Despite their limited impact on the actual preparation of legislative texts, the intellectual legacy of the theorists of the science of legislation was nevertheless critical in shaping the belief in legislation's duty to rationality.

Describing what is 'Recht als Gesetz', Hegel says:

> What is law (*Recht*) in itself is constituted (*gesetzt*) in its objective existence, ie determined by thought for the consciousness and known as what is right and valid, the legislation (*Gesetz*); and through this determination, law is positive law in general. To posit something as universal – ie to bring it to consciousness as a general thing is, as is well known, thinking; … in so reducing the content to its simplest form, it gives it its final determination. What is legal only receives not only the form of its universality but its true determination when it becomes a law (*Gesetz*).[168]

On the basis of these characteristics, legislation in turn becomes encyclopaedic, having to deal systematically with all the various needs expressed by society. The legislation is expected to respond to social demands through rational and long-lasting rules.[169] The rationality of the legislator derives from the deliberative dynamics inherent in the decision-making process of the parliaments. The free confrontation between parliamentarians is considered,

[165] D Baranger, *Penser la loi: Essai sur le législateur des temps modernes* (Paris, Gallimard, 2018) 78.

[166] ibid, 77, with obvious reference to the well-known work by Alexandre Koiré, *Du monde clos à l'univers infini* (Paris, Gallimard, 1993).

[167] Baranger (n 165) 279–90.

[168] GWF Hegel, *Grundlinien der Philosophie des Rechts* (Hamburg, Meiner, 2009–11) § 211 (translation mine).

[169] W Kluth, 'Entwicklung und Perspektiven der Gesetzgebungswissenschaft' in W Kluth and G Krings (eds), *Gesetzgebung. Rechtsetzung durch Parlamente und Verwaltungen sowie ihre gerichtliche Kontrolle* (München, CF Müller, 2018) 4.

as we have seen, to be capable of bringing out the common interest of the entire nation. From this perspective, legislation is therefore not a mediation between conflicting interests, but the result of a reasoning based on debate between competing arguments. As Carl Schmitt has remarked commenting the concept of law in liberal age:

> [I]f only those regulations which have come into effect with the cooperation and participation of the popolar assembly are called laws, then it is because the popular assembly, that is, the parliament, has taken its decisions according to a parliamentary method, considering arguments and counterarguments. As a consequence its decisions have a logically different charachter from that of commands which are only based on authority.[170]

Of course, this model of legislation linked to the encyclopaedic nature of nineteenth-century parliaments was interpreted in very different ways in the national contexts.

In Great Britain, legislation passed by the 'omnipotent' Parliament at Westminster only partially replaced common law regulations. Moreover, in the second half of the nineteenth century, the clear dominance of the government in legislative initiatives was also affirmed, with the parliamentary counsel (based in the executive offices) being responsible for the drafting of legislative texts. This dominance went hand-in-hand with the growing control by the government of the agenda of the chambers and of the time for carrying out parliamentary work. Even the defenders of the deliberative dimension of Parliament, such as John Stuart Mill, believed that the legislative function could be poorly exercised by a large assembly, more suited instead to carry out political debating and oversight functions over the work of the executive.[171] Even in Britain, however, parliamentary legislation marked important turning points in the social life of the country, as happened with the electoral reforms (the Reform Acts of 1832 and 1867) or with the great laws for the improvement of workers' welfare[172] and the relief of poverty.[173]

In conclusion, despite growing control over the content of legislation by governments and bureaucracies, the liberal constitutions of the nineteenth century confirmed the attribution of the legislative function to parliaments. This unanimity was based on the assumption that this option constituted the best response to a twofold need: on the one hand, to guarantee that the legislative command came from an institution representing the entire national community, and on the other, to ensure that the legislative will was the result of a rational decision as it was adopted in the course of free debate between parliamentarians who operated in the exclusive interests of the nation. The encyclopaedic structure of nineteenth-century parliaments operated within this paradigm of legislative production. The evident divergence between the actual operation of parliaments and this ideal approach features among the reasons for the crisis of liberal parliamentarism in the second half of the century, accompanied by a wide diffusion of anti-parliamentary opinion movements, often fed from within the political class itself. The last section of this chapter is dedicated to these developments.

[170] C Schmitt, *The Crisis of Parliamentary Democracy* (1st edn 1926) (Cambridge, MA, MIT Press, 1985) 43.

[171] Mill, 'Considerations on Representative Government' (n 121) 279.

[172] B Harris, *The Origins of the British Welfare State: Social Welfare in England and Wales, 1800–1945* (Basingstoke, Palgrave Macmillan, 2004).

[173] ME Rose, *The Relief of Poverty 1834–1914* (Basingstoke, Palgrave Macmillan, 1986).

XI. The Crisis of the Nineteenth-Century Encyclopaedic Parliament

In the preceding sections, we have seen how in many European countries' parliaments, as 'great theatres' of politics, played a fundamental role in nineteenth-century nation-building processes. Their symbolic function as an expression of the new liberal systems can hardly be underestimated.[174] Parliaments, however, were not only symbols, but established themselves as institutions genuinely capable of elaborating in reflexive terms the knowledge of the political community about itself. The parliamentary hemicycles became living cognitive maps of politics.

We have also observed how the cognitive value of parliamentary representation was strongly affirmed by many of the theorists of nineteenth-century parliamentarism. The ability to produce political knowledge was attributed to parliaments regardless of any similitude to the represented society. From this point of view, the first period of modern political representation is marked by a clear paradigm shift vis-a-vis pre-modern representatives institutions. The latter, like the *Etats generaux*, were censed to somehow replicate the social structure through a relationship of analogy and similitude. The first version of the modern parliamentary assemblies broke with this tradition in the name of the new principles of freedom of mandate and national representation. Early modern parliaments did not claim to resemble the society they represented. They aimed at a superior political synthesis of the essential values and interests of the nation. It was precisely this claim which enabled the chambers to express a circular and all-encompassing representation according to an encyclopaedic scheme that submitted to parliamentary debate any subject of political relevance.[175] From this point of view, for its rejection of any reference to the principle of analogy, the cognitive paradigm of early modern parliamentarism can be considered to be one of the late expressions of the epistemological scheme of the *âge classique*.[176]

[174] Mastropaolo (n 117) 782, emphasises that 'the parliamentary regime was most likely the institution which contributed most in Italy to unite the country, but its achievements were not even remotely recognised as such'. Mastropaolo points out that, on the contrary, Parliament was the subject of repeated attacks by the liberal political elite.

[175] 'Tout vient aboutir au parlement. Il discutera tour à tour les agissements d'un garde champêtre ou une grande réforme sociale; il doit tout contrôler, pouvoir à tout, tout connaitre, légiférer sur tout': A Prins, *La démocratie et le régime parlementaire* (Bruxelles, Librairie Européenne Muquardt, 1884) 16, quoted by M Gauchet, *La crise du liberalisme 1880–1914* (Paris, Gallimard, 2007). With reference to the British Parliament, Redlich (*The Procedure of the House of Commons* (n 120) Vol III, 8–9) noted that in Britain the unlimited powers of Parliament are 'translated into actual fact in the countless, almost unconceivable, number of subject brought before it'. 'Every imaginable interest from every part of the British Empire, every possible aspiration and tendency, material or personal, claims its share of the limited period of the session, each to the exclusion of the rest. They find expression in motions, in proposed laws, in questions and speeches, all going to swell the gigantic total of the business of the parliament; they range from subjects of the most trivial concern to matters of the highest: now some detail of local administration, now some problem of international policy calls for attention, or again some general principle of law, or the investigation, reconstruction, reform or abolition of some administrative arrangements or social institution'. 'The system converts all state business either directly or indirectly into parliamentary business'.

[176] I am referring to the chronological categories introduced by Michel Foucault's *archéologie du savoir*: M Foucault, *The Order of Things* (1st edn 1966) (New York, Routledge, 2002). According to Foucault the 'classical age' (early 17th century–early 18th century) marked a sharp break with the epistemological foundations of early modernity. The latter were oriented by the principle of resemblance: 'Up to the end of the sixteenth century, resemblance played a constructive role in the knowledge of Western culture. It was resemblance that largely guided exegesis and the interpretation of texts; it was resemblance that organized the play of symbols, made possible

The encyclopaedic parliament of the nineteenth century was not an 'omniscient' parliament, but rather a 'generalist' institution with a strong pedagogical inclination. The separation between the parliamentary sphere and the social sphere did not result in isolation of the former from the latter thanks to the strong ties of the members with local constituencies. A fundamental role was also played in this sense by the press, which offered broad resonance to the parliamentary debate, elevating it to one of the main factors responsible for the orientation of emerging national public opinion.

It should be noted, however, that, especially in Europe, the national pedagogy carried out by encyclopaedias and parliaments was mainly aimed at the elites. The many links between parliamentarism and encyclopaedism in the construction of the new public sphere had their common assumption in the very narrow nature of that sphere. For most of the nineteenth century, in many European countries, the liberal bourgeoisie at the helm of the nation-building processes represented a tiny minority compared with the rest of society. Even in the absence of a clear-cut distinction between the upper and the lower classes, it has been estimated that the bourgeoisie comprised between 5 and 15 per cent of the total population, depending on the countries and different criteria adopted.[177] Bourgeois culture has always been confronted with the contradiction between its claim of universality and its real exclusivity: 'the consequence was that it, despite its aspiration to cross its social boundary, has never completely stopped confirming them (at least downwards)'.[178] This contradiction was confirmed by the rules on suffrage, which restricted the electorate to a small fraction of the population.

The representative paradigm incarnated by parliaments in the liberal age faced growing criticism after the second half of the nineteenth century, when an increasing push emerged in many countries for the democratisation of parliamentary representation and the admission of new forces coming from outside the liberal monoculture.[179]

In Victorian Great Britain, there was a lively debate on how to make Parliament more representative, in order to make it a faithful 'mirror of the nation'. The great reforms that expanded the suffrage in 1832 and 1867 were accompanied – sometimes as an alternative to the interventions to expand the right to vote – by several proposals to make the House of Commons better able to reflect the diversity of the British nation: for example, via measures aimed at revising the boundaries of constituencies or via the more radical hypotheses of adopting proportional electoral systems.[180] Equally strong was the controversy over

knowledge of things visible and invisible, and controlled the art of representing them' (English translation: 19). During the Classical Age, the space of knowledge was then arranged in a totally different way: representation replaced resemblance and analogy as the universal foundation of all possible orders.

[177] Kocka (n 26) 13.

[178] ibid, 31–32.

[179] On this development, see S Rokkan, *State Formation, Nation-building, and Mass Politics in Europe* (Oxford, Oxford University Press, 1999).

[180] See G Conti, *The Parliament the Mirror of the Nation: Representation, Deliberation and Democracy in Victorian Britain* (Cambridge, Cambridge University Press, 2019). Conti emphasises that in the Victorian age, the different proposals to ameliorate the 'descriptive capacity' of parliamentary representation vis-a-vis social diversity were not always associated with democratic ideals. For a vocal group of authors of the age, the ideal of reaching a 'mirroring parliament' was to be pursued not through a simple enlargement of the suffrage, but rather with an electoral reform that deliberately varied the suffrage across the constituencies in order to ensure seats in the House of Commons for different classes, interest groups and ideological movements. This arrangement would have been capable of generating an assembly that was an 'epitome' of the diverse civil body. By contrast with this 'true liberal' option, according to these writers, a uniform suffrage entailed bestowing an illiberal hegemony on only one part of the

whether electoral reforms should favour or hinder the articulation of parliamentary representation by parties: the first thesis was supported by Bagehot, who considered the parties necessary to enable Parliament to choose a government; the second position was instead defended by John Stuart Mill who believed that electors should not vote for a candidate for his party membership, but because of his superior capacity for making independent judgements based on knowledge and wisdom.[181]

Also in France, the rules on suffrage followed a development that was anything but linear. The revolutionary assemblies were elected with an indirect system and without a procedure for formalising the candidacies: it was a system designed specifically to avoid the introduction of any 'aristocratic' degeneration in a process that was instead aimed at selecting representatives of the people inspired by the general interest of the nation alone.[182] With the restoration and the Orleanist monarchy a direct election system was adopted, but with the introduction of high census barriers for both the active and passive electorate: the new restrictive rules on suffrage marked 'the permanent tendency to pass from a meritocratic vision of representation to a flat consecration of the bourgeois order'.[183] This trend was corrected after the Revolution of 1848 and the introduction of universal male suffrage. After the Bonapartist authoritarian regime, the Third Republic reintroduced universal suffrage. This non-linear trend is also found in other countries, confirming the fact that the extension of suffrage did not always correspond with a real desire to expand the democratic bases of the state. It is well known that in Bismarck's Germany, the introduction of universal suffrage was inspired by paternalistic intentions and the desire to oppose a democratic evolution of the state.

Moreover, the great social and political transformations that took place between 1880 and 1914 highlighted the structural insufficiency of the liberal representative system to meet the new political demands coming from European civil societies. As Gauchet put it,

> in these years representative government was deeply challenged by the transformations of the communities that it is supposed to express and command. It had built itself on the basis of a society that disintegrated under it to be replaced by another: how could it not have been affected? In practice, it relied implicitly on mechanisms that ensured the 'natural' selection of representatives: it was undermined by the irruption of organization in place of hierarchies and memberships rightly, and wrongly, called 'natural'.[184]

Parliaments were at the centre of this crisis. The extension of suffrage had given rise to growing political expectations. In the face of these new demands, traditional parliamentary representation seemed incapable of adequately representing a society that had become more complex. The old liberal class appeared not up to the new challenges and detached from the 'real society'. Parliamentary politics was accused of transformism, lack of responsibility

body politic, the most numerous one. The best-known author belonging to the 'variety-of – suffrages' school is Walter Bagehot. According to him, the 1932 Reform Act had betrayed genuine Whig-liberalism by diminishing the variety of the franchise: the reform 'had decreased the multiformity of the suffrage, rendering the Commons membership less diverse and cutting the lower classes off the Parliament' (Conti, ibid, 34).

[181] A Carstairs, *A Short History of Electoral Systems in Western Europe* (London, George Allen, 1980) 194.

[182] P Rosanvallon, *Le peuple introuvable: Histoire de la représentation démocratique en France* (Paris, Gallimard, 1998) 58–59.

[183] ibid, 69.

[184] Gauchet, *La crise du libéralisme*, 1880–1914 (n 175) 170.

and opacity.[185] Parliamentary legislation itself increasingly appeared to be the result of the pressures imposed by self-interested oligarchic groups rather than of a rational deliberation. These shortcomings gave rise, in some countries, especially in Italy and France, to strong anti-parliamentarian stances.[186] The capacity of parliaments to offer a cognitive map of politics seemed to be deeply affected: confused parliamentary politics now seemed to offer a representation more of a condition of ignorance than of awareness about the orientation to be given to national politics. The void between parliaments and civil society was progressively filled by new formations, the mass-based parties, that viewed themselves as entities capable of transmitting the new social demands to the institutions. To the amateurism of the liberal political class they opposed the strength of organisation and ideological identities. These apparatuses were controlled by a new professional political personnel, specialised in political propaganda, in the organisation of militants, and in the activation of financing channels.

These great transformations called into question the model of liberal representation and, with it, the epistemological foundations and the very meaning of the parliamentary encyclopaedia that had come to be formed during the nineteenth century. We will see in the next chapter how the encyclopaedic structure of parliaments was profoundly affected by these developments.

[185] As Giuseppe Maranini put it (*Storia del potere in Italia* (Firenze, Vallecchi, 1983) 129: 'As for the institutions, their distorted dynamics, which we know well, could only be detrimental: the lack of a clear party alignments, the cabal of parliamentary combinations, the systematic corruption turned into the very foundation of the regime, the impossibility of establishing a transparent relationship between the elections and the formation of governments, the widespread feeling, even if in part unjust, of being dominated by inefficient and dishonest oligarchies, the lack of an opposition alternative within the system, the evident immorality of the parliamentary maneuvres, the periodic irresponsible interventions of the Crown, were not really what was needed to educate new generations of conscious voters, to whom to hand over the conquests of the Risorgimento'.

[186] For the anti-parliamentary stances in Italian culture and politics at the end of the 19th century, see: G Perticone, 'Parlamentarismo e antiparlamentarismo nel post-Risorgimento' in G Perticone, *Scritti di storia e politica del post-Risorgimento* (Milano, A Giuffrè, 1969); E Cuomo, *Critica e crisi del parlamentarismo (1870–1900)* (Torino, Giappichelli, 1996); TE Frosini, 'L'antiparlamentarismo e i suoi interpreti' in A Cerri, P Häberle, M Jarvad et al (eds), *Il diritto fra interpretazione e storia: Liber amicorum in onore di Angel Antonio Cervati* (Roma, Aracne, 2010). For the anti-parliamentary movements in France, see: J Defrasne, *L'antiparlementarisme en France* (Paris, Presses Universitaires de France, 1990); J-Y Mollier, 'Les racines de l'antiparlementarisme au début de la troisième République (1870–1900)' in M Vovelle (ed), *Révolution et République: l'exception française* (Paris, Kimé, 1994); B Jeanneau, 'L'antiparlementarisme d'hier à aujourd'hui' (1993) 64 *Pouvoirs* 23; In the UK the anti-parliamentary trends were far less widespread thanks to the stabilising effect played by the cabinet system; the same can be said with reference to the United States, where the growing political weight of the presidency counterbalanced the power of the Congress.

3

Encyclopaedic Parliamentarism in the Twentieth Century

I. Major Transformations in Twentieth-Century Parliaments

As early as the first decades of the century, the organisation of the parliamentary encyclopaedia was deeply affected by two major structural innovations: the party groups and the permanent specialist committees.

The first innovation was directly linked to the rise of large mass parties organised along strong territorial lines. These organisations were very different from their predecessors. As we have seen, in liberal times, the parties consisted mainly of local notables, whose power derived from their personal system of social relations and their prestige. By contrast, the membership of mass parties was characterised by a new breed of activists, ideologically homogeneous and bound to comply with strict party discipline.[1] In order to win the voters' support, parties had to propose political programmes shaped by comprehensive ideological visions. But ideologies are not only a matter of values. Rather, they are rooted in interpretations of the world aimed at responding to the main political issues of the time. To achieve this objective, party ideologies must be capable of producing political knowledge which is 'reusable' by the members of the organisation. The production of 'collective intelligence' is, typically, one of the functions of the twentieth-century party.[2]

These features had a strong influence on legislative assemblies. In particular, they challenged the traditional liberal ideology based on the freedom of the parliamentarians' mandate. According to some observers, this development was equivalent to the death of parliamentarism, given the transformation of parliamentary debates into mere repetitions of the ideological conflicts existing between the political parties.[3]

In reality, while these transformations certainly put an end to nineteenth-century parliamentarism, they actually heralded a new phase: that of party-based parliaments.[4]

[1] M Duverger, *Political Parties: Their Organization and Activity in the Modern State* (1st edn 1951) (New York, Wiley, 1954).

[2] On this subject, see the classical considerations of A Gramsci, 'Quaderno 13. Noterelle sulla politica di Machiavelli' in *Quaderni del Carcere*, a cura di V Gerratana (Torino, Einaudi, 1977) Vol III.

[3] As is well known, the most radical supporter of this opinion was Carl Schmitt: according to him modern mass democracy had rendered the fundamental principles of parliamentarism void and meaningless: C Schmitt, *The Crisis of Parliamentary Democracy* (1st edn 1926) (Cambridge, MA, MIT Press, 1985).

[4] On the literature regarding the shift from the 'Gentlemen's club Parliament', to the 'Representative Parliament' (dominated by political parties), see N Lupo, 'Le metamorfosi del Parlamento' (2019) 1 *Rassegna di diritto pubblico europeo* 1.

This development continued for most of the twentieth century, albeit with phases of resistance and backsliding – sometimes tragic in nature, such as the transformation of some European liberal regimes into dictatorships – but it ultimately resulted in a new type of parliamentarism. The new model recognised the existence of political parties – originally considered incompatible with the free mandate doctrine – as a necessary precondition for the functioning of parliaments.[5] Legislative assemblies very soon incorporated the changes under way, amending their own rules and formally regulating the existence of parliamentary groups, that is, the 'projections' of the political parties within the parliaments.[6] Membership of one of these groups became a mandatory requirement for MPs in many parliaments.

The parliamentary party groups constituted 'the linkage between mass suffrage, parties and parliaments, and are today accepted as necessary instruments of parliamentary business'.[7]

The parliamentary ecosystem was profoundly transformed. Parliamentary hemicycles were now divided into various segments, whose breadth varied depending on the size of the different political groups. Parliamentary plenary halls became the visual representation of each country's political system. Parliaments thus confirmed their 'encyclopaedic' calling not only as the place of democratic political debate, but also as a tangible and immediate representation of something that would otherwise have been quite elusive, that is, the national political system.

The prevalence of the new political parties led to another major development: professionalisation in politics. The parliamentarian ceased to be an 'amateur' and instead became a 'specialist' in politics on the basis of the experience acquired in the course of an often long political career.

This development ran parallel to the emergence, on the executive side, of the large administrative apparatus, typical of the twentieth century 'Big Government'. In order to effectively scrutinise and influence these new structures, parliamentarians needed to specialise, gaining expertise focused on certain areas of public policy. This need led to a major change in the structure of parliamentary assemblies, with the creation of specialist committees. The two parallel and interlinked phenomena of the emergence of parliamentary groups and permanent committees were at the heart of the 'great transformation' experienced by parliaments in the twentieth century. This change would influence the long-term cognitive structures of parliamentary assemblies.

We now analyse these two important developments in further detail.

[5] The parliamentarisation of political parties was part of a broader shift in the way that European constitutional systems viewed political parties from the first half of the 19th century to the second half of the 20th century. It is, in fact, an aspect of the *Inkorporierung* of parties, according to the categories introduced by H Triepel, who distinguished four stages in this development: *Bekämpfung; Ignorierung; Anerkennung und Legalisierung; Inkorporation*: H Triepel, *Die Staatsverfassung und die politischen Parteien* (Berlin, Liebmann, 1927). On this theory, see P Ridola, *Democrazia rappresentativa e parlamentarismo* (Torino, Giappichelli, 2014) 1–22.

[6] A broad variety of terms was and is still used to describe parliamentary party groups, like *parliamentary parties* in the United Kingdom; *congressional parties* in the United States; *Fraktionen* in Germany; *fracties* in the Netherlands; *groupe politique* in France; *gruppo politico* in Italy; and *grupos parlamentarios* in Spain. In Austria, the parliamentary groups are still called *parlamentarische Klubs*, which term is reminiscent of 19th-century use.

[7] K Heidar and R Koole, 'Representative Democracy and Parliamentary Party Groups' in K Heidar and R Koole (eds), *Parliamentary Party Groups in European Democracies: Political Parties Behind Closed Doors* (London, Routledge/ECPR, 2000) 1.

II. Party Parliaments

In the previous chapter, we observed how nineteenth-century parliaments were already shaped by the existence of parties. However, most of the parties originated in the same parliamentary chambers. The rise of parties as mass organisations triggered crucial transformations in the structure of the parliaments. This development took place within the context of a broader process of democratisation of European political systems under the pressure of a demand for greater political participation from new social layers. Organised political parties were among the main channels for meeting these new democratic needs. In this section, I analyse how the structure of parliaments adapted to the presence of these new actors in some European parliamentary regimes. I will consider the cases of Germany, Italy, France and the United Kingdom; a final section will be devoted to the European Parliament, which, despite being a rather young legislature, has rapidly replicated, with some variants, the organisation of the national parliaments.

A. Germany

In Germany, parliamentary party groups (*Fraktionen*) were formally recognised by the Reichstag of the Weimar Republic in 1922: the decision to do so, even without a formal modification of the standing rules, marked a major step towards the *Inkorporation* (incorporation) of the political parties in the German legal order. Following this reform, the Reichstag became an assembly dominated by party groups.[8] However, the newborn party democracy proved weak, also due to the uncertain support offered by the bourgeois parties.[9] The difficulties of the parliamentary regime encouraged the reappearance of traditional German dualism between the sphere of parliamentary representation and that of the government, controlled by the bureaucratic and military apparatuses.[10] This tendency contributed to the fatal crisis of the Weimar Republic.

After the fall of the Nazi regime, article 21 of the *Grundgesetz* (German Basic Law) (1949) recognised the role of the political parties in the formation of the political will of the people. The same article stipulates the possibility for the Federal Constitutional Court to dissolve parties that, 'by reason of their aims or the behaviour of their adherents, seek to

[8] P Jekewitz, 'Politische Bedeutung, Rechtsstellung und Verfahren der Bundestagfraktionen' in HP Schneider and W Zeh (eds), *Parlamentsrecht und Parlamentspraxis in Bundesrepublik Deutschland* (Berlin, De Gruyter, 1989) 1032.

[9] HA Winkler, *Weimar 1918–1933: Die Geschichte der ersten deutschen Demokratie* (München, Beck, 1993) 288. Thomas Mann's book, *Betrachtungen eines Unpolitischen* (Berlin, S Fischer, 1918), exerted a strong influence on the bourgeois elite's lukewarm support of democracy. Mann's text suggests that democracy, even if partially stemming from the principles of German philosophy, is not only 'un-German', but can even be viewed as 'anti-German'. Later, however, Mann became a staunch supporter of the Weimar Republic: this dramatic change of attitude towards the democratic principles was probably also due to the brutal assassination in June 1922 of the German Foreign Affairs Minister Walter Rathenau by a right-wing terrorist group: see JN Bade, 'The Magic Mountain of Weimar Politics: The Impact of the Assassination of Walther Rathenau on Thomas Mann's "Der Zauberberg"' (2014) 106, 1 *Monatshefte* 37, available at: www.jstor.org/stable/24549905.

[10] K von Beyme, 'Wandlungen des Parlamentarismus: Von Weimar nach Bonn' in HP Schneider and W Zeh (eds), *Parlamentsrecht und Parlamentspraxis in der Bundesrepublik Deutschland* (Berlin, De Gruyter, 1989).

undermine or abolish the free democratic basic order or to endanger the existence of the Federal Republic of Germany'. This provision was enforced by two landmark rulings of the Federal Constitutional Court in 1952 and 1956, when the Court declared unconstitutional the Sozialistische Reichspartei (SRP, a formation collateral to the Neo-Nazi Party NSDAP) and the Kommunistische Partei Deutschland (KPD) respectively.[11] Although isolated, these decisions contributed to shaping the German system, for a long time, as a 'protected democracy' against anti-establishment political forces.[12]

Beyond these ideological barriers, the parties also had to reach an electoral threshold of 5 per cent of the votes nationwide in order to be admitted to the Bundestag (or they have to win at least three seats in the single member constituencies).[13] Additionally, also as a consequence of these constraints for many years only three party groups were represented in the Bundestag (the Christian Democrats (CDU/CSU), the Social Democrats (SPD) and the Liberals (FPD)). This situation changed with the formation of the new groups of the Greens (1983) and of the Linke (1990, originally 'Partei des demokratischen Sozialismus – PDS).[14] More recently, the formation of the Alternative fuer Deutschland straddled the 5 per cent threshold, shattering the historical taboo against the presence of a far-Right party in the German Parliament.

The German system distinguishes itself by its significant degree of legal codification of party politics,[15] which also affects the parliamentary groups. Even if the latter are not directly mentioned in the *Grundgesetz*, the Federal Constitutional Court has long recognised the constitutional status of these organisations as key actors in political decision-making[16] and as 'necessary institutions of the constitutional life'.[17] This feature is confirmed by the groups' recognised right to appeal to the Federal Constitutional Court in the context of an *Organstreitverfahren* (organ controversy).[18] The German system has therefore been called a 'state of parliamentary party groups (*Fraktionenstaat*)'.[19] Consistently with these

[11] For the ban of the Sozialistischen Reichstpartei, see BVerfGE, 2,1; for the ban of the Kommunistische Partei Deutschland, see BVerfGE 5, 85.

[12] According to H Klein, 'Art 21' in T Mauntz and G Düring (eds), *Grundgesetz Kommentar* (München, Beck, 2009) § 490) the German system represents an 'abwehrbereite Demokratie' (a 'defence-ready democracy'), a definition that suits not only the first period of the Federal Republic, but also identifies a long-standing feature of the German constitutional order.

[13] The German electoral law combines the principles of majority voting with proportional representation with a system of 'personalised proportional representation': each elector may cast one vote for a candidate in one of the single member constituencies (first vote) and one vote for one party's list of candidates (second vote). In the constituencies the candidate who gets the most votes is directly elected to the Bundestag. The overall functioning of the system provides for proportional representation, since the number of seats won directly in the constituencies is deducted from the total number of seats allocated to a party according to the number of second votes received for that party's list of candidates. For more details, see the website of the German Ministry of Interior and Community, available at: www.bmi.bund.de/EN/topics/constitution/electoral-law/voting-system/voting-system-node.html.

[14] O Nidermayer, 'Nach der Vereinigung. Der Trend zum Fluiden Fuenfparteisystem' in OW Gabriel, O Nidermayer and R Stoess (eds), *Parteidemokratie in Deutschland* (Wiesbaden, Westdeutscher Verlag, 2002).

[15] T Poguntke, 'Parties in a Legalistic Culture: The case of Germany' in RS Katz and P Mair, (eds), *How Parties Organize: Change and Adaptation in Party Organization in Western Democracies* (London, Sage Publications, 1994).

[16] BVerfGE 80, 188 (219).

[17] BVerfGE 2, 143 (160); 20, 56 (104); 43, 142 (147); 70, 324 (362); 112, 118 (135).

[18] On the basis of the principles set by art 93, s 1, n 1 of the *Grundgesetz* (Basic Law) and art 63 of the Law on the Federal Constitutional Court.

[19] U Thaysen, 'Fraktionenstaat: Oder was sonst?' in P Haungs and E Jesse (eds), *Parteien in Krise?* (Köln, Verlag Wissenschaft und Politik, 1987), quoted by T Saalfeld, 'Bureaucratisation, Coordination and Competition: Parliamentary Party Groups in the German Bundestag' in K Heidar and R Koole (eds), *Parliamentary Party Groups in European Democracies: Political Parties Behind Closed Doors* (London, Routledge/ECPR, 2000) 37.

assumptions, the Bundestag's Rules of Procedure assign crucial organisational responsibilities to the parliamentary groups. These rules outline two basic requirements for the formation of a parliamentary group: its members must comprise no less than 5 per cent of the members of the Bundestag, and shall belong to the same party or to parties which, on account of their similar political aims, do not compete with each other in any Land.[20]

The groups submit the MPs to the significant constraints of party discipline, but also offer them crucial resources for institutional learning and political action.[21] The Bundestag's operation as a 'working parliament' (*Arbeitsparlament*) requires a high degree of specialisation, coordination and cohesion, for which the contribution of parliamentary party groups is crucial.[22] The *Fraktionen* play an important role in the mediation of the technical knowledge needed in the law-making process. The groups' experts regularly brief MPs within the several working groups corresponding to the policy sectors covered by the standing committees.[23] As we shall see later, they can also assist their members in the committees. In order to discharge these functions, the groups receive significant financial contributions from the Bundestag budget; since 1977, additional contributions have been provided for the groups belonging to the parliamentary opposition.[24]

B. France

There are some interesting similarities between the development of parliamentary groups in Italy and in France, due to the political history of the two countries.

In France, the emergence of modern parliamentary groups took place in connection with the establishment of parliamentary committees.[25] Parliamentary groups were officially recognised by a resolution adopted by the National Assembly on 1 July 1910.[26] This was an indirect recognition, since the resolution referred to the size of the groups as a criterion for the composition of parliamentary committees. Previously, the legislative process was based on the system of 'offices', in which parliamentarians were called upon to participate by drawing lots. This arrangement had given rise to several drawbacks: since the committees' majorities were essentially random, they did not reflect those of the Assembly, which in turn resulted in a legislative process characterised by chance and inconclusiveness. The 1910 reform recognised an already existing situation.[27] The parliamentary groups were

[20] See Rule 10, s 1 of the Rules of Procedure of the Bundestag. The possibility for MPs to form a group, despite belonging to different parties that 'do not compete with each other in any Land', allows for the constitution of the unitary group of the CDU and CSU MPs. Rule 10, s 4 admits also the formation of 'groupings' (*Gruppen*) for members whose number amounts to less than the 5 per cent of the Bundestag's membership, if the Bundestag majority agrees.

[21] SS Schuettemeyer, *Fraktionen im Deutschen Bundestag 1949–1997: Empirische Befunde und theoretische Folgereungen* (Opladen, Westdeutscher Verlag, 1998) 448 ff.

[22] Saalfeld (n 19) 37.

[23] ibid, 28.

[24] See art 50 of the Abgeordnetengesetz (AbgG).

[25] D Connil, *Les groupes parlementaires en France* (Issy-les-Moulineaux, LGDJ, 2016) 15.

[26] J-L Thiébault and B Dolez, 'Parliamentary Parties in the French Fifth Republic' in K Heidar and R Koole (eds), *Parliamentary Party Groups in European Democracies: Political Parties Behind Closed Doors* (London, Routledge/ECPR, 2000) 57.

[27] G Le Beguec, 'Naissance et développement des groupes parlementaires sous la IIIème République' (2003) *Parlement(s). Histoire et politique* 3, available at: www.parlements.org/parlements/num0_7_LeBeguec.pdf.

already active and present in both Houses of the French Parliament as structured entities, particularly those belonging to the left-wing blockade. After 1910, the French parliamentary rules further increased the groups' prerogatives by providing for the participation of their presidents in the Conference of Presidents and for the division of the plenary hall of the Chamber of Deputies into areas corresponding to the groups.

A persistent feature of French parliamentarism is the lack of correspondence between the geography of parliamentary groups and that of the political parties organised across the country.[28] The French parliamentary rules did not require any particular formality for the formation of groups, thus allowing the emergence of multiple formations arising from the division of previous groups or from political initiatives of a purely parliamentary nature. It was only in 1932 that all members of the same group not belonging to the same party had to sign a common political declaration of a programmatic nature. This situation explains both the large number of groups in the legislative assemblies of the Third Republic (11 groups in the Chamber of Deputies after the 1919, and 17 groups after the 1932, elections) and the highly fluid political framework offered by the these assemblies.

This picture did not change much with the advent of the Fourth Republic, which, heralded what some commentators refer to as the era of the 'triumph' of parliamentary groups.[29] The 1946 Constitution made explicit reference to the existence of parliamentary groups (without, however, expressly regulating them) that were given important functions by the new parliamentary rules. These provisions reflected the political reality of the new Republic, that, like the contemporary Italian one, was essentially a 'republic of the parties'. In France, however, the democratic legitimacy of the new regime was seriously flawed.[30] The Constitution approved by a popular referendum in October 1946 (after the rejection via referendum in May 1946 of the Constitution drafted by the first Constituent Assembly) introduced a parliamentary form of government centred on the figure of President of the Council of Ministers. The attempt made by the new Constitution to strengthen the head of the government with some institutional devices (for instance, his direct election by the Chamber of Deputies before the appointment of the other ministers) proved unsuccessful. The life of the new Republic was characterised by a high degree of governmental instability (22 executives in 12 years) and by the opposition to the regime expressed by two major political forces: the movement led by the hero of the French Resistance, Charles de Gaulle, and the Communist Party. The fate of the executives was at the mercy of a set of centre-left and centre-right parties that de facto represented the minority of the population. This 'government of the assembly' – in which 'le government rend compte [à l'assemblée] comme le serviteur à son maître'[31] – proved incapable of tackling the national emergency created by the Algerian war. The crisis was overcome with De Gaulle's return to

[28] ibid, 5.

[29] Connil (n 25) 20.

[30] For an explanation of the different outcomes of the constituent processes in Italy and France after the Second World War, see S Guerrieri, *Costituzioni allo specchio: la rinascita democratica in Francia ed in Italia dopo la liberazione* (Bologna, il Mulino, 2021).

[31] J Gicquel, 'La IV République: la République-Janus' in M Calamo Specchia (ed), *La Costituzione francese/La Constitution Française* (Torino, Giappichelli, 2009) 163.

power: his leadership imposed the introduction of a new constitution (approved by a popular referendum) that marked a radical shift in the balance of power between the Parliament and the government. The reform introduced a version of 'rationalized parliementarism'[32] that significantly strengthened the position of the government vis-a-vis the Assembly. The most emblematic innovation was Article 49.3 that allows the so-called *vote bloqué*, through which the government can ask the National Assembly to approve the law in discussion or to express its censure.[33] But, from our point of view, even more important modifications were those intended to radically reduce in parallel the power of the parliamentary groups and of the standing committees in the legislature. The first target was achieved through Article 48 of the Constitution, that granted the government power to set priorities in the parliamentary agenda. This innovation secured the executive absolute dominance in the agenda-setting of the Parliament, leaving a mere formal role for the Conference of the Presidents of the groups.[34] The other major innovation invested the core of the parliamentary decision-making: the standing committees. Their number was fixed directly in the Constitution and was reduced to six. Even more importantly, the legislative power of the committees was radically reduced, limiting their role to the preparation of a report on the bills, without the possibility of introducing any amendments. As is well known, the presidentialisation of the French constitutional system was completed in 1962 with the adoption of the direct popular election of the President and the parallel emergence of the *fait majoritaire*, through the use of a two-round system for both presidential and legislative elections.[35]

The first 50 years of the Fifth Republic confirmed the clear dominance of the executive over the Parliament, even if some limited but important reforms were introduced in order to establish some form of compensation in favour of the oppositions. Significantly, the most important modification consisted of the *saisine parlamentaire*, a procedure external to parliamentary decision-making, allowing a minority of 60 deputies or senators to challenge legislative acts before the Constitutional Council after their final approval by Parliament. The reform contributed to shaping an important component of the prerogatives of parliamentary opposition in France.[36]

A more extensive rebalancing of power between the legislature and the executive was, however, achieved by the constitutional reform promoted by President Sarkozy in 2008. The reform affected 47 Articles of the Constitution and was inspired by the main

[32] JL Quermonne, *Le Gouvernement de la France sous la Ve République* (Paris, Dalloz, 1987) 26. The term 'rationalisation', insofar as it relates to the form of government, was coined by B Mirkine-Guetzévich, *Les nouvelles tendences du droit constitutionnel* (Paris, Marcel Giard, 1931). In his later work, Mirkine-Guetzévich used the phrase 'parlamentarisme rationalisé' in order to define the constitutional arrangements intended to strengthen the position of the executive vis-a-vis the parliament: see B Mirkine-Guetzévich, 'Le régime parlementaire dans les récentes Constitutions européennes' (1950) 2–4 *Revue internationale de droit comparé* 605.

[33] JD Huber, *Rationalizing Parliament: Legislative Institutions and Party Politics in France* (Cambridge, Cambridge University Press, 1996) 23–37.

[34] P Hontebeyre, 'La fixation de l'ordre du jour prioritaire un pouvoir sans contre-pouvoirs' (1984) 34 *Pouvoirs: L'Assemblée* 13.

[35] On the majoritarian effects of the French electoral system, see A Blais and P Loewen, 'The French Electoral System and its Effects' (2009) 32 *West European Politics* 345.

[36] On the institutional consequences of this reform, see L Favoreu, *La politique saisie par le droit* (Paris, Economica, 1988).

objective of 'rééquilibrer les pouvoirs du Parlement par rapport à ceux de l'éxecutif'.[37] The constitutional amendments were followed by an extensive modification of the parliamentary Rules of Procedure implementing the new constitutional provisions. The reform operated decidedly for the opening of new spaces for parliamentary politics in the French system.[38] From this perspective, the main innovations were the introduction of special prerogatives in favour of the opposition and minority groups (to be defined by parliamentary rules of procedure); the increase in the number of standing committees, and more importantly, their empowerment with the possibility of introducing amendments in the legislative texts for the plenary; the reduction of the admissibility of the *vote bloqué*; and the attribution to the Conference of the Presidents of the power to set the agenda of the Chamber, with the reservation of only partial segments of parliamentary time to government proposals. Also important was the introduction of the oversight function and of the assessment of public policies among the core tasks of the Parliament.[39] Through these innovations, party groups recovered much of the ground lost when the 1958 Constitution came into effect. Such evolution is particularly evident in the agenda- setting function and in the new role assigned to the standing committees.

C. Italy

In Italy, the emergence of modern parliamentary groups took place with the reform of the Rules of Procedure of the Chamber of Deputies in 1920. The reform introduced some important innovations that shaped some long-lasting characters of Italian parliamentarism in the twentieth century and beyond.[40] For the first time, the new rules included the notion of a parliamentary group, making it compulsory for members to belong to a group from the beginning of each parliamentary term. In order to form a group, a purely quantitative requirement was set: the minimum was 20 members.

The emergence of new mass parties certainly reflected the political premise for the formalisation of parliamentary groups. Parties' presence in Parliament had become very clear following the adoption in 1919 of the new proportional electoral law and the preceding extension of the right to vote.[41] The link between the institutionalisation of political groups

[37] See President Sarkozy's *lettre de mission* to the Comité de reflexion et de proposition sur la modernisation et le rééquilibrage des institutions de la Ve République (7 July 2007), published in the special issue of the *Revue Française de droit constitutionnel, Aprés le Comitè Balladour. Réviser la Constitution en 2008?* (2008) 251.

[38] A Vidal-Naquet, 'La revalorisation du Parlement et l'équilibre au sein de l'exécutif. Vers un rééquilibrage au sein de l'exécutif?' in X Magnon, R Chevontian and M Stéfani (eds), *Pouvoir exécutif et Parlement: de nouveaux équilibres? L'impact de la révision constitutionnelle du 23 juillet 2008 sur le rééquilibrage des institutions* (Aix-en-Provence, Presses Universitaires d'Aix-Marseille, 2012).

[39] The new text of art 24 of the Constitution reads: 'Le Parlement vote la loi. Il contrôle l'action du Gouvernement. Il évalue les politiques publiques'.

[40] Orsina rightly emphasises the 'constitutional character' of the 1920 reform of the parliamentary standing rules: see 'L'organizzazione politica nelle Camere della proporzionale (1920–1924)' in F Grassi Orsini and G Quagliariello (eds), *Il partito politico dalla grande guerra al fascismo: crisi della rappresentanza e riforma dello Stato nell'età dei sistemi politici di massa* (1918–1925) (Bologna, il Mulino, 1986) 397.

[41] On these developments, see MS, Piretti, *La giustizia dei numeri: Il Proporzionalismo in Italia (1870–1923)* (Bologna, il Mulino, 1990).

and the adoption of the new electoral rules was immediately underlined by the commentators of the time.[42]

Despite this clear link with the emergence of large parties in Italian political life, the parliamentary rules did not include any legal requirement to verify the actual connection between the parliamentary groups and the parties outside Parliament. The new rules only required this link for authorising the formation of groups with fewer than 20 members (subject to the condition, however, that they reached the threshold of 10 members). In short, the new Italian rules regarding the formation of groups looked to the French model, which was characterised, as we have seen, by a very flexible parliamentary 'political geography',[43] albeit with a preference in Italy for a stronger rationalisation (eg, as regards the minimum number of members needed to form a group).

The other interesting aspect of the 1920 Italian reforms is the close link between the formalisation of the political groups and the establishment of the system of standing parliamentary committees. Indeed, the 1920 reform entirely abandoned the previous system, based on the random allocation of members to nine 'offices' in charge of the preliminary examination of draft laws.[44]

The new Rules of Procedure replaced the system of the 'offices' with a set of nine permanent committees responsible for the same number of areas of legislation and composed in proportion to the size of the parliamentary groups. In accordance with this criterion, it was up to each group to indicate its members of each committee. It should be pointed out that, when the new rules were adopted, the only function expressly assigned to the groups was in fact the appointment of the members of the committees.

The advent of Fascism and the end of political freedoms in Italy froze the transformation of the Italian Parliament into a parliament for groups. However, this major change was completed with the inauguration of the new democratic regime via the 1948 Constitution. The new Constitution recognised the central role of political parties as free associations of citizens to 'determine national politics'.[45] The constitutional recognition reflected the role effectively played by the mass parties as leading political institutions.[46] The Constitution also made explicit references to the parliamentary groups,[47] without, however, directly regulating their formation. Under the new democratic Republic,

[42] G Ambrosini, *Partiti politici e gruppi parlamentari dopo la proporzionale* (Firenze, La Voce, 1921).

[43] The analysis of the relationship between electoral lists and parliamentary groups in the 1919–21 and 1921–24 legislatures leads to a conclusion that – with the exception of the groups of the popular party, the communists and the socialists – there was almost no correspondence between the elections and the subdivision of the Chamber in groups (G Orsina (n 40) 470).

[44] Each office then appointed, by majority, a commissioner to be part of an ad hoc committee responsible for completing the examination of the draft law. These ad hoc committees did not in fact have any particular expertise on the subjects submitted to them, and even the majorities formed within them could be entirely random (see M Mancini and U Galeotti, *Norme ad usi del Parlamento italiano* (Roma, Tipografia della Camera dei deputati, 1887) 212–18).

[45] See art 49 of the 1948 Constitution.

[46] P Ridola, *Democrazia pluralistica e libertà associative* (Milano, Giuffré, 1987); P Scoppola, *La Repubblica dei partiti: Profilo storico della democrazia in Italia (1945–90)* (Bologna, il Mulino, 1991).

[47] See art 72, s 3, according to which the standing rules of the two chambers 'may establish when and how the consideration and approval of bills may be referred to Committees, including Standing Committees, composed so as to reflect the proportion of the Parliamentary Groups'. The same criterion of proportionality with reference to the size of the parliamentary groups is imposed by art 82 for the composition of the inquiry committees.

the Chamber of Deputies readopted the standing rules in force prior to the advent of Fascism, thus recognising the role of the political groups.[48] However, it was not until the major regulatory reform of 1971 that the Italian Parliament ultimately became a 'parliament for groups'. These new rules granted the groups broad powers over the parliamentary decision-making, from legislative, steering and monitoring procedures to agenda setting. This situation, albeit with a number of changes and innovations, still persists.

Also in the republican era, the provisions of the parliamentary Rules of Procedure continued to allow a wide margin of flexibility between the electoral vote and its translation into the parliamentary arena.[49] In particular, they also permitted the formation in Parliament of groups which had no connection with a pre-existing party, or which were created following the dissolution of parties which had stood for election. The groups thus formed could in turn serve as a basis for the emergence of new parties that would later present candidates in the next elections. The parliamentary groups were therefore far from offering a mechanical reflection of the nascent Italian party system. In fact, the reverse is true: over the course of Italy's political history, parliamentary groups contributed decisively to shaping and developing the country's political system.[50]

D. United Kingdom

In comparison to the history of the parliamentary party groups in Germany, France and Italy, the British case is characterised by some peculiarities. Party organisation 'is a long-established feature of the British House of Commons, predating the emergence of mass political parties'.[51] Writing in 1867, Walter Bagehot considered the existence of

[48] N Lupo, 'La continuità del diritto parlamentare. La riadozione del regolamento prefascista nella Camera dei deputati' in U De Siervo, S Guerrieri and A Varsori (eds), *La prima legislatura repubblicana: Continuità e discontinuità nell'azione delle istituzioni*, Vol II (Roma, Carocci, 2004). The Senate adopted a completely new set of standing rules (on the new standing rules of the Senate, see N Lupo, 'I regolamenti parlamentari nella I legislatura repubblicana (1948–1953)' (2008) 15 *Giornale di storia costituzionale* 117).

[49] A Manzella, *Il Parlamento* (Bologna, il Mulino, 2003) 91 ff.

[50] Some examples: during the Constituent Assembly mandate (1946–48), and as a consequence of a secession which occurred within the Socialist Party (PSIUP), a new social-democrat party was founded (PSLI) in January 1947, led by Giuseppe Saragat. The new party immediately constituted a parliamentary group at the Assembly; the new party obtained a good share of the vote at the following parliamentary elections on 18 April 1948. In January 1964, some left-wing MPs of the Socialist Party announced their departure from the party for they dissented about the party's decision to take part in the new centre-left government led by Aldo Moro. The rebels founded the Italian Socialist Party of Proletarian Unity and the corresponding parliamentary group in both chambers; the party participated in the 1968 parliamentary elections and elected 23 members to the Chamber of Deputies. In September 2019 the former Italian Prime Minister Matteo Renzi announced he was leaving the Democratic Party and founding a new party (Italia Viva, 'Living Italy'). In the following days 23 MPs left the Democratic Party Group of the Chamber of Deputies and entered the group corresponding to the new party; Italia Viva participated in the 2022 parliamentary elections in alliance with the centrist movement Azione and elected 13 members to the Senate and 21 to the Chamber of Deputies. On some of these developments, see L Verzichelli, 'I gruppi parlamentari dopo il 1994. Fluidità e riaggregazioni' (1996) 2 *Rivista italiana di scienza politica* 391. On the fluidity of the parliamentary groups as an adaptative reaction to the mutations in the political system, see A Palanza, 'La perdita di confini: le nuove procedure interistituzionali nel Parlamento italiano' in L Violante (ed), *Storia d'Italia: Annali 17. Il Parlamento* (Torino, Einaudi, 2001).

[51] P Norton, 'The United Kingdom. Exerting influence from within' in K Heidar and R Koole (eds), *Parliamentary Party Groups in European Democracies: Political Parties Behind Closed Doors* (London, Routledge/ECPR, 2000) 39.

parliamentary parties a quintessential feature of the constitutional role of the House of Commons:

> The moment, indeed, that we distinctly conceive that the House of Commons is mainly and above all things an elective assembly, we at once perceive that party is of its essence. There never was an election without a party ... The House of Commons lives in a state of perpetual potential choice; at any moment it can choose a ruler and dismiss a ruler. And therefore party is inherent in it, is bone of its bone, and breath of its breath.[52]

Bagehot associates the partisan nature of the House of Commons with the British form of government, based on the fundamental principle of executive accountability to the elected assembly. This system favours the division of the House into two parties, separated by their support of or opposition to the government of the day. Given the strong connection between the parliamentary majority and its government (according to the principle of the 'fusion of powers'),[53] the divide between majority and opposition became the primary structural feature of the British House of Commons.

Bagehot, however, emphasises that this system is functional only in the absence of strong ideological divisions within the House:

> [I]t may seem odd to say so, just after inculcating that party organisation is the vital principle of representative government, but that organisation is permanently efficient, because it is not composed of warm partisans. The body is eager, but the atoms are cool. If it were otherwise, Parliamentary government would become the worst of governments – a sectarian government.[54]

According to the author of the *English Constitution*, it is only by virtue of British politicians' moderate and pragmatic approach to policymaking that the possible risks of degeneration of parliamentary government have been avoided. In this context, even the opposition had to behave as 'His (or Her) Majesty's loyal opposition'.

As a consequence of these assumptions, the party labels were worn loosely by parliamentarians, and the organisation of the parliamentary parties was highly informal. The main organisational feature was represented by the party 'whips', that is, the members charged with the task of ensuring that the supporters of the ministry turned up and voted.[55] In the context of the British form of government, in which the members of His Majesty's government were, as a rule, MPs, a clear distinction emerged between the parliamentarian members of the government and all the other members, referred to as 'backbenchers' because they were (and are) physically seated behind the benches reserved to the members of the government. Over time, this distinction also applied to the parliamentarians from the opposition, with the intent of distinguishing the frontbenchers (the members of the Shadow Cabinet) from other members in the opposition parliamentary party.

The situation described by Bagehot changed significantly with the emergence of large mass parties. In Britain, this development preceded the advent of the Labour Party on the political scene. The widening of the franchise, deriving from the 1867 Reform Act, already

[52] W Bagehot, *The English Constitution* (1st edn 1867) (Oxford, Oxford University Press, 2009) 134.
[53] See ch 2 (n 88).
[54] Bagehot (n 52) 67.
[55] Norton, 'The United Kingdom' (n 51) 41.

favoured the transformation of the two main political parties of the day – the Conservatives and the Liberals – from cadre to mass membership parties. Moisey Ostrogorsky brilliantly described how the previously purely parliamentary parties had to set up external organisations in order to mobilise an ever-increasing number of electors.[56] The arrival of the working class-based Labour Party gave new momentum to this trend, marking a clear watershed in the imposition of new standards of party discipline within the Parliament: a development that can be attributed to the need to attract the support of a large extra-parliamentary party.[57] These events led, on the one hand, to the strengthening of the Cabinet, and on the other, to the increased role of the whips, as instruments of the leadership for maintaining discipline within the parliamentary party. At the turn of the century, voting discipline became the rule in British parliamentary life. This new political environment also had evident consequences for the organisation of the parliamentary parties. Parliamentary parties were (and still are) the 'party in Parliament'. This explains an apparent paradox of the British system: the coexistence of an extremely weak structure of the parliamentary party with a tradition of strong discipline of its members. Even today, the original nature of British parliamentary parties is reflected by the absence of statutory or parliamentary rules governing their formation or membership. Nevertheless, in the twentieth century, some organisational innovations have been introduced that have actually strengthened the structure of these entities. An interesting example on the Conservative side is represented by the 1922 Committee. In 1923, for the first time, some Conservative MPs formed a Conservative private members' committee.[58] Membership of the committee was soon extended to all the Conservative backbenchers. Even if still largely informal in nature, the 1922 Committee plays some vital functions, as a channel of communication between the leadership and MPs or for the development of the platforms for elections. It is also the forum where Conservative MPs can challenge the leadership of the party, as quite recently occurred in June 2022 with the failed attempt to dismiss the leadership of Boris Johnson. Curiously enough, this Committee very soon developed some sub-committees assembling the MPs interested in particular policy fields. The purpose of these subject committees was to bring together interested parliamentarians to discuss issues relating to major public policy areas (foreign affairs, welfare, farming, and so on). The same organisational solution was adopted by the Labour Party when it became the majority party in the House of Commons after the Second World War. A strong connection between parliamentary party groups and sectoral committees therefore emerged through these channels even in the British Parliament – an institution that still today lacks a system of permanent specialist committees for law-making.[59]

As regards the relationship between the parliamentary party groups and the political movements organised within the country, the UK case study is characterised by its uniqueness. On the one hand, there is virtually no phenomenon in the United Kingdom of purely parliamentary political groups, which are not the expression of a party that has presented

[56] M Ostrogorsky, *Democracy and the Organization of Political Parties* (London, Macmillan, 1902) Vol I, 183–286.

[57] J Brand, *British Parliamentary Parties* (Oxford, Clarendon Press, 1992) 20.

[58] On the history of the 1922 Committee, see P Norton, *The Voice of the Backbenchers: The 1922 Committee: The First 90 Years 1923–2013* (London, Conservative History Group, 2013).

[59] However, there has been a recent trend towards departmental select committees at Westminster reporting on draft legislation.

itself for election. From this point of view, therefore, the parliamentary groups are the exact reflection of the electoral result. However, the highly selective effects of the British electoral system, based since 1911 on the single-member constituencies and the strict majority rule of the first past the post, should also be highlighted. It is a system which, as is well known, overrepresents relative majorities on the basis of the so-called cube law.[60] Thanks to this system, parties that have strong regional support, such as the Scottish National Party or the Democratic Unionist Party, are also represented in the House of Commons. On the other hand, representation of 'opinion parties', including those which have broad support at the national level, but which can only count on a low regional concentration, as is traditionally the case for the Liberal Democrats, is severely penalised.

E. Political Groups in the European Parliament

The history and structure of the political groups in the European Parliament (EP) shows both similarities and differences with the evolution of political groups in national parliaments. The analysis of these characteristics can be interesting as it allows us to identify some recent trends affecting both the European and national spheres.

The birth of European parliamentary groups coincided with the foundation of the European Communities. The first European Parliamentary Assembly (as the European Coal and Steel Community Parliamentary Assembly) rapidly evolved from a house representing national parliaments to a political body organised along ideological lines. As early as 1953, three political groups (Christian Democrats, Liberals and Socialists) were formed in the Assembly; due to the growing salience of the political alignment as a distinctive feature, in 1958 it was decided to abandon the alphabetical order of seating and organize members by political groups.[61]

The internal rules of the Assembly played a crucial maieutic role in encouraging such evolution. In addressing this task, the rules had to take into account the peculiarities connected with the recognition of political groups in a multinational assembly. By contrast with what normally happens in a national parliament, the members of each group were not affiliated with the same party, but with multiple national party organisations sharing different degrees of ideological affinity. Against this backdrop, the regulatory framework gradually accompanied the formation of cohesive political groups within the legislature. The final outcome of this process, as shown by the current discipline, is inspired by two basic principles:[62] (1) formation of the groups on the basis of the MEPs' declaration of their 'political affinity' with their fellow colleagues; and (2) in order to be formally recognised, a group must consist of a minimum number of MEPs (currently, 23 members) coming from at least one-quarter of the Member States (currently, at least seven states). The rules therefore aim to prevent the formation of groups on a purely national basis, with the intent of favouring the integration into multinational groups of MEPs sharing 'political affinities'. The concept of 'political affinity' is clearly rather loose, and the Rules of Procedure do

[60] R Taagepera, 'Seats and votes: A generalization of the cube law of elections' (1973) 2 *Social Science Research* 257.

[61] A Ripoll Servent, *The European Parliament* (London, Palgrave, 2018) 23.

[62] Rule 33 of the EP Rules of Procedure.

not provide for any formal verification of the actual existence of such affinity on the basis, for example, of the political platforms presented by the national parties at the European elections. According to the official interpretation given to the Rules of Procedure,[63] in forming a group together, their members accept, by definition, that they have political affinity. Only when this is denied by the members concerned does it become necessary for Parliament to evaluate whether the group has been constituted in accordance with the Rules. Moreover, each political group has to make a formal statement to the presidency setting out the group's values and the main political objectives which its members intend to pursue together within the framework of the exercise of their mandate. The declaration has to describe the common political orientation of the group 'in a substantial, distinctive and genuine way'. These provisions exclude the formation of political groups on a merely 'technical' basis, as happened in the past (ie, with the intent of reaching the membership threshold in order to benefit from the several procedural privileges and logistical facilities accorded to the groups). Nevertheless, appreciation of the political affinity remains mainly a political decision in the hands of MEPs and of the groups' leadership. Such a decision raises the question of the 'triangular relationship' between EP political groups, the national parties and the European parties. On the one hand, European parties are recognised by the Treaty on European Union (TEU) as crucial democratic institutions for their contribution to 'forming European political awareness and to expressing the will of citizens of the Union'.[64] On the other hand, the elections for the European Parliament are still under the control of the national parties that usually present their candidates with the traditional party symbols. There have been some important experiments to Europeanise these elections with forms of transnational coordination between national parties through the common indication of individual personalities as candidates for the post of President of the European Commission (the *Spitzenkandidaten*). We cannot analyse here the institutional implications of these initiatives in the context of the form of government of the European Union (EU). Suffice it to say that the *Spitzenkandidaten* experience and other forms of political coordination have, to date, proven incapable of replacing the national parties as the real masters of the European elections, which continue to be perceived at the national level as 'second order' contests.[65] Lacking any real connection with the national electorates, European parties essentially remain federations of national parties, a kind of umbrella organisations whose political meaning derives mainly from their relationship with the corresponding political groups in the European Parliament. Even if the European rules make a clear distinction between the European parties and the EP groups (especially from the point of view of their funding by European financial resources), the parties can be considered 'emanations' of the groups, rather than the other way around. On the basis of their ascendancy, the EP groups play a crucial role in structuring European politics and in decision-making in Brussels.

[63] See the interpretation notes annexed to Rule 33.

[64] Art 10, s 4 TEU. The phrase about the democratic function of the European parties is repeated by art 12, s 2 of the Charter of the Fundamental Rights of the European Union.

[65] S Hix, A Noury and G Roland, *Democratic Politics in the European Parliament* (Cambridge, Cambridge University Press, 2007). For an assessment of the experience with the *Spitzenkandidaten*, see D Fromage, 'The *Spitzenkandidaten* procedure for the election of the European Commission President: a critical view' in T Marguery, S Platon and H van Eijken (eds), *Les élections européennes 40 ans après* (Bruxelles, Bruylant, 2020).

It must also be said that what happens within the European Parliament has increasingly evident effects on the third side of the triangle, that is, on the national political systems. The inclusion of the MEPs elected with the lists of the national parties in one or another EP political group has growing consequences for the political identity of the parties in the domestic arena. This trend is partially due to the fact that most of the major domestic political issues are today simultaneously European issues. The political dilemmas regarding transnational phenomena like immigration, climate change and energy transition are provoking ideological divides that affect national and European levels in parallel. The debates in the European Parliament therefore have an increasing correspondence with the controversial issues dealt with by national parliaments and member countries' public opinions. The EP political groups, representing the great European political families in the European Parliament, are consequently emerging as incubators of a nascent European political system, especially if we adopt a constructivist perspective *à la* Habermas about the possible emergence of a political *demos* at a European level.[66]

With the direct election of the European Parliament and the gradual expansion of its powers within the EU institutional framework,[67] the groups have become pivotal actors in the work of the legislature: they are 'the institutional cement pasting together the different units of the Parliament'.[68] This function has been officially recognised by the attribution, since 1993, to the Conference of the Presidents (including the EP President and the chairmen of the political groups) of the responsibility for the organisation of Parliament's work and for all the matters relating to legislative planning.[69] Beyond this agenda-setting function, the political groups are also pivotal in organising the legislative work of the Parliament: this role is particularly relevant at the committee stage, as we shall see in section III.

From the point of view of their structure, EP political groups show a higher degree of complexity in comparison to their national equivalents.[70] Their internal governance and decision-making need to take into account both the national delegations and the different political sensibilities of the national parties. Most of the decisions relating to the different topics in the parliamentary agenda are therefore fleshed out within the groups' working committees that reflect both these dimensions. In order to define their positions on highly technical issues, the groups are able to mobilise considerable cognitive resources, also thanks to the financial funds received from the EP budget. The preparatory work is inevitably highly complex as it involves a wide consultation process within the group: recent

[66] J Habermas, 'Remarks on Dieter Grimm's: 'Does Europe need a Constitution?' (1995) 1 *European Law Journal* 303.

[67] Due to these developments, today the EP 'deserves to be considered a "transformative" legislature capable of significantly impacting the decision-making and policy processes of the European union': A Kreppel, *The European Parliament and Supranational Party System: A Study in Institutional Development* (Cambridge, Cambridge University Press, 2002) 1.

[68] M William, 'The European Parliament: Political Groups, Minority Rights and the "Rationalization" of Parliamentary Organization. A Research Note' in H Doering, (ed), *Parliaments and Minority Rule in Western Europe* (Frankfurt, Campus, 1995) 395.

[69] Rule 24 of the EP Rules of Procedure.

[70] T Raunio, 'Understanding the European Parliament's Party Groups' in K Heidar and R Koole (eds), *Parliamentary Party Groups in European Democracies: Political Parties Behind Closed Doors* (London, Routledge/ECPR, 2000).

research has shown that the two major groups (EPP and S&D) have an effective bottom-up organisation designed to maximise internal agreement.[71]

Through their political work, the EP party groups have proven rather successful in reducing the complexity of national political arenas. For example, currently the EPP Party Group represents 48 different national parties, the S&P Group 36. It should also be borne in mind that, following the different phases of EU enlargement, the EP groups managed to successfully incorporate most of the national parties from new Member States.

In conclusion, it can be said that the EP groups have played an essential function in distilling, out of the fragmentation of the national political systems, a common basis of debate to be shared by all MEPs. These platforms have not remained purely ideological positions, but have been translated into the daily legislative work of a great 'transformative' assembly like the European Parliament. Most of this remarkable encyclopaedic work of synthesis and simplification is done at the intersection between the groups' working committees and the sectoral committees of the Parliament. In the next section, we will analyse in more detail the contribution to this complex machinery made by the committees in the national parliaments and in the European legislature.

III. Parliamentary Committees and the Professionalisation of Politics

The transition between the nineteenth and twentieth centuries saw the emergence of a new type of professional politician, in contrast with the 'generalist politician' who dominated the liberal parliaments. A key trigger of this phenomenon was the rise of mass parties. The parties and their several side organisations (trade unions, associations, newspapers) were the fora for the emergence of the new figure of the politician, as someone who lived – according to the classical Weberian description of this development – not only *for* politics, but also *off* politics. In some countries especially, a significant proportion of the parliamentarians were recruited from among the leading figures within the parties or trade unions. Those figures already received salaries from their organisations, well before the introduction of stable forms of remuneration for MPs.[72] Moreover, from the constitutional perspective,

[71] E Bressanelli, 'The Political Group as Organisations: The Institutionalisation of Transnational Party Politics' in P Ahrens, A Elomaki and J Kantola (eds), *European Parliament's Political Groups in Turbulent Times* (Cham, Palgrave, 2022) 65–66: 'Issues are first debated in the working group at the committee level. If important divergences remain, the issue is brought to the "standing" (EPP) or "horizontal" (S&D) working group, bringing together a number of policy-connected committees, under the aegis of a vice-president. Should significant divergences remain, the bureau of the presidency, with the heads of the national delegations, consider the issue. If tensions remain, the group plenary is the stage of last resort'.

[72] In the UK, the payment of members of the House of Commons was introduced in 1911, following a long debate during the nineteenth century about the opportunity to opt for this solution. Compulsory payment of MPs was predominantly supported by Liberals and opposed by Conservatives. The introduction of a stable salary was decided upon in 1911 after the Osborne Judgment, a judicial ruling which banned contributions to the Labour Party by trade unions (see E Hicks, 'MPs pay: the never ending controversy' in historyofparliamentonline.org, available at: thehistoryofparliament.wordpress.com/2013/12/09/mps-pay-the-never-ending-controversy/). In Germany, the indemnity for MPs (*Abgeordetenentschaedigung*) was introduced in 1906: see M Reiher, *Parlamentarier als Beruf: Rekrutierungswege und politische Karrieren am Beispiel des Deutschen Bundestages* (Baden Baden, Nomos, 2019) 51.

there was a gradual shift from the notion of attendance in Parliament as a purely honorary duty to the affirmation of the parliamentary mandate as a public office worthy of some form of remuneration.[73] This development partially challenged Weber's expectation that political professionalisation would have been accompanied by a radical shift of power from the parliaments to the parties: party democracy took root, not at the expense of parliamentarism, as Weber had expected, but rather *via parliamentarism*.[74]

The institutional environment in which the new 'professional' politicians developed their skills was offered by the parliamentary committees. The twentieth century, especially after the First World War, was the age, almost globally, of the 'big government', with executive powers being shaped in the form of large, specialised administrations.[75] In order to keep abreast of these transformations, parliaments also had to adapt, introducing the innovation of permanent committees capable of following and 'mirroring' the work of state bureaucracies. This implied, almost everywhere, the abandonment of the traditional organisation of legislative work, according to which draft laws were examined by ad hoc committees prior to debate in the plenary. This means of operation prevented the concentration of parliamentary expertise in specialised sectorial committees. Over the course of the twentieth century, many of the European legislative assemblies decided to establish such committees. This development was accurately described by Max Weber, who emphasised its importance for a well-functioning parliamentary form of government. In his view, the accumulation of expertise through the day-to-day work of parliamentarians in the committees was crucial for the purposes of offsetting the enormous power accumulated by ministerial bureaucracies.[76] Expertise and knowledge were the crucial resources at stake in this new division of powers.

The twentieth-century parliamentary encyclopaedia was thus structured on the basis of a dual analytical grid. On the one hand, the organisational structure of the political groups, and on the other hand, the specialised committees. The coincidence between these two developments was anything but accidental. The emergence of political parties and their projection within the elected assemblies – namely, the parliamentary groups – actually made it possible for parliaments to entrust the preparatory stages of their decisions to permanent committees with a stable allocation of competence.[77] The premise on which that solution

[73] In Germany, for example, until the 1975 Judgment of the Federal Constitutional Court ('Diaetenurteil': BVerGE 40, S 296, S 314), the parliamentary mandate, according to constitutional law theory and practice, was always seen as an honorary post and the payments to MPs were therefore designed to be tax-free expense allowances (see P Austermann, 'Die Entwicklung der Entschädigung und der Reisebezogenen Ansprüche im Deutschen Abgeordnetenrecht' (2014) 2 *Zeitschrift Für Parlamentsfragen* 270, available at: www.jstor.org/stable/24243398.

[74] J Borchert and L Golsch, 'Deutschland: von der "Honorationenzukunft" zur politischen Klasse' in J Borchert (ed), *Politik als Beruf: Die politische Klasse in westlichen Demokratien* (Opladen, Leske+Budrich, 1999) 118, quoted by Reiher (n 72) 59.

[75] On the rise of big government in Western democracies, see R Rose, *Understanding Big Government: The Programme Approach* (Beverly Hills, CA, Sage, 1984).

[76] See M Weber, *Parliament and Government in Germany under a New Political Order in* M Weber, *political Writings* (1st edn 1918) (Cambridge University Press, 1994). Of course, on the professionalisation of politics and its consequences, see also the famous *The Vocation Lectures: Science As a Vocation, Politics As a Vocation* (1st edn 1919) (Indianapolis, IN, Hackett Publishing, 2004). For the debate about the role of the parliament in the new German State, see C Senigaglia, 'The debate on democratization and parliament in Germany from 1871 to 1918' (2020) 3 *Parliaments, Estates and Representation* 290.

[77] K von Beyme, *Die parlamentarische Demokratie: Entstehung und Funktionsweise 1789–1999*, 4 Aufl (Wiesbaden, Springer, 2014) 182–83.

was based was the representativeness of the committees, as far as they were expected to reflect, to a smaller extent, the political composition of the plenum and the relative power relationship between the majority and the opposition.

The connection between party and committee organisation in parliaments is therefore very strong: 'It is in relation to the formation of standing committees that the modern party is recognised by Parliament'.[78] The new committees, composed on the basis of the strength of the parliamentary groups, formed a 'system'.[79] It was precisely in order to form a 'system' that the committees had to become permanent bodies with a stable remit of competence. This new systemic organisation is central to understanding the encyclopaedic pattern of modern parliaments. This major transformation occurred first in the US Congress in the first half of the nineteenth century, whereas in continental European parliaments it took place in the first decades of the following century.

A. United States

In the United States, the adoption of the system of standing committees (and of a very complex network of subcommittees) was already completed in the nineteenth century as one of the consequences of the political parties' predominance in the Congress.[80] Seniority and expertise were and are still crucial for participation in the committees:

> [H]owever large or small a committee, it is important that those nominated to it should serve for long enough to build up a sufficient knowledge to enable them to sustain an informed dialogue with official and non-official experts, and that their attendance should be regular.[81]

From a comparative perspective, the American Congress is usually cited as the legislature with the strongest committee system: 'the United States Congress makes most of its legislative and other decisions in committees and subcommittees. They are in almost every respect the eyes, ears, and hands of the Senate and of the House of Representatives'.[82] Writing in 1885, Woodrow Wilson asserted that 'congressional government is committee government' and he added that 'Congress in its Committees' rooms is Congress at work'.[83]

[78] L Elia, 'Commissioni parlamentari' in *Enciclopedia del diritto*, Vol VII (Milano, Giuffré, 1960) 896.

[79] By comparing the different models of parliamentary committees, Fasone rightly defines these models as 'systems', namely structures organised on the basis of a certain logic, for their different purposes. These structural characteristics are capable of deeply affecting the form of government of each country. See C Fasone, *Sistemi di commissioni parlamentari e forma di governo* (Padova, Cedam, 2012) 147. Fasone describes the system of parliamentary committees as 'the coherent and rational organisation of all parliamentary committees specialised in their mutual relations, in relations with other parliamentary bodies and with the government'.

[80] GW Cox and MD McCubbins, *Legislative Leviathan: Party Government in the House* (Berkeley, CA, University of California Press, 1993) 159. However, the foundation of today's committee system was established by the 1946 Legislative Reorganization Act.

[81] W McKay and CW Johnson, *Parliament and Congress: Representation and Scrutiny in the Twenty-First Century* (Oxford, Oxford University Press, 2010) 365.

[82] JD Lees, 'Committees in the United States Congress' in JD Lees and M Shaw (eds), *Committees in Legislatures: A Comparative Analysis* (Oxford, Martin Robertson, 1979) 11.

[83] TW Wilson, *Congressional Government: A Study in American Politics* (1st edn 1885) (Cleveland, OH, The World Publishing Company, 1956) 123.

In the House of Representatives, there are currently 20 permanent committees and five select committees. Most of the former committees have legislative capacity (for instance the Energy and Commerce Committee and Education and Labor Committee), whereas the latter have oversight and investigative functions (like the controversial Committee to investigate the 6 January 2021 attack on the US Capitol). Standing committees also have jurisdiction over appropriations (the Appropriations Committee), taxation (the House Ways and Means Committee and Senate Finance Committee), and a variety of other spending programmes. Committees are determinant in setting the Congress agenda, since the timing for the consideration of bills is almost entirely in their hands.[84]

Committees are rightly considered to be the most important safeguard of the separation of powers and of the independence of Congress from the executive. The way in which committees gather and process information is crucial to affirming this autonomy in the context of the American presidential form of government. The committees transform information into 'usable knowledge' for the benefit of Congress.[85] They do so with the support of a staff of specialists and policy advisers who are recruited on the basis of their party affiliations. In addition, a source of non-partisan expertise is provided by the Congressional Research Service and by other agencies that support the Congress (the Government Accounting Office and the Congressional Budget Office). Knowledge is an essential resource for leaders of the committees: to be successful, a committee chairman must gain the respect and support of committee members on the basis of his superior knowledge of the committee's subject matter.[86]

B. Germany

In Germany, after 1918, the Reichstag adopted a system of permanent committees relating to the main areas of government action.[87] After the end of the Nazi regime and under the new *Grundgesetz*, this precedent was followed by the Bundestag. Today, this assembly has a powerful system of standing committees, which mirror the government departments. From a comparative perspective, the Bundestag's committee system stands out as one of the strongest in Europe. As already stated, one of its main features is its strong relationship with the party groups: the membership of each committee is proportional to the division of party seats in the chamber and the chairs are also distributed according to the size of political groups (therefore, the representatives of the opposition also have their share in the

[84] 'Each committee has a nearly exclusive right to consider measures within its jurisdiction. In general, committees are not required to act on any measure, and a measure cannot come to the floor for consideration unless through the action or at least concurrence of a committee. A procedure to discharge a committee from consideration is rarely successful': J Schneider, *The Committee System in the US Congress* (Washington, DC, Congressional Research Service, 2009) 3.

[85] J Cooper, *The Origins of the Standing Committees and the Development of the Modern House* (Houston, TX, Rice University Studies, 1970).

[86] Lees (n 82) 29.

[87] N Johnson, 'Committees in the West German Bundestag' in J Lees and M Shaw (eds), *Committees in Legislatures: A Comparative Analysis* (Oxford, Martin Robertson, 1979) 102.

distribution of the chairs).[88] Moreover, all the decisions made by the committees are prepared in advance within the working groups of the parties. For German MPs, membership of one of these working groups and the possibility of acting as a rapporteur on a specific legislative subject constitute a crucial passage to obtaining visibility and reputation within the party group. Especially for backbenchers, an important part of their political status depends on the possibility of being perceived by their colleagues as experts on a given topic.[89] The committees therefore provide the institutional context where MPs display professionalism and a specialisation in politics.[90]

While committees of the German Bundestag used to meet in closed session, the reform of the rules of procedure in 2023 has brought about a cultural change. Since then, the committees decide for themselves whether they will meet in public or in closed session. The meetings are regularly attended by experts from public administration and other staff: this 'allows members to acquire expertise in a specific policy area and build informational ties to executive experts. This policy expertise is conducive to finding a common approach to political problems, hammering out technical compromises, and overseeing hostile ministries'.[91] The neutrality of the information provided by the executive experts, however, has been questioned, as they tend, as a rule, to support the policy choices proposed by the government.[92] For this reason, in 1989, a new rule was introduced in the standing orders of the Bundestag that also admits the presence within the committees of the experts of the political groups, including those belonging to the opposition.[93] The importance of the parliamentary committees is emphasised by the fact that some of them are expressly mentioned by the *Grundgesetz* (namely, the Committee on Foreign Affairs, the Petitions Committee, the Defence Committee, and the Committee on the Affairs of the European Union). As for the legislative process, all bills, after a formal first reading by the plenary, are deferred to a lead committee and normally to one or more co-advising committees. A special role is played by the Budget Committee, which is responsible for considering the draft federal budget submitted annually by the Federal government. The Budget Committee also provides other committees with binding opinions on the financial aspects of the bills they are examining. The committees have a considerable transformative power even in relation to the bills introduced by the executive. The complex system of the standing committees, therefore, represents the core of the Bundestag as an *Arbeitsparlament*. Indeed, this feature is also physically reproduced in Berlin by the building that hosts the committees. Designed in 1994 by Stephan Braunfels, the building vividly represents the notion of the committees as the 'factory of the laws': its appearance is reminiscent of a large and modern industrial plant, something between a nuclear power station and a chemical works.[94]

[88] S Linnand and F Sobolewski, *The German Bundestag: Functions and Procedures* (Rheinbreitbach, Neue Darmstadter Verlagsanstalt, 2015) 50 ff.

[89] J von Oertzen, *Das Expertenparlament: Abgeordetenrollen in den Fachstrukturen bundesdeutscher Parlamente* (Baden Baden, Nomos, 2006) 83.

[90] Johnson (n 87) 109.

[91] B Miller and C Stecker, 'Consensus by Default? Interaction of Government and Opposition Parties in the Committees of the German Bundestag' (2008) 17 *German Politics* 305, 310.

[92] W Ismayr, *Der Deutsche Bundestag*, 3 Aufl (Wiesbaden, Springer, 2012) 183.

[93] See Art 57, s 4 of the Bundestag Standing Rules.

[94] G Rizzoni, 'Political Architecture and the Seduction of Space: The Form of Parliaments and European Identity' in L Rorato and A Saunders (eds), *The Essence and the Margin: National Identities and Collective Memories in Contemporary European Culture* (Amsterdam, Rodopi, 2009) 191.

C. France

In the French Chamber of Deputies, the introduction of specialised standing committees was adopted in 1902.[95] Subsequently, in 1910, as already stated, a new reform of the standing orders called for a composition of committees in proportion to the size of the political groups. The committees rapidly became very powerful bodies. Writing in 1934, Joseph Berthélemy observed that, whereas in England the government was the true director of the legislative process, in France the government was obliged to share this power with the parliamentary committees.[96] The stability of the committees and the distribution of their responsibility for the different sectors of public administration enabled these bodies to exercise an effective control over the executive. The committees modified the balance of power among the branches of government to such an extent that their existence was considered 'inhérente au regime represéntatif français'.[97] The number of permanent committees kept increasing: in the 1930s the Chamber had 20 committees. The Assembly of Palais-Bourbon continued this complex system in the Fourth Republic without making any major changes. In keeping with the 'government d'assemblée' characterising the new regime, the standing committees were able to regularly modify the legislative texts of the government. According to Michel Debré, this practice was among the main causes of the weak position of the executive vis-a-vis the Parliament: 'la commission en fait éclaire le législatif, mais elle permet aussi au législatif de mieux empiéter sur l'éxecutif'.[98]

The radical 'rebalance' of power between the executive and the Parliament, mentioned earlier, brought about by the Constitution of the Fifth Republic, reduced the number of committees, fixing their number at six. The legislative capacity of the committees was also significantly curbed, limiting their function to a mere preparatory consideration of the bills. From this point of view, however, the already mentioned 2008 constitutional reform promoted by President Sarkozy marked a turning point. The reform restored the central place of the permanent committees (whose number was increased from six to eight), guaranteeing them sufficient time to be able to fulfil their mission under satisfactory conditions.[99] On the basis of the new constitutional provisions, the plenary debates are held on the texts prepared by the committees (with the exception of the constitutional revision bills, finance bills and social security financing bills; in these cases the plenary discusses the text presented by the Government). The cognitive function of the committees has also been significantly enhanced, with the *missions d'information* conducted by the committees and the impact

[95] The resolution of 17 November 1907 gave official recognition to 17 permanent committees, each composed of 33 members. This reform reflected 'la mutation de député omniscient vers le deputé specialiste': J Garrigues (ed), *Histoire du Parlement* (Paris, Colin, 2007) 296.

[96] J Berthélemy, *Essai sur le travail parlamentaire et le système des commissions* (Paris, Librairie Delagrave, 1934) 24.

[97] ibid. Barthélemy also reminds the criticism of the rise of a powerful system of permanent committees. On this point, he quotes the former President of the French Republic, Raymond Poincaré, who stated that 'ce qui entrave le plus le fonctionnement normal de notre regime, c'est l'existence des grand commissions'. Against this thesis, Berthélemy defends the need for permanent committees in a modern parliament, since 'le nombre, la complexité, le difficulté des problèmes actuels exige une division du travail et une spécialisation que l'on ne peut obtenir qu'avec la permanence' (ibid, 45).

[98] M Debré, 'Trois caractéristiques du système parlementaire français' (1955) 1 *Revue française de science politique* 21, 33.

[99] J-J Urvoas, 'La lente mais irrépressible renaissance des commissions parlementaires' (2013) 146 *Pouvoirs: Le renouveau du Parlement* 21.

assessment procedures.[100] As Pauline Türk has observed,[101] until 2008, the autonomy of the commissions vis-a-vis the government was the subject of a constant battle to take into account the contribution of the Parliament, whereas in 2008 a virtual inversion of the perspective took place: the autonomy so dearly conquered now seems to be guaranteed. It should be noted, however, that this new autonomy goes hand-in-hand with stronger control from the political groups on the organisation of the legislative process.[102]

D. Italy

In Italy, in some respects, the development of a system of modern parliamentary committees followed a parallel path to the French one. A set of stable committees with legislative competence was introduced, as already mentioned, via the 1920 reform of the Standing Rules of the Chamber of Deputies. This innovation occurred in parallel with the formal recognition of the party groups, a necessary step to guarantee a composition of the committees in line with the political majorities in the Chamber. The reform was short-lived, since, with the advent of the Fascist regime, the standing committees were abolished and the Chamber resumed its traditional system of 'offices'. The replacement in 1938 of the Chamber of Deputies with the 'Chamber of fasces and corporations' ended any appearance of parliamentary representation in Italy. The new chamber reflected the corporatist [illegible] of fascist ideology: the Assembly comprised representatives of the Fascist Party and professional organisations appointed by the regime. However, the new chamber introduced a major innovation regarding the committees that would have outlived the Fascist regime. The standing committees were granted the power to pass laws directly, without their passage in the plenary. This 'decentralised' legislative procedure was retained by the new republican Constitution of 1948, within certain limits. Article 72 of the Constitution renders mandatory the preliminary consideration by a committee of every bill introduced in each of the two Houses (the Chamber of Deputies and the Senate), and allows the standing rules of each House to establish in which cases and in what manner the examination and approval of bills is deferred to committees composed so as to reflect the proportion of parliamentary groups.[103] This possibility has been used extensively in practice, especially

[100] The function of the assessment of public policies, introduced by the already mentioned new text of art 24 of the Constitution, has been implemented by the rules of procedures of the National Assembly (art 98.1 and arts 146.1 to 146-7) through the institution of a *Comité d'évaluation et de contrôle*. The Committee is chaired by the President of the National Assembly and comprises 36 members appointed in such a way as to ensure a proportional representation of the political groups and a balanced representation of the standing committees. The committee may, on its own initiative or at the request of a standing committee, carry out work on cross-cutting subjects. Its annual programme gives special prerogatives to the opposition, since, on the one hand, each political group can freely choose one evaluation study per year, and, on the other, each subject is dealt with by two co-rapporteurs, including one from the opposition.

[101] P Türk, 'Les commissions parlementaires et le gouvernement' in F Fraysse and F Hourquebie (eds), *Les Commissions parlementaires dans l'espace francophone* (Paris, Montchrestien, 2011) 102.

[102] P Avril, 'Les commissions parlementaires, entre groupes politiques et gouvernement' in F Fraysse and F Hourquebie (eds), *Les Commissions parlementaires dans l'espace francophone* (Paris, Montchrestien, 2011) 91–93.

[103] Art 72 Cost provides that, in the event of the deferral of a bill to a committee for consideration in its legislative capacity, the bill, until the moment of its final approval, may be submitted to the plenary, if the government or one-tenth of the members of the House or one-fifth of the committee's members request that it be debated and

during the early decades of the Republic, and has encouraged the expansion of legislation aimed at circumscribed social or economic groups (the *leggine*).[104] This system allowed the development of a vertical integration between the competent ministry, the corresponding parliamentary committee and the social or professional groups relevant to that sector. On this basis, parliamentary committees in Italy became very powerful bodies, with a wide margin of autonomy. In their legislative capacity, they were the real engine of most Italian legislation, and it is unsurprising that, in a comparative analysis carried out at the end of the 1970s, the standing committees of the Italian Parliament found themselves in second place, immediately behind those of the US Congress, in a ranking that attempted to measure their 'importance'.[105] They constituted the forum where, behind closed doors, a substantial quota of state legislation was passed on the basis of a consensual and inclusive approach.[106] This situation has now changed, especially since the adoption of rigid budgetary constraints deriving from Italy's membership of the Eurozone.[107] The legislative process is now much more concentrated in the hands of the executive, with overarching control exercised by the Minister of Economy regarding every legislative measure with financial consequences for the state budget.[108] A significant role is played by the 'filter committees' as well, such as the Budget Committee or the Constitutional Affairs Committee, responsible for verifying the compliance of every bill with criteria relating to financial and constitutional compatibility respectively. It remains true, however, that the committees of the Italian Parliament still retain a considerable degree of 'transformative power' on legislation: in most cases the committees substantially amend the original text of the bill that is considered by the plenary in the version as amended at the committee stage. Committees are also the cognitive hub of the Parliament: through hearings of experts and stakeholders, investigations and other oversight procedures, they acquire and process a huge amount of information [illegible]

voted on by the House itself or that it be submitted to the House for final approval by means of a call for votes [illegible] The regular procedure for examination and approval directly by the House is mandatory for bills regarding constitutional and electoral matters, the ratification of international treaties, the approval of budgets and expenditure accounts and for those delegating legislative powers to the government.

[104] M Morisi, *Le leggi del consenso: Partiti e interessi nei primi parlamenti della repubblica* (Soveria Mannelli Rubbettino, 1992).

[105] M Shaw, 'Conclusion' in M Shaw and J Lees (eds), *Committees in Legislatures: A Comparative Analysis* (Durham, NC, Duke University Press, 1979) 384: by 'importance', the author means 'the ability of the official committees in the legislature to influence or determine the outputs of the legislature and the polity'.

[106] F D'Onofrio, 'Committees in the Italian parliament' in M Shaw and J Lees (eds), *Committees in Legislatures: A Comparative Analysis* Durham, NC, Duke University Press, 1979); A Pizzorno, 'Opposition in Italy' (1997) 4 *Government and Opposition* 61, 64 ff.

[107] N Lupo and G Rizzoni, 'Foreign influences on (the procedure and content of) the Italian legislative process' in N Lupo and L Scaffardi (eds), *Comparative Law in Legislative Drafting: The Increasing Importance of Dialogue Amongst Parliaments* (The Hague, Eleven International Publishing, 2014) 128.

[108] M Cotta, 'The Rise and Fall of the "Centrality" of the Italian Parliament: Transformations of the Executive-Legislative Subsystem After the Second World War' in GW Copeland and SC Patterson (eds), *Parliaments in the Modern World: Changing Institutions* (Ann Arbor, MI, University of Michigan Press, 1994).

[109] The process to be followed by the committees for the collection of information in their legislative capacity is regulated by art 79 of the Chamber of Deputies' standing rules: according to this provision, during consideration of the bill at the reporting stage, the Committee shall send for any information needed to verify the quality and efficacy of the provisions contained in the text. For this purpose, the pre-legislative scrutiny and consultation shall take the following aspects into consideration: (a) whether the legislation is necessary, or whether the same ends might be achieved through regulatory provisions other than an Act of Parliament; (b) whether the proposed legislation conforms to the Constitution, whether it is compatible with European Union legislation and whether it respects the areas of competence of the regions and local government; (c) the objectives of the new legislation

As for their number and remit, the system of the standing committees in the two Houses corresponds to the structures of the Italian ministries, with some asymmetries between the two chambers: in the Chamber of Deputies, there are 14 committees, whereas in the Senate, their number was recently reduced to 10 with the merging of some of the original committees.[110]

E. United Kingdom

An exception to the general trend towards a progressive empowering of committees in the law-making process is represented by the British Parliament. In the United Kingdom, the tendency in the legislative process to enhance the role of the plenary at the expense of the committee stage continued to prevail for a long time, via the tradition of entrusting the preliminary examination of draft laws to ad hoc committees or to the Committee of the Whole House. This is also the current practice: one of the procedural features that distinguishes Westminster from many other legislatures

> is that permanent, specialist committees do not formally consider the 'committee stage' of legislation … this stage is instead usually taken in temporary 'public bill committees' in the House of Commons, convened individually for each bill, and either on the floor or in grand committee in the House of Lords.[111]

However, committees of a stable nature were introduced by the regulatory reforms of 1979, with the aim of ensuring parliamentary scrutiny of the government's work.[112] This was the case for the departmental select committees responsible for monitoring the activities of the main ministries. According to the House of Commons Standing Rule 152, select committees are appointed to examine the expenditure, administration and policy of the principal government departments and associated public bodies. They therefore 'mirror' the structures of the executive: however, they 'have gradually extended their remit beyond the narrow consideration of the work of the relevant government department and its associated public bodies to include wider matters of public concern'.[113] These bodies work in a largely non-partisan manner and publish their reports on a unanimous

and the suitability of the means identified to achieve them; whether the deadline envisaged for implementation is adequate; the costs to the public administration, citizens and business; (d) lack of ambiguity and clarity of meaning of definitions and provisions, as well as the appropriate arrangement of the subject in sections and paragraphs. To obtain the information needed, the Committee may ask the government to provide data and information, and if necessary to draw up a technical report.

[110] The revision of the number and the remit of the committees in the Italian Senate was introduced in 2022 through a modification of the Senate's standing rules. The reform was introduced as a consequence of the reduction of over one-third of the members of the Senate with the 2020 revision of the Italian Constitution. Even if the constitutional revision also brought about a parallel reduction of the number of members of the Chamber of Deputies, it did not trigger any modification in the number of committees in this Chamber.

[111] M Russell and D Gover, *Legislation at Westminster: Parliamentary Actors and Influence in the Making of British Law* (Oxford, Oxford University Press, 2017) 205.

[112] P Norton, 'Nascent Institutionalisation: Committees in the British Parliament' (1988) 4 *Journal of Legislative Studies* 143.

[113] House of Commons. Liaison Committee, *The Effectiveness and Influence of the Select Committee System* (HC 2017–19, Fourth Report of Session 2019) 5.

cross-party basis.[114] Through their enquiries, they collect research evidence from the executive departments and other agencies, experts and academics. Select committees are also routinely the forum for a wide range of digital and face-to-face public engagement activities.[115] Even if select committees do not have a direct role in the legislative process, they exercise 'various interconnected, and often subtle, forms of power': their recommendations very often result in amendments to bills and their influence 'continues after the formal decision-making stage, to include evaluation of policy once it is in place'.[116] Select committees are a fundamental cognitive tool for Parliament: 'they exercise influence rather than power, and the extent of that influence rests on the quality of the evidence that they gather and the use they make of it in construing well-argued reports'.[117] The success and the reputation of the select committees as permanent, specialist and valuable bodies for their consensual cross-party operation, have made the traditional system of the public bill committees appear increasingly out of step. As a result, 'whereas the select committees have clearly sharpened the Commons' retrospective review of government performance, the same organisation and bite has not been displayed in the case of reviewing prospective government action in the case of government bills'.[118]

F. The European Parliament

The example of the European Parliament confirms the centrality of the committee system for the legislative activity of the Assembly. The EP committees have become more powerful and structured in parallel with the extension of the Parliament's legislative powers.[119] Seven committees had already been established in the common Assembly by 1953. After the European Parliament direct elections in 1979, 16 committees were installed, and by 1999 their number had increased to 20.

The number and responsibilities of the standing committees are defined by the Parliament following a proposal from the Conference of the Presidents.[120] The remit of the current 20 standing committees reflects the main EU policies and priorities in an encyclopaedic setting: they are the 'legislative backbone'[121] of the Parliament, since

[114] Russell and Gover (n 111) 206.

[115] C Leston-Bandeira and A Walker, 'Parliament and Public Engagement' in C Leston-Bandeira and C Thompson (eds), *Exploring Parliament* (Oxford, Oxford University Press, 2018) 312–3: 'public engagement is now explicitly part of select committees' core task, with social media regularly used to inform and consult the public about inquiries'. On these aspects, see ch 4 in this volume.

[116] Russell and Gover (n 111) 229–30.

[117] R Kelly, 'Select Committees: Powers and Functions' in A Horne, G Drewry and D Oliver (eds), *Parliament and the Law* (Oxford, Hart Publishing, 2014) 162.

[118] M Russell, B Morris and P Larkin, *Fitting the Bill: Bringing Commons Legislation Committees into Line with Best Practice* (London, The Constitutional Unit, 2013) 15: the paper, based on recent reviews of the UK system, and examination of the international evidence, recommends a number of changes to the public bill committees.

[119] R Whitaker, *The European Parliament's Committees: National Party Influence and Legislative Empowerment* (London, Routledge, 2011) 48.

[120] Art 206 of the Rules of Procedure and Annex VI.

[121] M Westlake, *A Modern Guide to the European Parliament* (London, Pinter Publishers, 1994) 191.

everything that could conceivably be dealt with by the European Parliament falls within their competence.[122] They also play an important role in the appointment of the members of the European Commission: before the election of a new commission, all new commissioners-designate have to be assessed by the committees that deal with their respective portfolios.

Since the Lisbon Treaty came into force, the European Parliament has strengthened its role as a 'transformative' parliament, with a clear division of labour between the committees (charged with the definition of the political and technical content of the legislative proposals) and the plenary (specialised in the political debate). The committees deal with legislative proposals through the adoption of reports, proposing amendments to the plenary and appointing a negotiating team to conduct negotiations with the Council on EU legislation. In discharging the committees' workload, a crucial role is played by the rapporteurs, as the MEPs charged with following all the stages of consideration of the legislative and non-legislative acts assigned to the committees. Having regard to the key importance of these figures, their choice is the result of complex negotiations between the political groups that reflect partisan elements as well as a dimension of expertise. By selecting rapporteurs and directing their work in party group meetings, party groups act as crucial agenda-setters in shaping the legislative output of the committees.[123] For each report, the political groups can also designate a shadow rapporteur to follow the progress of the relevant report and find compromises within the committee on behalf of the group.[124] The rapporteurs act, on the one hand, 'as floor managers pursuing goals in the interests of party blocs; on the other, they are technical experts who form and shape consensus'.[125] In the selection of rapporteurs, seniority plays an important role. The high level of continuity in committees' membership has supported the growing specialisation in the European Parliament: as a result, 'the legislature can now rely on long-serving, experienced legislators and staff members to draft well-informed policies'.[126] Rapporteurs and shadow rapporteurs also play a critical role in the 'trilogues' with the Commission and the Council, that is, the informal meetings aimed at finding acceptable compromises on the legislative proposals issued by the Commission. The use of these early agreements has increased dramatically in recent years, due to the complexity of the EU legislative process, particularly the co-decision procedure with its three rounds of readings. If the use of 'trilogues' has enhanced the efficiency of the legislative process, these kinds of negotiations have, in contrast, been accompanied by a reduction in transparency and a shift in the decision-making process away from the traditional arenas of parliamentary debate.[127]

In conclusion, EP committees are characterised by a highly structured machinery that operates at the intersection between technical expertise and political affiliation.

[122] C Neuhold and P Settembri, 'The Role of the European Parliament Committees in the EU Decision-making Process' in T Christiansen and T Larsson (eds), *The Role of Committees in the Policy-Process of the European Union* (Cheltenham, Edward Elgar, 2007) 153.

[123] N Yordanova, *Organising the European Parliament. The Role of Committees and their Legislative Influence* (Colchester, ECPR Press, 2013) 123.

[124] Art 215 of the EP Rules of Procedure.

[125] A Yoshinaka, G MCelroy and S Bowler, 'The Appointment of Rapporteurs in the European Parliament' (2010) 4 *Legislative Studies Quarterly* 457, 477.

[126] Yordanova (n 123) 122.

[127] ibid, 88.

Their centrality is one of the major arguments traditionally raised to support the similarity between the European Parliament and the US Congress. Undoubtedly, there are some interesting analogies between the two legislatures, although one major difference clearly relates to the context in which committees operate: in the multiparty environment of the European Parliament, the committees are normally oriented towards a consensus-building activity, unknown in the US system. The encyclopaedic system of the EP committees, in any event, plays a crucial role in addressing the multidimensional complexity of the European decision-making process.

IV. Bicameralism as a Resource for the Parliamentary Encyclopaedia

Bicameralism is another feature through which parliaments articulate their encyclopaedic calling. In the nineteenth century, the presence of the second chamber was often functional to the dual form of government in place in many European countries. The elective chamber was counterbalanced by another assembly whose members were appointed by the monarch or, as in the case of Britain, were in part hereditary members. For this reason, the supporters of a radically democratic view of parliamentarism were in principle 'monocameralist': according to them, the will of the people could be expressed only by a national assembly.[128] In the twentieth century, many national constitutions retained or introduced the second (or 'higher') chambers with the intent of allowing the representation of a different set of interests from those that existed in the 'lower' chambers.[129] Today, of the 190 national parliaments around the world, 78 are bicameral and 112 are unicameral; in the European Union, 13 of the 27 Member States have a bicameral parliament.[130]

Second chambers differ from first chambers in respect of their composition and functions. Several of them specialise in territorial representation. Consequently, their members are elected or appointed to represent sub-national governments: provinces, regions or states. This solution is adopted in several federal systems, in which one of the two chambers represents the member states of the federation.[131] As is well known, this option was chosen by the Philadelphia Convention to solve one of the most controversial aspects of the drafting of the new US Constitution. The 'Connecticut compromise' opted for the equal representation in the Senate of the 13 colonies, irrespective of their population. The solution adopted for the US Senate is the most radical one, with the aim of preserving the absolute equality of all the member States of the Federation. Other federations, like Germany, have preferred an intermediate option, allocating to each state a number of seats that only partially takes into account their respective populations.[132] The membership of a minor number of second

[128] M Decaro, 'I bicameralismi nell'Unione europea' in M Decaro, *Il bicameralismo in discussione. Regno Unito, Francia, Italia: Profili comparati* (Roma, Luiss University Press, 2008) 31.

[129] M Russell, 'What Are Second Chambers For?' (2001) 54(3) *Parliamentary Affairs* 442, 443.

[130] Source: Inter-Parliamentary Union website, available at: www.ipu.org/national-parliaments.

[131] G Tsebelis and J Money, *Bicameralism* (Cambridge, Cambridge University Press, 1997) 15 ff.

[132] According to art 52 of the German Basic Law, each *Land* has at least three votes. Länder with more than two million inhabitants have four; Länder with more than six million inhabitants have five; and Länder with more than seven million inhabitants have six votes.

chambers is selected according to criteria that differ from territorial representation. The most remarkable example by far is the British House of Lords, whose members have a life mandate: most of them are appointed on the basis of their political affiliation or having regard to their professional or scientific merits.[133] Thanks to its composition, the House of Lords is reputed for its expertise and political wisdom, especially when it comes to the oversight of public policies. The House of Lords model has been replicated in some Commonwealth countries, such as Canada, where the 105 members of the Senate are appointed[134] according to criteria that combine political affiliation with expertise in specific policy fields. Similarly, the composition of the Irish Senate is based on mixed criteria: 11 members are appointed by the Prime Minister (Taoiseach); six are elected by the graduates of certain Irish universities; the remaining 43 are elected from five 'vocational panels' by an electorate including members of the lower chamber (Dáil Éireann), outgoing senators and members of city and county councils. The candidates should, in theory, have special expertise in the fields of each of the five panels (for instance, education, public administration, industry) but, in practice, the election is almost systematically made on the basis of political affiliation. In Italy, five senators are appointed by the President of the Republic for having 'honored the Nation through their outstanding achievements in the social, scientific, artistic and literary fields'; former Presidents of the Republic too are senators by right and for life.[135] The remaining 200 senators are elected via a system which is very similar to that of the lower chamber. In India, the President can appoint 12 members of the Council of States (Raiya Sabha), having regard to their contributions to art, literature, science and social services, whereas the remaining 238 are elected by the legislatures of the states and union territories.[136] In these systems, the higher chamber 'to some extent represents "the great and the good", who bring a different perspective to policy making than the elected members of the lower house'.[137]

In most countries senators enjoy a longer term than their colleagues in the lower chamber: for instance, six years in the United States, France and India. Moreover, the renewal of their members takes place in parts: one third of the US senators are elected every two years; half of the French Senate is renewed every three years; in India one third of the members of the Rajya Sabha are elected every two years. When adopted, this system makes the higher house a continuous chamber, which is therefore not subject to dissolution. This contributes to the fact that the higher chambers sometime have a distinct party balance from that in the lower house. More generally, these chambers often introduce a counter-majoritarian and

[133] The 1999 House of Lords Act ended hereditary peers' right to pass membership down through family. Currently (July 2023), there are 779 sitting members of the House of Lords, of whom 663 are life peers; 92 are hereditary peers; and 26 are bishops and archbishops (Lords spiritual). The life peers are appointed by the monarch on the advice of the Prime Minister or of the House of Lords Appointments Commission. The peers appointed on the advice of the Prime Minister have a political affiliation, but the Prime Minister also has to consider nominations presented by opposition parties. The House of Lords Act created the House of Lords Appointments Commission with the task of recommending individuals for appointment as non-party political life peers. The Commission also has the power to vet nominations for life peers, including those nominated by the UK political parties, to ensure adequate standards of propriety. For an overview of the complex history of the House of Lords, see M Russell, 'The British House of Lords: A Tale of Adaptation and Resilience' in J Luther, P Passaglia and R Tarchi (eds), *A World of Second Chambers: Handbook for Constitutional Studies on Bicameralism* (Milano, Giuffré, 2006).

[134] By the Governor General via the recommendation of the Prime Minister.

[135] Art 59 of the Italian Constitution.

[136] Art 80 of the Indian Constitution.

[137] Russell, 'What Are Second Chambers For?' (n 129).

consensual factor to parliamentary decision-making. This element need not depend only on partisan diversity. It can also result from other territorial, linguistic or other perspectives that the second chamber can introduce into the policymaking process.[138]

These peculiarities in their composition are reflected by the functions attributed to the second chambers.[139] Following Montesquieu's opinion,[140] in several countries, these assemblies play a 'moderating role' vis-a-vis the more political lower houses. They are rarely on an equal footing with the latter when it comes to legislation and financial decisions. Moreover, in most parliamentary systems, they lack the ability to force a confidence vote on the executive. These features, however, enhance their political independence, and often contribute to strengthening their scrutiny and oversight functions. This is obvious in the case of the British House of Lords, which has created a small number of specialist committees that cover subjects not dealt with by the House of Commons departmental select committees.

Even if their democratic legitimacy is sometimes questioned,[141] all in all, the second chambers enrich the parliamentary encyclopaedia, with their relative independence, closer scrutiny of government and different categories of analysis from those offered by the lower chambers. In this way, they contribute to the management of social and political complexity: significantly, most of the democratic countries with large populations (and multiple political cleavages) have a bicameral parliament.[142] To be effective, however, second chambers 'must achieve the right balance of formal powers, distinct composition and perceived legitimacy'.[143] These difficult tasks are pursued in national contexts through very different solutions: 'the cultural diversity of second chambers is as obvious as it is fascinating. Every nation has its own model of bicameralism and every second chamber symbolises aspects of its political identity'.[144] For the future, some political thinkers propose the creation of a new type of 'second chambers', capable of giving voice to 'objective' interests and issues that do not find adequate representation in traditional parliamentary assemblies.[145]

V. The New Knowledge Systems Supporting Parliaments

Interestingly, the internal knowledge systems supporting parliamentary work have also evolved in connection with the emergence of the twentieth-century 'expert Parliament'.[146] As we have seen, individual parliamentarians were ideal users of the nineteenth-century parliamentary libraries. MPs were regarded as cultivated persons interested in deepening

[138] ibid.

[139] For an overview, see J Luther, 'The Search for a Constitutional Geography and Historiography of Second Chambers' in J Luther, P Passaglia and R Tarchi (eds), *A World of Second Chambers: Handbook for Constitutional Studies on Bicameralism* (Milano, Giuffré, 2006) 25 ff.

[140] C-L Montesquieu, *Esprit des lois* in *Œuvres Complétes*, vol II (Paris, Gallimard, 1951).

[141] The question of the reform (or even of the abolition) of the higher chambers is a permanent topic of debate in many countries, as is the case in the United Kingdom, Italy and France.

[142] A remarkable exception is Turkey.

[143] Russell, 'What Are Second Chambers For?' (n 129).

[144] Luther (n 139) 24.

[145] B Latour, 'From Realpolitik to Dingpolitik, or How to Make Things Public' in B Latour and P Weibel (eds), *Making Things Public: Atmospheres of Democracy* (Cambridge, MA, MIT Press, 2005).

[146] For more details about the subject of this section, see G Rizzoni, 'Parliamentary Administrations and the Provision of Scientific Expertise' in T Christiansen, E Griglio and N Lupo (eds), *The Routledge Handbook of Parliamentary Administrations* (London, Routledge, 2023).

their knowledge with respect to any legislative subject from a generalist perspective. The changes which occurred within the parliamentary environment accompanying the transition to the twentieth century triggered new cognitive demands. The full-time professional politicians working in the standing committees very rarely had the time or opportunity to conduct research on their own. They required briefings with new kinds of information products specifically prepared in a timely manner for the parliamentary consideration of a given topic. MPs could rely upon a variety of sources, including their own parties, the executive departments, or the parliamentary administration, for the purpose of satisfying these new needs. As a result, MPs began working closely with experts. Some of these new figures like the party functionaries were clearly pursuing specific political agendas. Others were active in parliamentary administration and were committed to the objective of political neutrality.

In particular since the second half of the twentieth century, in both parliamentary and presidential systems, parliaments have established their own administrative units, whose role was to produce and digest knowledge for the benefit of parliamentary bodies (committees, commissions, political groups) or individual parliamentarians. In many parliaments, these structures were created as 'spin offs' of the parliamentary libraries and were constituted as autonomous research services. The creation in 1914 of the Legislative Reference Service within the Library of the US Congress paved the way. The Service was created for the purpose of employing competent researchers to gather data and to 'render such data serviceable to Congress and committees and members thereof'.[147] In 1970, the Service was renamed the Congressional Research Service (CRS). The CRS staff currently comprises more than 400 policy analysts, attorneys and information professionals working across a variety of disciplines in one of the Service's five research divisions.[148] The size and research capacity of the CRS are unique from a worldwide perspective. The only other comparable parliamentary research service is the European Parliamentary Research Service (EPRS). Created in 2013, the EPRS currently employs a staff of around 300 people. Other European parliaments also introduced parliamentary research services, particularly during the second half of the twentieth century, such as the German Bundestag (1964) and the Italian Chamber of Deputies (1976). In the case of the Greek Parliament, the Research Service is expressly mentioned in the text of the 1975 Constitution.

Of course, the form of a nation's government affects the mission of the parliamentary research services (PRSs). Reflecting the presidential systems' separation of powers doctrine, PRSs are expected to provide parliamentarians with autonomous and first-hand information aimed at securing an independent cognitive underpinning for congressional law-making and oversight functions. The operation of the CRS very clearly reflects this principle: 'If the executive branch could control what Congress knows, it might largely

[147] V Langley 'CRS at 100 – Informing the Legislative Debate Since 1914' (2014) 3 *Library of Congress Magazine* 14. See also JY Cole, 'The Congressional Research Service' in JY Cole and J Aikin (eds), *Encyclopaedia of the Library of the Congress: For Congress, the Nation and the World* (Washington, DC, Library of the Congress, Bernan Press, 2004) 25.

[148] Congressional Research Service, *Organizational Structure*, available at: www.loc.gov/crsinfo/about/structure.html. For a description of the key components of contemporary parliamentary research services, see the Inter-Parliamentary Union (IPU) and the International Federation of Library Associations and Institutions (IFLA), *Guidelines for parliamentary research services* (IPU, Geneva, 2015), available at: www.ifla.org/files/assets/services-for-parliaments/publications/guidelines-for-parliamentary-research-services-en.pdf.

nullify Congress's independent exercise of its powers and its ability to oversee the exercise of executive powers'.[149] In undertaking this role, the CRS is flanked by other powerful congressional watchdogs, like the Congressional Budget Office[150] and the Government Accounting Office.[151] By contrast, in a parliamentary system, it is normally assumed that much of the politically relevant information reaches parliament through the government. The PRSs therefore focus instead on offering a 'second opinion' on the information provided by the government, and assume responsibility for preparing briefings on the bills proposed by the government and ex ante or ex post impact assessments on the policies proposed by the executive branch. These varying functions also have consequences for the composition of staff. In presidential systems, PRSs are predominantly staffed by specialists in a wide range of subjects, whereas in the PRSs of parliamentary systems, the majority of staff have generalist skills, especially in law, social sciences and economics.

Very active international networks, such as the European Centre for Parliamentary Research and Documentation (ECPRD), facilitate mutual contacts and exchanges of experience between the PRSs' different parliaments. Today, the ECPRD constitutes a true 'community of knowledge' through which PRS members of the network connect on a daily basis.

Organisations such as the Inter-Parliamentary Union (IPU) and the International Federation of Library Associations and Institutions (IFLA) also support international cooperation between PRSs on a global scale.[152]

When turning to a more detailed analysis of the functions of PRSs, it should be noted from the outset that their activity is guided by a set of common principles: capacity to provide independent, timely and authoritative analysis, lack of advocacy, pursuit of 'usable knowledge', transparency, and confidentiality. Generally, both governing and opposition parties may be the recipients of the services provided by PRSs, with the aim 'to inform the parliamentary and public debate on issues facing the parliament, not to lead the debate'.[153]

One of the PRS's implied functions is the preservation of the parliament's institutional memory and accumulation of knowledge. This mission is invaluable in an age dominated by the decline of parliamentary seniority and by an accelerated turnover in the composition of parliamentary assemblies.

[149] IA Brudnick, *The Congressional Research Service and the American Legislative Process*, CRS Report to the Congress, March 2008, 5, available at: ecommons.cornell.edu/bitstream/handle/1813/77742/RL33471_20080319.pdf?sequence=1.

[150] Created in 1975, the CBO produces independent analyses of budgetary and economic issues to support the Congressional budget process. The CBO tracks bills for which it provides estimates, generally at the committee report stage: P Posner, *The Politics of Unfunded Mandates* (Washington, DC, Georgetown University Press, 1998) 181.

[151] The GAO was created in 1921. As stated on its institutional website (www.gao.gov), the GAO, as the investigative arm of Congress, is 'an independent, nonpartisan agency that exists to support Congress in meeting its constitutional responsibilities … The agency examines the use of public funds; evaluates federal programs and policies; and provides analyses, recommendations, and other assistance to help Congress make informed oversight, policy, and funding decisions. GAO provides Congress with timely information that is objective, fact-based, non-ideological, fair, and balanced. GAO's commitment to good government is reflected in its core values of accountability, integrity, and reliability'.

[152] IPU and IFLA, *Guidelines for Parliamentary Research Services* (n 148).

[153] IPU, *Informing Democracy: Building Capacity to Meet Parliamentarians' Information and Knowledge Needs*. (Geneva, IPU, 2008), available at: www.ipu.org/PDF/publications/inform_dem_en.pdf.

Parliamentary committees are, in some cases, the primary beneficiaries of PRS activity. In other parliaments, individual parliamentarians are PRSs' main clients. In addition to the institutional recipients of PRS products, however, there are a range of other beneficiaries of their work, such as media actors, representatives of established interests, and parliamentary monitoring organisations. Beyond these stakeholders, the public too, via parliamentary sites and search engines, increasingly benefits from PRS products. Some PRSs, such as the House of Commons Library, are devoting increasing energy and resources to improving their capacity to connect with the public at large.

There are, of course, other actors, who also play a role in meeting parliamentary demands for information, whose existence and activities reduce the scope of the fields covered by the PRSs. For example, the presence of parliamentary political groups with their own knowledge-processing structures can make a significant contribution to defining the content of parliamentary decisions.

PRSs must therefore find their niche within a complex cognitive ecosystem in which MPs have access to multiple sources of information. One of the main conflicts within this environment arises due to the difference in the nature of the information which MPs receive. On the one hand, MPs are provided with politically biased information from their own political party or from representatives with vested interests. On the other hand, MPs receive information of a non-partisan and neutral nature from sources like PRSs, which are obliged to adopt such an approach. It is up to the parliamentarians themselves to identify the most convenient blend of information provided by these different sources. In some countries (eg, Brazil and the United States),[154] partisan sources are increasingly gaining ground – in terms of both audience and capacity to influence parliamentary decision-making – vis-a-vis the services provided by PRSs.

Finally, the 'encyclopaedic' mission of PRSs, within the complex cognitive system activated by parliamentary procedures, warrants mention. We have already noted that PRSs are given the function of digesting the rich flow of information conveyed to parliaments: they operate with the aim of transforming this flow into 'usable knowledge' for the benefit of MPs. In order to discharge this function, most PRSs use complex cognitive grids devoted to the classification and retrieval of the information made available to the parliament. In doing so, PRSs respond to the need to connect each individual action taken by the parliament to broader areas of intervention articulating the major contemporary public policies (such as the fight against climate change, women's empowerment, digitalisation, etc). In some cases, PRSs are responsible for preparing and continuously updating a list of the major legislative topics. While the architecture of these platforms can vary, they share the same objective of offering a cognitive map for the navigation of the immense ocean of information faced by parliamentary business.

[154] F Santos and F Saboia Vieira, 'Brazil's Parliamentary Administration' and BG Peters, 'The United States Congressional Administration' in T Christiansen, E Griglio and N Lupo (eds), *The Routledge Handbook of Parliamentary Administrations* (London, Routledge, 2023).

VI. Legislative Rationality in the Twentieth Century

The concept of legislative rationality in the twentieth century is very different from that which prevailed during the previous century.[155] It is no longer sufficient for the law to be an expression of the people's general will.[156] On the one hand, the recognised presence of parties in parliament makes it that the law is the outcome of a negotiation between different interests and between different ideological stances. Accordingly, political scientists have modelled different theories about the dynamics of legislative bargaining.[157] Moreover, empirical research shows that, in addition to the parties, other actors emerge as capable of exerting a, more or less, direct influence on legislative decision-making, such as interest groups, trade unions and non-governmental organisations.[158] On the one hand, the very essence of parliamentarism is now recognised in the ability to find a compromise between diverging ideological positions and interests.[159] On the other hand, the complexity of legislation makes it increasingly necessary for parliaments to identify the knowledge they need to support the legislative decision. We have seen how these needs have been met by the new structure of the parliamentary encyclopaedia, based on the intersection between party groups and specialised committees. Committees, in particular, have emerged as the most suitable institutional environment for reaching a compromise position between the various parliamentary groups and for acquiring the necessary knowledge for law making. As a result of these changes, the legislative process necessarily becomes more structured, through the participation of several actors, both internal and external to the parliamentary institutions: this phenomenon confirms the tendency of modernity to include social complexity in the legislative decision through increasingly complex procedures.[160] The rationality of the law becomes also subject to external scrutiny by the constitutional courts. The judicial review of legislation in its centralised form was established in the second post-war period in many European countries, following the various waves of democratisation affecting the continent and the adoption of rigid constitutions. The Constitutional Courts scrutinise the law by checking whether the legislature has appropriately balanced different constitutional principles.[161] Courts often perform a reasonableness test too: they verify the proportionality between the objectives pursued

[155] M Atienza, *Contribución a una teoria de la legislación* (Madrid, Civitas, 1997) 28–39, distinguishes five levels of legislative rationality: linguistic (intelligibility); systematic (consistency); pragmatic (efficacy); teleological (adequacy to reach the legislative goals); and axiological (ethical acceptability of the legislative goals).

[156] P Brunet, 'Que reste-t-il de la volonté générale?' (2005) 114 *Pouvoirs: La Loi* 5.

[157] On the different approaches of political science to the study of law-making, see C Benoit and O Rozenberg, 'Political Science Approaches to Legislatures' in C Benoit and O Rozenberg (eds), *Parliamentary Studies: Interdisciplinary Approaches to Legislatures* (Cheltenham, Edward Elgar, 2020).

[158] For an overview of the scholarly research on interest-group lobbying of parliaments, see A Skorkiaer Binderkrantz, 'Legislatures, Lobbying, and Interest Groups' in S Martin, T Saalfeld and KW Strom (eds), *The Oxford Handbook of Legislative Studies* (Oxford, Oxford University Press, 2014) 528–29.

[159] H Kelsen, *The Essence and Value of Democracy* (1st edn 1929) (Lanham, MD, Rowman and Littlefield, 2013) 47–57.

[160] This aspect of the legislative procedure has been analysed in depth by N Luhmann, *Legitimation durch Verfahren* (Frankfurt am Main, Suhrkamp, 1983) 189–202.

[161] G Marcilla Córdoba, 'Argumentación jurídica y racionalidad legislativa en el Estado Constitucional' [2004] *Anuario de filosofía del derecho* 337, 344–45.

and the means used to achieve them.[162] The rationality of the legislator's choices is therefore subject to increasingly stringent external controls, including of a judicial nature, as well as by the public. As a result of these developments, the rationality of the legislator is no longer subject to an irrebuttable presumption, but is necessarily limited, subject to correction and review.[163]

VII. The Basic Structure of the Twentieth-Century Parliamentary Encyclopaedia

In this chapter we have seen how twentieth-century parliaments emerged as 'expert legislatures' as a result of the intersection of a double cognitive grid formed by political groups and the sectoral standing committees. These two major structural innovations can be viewed as two sides of the same coin, reflecting a radical paradigm shift in parliamentary representation. On the one hand, the organisation based on political groups marked the direct link between the parliamentary assemblies and the new plebiscitary dynamics of the party democracy. On the other hand, the gradual institutionalisation of standing committees allowed parliaments to set up powerful tools needed to manage the legislative decision-making process and hold executives accountable vis-a-vis the growing complexity of contemporary public policies.

As for parliamentary groups, our review of some national cases has indicated that, in many European countries, parliamentary groups were the first form of institutional recognition of modern political parties as mass organisations. In some national contexts, this process was interrupted by the advent of authoritarian regimes, as was the case in Italy and Germany. With the second wave of democratisation following the end of the Second World War, many new democratic constitutions explicitly recognised the role of political parties. This resulted in a further strengthening of the legal status of parliamentary groups, as an expression of parties in parliament. We have seen, however, that in the context of the parliamentary arena, the groups represented, and still represent, the political system not mechanically, but with a margin of flexibility which, for example, is particularly prominent in the Italian and French legislatures, while being practically absent in the English tradition. Looking at their practical role in the political history of the different countries, we can see that, in many cases, the map of the political groups has helped shape the political system and plays a prominent role in structuring political pluralism in national contexts.

Towards the end of the twentieth century, the crisis of large mass parties did not lead to a decline in the role of parliamentary groups: if anything, the opposite occurred. With the disappearance of the party model based on large territorial organisations and extensive membership with a strong ideological commitment, parliamentary groups have gained an

[162] J Sieckmann, 'Legislation as Implementation of Constitutional Law: A Foundation for the Demand of Legislative Rationality' in LJ Wintgens and AD Oliver-Lalana (eds), *The Rationality and Justification of Legislation: Essays in Legisprudence* (Dordrecht, Springer, 2013); see also, K Masserschmidt and D Oliver-Lalana (eds), *Rational Lawmaking under Review: Legisprudence according to the German Constitutional Court* (Berlin, Springer, 2015).

[163] F Ferraro, *Razionalità legislativa e motivazione delle leggi: Un'introduzione teorica* (Milano, Giuffré Francis Lefebvre, 2019) 139.

even greater role in defining the identity and structure of parties and of the entire political system. In this new context, the parliamentary group is confronted with a dual task: not only must it take care of the 'ordering function' between parliament and government, but it will also, more than ever, have to play the intermediary role between citizens and the state.[164] This new role is confirmed by the evolution of parliamentary groups in the European Parliament, where they make a crucial contribution to reducing the complexity of the political space 'by creating correlations between the different dimensions of politics'.[165] It remains true that the parliamentary groups are 'the engines of learning and pursuing professional politics' in parliament since they offer an opportunity for *specialisation and information-gathering*. In doing so, they help to manage the complexity of political life.[166] As such, they are a crucial component in the parliamentary encyclopaedia of the twentieth century. They play this role in strict combination with the system of standing committees established in most modern parliaments.

As for parliamentary committees, their importance can be properly appreciated only in the context of the institutional architecture of each country.[167] Our analysis of some national cases has, however, confirmed a common feature that already emerges from broader comparative studies: the committee system is at the heart of the cognitive machinery of parliament.[168] The gathering of wisdom and expertise for collective decision-making is the 'raison d'etre for a committee system'.[169] As a member of a committee, an MP has access to 'relevant information through formal committee hearings, relationships with interest groups and executive agents in issue networks, and also from the party resources to which expert status helps him gain access'.[170] MPs acting in committees perceive themselves, first and foremost, to be 'experts' on the basis of their distinctive knowledge on a given public policy topic. This feature constitutes a critical aspect of their identity as professional politicians, together with other capabilities (such as the ability to convey the political demands being made by their constituencies).[171]

This fundamental cognitive function is ideally located in the parliamentary committees for a variety of reasons. The first has a bearing on the stability of these bodies, which enable their members to acquire considerable expertise over time on matters falling within the committees' remit. Of course, such expertise is often acquired in addition to the scientific and professional knowledge already independently held by parliamentarians, who are

[164] K Heidar and R Koole, 'Parliamentary Party Groups Compared' in K Heidar and R Koole (eds) *Parliamentary Party Groups in European Democracies: Political Parties Behind Closed Doors* (London, Routledge, 2000) 269.

[165] S. Hix, *Democratic Politics and the European Parliament* (Cambridge, Cambridge University Press 2007) 9.

[166] Heidar and Koole, 'Parliamentary Party Groups Compared' (n 164) 266–68.

[167] Fasone (n 79) 23.

[168] 'Les commissions sont en effet des structures adaptées à l'acquisition d'expertise. Elles ont l'expérience des lois passées portant sur un sujet similaire. Elles regroupent des élus maitrisant le sujet. Elles ont une plus grande souplesse organisationnelle que la séance ce qui leur permet d'adapter leur travaux, par exemple le nombre d'auditions requis, aux spécificités de l'enjeu': C Benoit and O Rozenberg, 'Les Legislatives Studies: de l'art de couper des bûches et de collectionner les barils de porc' in O Rozenberg and E Thiers (eds), *Traité d'études parlementaires* (Bruxelles, Bruylant, 2018) 324.

[169] KE Hamm, RD Hedlund and SS Post, 'Committee specialization in US State Legislatures during the 20th Century: Do legislatures tap the talents of their members?' (2011) 11 *State Politics and Policy Quarterly* 299, available at: eds.s.ebscohost.com/eds/pdfviewer/pdfviewer?vid=6&sid=83bbecc8-21ae-463e-9545-dbf65a930faf%40redis.

[170] K Strøm, 'Parliamentary Committees in European Democracies' (1998) 14 *Journal of Legislative Studies* 64.

[171] Von Oertzen (n 89) 85. Von Oertzen distinguishes between the profile of the expert (based on knowledge) and that of the specialist (based more on 'know how' capacity).

ordinarily assigned to committees which can benefit from their particular education or background. This synergy creates a virtuous circle which strengthens, on the one hand, the political professionalism of MPs and, on the other, the cognitive depth of parliamentary procedures.

The flow of knowledge produced by each committee is then put into circulation – with encyclopaedic dynamics – through the complex connections linking each committee to the system of the other standing committees. This dynamic unfolds through different channels, such as the opinions that a committee may be required to give on subjects primarily falling within the remit of other committees, or the holding of joint meetings between different committees. These procedures provide the 'synapses' of the parliamentary encyclopaedia through which the representative assemblies are able to deal with all kinds of topics.

Having regard to these assumptions, we can enrich the traditional theory regarding the professionalisation of politics. The existing literature emphasises two primary meanings implied by the concept of professionalisation of legislatures.[172] The first form of professional parliamentarian is connected mainly with the appearance of the socialist parties in the European political systems between the nineteenth and the twentieth centuries: a significant quota of the socialist MPs were recruited from among the functionaries of the party or from other affiliated organisations (trade unions, newspapers etc). The growing presence of this political personnel was therefore seen as an indication of a *political-bureaucratic professionalisation* of legislatures. This phenomenon was well described by the first observers (and critics) of the rise of political parties as predominant actors in Western politics, such as Ostrogorsky and Michels. In addition, during the twentieth century, another type of politician emerged: a person who entered the parliament with a previous scientific or professional background, which was often the main reason for his or her recruitment by the party's electoral machine. This phenomenon marks a trend towards a more *intellectual-technocratic professionalisation* of legislatures. Some common features underpin each of these models of professional legislatures, like the mobilisation of passive masses of citizens, the differentiation of legislative work, and the quantitative increase in the workload of the legislatures.[173] In my opinion, these analyses should be complemented by the consideration of another crucial form of professionalisation of parliamentarians: namely, that developed via the learning process to which MPs are exposed during their participation in standing committees. The committee environment contributes to the development of individual experienced parliamentarians. In particular, it encourages the socialisation of parliamentarians belonging to the same committee and, therefore, necessarily, also the sharing of their knowledge. On this basis, committees also represent the forum in which fact-finding procedures are normally carried out, such as investigations and hearings enabling parliamentarians to acquire data and information from external sources, both scientific and other. Committees are also the places where parliamentarians are exposed to the information provided by special interest representatives or where they get impartial advice from experts and parliamentary research services. For all these reasons, the

[172] A Panebianco, *Modelli di partito: Organizzazione e potere nei partiti politici* (Bologna, il Mulino, 1982) 412 ff.

[173] KA Eliassen and MN Pedersen, 'Professionalization of Legislatures: Long-Term Change in Political Recruitment in Denmark and Norway' (1978) 2 *Comparative Studies in Society and History* 286, 292–93, available at: www.jstor.org/stable/178050.

committees constitute a crucial institutional environment where the professionalisation of politics takes place.

The interaction between the party groups and the standing committees therefore configures the core of the twentieth-century parliamentary encyclopaedia. This double grid was integrated in many countries by the bicameral structure of the parliament: a solution meant to provide different forms of representation to territorial diversity or to expertise in specialist fields of scholarship. The combination of these different criteria was peculiar to each country, but, in general, this complex system proved capable of processing a huge amount of information with the result of producing new knowledge for the benefit of the democratic polity. However, the cognitive synthesis provided by parliamentary procedures is very different from a neutral scientific assessment. The necessary incorporation of scientific evidence and fact-finding procedures in parliamentary decision-making is not meant to elide, but to better illuminate, the different choices facing political decision-making. The legitimacy of political representation is intrinsically conditioned to the capability of opening a common platform of debate on issues involving political actions that remain inevitably controversial. The encyclopaedic structure of modern parliaments is functional to articulating such a sphere. In the contemporary age, this paradigm is confronted with powerful pressures operating against any encyclopaedic composition of the social pluralism. In the next chapter I analyse the terms of this crucial challenge.

4

Crisis and Transformation of the Encyclopaedic Model

I. Encyclopaedias in the Twentieth Century between Crisis and Innovation

A. Philosophical Visions

The growing specialisation of sciences, the fragmentation of knowledge, and the difficulty of facilitating a productive exchange between different fields of research were already widespread phenomena in the nineteenth century. In the first half of the twentieth century, however, they also became acutely perceived by the non-specialist public. Philosophers and writers expressed their concerns regarding the possible negative consequences of these trends for the progress of sciences.

Within the Vienna Circle, Otto Neurath advocated the need for a new encyclopaedic enterprise intended to revive the spirit of Diderot's *Encyclopédie*. The new encyclopaedia envisioned a systematisation of knowledge based on interconnectedness between the different disciplines. The project had its centre on the analysis of the methodological questions raised by the ever-expanding fragmentation of sciences (construction and confirmation of theories, induction, historical attempts at scientific integration).[1] The programme was implemented via the publication in 1938 of an *International Encyclopaedia of Unified Sciences*, intended to offer a complete and up-to-date overview of the state of the art of the major scientific disciplines. The *Encyclopaedia* was published only partially, with the issue of the first two volumes,[2] which featured in-depth articles devoted to different scientific domains and written by some of the most renowned scholars of the age, like Rudolf Carnap (*Foundations of Logic and Mathematics*), Otto Neurath (*Foundations of Social Sciences*) and Thomas S Kuhn (*The Structure of Scientific Revolutions*).

The need for a new encyclopaedic systematisation of knowledge was theorised during the same years by HG Wells. For him, the fragmentation of the contemporary sciences was a serious obstacle to tackling the 'terrifying gap between available knowledge and current social and political events'. Against this backdrop:

> A great new world is struggling into existence. But its struggle remains catastrophic until it can produce an adequate knowledge organisation. It is a giant birth and it is mentally defective

[1] C Morris, 'On the History of the International Encyclopedia of Unified Science' (1960) 4 *Synthese* 517.

[2] The original plan drafted by Neurath consisted of 26 volumes containing 260 monographs supplemented by a 10-volume 'Visual Thesaurus'.

> and blind. An immense and ever-increasing wealth of knowledge is scattered about the world today, a wealth of knowledge and suggestion that – systematically ordered and generally disseminated – would probably give this giant vision and direction and suffice to solve all the mighty difficulties of our age, but that knowledge is still dispersed, unorganised, impotent in the face of adventurous violence and mass excitement.[3]

Wells maintained that a 'world encyclopaedia' would be a viable solution:

> I want to suggest that something – a new social organ, a new institution – which for a time I shall call World Encyclopaedia, is the means whereby we can solve the problem of that jig-saw puzzle and bring all the scattered and ineffective mental wealth of our world into something like a common understanding, and into effective reaction upon our vulgar everyday political, social and economic life.[4]

Wells describes the new world encyclopaedia with visionary accents:

> A World Encyclopaedia no longer presents itself to a modern imagination as a row of volumes printed and published once for all, but as a sort of mental clearing house for the mind, a depot where knowledge and ideas are received, sorted, summarised, digested, clarified and compared. It would be in continual correspondence with every university, every research institution, every competent discussion, every survey, every statistical bureau in the world. It would develop a directorate and a staff of men of its own type, specialised editors and summarists. They would be very important and distinguished men in the new world. This Encyclopaedic organisation need not be concentrated now in one place; it might have the form of a network. It would centralise mentally but perhaps not physically. Quite possibly it might to a large extent be duplicated. It is its files and its conference rooms which would be the core of its being, the essential Encyclopaedia. It would constitute the material beginning of a real World Brain.[5]

This comparison of the world encyclopaedia with a 'world brain' – a kind of decentralised network for the communication of knowledge – foreshadows some aspects of the worldwide web and the collaborative structures adopted by the Wikipedian project. It should be emphasised, however, that the internet-based media do not seem to meet Wells' expectations of the future 'world encyclopaedia': according to him the latter should not have been 'a miscellany, but a concentration, a clarification, and a synthesis'. It is difficult to discern such qualities in the web or even in the ever-expanding entries of *Wikipedia*, as we shall see shortly.

B. Encyclopaedias in the Twentieth Century

Against the backdrop of these intellectual visions, real-life encyclopaedias as reference works continued to be extensively published during the twentieth century. The context was, however, profoundly changing. Encyclopaedias had to adapt to the demands of a mass market that was increasingly globalised. The case of the *Encyclopaedia Britannica*

[3] HG Wells, 'The Brain Organization of the Modern World. Lecture delivered in America, October and November, 1937' in HG Wells, *World Brain* (1st edn 1938) (North Haven, CT, Read Books, 2016) 62.

[4] HG Wells, 'World Encyclopaedia. Lecture delivered at the weekly evening meeting of the Royal Institution of Great Britain, November 20th, 1936' in HG Wells, *World Brain* (1st edn 1938) (North Haven, CT, Read Books, 2016) 27.

[5] Wells, 'The Brain Organization of the Modern World' (n 3) 64.

is particularly telling from this point of view: the rights to this work were bought by an American publisher in 1901, with the intent of exploiting the prestigious brand worldwide, targeting the broad international public of English speaking readers.

Other important encyclopaedic works initiated during the nineteenth century, like the *Larousse* and the *Brockhaus*, were regularly published and updated through several new editions. For some of these works, pocket editions were sold in millions of copies. The volumes were often enriched with illustrations that enhanced the accessibility of the written text.

In the pursuit of completeness, the most important encyclopaedias seemed to revive the universalistic and cosmopolitan spirit of eighteenth-century encyclopaedism: a sort of return to the origins inspired by the awareness of an increasing interconnectedness of world cultures and by the emergence of international communities of scholars and scientists across the different disciplines. This universalistic approach was also adopted by some encyclopaedias launched in the twentieth century with a strong national focus, such as the *Espasa*.

Another key aspect of the classical encyclopaedic tradition was resumed by some new publications in the second part of the century: the proposal of a systematisation of knowledge as opposed to the mere alphabetical order of the entries. These works were also accompanied by overviews and 'maps of knowledge' intended to offer a guide to the reading of the articles. This was the case, for example, in the fifth edition (1952–56) of Herder's *Konversations-Lexicon* and in the Italian *Enciclopedia Einaudi* (1977–84), which devoted two volumes to diagrams and interdisciplinary treaties meant to overcome the fragmentation deriving from the over-specialisation of knowledge.[6] Even the *New Encyclopaedia Britannica* (1974) was divided into three parts (*Propædia*, or *Outline of Knowledge*; *Micropædia*, or *Ready Reference and Index*; and *Macropædia*, or *Knowledge in Depth*). The work devoted a full volume, entitled *Propaedia*, to an overview of knowledge, with the intent of offering 'a reader's version of the circle of learning on which the set had been based and was organized in such a way that a reader might reassemble in meaningful ways material that the accident of alphabetization had dispersed'.[7]

However, the intellectual and editorial projects aimed at renovating the encyclopaedic ideal in the twentieth century were seriously challenged by some powerful cultural trends pushing in opposite directions.

On the one hand, the growing specialisation of sciences and the ever-expanding new fields of research seemed to frustrate the aspirations towards the construction of a new map of knowledge. According to its critics, such a map would need to be too detailed, risking its overlap with the territory sought to be described, like the fictional map of the empire on a scale of 1:1 mentioned by JL Borges in *On Exactitude in Science*, a short story published in 1946.[8]

[6] W Barberis, 'L'Enciclopedia einaudiana' in *Enciclopedismo antico e moderno* (Bari, Fondazione Gianfranco Diogaurdi, 2020).

[7] R Collison, *Encyclopaedias: Their History throughout the Ages* (New York, Hafner, 1966).

[8] The English translation of the story is included in the volume JL Borges, *A Universal History of Infamy* (London, Penguin Books, 1975).

On the other hand, one of the main cultural objectives of encyclopaedism between the eighteenth and nineteenth centuries – that is, the dissemination and communication of knowledge – was apparently better achieved in the twentieth century by the new electronic media, like the radio and television. These media had the possibility of reaching an immensely wider public than the readers of the printed encyclopaedias: they were therefore intensively used by governments and other educational agencies – especially in Europe in the first half of the century – with a view to implementing vast pedagogic programmes. In Britain, the British Broadcasting Company (BBC) had the mission of bringing 'into the greatest possible number of homes … all that is the best in every department of human knowledge, endeavour and achievement'.[9] In France, Italy and Germany, radio and later television programmes were broadcast by public service organisations whose objectives focused on education and the strengthening of a national cultural identity.

C. The 'Wikipedian' Model

It was, however, the advent of digitalisation that posed an apparently deadly challenge to printed encyclopaedias.

Electronic encyclopaedias appeared in the early 1990s: in the middle of the decade the market was already dominated by the Microsoft *Encarta* that was offered on a CD-ROM.[10] The new format had obvious advantages over paper publications: it allowed readers to spare space and offered rich multimedia contents like moving images and sounds. Readers had to pay a much lower cost to access a wider set of data: as a consequence, even the most prestigious works, such as the *Britannica*, suffered a dramatic drop in the number of copies sold worldwide.[11]

An even more radical change occurred with the advent of the worldwide web and of the digital media.

The 'internet revolution' in the world communication calls into question any encyclopaedic arrangement of knowledge. The digital ecosystem repudiates the ancient ideal of a circular knowledge synthesis, promoting in its place a 'network' model open to the development of potentially infinite interconnections. The internet is the environment in which this model has been established and evolved. This dimension is extremely complex and, despite being man-made, is such as to elude any attempt at systematic organisation. The web appears to be a new, enormous *ingens sylva*, such as that imagined by

[9] John Reith, Director General of the BBC (1927–38), quoted by A Briggs and P Burke, *A Social History of the Media from Gutenberg to the Internet* (Cambridge, Polity Press, 2009) 201.

[10] G Roncaglia ('Encyclopedias and encyclopedism in the era of the Web' (2021) 12 *JLIS.it, Italian Journal of Library and Information Science* 69, 71, available at: doi.org/10.4403/jlis.it-12757) distinguishes four main stages in the process of development of digital encyclopaedias: the age at the beginning of the 1980s of the first text-based online services such as Minitel, Prestel and CompuServe; the age of multimedia CD-ROMs, between the end of the 1980s and the end of the 1990s; the first generation of web encyclopaedias, that at the turn of the last millennium gradually replaced CD-ROMs: this period encompassed the emergence of *Wikipedia*; and the age of data-oriented, semantic-aware encyclopaedias: a development that is still ongoing.

[11] J Loveland, *The European Encyclopedia: From 1650 to the Twenty-First Century* (Cambridge, Cambridge University Press, 2019) 358.

Giovan Battista Vico,[12] which extends to the deep recesses of the web. The worldwide has been seen as a universal encyclopaedia taken to extremes:[13] in this new dimension, internet users' need to find data and information is primarily met by search engines, among which, as is well known, Google has assumed absolute primacy, thereby imposing a true global monopoly (at least in the Western world) in the field of information mediation. This has highlighted the problem of the transparency of search criteria, starting with the famous algorithms that determine the ranking of queries' outcomes.

One of the 'side effects' of these developments is the seemingly irreversible crisis of great traditional encyclopaedias. The symbolic date of this crisis is 13 March 2012, when the *Britannica* announced the end of its paper publications. Some encyclopaedias continued to be published online only, like the *Enciclopedia Treccani* and the *Britannica*: they still provide free access to high quality entries on a very wide number of subjects. Furthermore, some specialist encyclopaedias, like the Italian *Enciclopedia del diritto*, continue to be published on paper with regular updates of their entries.

In contrast, the crisis of the classical encyclopaedias has led to the emergence of a new encyclopaedic model based on radically different criteria from the traditional ones. I refer to the great success of *Wikipedia*, an online encyclopaedia continuously updated by users and available to date in 174 different languages.[14] *Wikipedia* is currently the seventh most visited website in the world:[15] millions of users use it every day to access quick information on the most diverse topics. The limits of this project are rather clear today, over 20 years after its launch: the progressive limitation of most of the contributors to a rather small 'Wikipedian club', the presence of a Western cultural bias even though *Wikipedia* is intended to be a source for people from all nations and cultures[16] and serious gender imbalances (only 19 per cent of people's voices relate to women).[17] There are also countless entries which, as expressly stated in the text, demonstrate inadequacies from the point of view of the reliability of the sources supporting the articles. Despite these problems, *Wikipedia* certainly represents a cognitive tool of the utmost interest having regard to the values of an epistemic 'participatory democracy' embodied by it. This model certainly poses a radical challenge to the traditional encyclopaedic scheme, particularly in two respects: the refusal of an authorial approach in favour of a bottom-up, spontaneous participation in the drafting of the texts; and the absence of any underlying hierarchical organisation in the selection and arrangements of the articles. *Wikipedia* has its strength in numbers as a product of collective intelligence, in which the abundance of editors

[12] GB Vico, *Scienza nuova*, in *Opere filosofiche* (Firenze, Sansoni, 1971).

[13] DR Headrick, *When Information Came of Age: Technologies of Knowledge in the Age of Reason and Revolution, 1700–1850* (Oxford, Oxford University Press, 2000) 172.

[14] On Wikipedia, see: A Lih, *The Wikipedia Revolution: How a Bunch of Nobodies Created the World's Greatest Encyclopedia* (New York, Hyperion, 2009); N Tkacs, *Wikipedia and the Politics of Openness* (Chicago, IL, University of Chicago Press, 2014); P Burke, *A Social History of Knowledge II: From the Encyclopédie to Wikipedia* (Cambridge, Polity Press, 2012); D Jemielniak, *Common Knowledge? An Ethnography of Wikipedia* (Stanford, CA, Stanford University Press, 2014); M Profitt (ed), *Leveraging Wikipedia, Connecting Communities of Knowledge* (Chicago, IL, ALA, 2018).

[15] Source: Similarweb, *Top Websites Ranking* (April 2023), available at: www.similarweb.com/top-websites/.

[16] C Hube, 'Bias in Wikipedia' in *Proceedings of the 26th International Conference on World Wide Web Companion (WWW '17 Companion)* (Geneva, International World Wide Web Conferences Steering Committee, 2017) 717, available at: doi.org/10.1145/3041021.3053375.

[17] *Wikipedia*, sv 'Gender bias on Wikipedia', available at: wikipedia.org/wiki/Gender_bias_on_Wikipedia.

allows errors to be promptly corrected. The collaborative method allows *Wikipedia* to reach a level of accurateness comparable to that of 'authorial' encyclopaedias, as a famous test conducted in 2005 by the journal *Nature* has shown.[18] Continuous controls by human editors and automatic systems (bots) protect the articles from acts of vandalism and contribute to maintaining the ideal of the neutral point of view (NPOV) proclaimed to be one of the founding principles of the enterprise.[19] Another clear advantage of *Wikipedia* vis-a-vis traditional encyclopaedias is the absence of limits of space which makes the work a continuously expanding universe, even canvassing items of popular culture or everyday news events.[20]

Despite all its innovations, it must be said that *Wikipedia* nevertheless remains explicitly anchored to the great encyclopaedic tradition. It rejects the idea of being an 'indiscriminate collection of information or a mere web directory'.[21] Its thousands of entries aim to serve an audience of readers who are looking for concise, updated and reliable information in the various fields of human knowledge.

The 'day after' *Wikipedia*, however, has already begun. The traditional concept of an encyclopaedia is likely to be replaced by new applications, relying on highly structured databases built on formal, rigorous ontologies (linked data). This development is the fundamental requirement of

> the transition from the web mainly oriented to consultation by human agents, to the 'semantic' web, which can also be used (and perhaps will mainly be used) by software agents, and in which the relationships between elements – and so, also among the entries of an encyclopedia – are explicit and in turn formalized.[22]

These innovations are already implemented in support of popular applications such as *Google Assistant*, *Amazon Alexa*, and *Siri*, which allow the users to formulate their questions in natural language. Through the use of artificial intelligence, these systems are able to improve the quality of their answers, learning from the feedback given by their users. These new developments combine user-friendly interfaces with complex systems of algorithms able to 'read' the content of every piece of information and the semantic relationship between the data.

As is well known, the latest and probably most disruptive innovations in this field are driven by generative artificial intelligence (AI) applications capable of generating original content based on training from massive AI models. The most popular of these new

[18] The test was conducted on a sample of 42 scientific entries taken from both *Wikipedia* and the *Encyclopaedia Britannica*. The selected entries were examined 'blindly' by a group of experts who did not identify any evident differences between the quality and reliability of the articles taken from *Wikipedia* and from the *Britannica* respectively.

[19] The five 'pillars' are described at *Wikipedia*, sv, 'Wikipedia: Five pillars', available at: en.wikipedia.org/wiki/Wikipedia:Five_pillars. Besides the NPOV, the other principles are: the encyclopaedic character of *Wikipedia*; the free content that anyone can use, edit and distribute; the editors' duty to treat each other with respect and civility; and the absence of rigid rules.

[20] This trend approximates *Wikipedia* to journalism: it must be said, however, that this practice is not welcomed by all the *Wikipedia* editors who are divided into groups of 'inclusionists' (more open to the coverage of trivia and the news) and 'deletionists' (who want to stick to the criterion of notability for the selection of the entries): see Loveland (n 11) 384.

[21] See 'Wikipedia: Five pillars' (n 19) fn 13.

[22] Roncaglia, 'Encyclopedias and encyclopedism in the era of the Web' (n 10) 84.

AI applications is OpenAI's *ChatGPT* (openai.com/blog/ chatgpt/) a conversational text-writing chatbot launched in November 2022.[23] Accessible via a free, intuitive, conversational web interface, *ChatGPT* 'can create new text or an essay on the fly in response to the user's prompts or questions. As a result, ChatGPT can revolutionize everything from writing and customer service to coding'.[24]

The opportunities offered, and the risks posed, by these new tools are at centre of a lively debate between academics,[25] politicians[26] and some of the top managers of the companies developing the new technologies.[27] Currently, the European institutions are considering a new regulatory framework that will establish obligations for providers and users depending on the level of risk posed by AI.[28] The final outcomes of the technological and regulatory developments in this field can hardly be foreseen. At the moment, perhaps the most interesting question posed by these innovations concerns their impact on human cognitive models. In the aftermath of the advent of the internet, some commentators maintained that the worldwide web promoted the rise of a 'new kind of mind that wants to and needs to take in and dole out information in short, disjointed, often overlapping bursts'.[29] According to this opinion, the information conveyed through the internet is inherently incompatible with complex content, and therefore poses serious constraints on our intellectual capacities. Others maintain, more persuasively, that digital content will not ultimately remain short, fragmented and granular. Rather, complexity, via the proper means, can also be reconstructed and communicated in the digital infosphere.[30]

II. Deconstruction of the Parliamentary Encyclopaedia

At present, the parliamentary encyclopaedia too is facing serious challenges. Parliamentary institutions are apparently experiencing a new crisis affecting their capacity to offer a politically meaningful synthesis of social pluralism. The cognitive role of parliaments in relation to politics is the subject of significant questioning. Traditional parliamentary

[23] M Harrison, 'ChatGPT's explosive popularity makes it the fastest-growing app in human history' (*The Byte*, 3 February 2023) 2, available at: futurism.com/the-byte/chatgpts-fastest-growing-app-human-history. Google is currently developing its own conversational Chatbox, named Bard.

[24] S Murugesan and A Cherukuri, 'The Rise of Generative Artificial Intelligence and Its Impact on Education: The Promises and Perils' (2023) 56(5) *Computer* 116, 117, available at:. www.computer.org/csdl/magazine/co/2023/05/10109305/1MET4MpWNZS.

[25] K Manheim and L Kaplan, 'Artificial Intelligence: Risks to Privacy and Democracy' (2019) 21 *Yale Journal of Law and Technology* 106; X Cheng, X Lin and XL Shen et al, 'The dark sides of AI' (2022) 32 *Electronic Markets* 11, available at: link.springer.com/article/10.1007/s12525-022-00531-5.

[26] See, eg, the report presented in June 2023 by the Tony Blair Institute for Global Change, *A New National Purpose: AI Promises a World-Leading Future of Britain* (June 2023), available at: www.institute.global/insights/politics-and-governance/new-national-purpose-ai-promises-world-leading-future-of-britain. The report maintains that the safe and successful development of artificial intelligence (AI) is 'a matter becoming so urgent and important that how we respond is more likely than anything else to determine Britain's future'.

[27] On 22 March 2023 more than 1,800 signatories – including Elon Musk, the cognitive scientist Gary Marcus and Apple co-founder Steve Wozniak – called for a six-month pause on the development of systems 'more powerful' than that of GPT-4. Engineers from Amazon, DeepMind, Google, Meta and Microsoft also lent their support: *Guardian* (1 April 2023).

[28] On 14 June 2023, the European Parliament adopted its negotiating position on the AI Act.

[29] N Carr, *The Shallows: What the Internet is Doing to Our Brains* (New York, Norton, 2011) 10.

[30] G Roncaglia, *L'età della frammentazione: Cultura del libro e scuola digitale* (Bari, Laterza, 2018) 12.

structures struggle to keep pace with the major transformations under way. Multiple and interlinked factors converge in deconstructing the traditional forms of parliamentarism. I try to briefly analyse here some of these phenomena.

A. Crisis of Institutional Representation

From the 1980s, political scientists observed the emergence of growing tensions between the party systems and value orientations in Western societies.[31] For some, these phenomena were the result of a shift from a class-based to a value-based political polarisation. In advanced industrial societies, the new polarisation cut across the conventional Left–Right axis and focused on a materialist–postmaterialist dimension. The issue-oriented cleavages generated new political movements centred on topics like women's empowerment, environment protection, the models of economic and social development.[32] The resulting stress on the traditional party systems produced increasing pressure towards political dealignment with a gradual decline in party loyalty and party identification. Today, over 40 years after these studies, the very possibility of analysing Western societies as being divided according to some comprehensive cleavages has become controversial. In the last decades, electors' behaviour has revealed a steady decline in the class and religious vote and the rise, instead, of a trend toward a rather oxymoronic 'individualisation of politics' resulting from the increasing heterogeneity of individual life and the fragmentation of the social structure.[33]

Political parties are in a significant crisis vis-a-vis these phenomena, at least if we look at the classical model of the party as a mass organisation, made up of ideologically homogeneous activists with pervasive territorial roots. Such a party no longer exists, apart from a few exceptions.[34] As a result, the parties did not disappear, but turned into much smaller organisations focusing essentially on two functions: participation in election campaigns, which have become 'permanent' and no longer limited to particular stages of political life; and presence and action in institutions, first and foremost legislative assemblies and executive bodies. To some extent, such development seems to lead to a return to the past: the progressive coincidence between the political party and its parliamentary projection, in the form of a political group.[35]

From the citizens' perspective, these phenomena result in growing mistrust regarding representative institutions. The representative image projected by parliaments is believed to resemble the political elite rather than social reality. This widespread belief leads to a

[31] M Kaase and H-D Klingemann, 'Social structure, value-orientations and party system' (1982) 10 *European Journal of Party Research* 367.

[32] R Inglehart, 'The Changing Structure of Political Cleavages in Western Society' in RJ Dalton, PA Beck and C Flanagan (eds), *Electoral Change in Advanced Industrial Democracies: Realignment or Dealignement?* (Princeton, NJ, Princeton University Press, 1984).

[33] P Mair, *Ruling the Void: The Hollowing of Western Democracy* (London, Verso, 2013).

[34] T Paguntke, 'Party Organizational Linkage: Parties without Firm Social Roots?' in KR Luther and F Mueller-Rommel (eds), *Political Parties in the New Europe: Political and Analytical Challenges* (Oxford, Oxford University Press, 2002).

[35] On these developments, see R Dalton and MP Wattenberg (eds), *Parties Without Partisans: Political Change in Advanced Industrial Democracies* (Oxford, Oxford University Press, 2002).

lack of confidence in the parliamentary institutions and their political mediation role. Mediation implies a certain degree of distance between the representatives and the represented: the digital age, however, seems to reject any idea of distance and to embrace the myths of immediacy and permanent connection.[36] As a consequence, and somehow paradoxically, mistrust affects the most open and transparent institutions, such as parliaments, which have the historical function of making political conflict public. Instead, more closed or monocratic institutions regularly gain a higher degree of public trust in opinion polls.[37]

Against this backdrop, unsurprisingly, a growing percentage of citizens are reluctant to identify themselves with any party organisation, with an increasing quota abstaining from the vote, an option that is particularly attractive for groups with fewer civic skills.[38]

Conversely, there is evidence of strong waves of political participation, especially in the form of protests, of a temporary nature in connection with particular events, such as the recent anti-vax movements or the various demonstrations following the Russian aggression against Ukraine. Mass anti-establishment revolts become increasingly frequent also in advanced democracies like France and Israel. In connection with these events in particular, individual leaders, proclaiming their distance from the political elite, raise 'representative claims' in defence of diffused interests that are allegedly ignored by the elective representative institutions. According to Michael Saward, these phenomena demonstrate that the representative function has not disappeared from our social horizon, but has instead become more 'nomadic' and ubiquitous, often displacing the institutionalised forms of political representation.[39] In contrast to the established forms of institutionalised political representation, Saward emphasises the *performative aspect* of representation, according to which the representative *creates* his constituency: 'political representation can be conceived as an ongoing funding, as the constitution of community'.[40]

In fact, the actual development of collective perceptions has gone even further, with individuals increasingly refusing *any kind of representation* and rejecting any possibility of recognising someone else's right to speak on their behalf. This new attitude is based on a somewhat paradoxical mass adherence to values of 'uniqueness' and 'specialness' that are carefully *curated* by individuals:[41] an attitude that is crucially fostered by the omnipresent

[36] Byung-Chul Han, *In the Swarm: Digital Prospects* (Cambridge, MA, MIT Press, 2017) 20 ff.

[37] On this 'confidence paradox', see G Rizzoni, 'How Can Parliaments Improve Citizens' Confidence in Legislation?' in M De Benedetto, N Lupo and N Rangone (eds), *The Crisis of Confidence in Legislation* (Baden Baden, Nomos, 2020) 232–33.

[38] AC Goldberg, 'The evolution of cleavage voting in four Western countries: Structural, behavioural or political dealignment?' (2020) 59 *European Journal of Political Research* 68, 72.

[39] M Saward, *The Representative Claim* (Oxford, Oxford University Press, 2010) 79–81.

[40] NL Schwartz, *The Blue Guitar* (Chicago, IL, University of Chicago Press, 1988) 127, quoted by Saward, ibid, 53.

[41] A Reckwitz, *Die Gesellschaft der Singularitäten. Zum Strukturwandel der Moderne* (Berlin, Suhrkamp, 2017); English translation, *The Society of Singularities* (Cambridge, Polity Press, 2020). On these phenomena, see also D Martuccelli, *La societé singulariste* (Paris, Colin, 2010). Whereas Reckwitz adopts a cultural critic approach that emphasises the role of contemporary industrial production and of communication technologies in imposing the individualisation processes, Martuccelli offers a more positive reading that interprets singularism as an ubiquitous phenomenon that simultaneously invests the economy, the institutions and private life. The French sociologist maintains that, to be fully understood, the heuristic hypothesis of singularism must be distinguished from Tocqueville's diagnosis of individualism. In individualism, the link between the individual and the collective is essentially political and based on the emergence of new core values: equality and autonomy. The diagnosis of singularism is based on a shift from the central value of equality to that of singularity, which emphasises how individuals

social media.[42] Late modernity has turned out to be a culture of the *authentic* that defies the translation of individual ideas and values into collective narratives. Apparently in countertendency with a world that is increasingly globalised and interdependent, it is only by reference to our own experiences that social ties make – or do not make – sense. Moreover, the institutional response to social needs – in such crucial domains as healthcare and education – adapts to these new demands with an increasing individualisation of the services that tend to be provided in the form of 'listening'.[43] This approach is consistent with an institutional setting that claims to valorise individual opinions in the context of participative democracy: the expansion of singularity strengthens the assumption that every individual has something original to say, even vis-a-vis the experts.[44]

B. Transformations of the Public Sphere

In the mid-1990s, Bernard Manin observed that representative democracy had entered a new phase: that of 'audience democracy'.[45] This configuration differs significantly from 'party democracy', which had dominated during the twentieth century. The main features of audience democracy are the personalisation of political leadership, the volatility of the voters' preferences that tend to respond differently to particular terms offered at each election, and the rise of a new elite which is present in both the media system and in the representative institutions. The 'image' of political leaders has assumed a crucial role, replacing the traditional party platforms: elections are more likely to be decided on the basis of the leaders' capacity to inspire trust in the electors, than on rational consensus reached on a set of measures to be implemented once in office.[46] Manin describes this new development in the context of the communicative environment of the 1990s, still dominated by the television and the press. Against this background, Manin's discussion is based on two fundamental assumptions: (a) the public has an essentially passive attitude vis-a-vis the mass media, in the sense that they are recipients of messages broadcast from above; and (b) the media system enjoys relative autonomy from the political sphere, in the sense that it is not structurally linked to parties that compete for votes. On the basis of the latter assumption, Manin maintains that, in this new age, the perception of public issues is more homogenous and less dependent on partisan preferences. The political neutralisation of the channels of communication through which the public is informed favours the emergence of an educated and interested electorate:

> [D]iscussion of specific issues is no longer confined to parliament (as in parliamentarianism), or to consultation committees between parties (as in party democracy); it takes place within the

perceive themselves as being different from their peers. Taking note of this change, however, Martuccelli admits that *even singularism must recognise a common horizon from which the individual can be defined as singular*. On the idea of the 'individualism of singularity', see also P Rosanvallon, *La Societé des égaux* (Paris, Seuil, 2011).

[42] Reckwitz, *The Society of Singularities* (n 41) 3.

[43] Martuccelli (n 41) 12.

[44] ibid, 22. On the importance of a 'listening' approach to democracy, see A Dobson, *Listening for Democracy: Recognition, Representation, Reconciliation* (Oxford, Oxford University Press, 2014).

[45] B Manin, *The Principles of Representative Government* (Cambridge, Cambridge University Press, 1997).

[46] ibid, 226.

> public. Thus the form of representative government that is emerging today is characterized by a new protagonist of public discussion, the floating voter, and a new forum, the communication media.[47]

In the two decades since the publication of Manin's book, some of the conditions assumed by his analysis have dramatically changed.

As we have already seen in connection with the decline of traditional encyclopaedias, the advent of the internet has introduced a global communicative platform that favours the convergence of multiple media into a single and pervasive 'infosphere'.[48] The new platform makes an incredible amount of information, provided in different formats (texts, images, sounds, videos etc), easily accessible. It also makes it possible for the users to produce and exchange any piece of information: the boundaries between the producers and the users of the media are fading away.

However, far from creating a common basis for public debate, the new infosphere seems to foster the segmentation of the public into a variety of 'echo-chambers' that tend to reinforce homogeneity exclusively within communities of like-minded people. The creation of 'gated communities', made possible by the extensive use of social media, risks promoting self-insulation with the result that falsehoods are spread, and polarisation and fragmentation are encouraged.[49] Conversely, the traditional mass media, even in established democracies, have often adopted overtly partisan stances, as was demonstrated by some US major TV networks. The 'mediatisation'[50] of the political process is more advanced than ever with political actors having to 'increasingly adapt to media demands, media logics and media perspectives on politics itself'.[51] This process is promoted by converging trends according to which, on the one hand, political leaders tend to circumvent mainstream media via channels of more direct contact with the voters, while on the other hand, citizens are no longer mere recipients of messages but have become active communicators themselves via different social media channels. As a result of these developments,

> the political communication system seems more fragmented than in the past, more centrifugal than centripetal, shot through with multiple communication outlets, multiple voices, and multiple issue agendas all cycled (thanks especially to the ever-changing role of the news values) and scene shifted swiftly from one short time period to the next.[52]

[47] ibid, 232. The same development is viewed by Nadia Urbinati as evidence of the 'plebiscitarian turn' taken by the audience democracy. According to Urbinati, the plebiscitarian nature of the audience democracy derives from the collapse of the distinction between the private individual and the citizen. The plebiscitarian project assumes members of the public to be passive subjects and rejects the idea of popular participation as an active and autonomous decision-making force. Such change leads to a 'disfiguration' of the traditional system of representative democracy. See N Urbinati, *Democracy Disfigured: Opinion, Truth, and the People* (Cambridge, MA, Harvard University Press, 2014).

[48] On this concept, see L Floridi, *The Fourth Revolution: How the Infosphere is Reshaping Human Reality* (Oxford, Oxford University Press, 2014).

[49] C Sunstein, *Republic Divided. Divided Democracy in an Age of Social Media* (Princeton, NJ, Princeton University Press, 2017) 5.

[50] Mazzoleni and Schulz distinguish between 'mediation' and 'mediatization', where the former means the transmission of messages through media technologies, whereas the latter describes a much more complex situation in which political institutions are 'increasingly dependent and shaped by the media': G Mazzoleni and W Schulz, 'Mediatization of Politics: A Challenge for Democracy?' (1999) 16 *Political Communication* 247.

[51] JG Blumer, 'In Praise of Holistic Empiricism' in K Brants and K Voltmer (eds), *Political Communication in Postmodern Democracy: Challenging the Primacy of Politics* (New York, Palgrave Macmillan, 2011) II.

[52] ibid, IV.

C. The New Formats of Public Policies

The cognitive system developed by parliaments during the course of the twentieth century appears to be increasingly incapable of framing and effectively processing the new public policies. As we have seen, basically, the traditional parliamentary categories were structured on the intersection between the political grid of the party groups and the expert machinery of the sectorial committees. The committees controlled their legislative domain thanks to a strong vertical integration with the ministerial departments. Moreover, the territorial dimension of the public policies generated by this machinery was typically the national state. With the exception of the polities originally shaped according to a federal arrangement, this gave considerable power to a hierarchical administrative structure controlled by central government. The centralised national state was therefore the ideal environment in which modern parliaments played an active role in managing important aspects of major public policies. These basic assumptions faced a gradual but radical change from the mid-twentieth century.

Since the 1970s subnational and supranational entities have been acquiring increasing power in the shaping of public policies.

On the one hand, decentralisation, in its various forms, has emerged as a powerful transforming factor even in states with a consolidated centralistic structure. Different and often interconnected factors underpin this trend. The phenomenon of social autonomisation that we have seen emerging in Western society is perhaps the most powerful propellant for this development, provided that 'the essence of federalism lies not in the institutional or constitutional structure, but in society itself. Federal government is a device by which the federal qualities of the society are articulated and protected'.[53] The expansion of self-government schemes (regionalism, quasi-federal arrangements, fully-fledged federations) is consistent with the pressure for an ever more advanced social differentiation.

On the other hand, the size of the major political issues of our age (like environmental protection, cybersecurity, immigration) promotes the growing role of supranational institutions in setting standards and directives for coordinated public intervention.

In this respect, the European Union must of course be mentioned first. The Member States retain the competence to implement EU policies, but their margin of choice is often rather limited: the reform policies of each country often appear to be 'dictated' by Brussels through monitoring and verification mechanisms that have been strengthened over the years.[54] Europeanisation of domestic policies is, however, a phenomenon that extends beyond the mere implementation of EU policies at a national level: it is a much more complex process that encompasses the

> a) construction; b) diffusion; and c) institutionalization of formal and informal rules, procedures, policy paradigms, styles, 'ways of doing things', and shared beliefs and norms which are first

[53] WA Livingston, 'A Note on the Nature of Federalism' (1952) 67 *Political Science Quarterly* 81, 84, quoted by F Palermo and K Kössler, *Comparative Federalism: Constitutional Arrangements and Case Law* (Oxford, Hart Publishing, 2017).

[54] The European Semester mechanism has placed national fiscal policies under close European surveillance. More recently, the Next Generation EU programme, developed in the wake of the pandemic crisis, provided that the beneficiary states of the programme must comply with a clear roadmap for the implementation of the objectives financed by European resources.

> defined and consolidated in the making of EU policy and politics and then incorporated in the logic of domestic discourse, identities, political structures, and public policies.[55]

These phenomena affect the political systems of the Member States, undermining the salience of the traditional internal political divisions of each country. This trend is imposing itself while the European Union as a political entity seems unable to provide true European political parties capable of mobilising public opinion on a continental scale. Political systems are still modelled on strictly national formats, although a transnational confrontation between pro-European and Eurosceptic, or openly anti-European, parties has begun to emerge. The effect of these developments is a situation in which the European Union offers an example of 'split-level democracy', in which 'policies are without politics', whereas the national states remain dominated by 'politics without policies'.[56] The lack of coordination in European policies with the formats of the national political debate is a further manifestation of the 'democratic disconnect' that affects the European polity.[57] At a national level, this development leads to a crisis of the majority–opposition divide, since any real alternative to the major public policies seems to be pre-empted by the pervasiveness of EU policies.[58] In contrast, the European Union as a political system – dominated by a kind of permanent grand coalition – seems impervious to the emergence of an institutionalised opposition.[59]

The European policies challenge the traditional, state-centred policymaking process on the basis of another crucial aspect: the frequent, systematic involvement of regional and local authorities. The latter are required to implement European targets in some critical fields, like sustainable development or cohesion policies.[60] Local authorities are increasingly involved (often together with private actors) in different forms of strategic partnerships aimed at coordinating the different levels of government.[61] As a 'compound democracy', the European Union is characterised by a highly dispersed decision-making process, since 'the loci where decisions are taken are a multitude, with each institution multiplying at its own

[55] CM Radaelli, 'The Europeanization of Public Policies' in K Featherstone and CM Radaelli (eds), *The Politics of Europeanization* (Oxford, Oxford University Press, 2003) 30.

[56] VA Schmidt, *Democracy in Europe: The EU and National Polities* (Oxford, Oxford University Press, 2006) 223.

[57] R Bellamy and S Kröger, 'The politicization of European integration: National parliaments and the democratic disconnect' (2016) 14 *Comparative European Politics* 125.

[58] We have seen that the divide between majority and opposition in parliamentary systems is not only an inherent feature of parliamentary government, but also offers a fundamental cognitive key to understanding the principle of political accountability. Through this divide, the parliament produces politically qualified information on the fundamental choices of each country's policy. However, this political and conceptual divide between majority and opposition also seems to be declining in contemporary democracies. At the beginning of the 1950s, Otto Kirchheimer had already observed ('The Waning of Opposition in Parliamentary Regimes' (1957) 24 *Social Research* 127) the phenomenon of the 'waning political opposition': this trend stemmed from the same political programme underpinning the construction of welfare states, aimed at overcoming class conflict and fostering convergence of society towards the centre.

[59] G Rizzoni, *Opposizione parlamentare e democrazia deliberativa: Ordinamenti europei a confronto* (Bologna, il Mulino, 2012) 307–12; C Rauh and P de Wilde Pieter, 'The opposition deficit in EU accountability: Evidence from over 20 years of plenary debate in four member states' (2017) 57 *European Journal of Political Research* 194.

[60] E Domorenok, *Governing Sustainability in the EU: From Political Discourse to Policy Practices* (Abingdon, Routledge, 2019).

[61] P Glasbergen, F Biermann and A Mol (eds), *Partnerships, Governance, and Sustainable Development* (Cheltenham, Edward Elgar, 2007).

turn the locus within itself'.[62] The inherently multilevel structure of the European policy-making environment creates obvious asymmetries between national executives and 'their' parliaments. On the one hand, governments are directly involved in EU decision-making through their presence in the Council. On the other hand, they have privileged channels of dialogue and negotiation with the country's regional and local authorities. Systematic reforms have been introduced – especially with the Lisbon Treaty – to enhance the participation of national parliaments in the European decision-making process.[63] Until now, the results of these institutional changes have, however, been rather mixed.[64]

Moreover, it is the very concept of sectorial public policies which has been radically destabilised by the supranational public policies that tend to take on new formats, focused on the definition of broad intervention programmes linking a multitude of sectors in broad 'encyclopaedic' syntheses.

The European Union is also at the forefront in this respect. A recent macro-example is offered by the programmes of action developed by the launch in 2020 of the Next Generation EU Strategy that provides the financial framework for the policies to be adopted by the Member States for the purpose of overcoming the economic crisis caused by the Covid-19 pandemic. The EU Plan sets out a few broad objectives (green transition, digital transition, equity and social and territorial cohesion, macroeconomic stability) that must be implemented through the Member States' national plans. The whole policy and decision-making process (and its implementation) will be submitted to a periodic review that involves the Member States' governments and the EU Commission.

At a global level, the same trend can be identified with reference to the shaping of 'global public policies' intended to protect and develop 'public goods'[65] like human health, the fight against poverty, and the reduction of the emissions driving climate change. According to a broad international consensus, these targets can only be achieved through transnational coordinated efforts encompassing a panoply of measures across different sectors. Organisations like the United Nations (UN), the World Bank and the UN Development Programme have consequently promoted global international agreements intended to engage national states in long term policy programmes.

The most comprehensive example of this approach is the Agenda for Sustainable Development, approved by the UNs General Assembly in 2015. The Agenda defines the broad lines of public policy action, which commit all acceding states to reach 17 objectives, which in turn are divided into 169 sub-targets, by 2030.[66] The novelty of the Agenda is

[62] S Fabbrini, *Compound Democracies: Why the United States and Europe are Becoming Similar* (Oxford, Oxford University Press, 2007) 271.

[63] The Lisbon Treaty not only explicitly mentions the role of national parliaments (Art 12 TEU regarding the 'Provisions on Democratic Principles' of the Union), but it also gives national parliaments information rights with respect to the draft legislative acts and other policy documents of the Commission (see the Protocol on the role of national parliaments in the European Union), as well as a role within the EU's legislative process, in particular through the subsidiarity control procedure (see the Protocol on the application of the principles of subsidiarity and proportionality).

[64] For an assessment, see K Auel and T Christiansen (eds), 'After Lisbon: National Parliaments in the European Union (2015) 38 *West European Politics* 261.

[65] On the nature of the 'global public goods', see I Kaul, I Grunberg and MA Stern (eds), *Global Public Goods: International Cooperation for the 21st Century* (New York, Oxford University Press, 1999).

[66] See United Nations, Resolution adopted by the General Assembly on 25 September 2015. Transforming our world: the 2030 Agenda for Sustainable Development, available at: www.un.org/ga/search/view_doc.asp?symbol=A/RES/70/1&Lang=E.

represented by the fact that it binds both developed and developing countries in a multilateral effort that sets a variety of ambitious goals, from gender equality to creating decent work for all, from the reduction of inequality to the promotion of responsible consumption and production. For its amplitude and ambition, the Agenda has been criticised as being a 'fairy tale' devoid of any binding effect on the actions of the states.[67] Against this criticism, it has been correctly observed that the 2030 Agenda provides a global platform for comparing the capacity of national policies to achieve some basic public goals. Critical to the success of this effort are the interlinkages 'across sectors (eg, finance, energy, technology and transport); across societal actors (local authorities, government agencies, private sector, and civil society); and between and among low, medium, and high income countries',[68] as well the definition of clear parameters and indicators capable of measuring the outcome of the policies implemented at national level.

A more advanced example of a global policy platform originates from the UN Framework Convention on Climate Change, which entered into force on 21 March 1994. Under the Framework created by the Convention, in 2015, 196 states signed the Paris Agreement as a legally binding international treaty on climate change with the purpose of limiting global warming to well below 2, preferably to 1.5, degrees celsius, compared to pre-industrial levels.[69] The Paris Agreement requires each party to prepare, communicate and maintain the successive nationally determined contributions (NDCs) that it intends to achieve. An annual Conference of the Parts (COP) is regularly held in order to review the implementation of the Convention and to take the decisions needed to promote the goals envisaged by the Agreement. The measures taken by the states thus far affect multiple sectors, like energy production, public transportation, housing etc, but a growing role is also played by non-state actors, by civil society, industry and other international and national players.[70]

The three global policy platforms mentioned above have the following characteristics in common: (a) being mutually interconnected (the climate change agreements can in fact be viewed as a section of the 2030 UN Agenda for Sustainable Development, whereas one of the main political objectives of the Next Generation EU Plan is to position the European Union as a global front-runner in the implementation of the Sustainable Development Goals (SDGs); (b) engaging multiple policy sectors and state and non-state agencies in the pursuit of a few comprehensive goals; and (c) being oriented towards the future on a long-term basis. Having regard to these features, they can be viewed as components of a 'world encyclopaedia' of public global policies, whose importance should be appreciated, not only for its binding effect on state policymaking, but for its cognitive value as a standard setting factor at an international level. The new encyclopaedia is built on the basis of four fundamental assumptions: (a) the key political questions of our age can be addressed only by overcoming

[67] R Horton, 'Offline: why the Sustainable Development Goals will fail' (2015) *Lancet* 383(9936).

[68] M Stafford-Smith, D Griggs, O Gaffney et al, 'Integration: The key to implementing the Sustainable Development Goals' (2017) 12 *Sustainable Science* 911, 913.

[69] For more details, see the website of the Secretariat of the United Nations Framework Convention on Climate Change (UNFCCC), available at: unfccc.int.

[70] On the role of non-state actors for the implementation of the Paris agreement, see P Pattberg, C Kaiser, O Widerberg et al, '20 Years of global climate change governance research: Taking stock and moving forward' (2022) 22 *International Environmental Agreements* 295.

the fragmentation of the sectorial policies with the adoption of a holistic approach; (b) such an approach can only be implemented by turning fragmentation into complexity; (c) scientific evidence should play a central role in shaping public policy; and (d) it is equally important to generate visions and imagined futures capable of giving a real transformative value to political action. In other words, world politics, including the collective actions regarding sustainability and climate change, is best addressed 'as a complex system, with open boundaries, emergent properties, and self-organizing adaptive behaviour'.[71]

D. The Crisis of Legislative Rationality

The rationality of parliamentary legislation is profoundly challenged by these developments. The role of legislatures as authoritative sources of statutory law is called into question, with the effect of undermining the confidence in traditional forms of legislation as coherent and effective tools for addressing societal problems.[72] Executives exert a growing control over legislative production, the content of which often risks being de facto captured by ministerial bureaucracies.[73] The parliamentary legislation assumes an increasingly limited and partial role within the system of legal sources, facing competition from the rules of supranational authorities, territorial self-government, or independent regulatory authorities.[74] Above all, legislation appears to be less and less capable of producing an effective political synthesis of social interests: it intersects only some segments of the more complex decision-making processes to which we have referred in the previous section. At the same time, the phenomenon of legislative inflation[75] goes hand-in-hand with a decline in the quality of legislative production.[76] The grand plans of rationalising legislation, which have accompanied modernity, are in crisis: we live in the 'age of de-codification', with the emergence of autonomous regulatory systems focused on particular areas of legislation.[77] Emergency situations involving governments and parliaments play an important role in feeding these phenomena. Recent cases of financial crises, the Covid-19 pandemic, and the war in Ukraine are just a few examples of how dramatic, unforeseen situations are forcing exceptional interventions that are disruptive for the political agenda. Paradoxically, while major political problems increasingly appear to assume a systemic and cross-sectoral character, parliamentary legislation seems to have become more fragmented and disorderly.

[71] A Orsini, P Le Prestre, PM Haas, M Brosig, et al, 'Forum: Complex systems and international governance' (2020) 22(4) *International Studies Review* 1008.

[72] M De Benedetto, N Lupo and N Rangone (eds), *The Crisis of Confidence in Legislation* (Baden Baden, Nomos, 2020).

[73] 'In parliamentary democracies, governments usually propose at least 70 percent of the legislative agenda, and roughly 80 percent of what they propose is actually adopted': SM Saiegh, 'Lawmaking' in S Martin, T Saalfeld and KW Strom (eds), *The Oxford Handbook of Legislative Studies* (Oxford, Oxford University Press, 2014) 484.

[74] U Karpen, 'Gesetzgebung in Rechtsvergleich' in W Kluht and G Krings (eds), *Gesetzgebung: Rechtsetzung durch Parlamente und Verwaltungen sowie ihre gerichtliche Kontrolle* (Heidelberg, Müller, 2014) 188.

[75] On the phenomenon of legislative inflation, see J-P Camby, *La loi* (Issy-les-Moulineaux, LGDJ, 2015) 108–13 (with data regarding France).

[76] 'The law has become, in fact, a rite like an incantation, overloaded with details, often imprecise, which beats around the bush … and is, therefore, ineffective': Pierre Mazeaud, former President of the Constitutional Council of France, quoted by B Mathieu, *La loi* (Paris, Dalloz, 2010) 61.

[77] N Irti, *L'età della decodificazione* (Milano, Giuffré, 1989).

III. 'Resistance' (and Resilience) of the Parliamentary Encyclopaedia

How has the twentieth century parliamentary encyclopaedia reacted to these developments?

It appears that parliaments have thus far adopted a rather conservative approach and have chosen to stick to the traditional structures based on the intersection between party groups and sectorial committees. However, many legislatures around the world have promoted interesting innovations that have pervaded the three domains we have considered in the previous section: the structural components of political representation; the relationship with the public sphere; and the capacity to influence and shape the new public policies. This section is devoted to a brief overview of the most promising initiatives taken in these three sectors.

A. Parliamentary Representation between Conservation and Innovation

The conservative stance adopted by most legislatures applies, first, to the 'political encyclopaedia' of parliamentary groups, which still remains firmly a criterion for organising legislative assemblies. The traditional structural difference between the 'Westminster model' (based on the parliamentary party) and the 'continental' model (based on political groups) continues to mark a clear divide among legislatures. Both models, however, tend to structure the parliamentary assembly in a way that allows it to reflect the relative strength of the parties that have participated in the elections. Similar considerations can be made about the majority–opposition divide that remains a fundamental structural distinction in most parliamentary systems. In some cases, the majority–opposition divide can affect the geography of the parliamentary groups in order to take electoral coalitions into account. A recent example is offered by France, where, in May 2022, the coalition of four left-wing parties (Nouvelle Union populaire, écologique et sociale – Nupes) announced – in preparation for the legislative elections – that, in the event of victory, the parliamentary majority would comprise different political groups united in an 'intergroup', as a platform for debate and permanent coordination between the groups participating in the coalition. After the election, the intergroup met in order to select common candidates for the positions of President of the National Assembly, President of the Finance Committee, and the components of the assembly Bureau.[78] A similar initiative was taken some years ago by the opposition groups in the Italian Parliament.[79]

Another form of 'intergroups' are the thematic groups constituted on a voluntary basis in some parliaments by members with different party affiliations, who are interested in

[78] Julie Carriat and Mariama Darame, 'A l'Assemblée nationale, la Nupes à l'épreuve de la lutte des places' *Le Monde* (30 June 2022), available at: www.lemonde.fr/politique/article/2022/06/30/a-l-assemblee-nationale-la-nupes-a-l-epreuve-de-la-lutte-des-places_6132633_823448.html.

[79] On this experience, see G Rizzoni; 'Un nuovo tentativo di "stabilizzazione dell'opposizione": lo statuto della coalizione parlamentare dell'Ulivo' (2003) Associazionedeicostituzionalisti.it, available at: www.associazionedeicostituzionalisti.it/old_sites/sito_AIC_2003-2010/dibattiti/partiti/rizzoni-20030207.html.

promoting informal exchange and public debate on some specific topics. The European Parliament has the most formalised discipline of these groups:[80] currently it has 27 intergroups focused on a wide variety of fields (for instance, disability, anti-corruption, and LGBT rights). This practice is well established in other parliaments, as in the French National Assembly and the Italian Chamber of Deputies, where, however, intergroups remain purely informal, without any recognition by the parliamentary standing rules.[81] Another kind of intergroup that is widespread in many parliaments is the friendship group, formed with the parliaments of other countries.

These partial deviations, however, do not destabilise the backbone of the political geography in parliaments, which remains fundamentally based on the party groups. In a sense, today this articulation seems more democratically necessitated than in the past. The trend towards the coincidence between the political party and its parliamentary projection, mentioned earlier, makes parliaments crucial catalysts for political representation, in the sense of being the places where representation takes concrete shape. This development increases the cognitive value of parliamentary representation, especially in our age when political public debate has become monopolised by communication and entertainment and the public sphere is infinitely fragmented and dispersed. The anchoring of political debate to the parliamentary dimension, where power relations are measured through interactions between the different political groups, seems as necessary as before in order to render politics understandable and accountable:

> [F]aced with the disintegration of the represented, parliament is one of the few places where one can try to restore coherence and unity to a pluralism that is enormously disjointed. Representation, in other words, appears still today an essential tool for giving a *political form* to civil society.[82]

It is clear, however, that parliaments cannot simply stick to the representative model developed during previous centuries. Political representation is, per se, something that requires continuous adaptation and innovation in order to preserve the capacity to give political form to social pluralism. As mentioned above, Michael Saward has emphasised the dynamic and even 'creative'

[80] See the rules adopted by the Conference of Presidents on 16 December 1999 (last updated on 11 September 2014), according to which intergroups are not parliamentary bodies and therefore may not express Parliament's opinion. However, technical facilities, conference rooms and interpretation services are made available for the intergroups' activities.

[81] On the intergroups in the French National assembly, see J-M Pontier, 'Le rôle des intergroupes au Parlement français' (1982) 32 *Revue française de science politique* 810: the author emphasises that the practice of the intergroups dates back to the early twentieth century and has sometimes triggered critical evaluations of the possible ties between the deputies and extra-parliamentary pressure groups interested in promoting specific public policies. For this reason – and in order to comply with art 23 of the Assembly standing rules, which forbids 'the formation of special, local or professional interest groups, entailing acceptance by their members of a mandatory mandate', as well as 'the meeting within the Palace of permanent groups … aimed at the defence of the same interests' – the current practice of the national assembly encourages the formation of 'study groups' composed of deputies from different parties and aimed at studying and debating subjects of common interest. The formation of a study group is submitted for authorisation by the Bureau that grants some logistical support to the group's operation. In the 14th (2012–17) and 15th (2017–22) legislatures, over 100 study groups were formed on a variety of subjects (tourism, regional languages, prisons, animal protection etc): see, 'Les groupes d'étude' in the National Assembly website, available at: www2.assemblee-nationale.fr/16/les-groupes-d-etudes.

[82] M Luciani, 'Il Parlamento negli anni Novanta' in L Violante (ed), *Storia d'Italia: Annali 17. Il Parlamento* (Torino, Einaudi, 2001) 423. Luciani maintains that the real origins of this crisis should be traced in a 'crisis of the represented' and in the vanishing of the collective identities (that, in turn, reflects the crisis of individual identities as consequence of the decline of social roles).

aspect of representation, not to be limited exclusively to the institutional sphere. Conversely, contemporary political theory has shown that, within the institutions themselves, their 'instituting' aspect should be reassessed as a factor for change and shaping political conflict. I shall return to this point in the final part of this volume. For several legislatures, actions meant to open parliaments to citizens, with the introduction of participative and deliberative procedures, have been the most promising responses to the legitimisation crisis of parliamentary representation. In international comparisons, public engagement is seen as key to overcoming the disconnect between the people and parliaments.[83] The use of digital innovation is considered crucial in this respect. In the following sections, I discuss some of the projects implemented in this field.

B. Public Engagement: A Panacea for Delegitimisation?

'Public engagement' has become a buzzword for different actions, within a wide range of options that extends from simply providing information, to introducing procedures allowing citizens to have a direct role in institutional decision-making.[84] In this context, contemporary parliaments are today engaged in finding the best combination of informing, educating, consulting and participative procedures. To be successful, public engagement should satisfy some key conditions: it should not limit itself to a 'broadcast' mode, but should promote an interactive relationship between citizens and parliament; it should be integrated within the ordinary parliamentary functions and connected with core parliamentary business; and it should make clear the expected effects of the public's involvement from the very outset of the process.[85] This last point is crucial: the benefits expected to derive from public engagement actions should be evaluated with a realistic lens. Moreover, public engagement can hardly be seen as a panacea for the legitimisation crisis of parliamentary representation. The number of citizens normally involved in these initiatives remains limited and is often affected by self-selection phenomena. The interactions of different democratic forms (deliberative, participative, representative) can be problematic. Without properly being inserted into the complex parliamentary ecosystem 'by design', participative procedures risk disrupting parliamentary deliberation, with the effect of increasing, rather than diminishing, the delegitimisation of the institution.[86] Public engagement procedures,

[83] See Inter-Parliamentary Union (IPU) and United Nations Development Programme (UNDP), *Global Parliamentary Report 2022. Public engagement in the work of parliament* (Geneva, IPU, 2022). The report (at 7) 'recognizes that parliaments have a vital role to play in addressing the challenges of today's rapidly changing world, by enabling people to connect with and participate in the law-making, policy formulation and oversight processes that impact their lives now and into the future'. 'Effective engagement can help avoid a disconnect between elected representatives and the public they serve. It can show the community it is being listened to and heard, countering rising public distrust and negativity … it supports parliament's main functions by giving access to the breadth and depth of information and ideas that are needed for representation, law-making, public policy formulation and oversight that meet people's expectations and aspirations'.

[84] C Leston-Bandeira and A Walker, 'Parliament and Public Engagement' in C Leston-Bandeira and L Thomson (eds), *Exploring Parliament* (Oxford, Oxford University Press, 2018).

[85] ibid, 310–11.

[86] eg, with regard to the impact of e-petitions, a recent survey conducted among British MPs has revealed a 'degree of apathy – occasionally outright antipathy – on the part of parliament's political elites' towards this tool; 'MPs have welcomed e-petitions for providing additional information about constituents' concerns and have used e-petitions as a way of leveraging these concerns from within Parliament, particularly via petition debates. However, the research demonstrates that traditional forms of constituent-to-Member engagement remain regarded as the most

however, can be extremely useful for expanding the informative basis of parliaments. They usually allow participants to share not only their preferences, but their knowledge, with the effect of revealing the knowledge implicitly held by the people. This appears to be a very important feature in an age in which there is a growing reaction against 'expertocracy': an attitude that reveals a social demand for finding new ways of combining specialised knowledge with common sense. Parliamentary decision-making should include due consideration given to the common knowledge of ordinary people through inclusive and creative procedures, for example via outreach actions ('the parliament should go to where people are') and listening sessions capable of making legislative assemblies operate as '*le parlament des invisibles*'.[87]

Parliamentarians cannot today claim to hold the absolute representative presumption enjoyed in the past by their nineteenth-century colleagues. As we have seen, that presumption was based on a 'closed' representative paradigm, according to which MPs (or in the twentieth century, the political parties) were assumed to interpret the citizens' will in the name of the national interest or of holistic ideologies. A new paradigm is needed in order to preserve democracy in the face of the above-mentioned phenomena of singularisation of individual identities that push for adequate political recognition. This implies the abandonment of the traditional closed and self-sufficient model of political representation, in order to open up the parliamentary encyclopaedic framework to the participation not only of experts, but of ordinary citizens.[88] In this field, there are parliaments with very interesting experiences: some of them are focused on the revaluation and updating of traditional tools, like petitions, while some others have launched new forms of interaction between parliament and citizens, through consultative or deliberative processes. In the following sections I analyse some of these experiences.

i. E-Petitions

The right to petition has a long institutional history that dates back to the Middle Ages, when it was one of the first rights to be formally recognised in constitutional documents. Before being presented to the parliament, petitions were presented directly to the monarch by people from levels of society seeking redress, mercy or advancement. As the only acceptable way to address the authorities, 'it was a crucial mode of communication between the "rulers" and the 'ruled"'.[89] In England, by the fifteenth century most petitions were directed

effective means for constituents to have their concerns heard. Because of this, there are significant concerns that e-petitions foster unrealistic expectations of policy change risks exacerbating, rather than ameliorating, public distrust and democratic disengagement. Finally, the research findings temper the optimism often associated with such initiatives, with important concerns expressed regarding the quality of democratic engagement and of the capacity of parliamentary e-petitions to provide a voice for the less vocal and more marginalised groups in society': F Matthews, 'The value of "between-election" political participation: Do parliamentary e-petitions matter to political elites?' (2021) 2 *British Journal of Politics and International Relations* 425.

[87] P Rosanvallon, *Le Parlement des invisibles: Déchiffrer la France* (éd augmentée et mise à jour, Paris, Seuil, 2020).

[88] On these developments, see R Rubio and R Vela, 'Open Parliaments around the World. Open Parliaments Tools in Comparative Perspective' (2019) 49 Luiss School of Government Working Papers, available at: sog.luiss.it/sites/sog.luiss.it/files/WP%2049%20Rubio-Vela.pdf.

[89] 'The Power of Petitioning in Seventeenth-Century England', website of the British Arts and Humanities Research Council that examines petitioning systematically at all levels of English government over the whole century, available at: petitioning.history.ac.uk/. See the English Petition of Rights (1628) and the Bill of Rights (1689), which explicitly protected the right to petition.

to Parliament, and they became important drivers for the legitimisation of Parliament as a representative institution. In nineteenth-century parliamentarism, the right to petition was widely recognised, even with differences deriving from the cultural and constitutional features of each country. One important role played by petitions was connected with the integration of the disenfranchised into the political system, since in some countries, like the United Kingdom, even those citizens who did not have the right to vote, could present petitions. The history of petitioning also shows that 'it performs an important role of mobilisation, as illustrated by the very large 19th century petitions, such as the Chartists petitions which gathered millions of signatures'.[90] In the twentieth century, the importance of petitions declined, in parallel with the progressive enfranchisement of the population and the leading role played by political parties as connecting agencies between citizens and political institutions.

Quite recently, petitioning has been rediscovered, mainly thanks to the success of initiatives directed at digitalising the right to petition. Interestingly, these projects were implemented in parallel with the rise of some popular non-institutionalised petitioning platforms such as Avaaz.org, MoveOn.org and Change.org. The newly opened Scottish Parliament was the first legislature to introduce the e-petitions in 1999,[91] then followed by many other European and extra-European parliaments. In the new digital environment, e-petitions are proving to be an interesting tool of participative or advocacy democracy that can potentially fulfil multiple roles in mediation between citizens and policymaking. In this regard, Cristina Leston Bandeira has identified four possible roles of petitioning: providing a linkage between the parliament and citizens; campaigning for public mobilisation on specific issues; scrutinising the executive; and influencing policymaking.[92] In this section I analyse some experiences conducted in this field.

Since 2008, the German Bundestag has introduced the possibility for citizens to file public petitions electronically through the parliamentary website, where they can also be signed by supporters and be discussed in a forum. All the petitions are dealt with by the Petition Committee, whose institution is provided directly by the *Grundgesetz* (German Basic Law).[93] On a monthly basis, the Committee submits a report to the Bundestag on the petitions received, in the form of a list together with a recommendation. A debate is held in the plenary on request of one parliamentary group.[94] If a petition receives at least 50,000 signatures, a representative of the petitioners is heard by the Committee. Today the petitioning platform of the Bundestag website has more than four million registered users.[95] An analysis conducted on the platform combined with the results of an online-based

[90] C Leston Bandeira, 'Parliamentary petitions and public engagement: An empirical analysis of the role of e-petitions' (2019) 47 *Policy & Politics* 415, 427.

[91] L Beddie, A Macintosh and A Malina, 'E-democracy and the Scottish Parliament' in B Schmid, BK Stanoevska-Slabeva and V Tschammer (eds), *Towards the E-Society* IFIP International Federation for Information Processing, Vol 74 (Boston, MA, Springer, 2001).

[92] Leston Bandeira, 'Parliamentary petitions and public engagement' (n 90) 429.

[93] See art 45c.

[94] See arts 108–12 of the Bundestag Rules of Procedure.

[95] Deutscher Bundestag Drucksache 20/2200, 20. Wahlperiode, Bericht des Petitionsausschusses (2. Ausschuss): Bitten und Beschwerden an den Deutschen Bundestag; Die Tätigkeit des Petitionsausschusses des Deutschen Bundestages im Jahr 2021 (22.06.2022), available at: dserver.bundestag.de/btd/20/022/2002200.pdf. The report states that in 2021, 11,667 petitions were submitted to the Bundestag, 42% of which were through the electronic platform.

user-survey has revealed that, somewhat paradoxically, the users of the platform 'show a critical and sceptical attitude towards "politics" in general, but make use of an institutionally regulated form of political participation at the same time'.[96]

In 2014 the European Parliament Petition Committee activated the Petition Web Portal through which European citizens, as well as residents on EU territory, can submit a petition electronically, regarding issues that fall within the EU's fields of activity.[97] Thus far, a growing number of petitions have been registered via the portal: this participatory channel has proved rather effective in mobilising, through the filter of the Petition Committee, the European Parliament and the other EU institutions, to address citizens' concerns especially on 'orphan' or 'dormant' issues. It must be said, however, that the number of petitions and users registered at the portal remains very low, if compared with the total EU population.[98]

The most successful (and most studied) example of an e-petitions system is the one introduced by the British House of Commons in 2015. The system replaced an earlier arrangement set up by the British government in 2012 and intended to offer citizens the possibility of sending petitions directly to the executive via a dedicated web portal. The management of the portal, however, proved rather problematic due to the lack of adequate moderation and timeliness in responding to petitioners' demands. The experience therefore resulted in the launching in 2015 of a new petition portal managed jointly by the government and Parliament. For the purpose of considering the petitions, the House of Commons constituted a new Petitions Committee, that was granted powers comparable to those of a standing committee, including the possibility to receive evidence and undertake enquiries on issues raised by e-petitions. The rules governing the use of the portal provide that, once a petition is accepted, it is made accessible online for supporters to sign it. When an e-petition reaches 10,000 signatures, the government must respond to it within 21 days; once it reaches 100,000 signatures, the Petitions Committee considers whether to debate it. Such debate is therefore not automatic but, as a rule, it takes place regularly unless the topic has recently been debated in Parliament. Since their introduction, e-petitions have proved to be extremely popular: during the 2015/17 and 2017/19 parliaments, a total of 59,833 e-petitions were signed. Of these, 19,104 were published, 939 received government responses and 140 were debated in Westminster Hall. Eight e-petitions received over

[96] J-H Schmidt and K Johnsen, 'On the Use of the E-Petition Platform of the German Bundestag' (2014) 3 HIIG Discussion Paper Series, available at: ssrn.com/abstract=2444672 or dx.doi.org/10.2139/ssrn.2444672. The same remark is also made by C Puschmann, M Bastos and J-H Schmidt, 'Birds of a feather petition together? Characterising e-petitioning through the lens of platform data' (2017) 20(2) *Information, Communication & Society* 203. On the users of the Bundestag platform, see also A Steffen, *Teilstudie 3: Befragung der Nutzer der Bundestags- Webseiten zu den öffentlichen Petitionen. Follow-up-Studie zu den Öffentlichen Petitionen des Deutschen Bundestags. Gutachten im Auftrag des Deutschen Bundestages vorgelegt dem Büro für Technikfolgen-Abschätzung beim Deutschen Bundestag (TAB)* (Berlin, Zebralog GmbH & Co, 2010). For a comparison between the e-petitions systems in the European Parliament and the British House of Commons, see U Riehm, K Böhle and R Lindner, *Elektronische Petitionssysteme: Analysen zur Modernisierung des parlamentarischen Petitionswesens in Deutschland und Europa* (Berlin, Edition Sigma, 2013).

[97] The right to petition is guaranteed by Arts 20, 24 and 227 of the TFEU and Art 44 of the EU Charter of Fundamental Rights. The details of the parliamentary procedure and the functions of the Committee for petitions are regulated by art 226 of the European Parliament's Standing Rules.

[98] J Heezen and O Marzocchi, *Achievements of the committee on petitions during the 2014–2019 parliamentary term and challenges for the future* (European Parliament Policy Department for Citizens' Rights and Constitutional Affairs, Brussels, 2020).

500,000 signatures. The title of the petition which received the most signatures during the 2017/19 Parliament was: 'Revoke Article 50 and remain in the EU': it was signed by over 6.1 million people.[99] According to the Hansard Society survey of political engagement in 2018, 28 per cent of the population had created or signed at least one e-petition in the previous year.[100]

In the British example, the role of e-petitions in fostering political participation and the relationships between Parliament and the public is widely acknowledged. E-petitions can support the perception that the institution listens to the public's concerns.[101] The British petitioning system has proven excellent from the point of view of its transparency and accessibility, performing particularly well in its linkage and scrutiny roles, also thanks to the positive cooperation between the government and Parliament.[102] However, effective public understanding of the petitions system remains rather low.[103] Besides, the fairness of the parliamentary process through which petitions are considered has been emphasised as a key factor for enhancing engagement with Parliament: from the petitioners' perspective, the effective impact on the decision-making process is often less important than the perception that petitions have been adequately considered by Parliament.[104] In sum, the 'success' of a petition should not only be measured having regard to the fulfilment of the petitioners' requests, but also taking into consideration other outcomes, like

> awareness raising on the topic of the petition, promoting the petition to wider audiences, perhaps through a debate or an inquiry, getting their issue on the agenda of the Parliament or Assembly by it being discussed by a petitions committee, being able to collect further information on the topic of their petition, and having an opportunity for written and potentially face to face dialogue with members.[105]

ii. Consultative and Deliberative Procedures

Another emerging channel of communication between parliaments and citizens is centred on the procedures of public consultation conducted mainly at the committee stage.

Public consultation is one of the key practices systematically employed by regulatory agencies to improve the transparency, efficiency and effectiveness of regulation alongside other tools such as the Regulatory Impact Analysis (RIA). The use of such tools is normally connected with the unelected nature of agencies that lack a direct democratic legitimisation. In this context, a fair public consultation is expected to follow a process that can include different forms: from simple communication, through which the public is informed about the regulatory decisions of the agencies, to consultation, as a two-way flow of information

[99] For the data on e-petitions in the UK Parliament, see House of Commons Library, *E-Petitions in the UK*, July 2019, available at researchbriefings.files.parliament.uk/documents/CBP-8620/CBP-8620.pdf.

[100] Hansard Society, *Survey of Political Engagement 15. The 2018 Report* (London, Hansard Society, 2018) 29.

[101] M Asher, C Leston-Bandeira and V Spaiser, 'Do Parliamentary Debates of e-Petitions Enhance Public Engagement with Parliament? An Analysis of Twitter Conversations' (2019) 11(2) *Policy & Internet* 149.

[102] Leston Bandeira, 'Parliamentary petitions and public engagement' (n 90) 434.

[103] T Caygill and A-M Griffiths, 'Parliament and Petitions' in C Leston Bandeira, and L Thompson (eds), *Exploring Parliament* (Oxford, Oxford University Press, 2018) 327.

[104] C Carman, 'The Process is the Reality: Perceptions of Procedural Fairness and Participatory Democracy' (2010) 58 *Political Studies* 731.

[105] C Bochel, 'Petitions Systems: Outcomes, Success and Failure' (2020) 73(2) *Parliamentary Affairs* 250.

that involves actively seeking the opinions of interested and affected groups, to participation, as active involvement of interest groups in the formulation of regulatory policies.

Quite recently, parliaments too have introduced public consultation procedures as a measure intended to strengthen their public engagement strategies. These innovations, where adopted, have the objective of complementing other more traditional tools, such as the public hearings held by parliamentary committees. Hearings can be held in the context of the committees' legislative or oversight functions as they are typically aimed at gathering factual evidence or more political opinions from experts or interest groups. Parliamentary public consultations have a rather different objective since they are intended to address the public at large through different forms of involvement. For the development of these new procedures, the use of digital technologies also represents a crucial asset.

The British Parliament is also at the forefront in this field. During the last decade, the 'mother of parliaments' has launched a wide range of public engagement procedures mainly conducted by its select committees. The richness and variety of the experiences is impressive. Within the administration of the British Parliament, a Select Committees Engagement Team has been constituted which works with people and communities across the United Kingdom to increase public understanding of, and engagement with, select committees. Committees are continually innovating in their approach: beyond round tables and 'town hall' methods, deliberative workshops, using voting pods and 'go to democracy', are employed.[106] There is also significant recourse to digital engagement, through web forums or online surveys, in order to find out more about the public's views on an issue. An example is given by the MYScience inquiries launched in 2017 and 2019 by the Science and Technology Committee:

> Using social media platforms, the public were invited, via written submissions or through video submissions using #MyScienceInquiry on Twitter, to put forward their ideas on what the committee should launch an inquiry. Submissions covered a broad range of subjects and came from individuals, universities, learned societies, charities, and civil society organisations. The Committee shortlisted submissions and invited submitters to pitch their proposal in person to the Committee. The Committee subsequently launched some of these as full inquiries and acted on the others through writing letters to Ministers and incorporating relevant questions into future evidence sessions.[107]

The devolved assemblies in the United Kingdom, like the Scottish Parliament and the National Assembly for Wales, have had similar experiences, as have the assemblies of other European and extra-European countries. The Brazilian Chamber of Deputies and Senate are among the most advanced parliamentary assemblies from this point of view, with the creation of a set of digital platforms (e-*Democracia*, e-*Cidania*, *Wikilegis*) designed to engage with constituents and representatives through surveys, forums and collaborative 'Wiki tools'. With the *Ulysses* smart analysis platform, the Brazilian Chamber of Deputies has applied an AI-based tool to conduct a 'smart' analysis of all comments submitted by citizens regarding the positive and negative aspects of a piece of legislation.[108]

[106] House of Commons Liaison Committee, *The effectiveness and influence of the select committee system. Fourth Report of Session 2017–19*, HC 1860, available at: publications.parliament.uk/pa/cm201719/cmselect/cmliaisn/1860/1860.pdf, 53.

[107] ibid, 54.

[108] Inter-Parliamentary Union (IPU), *Brazil, A Digitally Mature Parliament* (June 2022), available at: www.ipu.org/news/case-studies/2022-06/brazil-digitally-mature-parliament.

In Italy, in 2015, a special commission set up by the Speaker of the Chamber of Deputies with a mixed membership (comprising parliamentarians and experts) approved a non-binding Declaration of internet rights.[109] Before its final drafting, the declaration was submitted for broad public consultation via the Chamber's internet website. The text was consequently reworked in order to take into account the results of the consultation.

Beyond public consultation, some parliamentary assemblies have also experimented with deliberative procedures, involving the participation of citizens' assemblies, conventions and focus groups.[110] The most advanced examples of this kind are offered by countries like Iceland and Ireland, which have launched participatory procedures aimed at involving groups of quasi-randomly selected citizens tasked with making decisions regarding important constitutional reforms in a deliberative setting.[111] Common to the two cases is the combination of deliberative moments with the participation of citizens' assemblies, the work of parliamentary committees and assemblies and the celebration of referendums. The success of these experiments has been mixed. In Iceland, the outcome of the complex deliberative exercise involving some thousands of citizens in the revision of the Constitution, which was confirmed by a referendum, was not finalised by the parliament. In Ireland, in 2014, a constitutional convention comprising 66 randomly selected citizens and 33 members of the Irish Dail and Seanad approved several recommendations, some of which were submitted to referendums as constitutional amendments: two of them were approved (removal from the constitution of the offence of blasphemy and introduction of clauses permitting same-sex marriage), whereas a third one was rejected (reduction of the minimum age for presidential candidates).

iii. Parliaments between Digitalisation and Physical Presence

Fostering public engagement is crucial to revitalising the representative function of parliaments and of their members. The opening of participative, deliberative and consultative procedures can provide a significant contribute in shaping the cognitive basis of the new 'Wikipedian parliament'. The digital interactive media offer invaluable new opportunities for renegotiating the relationship between legislatures and citizens. Moreover, digitalisation and AI applications can render parliamentary decision-making more transparent, responsive and efficient.

[109] The text is available at: www.camera.it/application/xmanager/projects/leg17/commissione_internet/testo_definitivo_inglese.pdf.

[110] For an international comparison of 'deliberative representative' procedures involving citizens in public decision-making, see OECD, *Innovative Citizen Participation and New Democratic Institutions: Catching the Deliberative Wave* (OECD Publishing, Paris, 2020), available at: doi.org/10.1787/339306da-en. The study, however, assumes a rather unproblematic relationship between deliberative democracy and representative democracy, without considering the difficult challenges posed by the insertion of deliberative and participative procedures into the context of parliamentary decision-making. For an overview of the participative 'best practices' in contemporary parliaments, see IPU, UNDP, *Global Parliamentary Report 2022* (n 83).

[111] S Suteu, 'Constitutional Conventions in the Digital Era: Lessons from Iceland and Ireland' (2015) 38(2) *Boston College International and Comparative Law Review* 251, 259. In July 2023 the German Bundestag launched its first 'Citizens Assembly' (*Bürgerrat*) on the topic 'Nutrition in transition'. The Assembly is composed of 160 randomly selected participants and is expected to present its recommendations to the Bundestag in 2024. For more details, see the Assembly website: www.buergerrat.de/en/news/citizens-assembly-on-nutrition-randomly-selected/.

The benefits to be expected from these innovations should, however, not be overestimated. On the one hand, the number of citizens actually participating in public engagement activities remains limited to a tiny minority in comparison with the rest of the population. On the other hand, a massive use of participative procedures is likely to be disruptive for the complex parliamentary ecosystem. The insertion of these procedures must be carefully designed in order to offer successful new channels of access to parliamentary decision-making.

As for the perspective of a full digitalisation of parliamentary procedures, the unprecedented challenge posed to parliaments by the Covid-19 pandemic has given parliaments a dramatic incentive to embrace new technologies and remote sittings in order to keep functioning through the crisis. In several legislatures the pandemic has left a legacy of innovation that will be further developed in the future.[112] The Covid emergency has, however, also confirmed that digital technology overcomes distance, but it does not always bring nearness.[113] Informal off-the-record contacts, face-to-face interactions, the physical compresence of the parliamentarians in the assembly could not be permanently substituted by digital platforms without destroying the essence of parliamentary institutions. The archaic nature of the assemblies as places for human gathering is likely to represent the core of parliamentarism also in the new century. As Marcel Detienne has observed, the gathering of the assembly, as a social formation for the debate of issues of interest to the whole community, is the crucial decision through which human beings, in different ages and civilisations, have given origin to the *res publica*.[114] In keeping with this origin, the future of parliaments is not in a virtual dispersion, but in a combination of digitalisation and physical presence, where 'the challenge is to find new modalities of accommodation between our digital and lived bodies, acknowledging their differences while exploring modes of mutually enhancing symbiosis'.[115]

C. New Forms of Relationship with the Public Sphere

We have seen that most of the participative channels opened by parliaments are supported by digital technologies and rely on the internet to reach the public. This development is part of the communicative trend initiated by parliaments at the end of the last century. Prior to this, parliaments were still dominated by the Gutenberg culture based on printing. This meant that documents relating to parliamentary business were published in paper format and very few copies were circulated. This made it very difficult for most citizens to practically access parliamentary documentation, in contrast to the principle of publicity informing parliamentary work. The advent of twentieth-century mass media did not significantly improve this situation. Radio and TV broadcasting did not prove to be a parliamentary-friendly

[112] IPU, *World e-Parliament Report 2022* (Geneva, IPU, 2022), available at: www.ipu.org/resources/publications/reports/2022-11/world-e-parliament-report-2022.

[113] R Kearney, *Touch: Recovering our Most Vital Sense* (New York, Columbia University Press, 2021) 5.

[114] M Detienne, 'From Assembly Practices to Forms of Politics. A Comparative Approach' in M Detienne, *Comparing the Incomparable* (Stanford, CA, Stanford University Press, 2008) 79ff.

[115] ibid.

medium, as these media are ordinarily unable to convey the complexity of parliamentary work. Due to its very nature, television tends to oversimplify the diverse parliamentary environment, overexposing some stages of parliamentary work – not necessarily the most important – like the debates in the plenary. Parliamentary debates themselves are normally reduced to 'sound bites' – fragments of political leaders' speeches – for the benefit of prime-time TV news.

Conversely, the advent of the internet seemed to offer a new and more promising medium for parliaments. Very soon legislatures all over the world set up their own websites, since this move offered multiple communicative opportunities.[116]

On the one hand, this new medium seemed to open the disintermediation of parliamentary communication. Websites activate an interface of direct contact with the public, covering the whole complexity of parliamentary work in its different stages and articulations. The gains in terms of transparency and accessibility are enormous. Moreover, parliaments discovered the advantages offered by social media like *Facebook* or *Twitter*, with the effect of rendering their communicative strategy decidedly more multichannel.

On the other hand, the use of the internet made possible a two-way communication flux between legislatures and citizens. We have seen that parliaments were much more reluctant – sometimes with good reason – to fully exploit this opportunity. More recently, however, a handful of legislatures have opted for a more systemic use of these practices, promoting a virtually radical shift in the concept of parliamentary publicity from mere broadcasting to an interactive relationship with the public.

However, the advent of the internet and the introduction of new information technologies marked a turning point for parliaments, not only from the communicative point of view. Over the last two decades, these innovations have produced a transformative impact even on the core parliamentary procedures, as we have seen with the new participative and deliberative practices launched by several legislatures. More generally, the internet and IT allowed a dramatic shift in the way in which parliaments and their administrations manage information.[117] The production of digital databases and the introduction of AI applications play a crucial role in rendering the parliamentary cognitive machinery far more systematic, accessible and interconnected. The most visible example of this huge effort in innovation is shown by parliamentary websites. In building their websites, parliaments were compelled to rethink their inherent complexity in terms of a system. In a sense, websites made explicit – visible and practically usable – the long-standing implicit parliamentary encyclopaedia. The democratic value of the free and easy access to this new digital encyclopaedia can hardly be overestimated. Even if most users normally retrieve parliamentary documents via search engines rather than by directly consulting parliamentary websites, this practice could not be viable without the establishment of a strong and cyber-safe IT infrastructure on the part of parliaments. From this point of view, the availability of parliamentary documents in the format of open linked data appears crucial.[118]

[116] For an analysis, in historical context, of the relationship between the UK Parliament and the internet, see A Blick, *Electrified Democracy, the Internet and the United Kingdom Parliament in History* (Cambridge, Cambridge University Press, 2021).

[117] C Leston Bandeira, 'The Impact of the Internet on Parliaments: A Legislative Studies Framework' (2017) 60(4) *Parliamentary Affairs* 655.

[118] On this aspect, see Inter-Parliamentary Union (IPU), *The state of open data in parliaments in 2022*, available at: www.ipu.org/innovation-tracker/story/state-open-data-in-parliaments-in-2022.

D. Parliaments and the New Public Policies

In most assemblies, legislative committees remain fundamentally organised according to the structure of the ministries in the national government.[119] Some parliaments have, however, made interesting attempts to reorganise their remit and the number of permanent committees with the intent of taking into account cross-cutting public policies. As already mentioned, the Italian Senate, for example, as a consequence of the reduction in its members from 315 to 200, has recently revised its system of committees.

Another example of variation from the traditional model of departmental committees is represented by the introduction in some parliaments of committees whose remit is defined on the basis of different interests and values. The reference to a ministerial department has the obvious advantage of allowing the committees to match the legislative function with oversight activities of ministerial structures. However, such articulation has serious difficulties in framing emerging and cross-cutting issues within the ordinary cognitive categories of the parliament and its committees. Another possible shortcoming of the traditional approach is 'short-termism' or a 'presentist bias', that is the tendency to prioritise short-term interests over long-term objectives. This tendency hinders the capacity of representative institutions to deal with some of the major problems of our age, like climate change, the social consequences of technological innovation, demographic trends, and so on. Short-termism seems in contrast to the fundamental mission of the parliaments to legislate for tomorrow: the orientation towards the future is inherent in the core function of parliamentary representation. A forward-looking approach is now also required by some national constitutions that have included, among the interests to be considered by public policies, the 'interest of future generations'.[120]

The need for this approach is not contradicted by the fact that, in our age, we are confronted with a succession of 'black swans', the often dramatic emergence of unexpected events that seem to disrupt any attempt to plan the legislative agenda from a long-term perspective. On the one hand, the difficulty of tackling these emergencies can be taken as an additional confirmation of the need to set up cognitive tools and political bodies capable of intercepting the 'weak signals'" that are often preludes to the outbreak of great catastrophes. On the other hand, unexpected events – precisely because they are unexpected – are usually very rich in informative content: they should therefore be comprehensively studied and interpreted in order to be fully exploited to improve our social preparedness for the future.[121]

Against this backdrop, there is a growing awareness of the need to overcome political myopia with the design of institutions supporting far-sighted politics in a context of

[119] C Fasone, *Sistemi di commissioni parlamentari e forme di governo* (Padova, Cedam, 2012) 390 ff.

[120] See art 20a of the German Basic Law: 'Mindful also of its responsibility towards future generations, the state shall protect the natural foundations of life and animals by legislation and, in accordance with law and justice, by executive and judicial action, all within the framework of the constitutional order'. See also art 9, s 3, of the Italian Constitution: 'The Republic ... shall safeguard the environment, biodiversity and ecosystems, also in the interest of future generations'.

[121] This is the lesson deriving from the last book of the great semiotician Juri Lotman, *Culture and Explosion* (1st edn 1992) (Berlin, Mouton de Gruyter, 2009); see ch 11: 'The Logic of Explosion'.

'anticipatory governance' to better address complexity and uncertainty for high-level policy decision-making.[122]

At the parliamentary level, the first parliament to address these demands was the Finnish Eduskunta with the introduction in 1993 of a 'Committee for the Future'. This Committee is one of the Finnish Parliament's permanent committees, which 'serves as a think tank for futures, science and technology policy in Finland'.[123] It generates dialogue with the government, especially on the occasion of the presentation of the government's 'Future Report' (which is normally issued once each legislative term) on long-term policy options for the country. The Committee also autonomously produces reports on subjects of its choice and, when requested, issues statements on government bills to the other standing committees. The Committee's reports and statements are not binding: nevertheless, the well-established nature of the Committee and the non-partisan, deliberative style of its proceedings exert a largely indirect effect on the shaping of some of the major political choices of the country.[124]

The interest in developing such advisory bodies in legislatures seems to be expanding: quite recently, similar committees have been established by other parliaments, like the Parliament of Uruguay (2017), the Senate of the Philippines (2019), the Lithuanian Seimas (2020), the Parliament of Iceland (2021) and the Chamber of Deputies of Paraguay (2022).

In a global environment in which uncertainty has become the 'new normal', the committees for the future share the common intent of enlarging the analytical capacity of the parliamentary encyclopaedia leading to a paradigm shift in public governance. In their efforts to meet this objective, most of these committees make extensive use of external expertise and international evidence when addressing long-term future prospects. Such evaluations very often have scientific and technological implications. From this point of view, the remit of the committees for the future overlaps with that of the parliamentary bodies which specialise in the assessment of technological choices.[125] Some of these bodies have a hybrid nature, with a membership that combines the presence of parliamentarians and external experts,[126] whereas some other legislatures have opted for a full externalisation of the technological assessment, delegating this function to scientific bodies located

[122] On anticipatory governance see: J Boston, J Bagnall, A Barry, G Hellyer and P Sharma, P, *Foresight, Insight and Oversight: Enhancing Long-term Governance through Better Parliamentary Scrutiny* (Institute for Governance and Policy Studies, Victoria University of Wellington 2019); J Boston, *Governing for the Future: Designing Democratic Institutions for a Better Tomorrow* (Bingley, Emerald Publishing, 2017); S Caney, 'Political Institutions for the Future: A Fivefold Package' in I González-Ricoy and A Gosseries (eds), *Institutions for Future Generations* (Oxford, Oxford University Press, 2016).

[123] See the Committee website: www.eduskunta.fi/EN/valiokunnat/tulevaisuusvaliokunta/Pages/default.aspx.

[124] For a recent assessment of the committee work, see V Koskimaa and T Raunio, 'Encouraging a longer time horizon: The Committee for the Future in the Finnish Eduskunta' (2020) 26 *Journal of Legislative Studies* 159.

[125] For a comparison between the different models adopted by parliaments, see J Ganzevles, R van Est and M Nentwich, 'Embracing variety: Introducing the inclusive modelling of (Parliamentary) technology assessment' (2019) 1(3) *Journal of Responsible Innovation* 292. The recent literature about technological assessment bodies in parliaments is reviewed by M Acosta, M Nestore, ME Jarquín-Solís and R Doubleday, 'A typology of advisory bodies in legislatures and research perspectives' [2022] *Journal of Legislative Studies* 1, available at: doi.org/10.1080/13572334.2022.2070985. EPTA (European Parliamentary Technological Assessment) is the network of the bodies specialising in technological assessments for parliaments (see the EPTA website at: eptanetwork.org/).

[126] See, eg, in the UK, the Parliamentary Office of Science and Technology (POST).

outside the parliament.[127] In any case, one of the most serious challenges faced by these bodies relates to their relationship with the standing legislative committees. The actual use of the expertise delivered by the technological assessment in the everyday work of the standing committees can sometimes prove difficult: in some cases, the reports prepared by the technological assessment bodies 'could lead to too forward-looking topics disconnected from policy impact or challenges that are not genuinely on the horizon but are already being treated through policies'.[128] There is, therefore, the need to strike an adequate balance between future-oriented and current political issues. Another challenge relates to the inclusion of politically controversial topics in the technological assessment agenda. Organising a functional knowledge brokerage between the scientific communities and the policymaking institutions is not an easy task: it demands the right timing (capacity to deliver the useful information at the right moment) and advanced communication skills to convey complex contents in a concise form (for instance, data visualisation). Moreover, when it comes to the social consequences of technological choices, the knowledge to be conveyed to legislators should not be limited to the advice coming from the scientific communities, but should be expanded to also include the opinions of the citizens to be affected by the decisions at stake. In order to respond to this need, some participatory phases have been introduced into the technological assessment processes.[129]

E. Parliaments and the Challenges of Multilevel Governance

As regards the ability of parliaments to intercept the dynamics of multilevel governance, a distinction must first be made between federal and non-federal systems. Federal constitutions normally provide for bicameral parliaments in which one of the two chambers represents the member states of the federation. Even if this option is implemented via a wide range of different arrangements, the numerous variants are all inspired by the same intent: allowing the territorial components of the federation to have direct participation in the law-making function. This solution is suggested by some basic democratic values that conceive federalism as fundamentally based on the principles of 'self rule' and 'shared rule'. The involvement of the member states, however, also has a functional meaning, since it is expected to improve the coordination between the different levels of government. If the main benefit of multilevel governance lies in its scalable flexibility, its chief

[127] This is the case of the German Büro für Technikfolgen-Abschätzung (TAB). TAB is operated by the Institute of Technology Assessment and Systems Analysis (ITAS) of the Karlsruhe Institute of Technology (KIT) on the basis of a contract with the German Bundestag. The head of TAB is appointed by KIT in agreement with the Bundestag's Committee on Education, Research and Technology Assessment, which is responsible as the steering committee. Since September 2013, KIT has been cooperating with IZT – Institute for Futures Studies and Technology Assessment gGmbH and VDI/VDE Innovation + Technik GmbH in the operation of TAB. See the TAB website: www.tab-beim-bundestag.de/index.php.

[128] KM Weber, N Gudowsky and G Aichholzer, 'Foresight and technology assessment for the Austrian parliament – finding new ways of debating the future of industry 4.0' (2019) 109 *Futures* 240, available at: doi.org/10.1016/j.futures. 2018.06.018.

[129] ibid.

problem lies in the transaction costs of coordinating multiple jurisdictions.[130] In such contexts, the presence of a chamber specialising in territorial representation can help prevent conflicts between the different members of the federation. In federal systems, the parliament therefore usually also has the encyclopaedic role of summarising the nation's different levels of democracy. It should be recalled, however, that in some federations the representation of the member states in one of the two chambers is sometimes 'doubled' by the presence of coordinating bodies at the executive level, as occurs, for example in the United States and in Germany. In these bodies, the representatives of the state executives liaise directly with the federal government.

In some centralised states, parliaments have also recently launched new procedures for coordination and consultation with the system of territorial autonomies. These initiatives are intended to respond to the aforementioned phenomena of devolution of powers or of transformation into quasi-federal systems, which have recently affected states with a long-standing centralist tradition.

In the UK Parliament, for example, the devolution of powers to the Scottish Parliament has been accompanied since 1998 by the Sewel Convention, which provides that the Parliament legislates on a matter devolved to the Scottish Parliament only if the latter has given its consent. The Convention was conceived as a tool for coordinating the legislative activity between the British Parliament and the Scottish Parliament.[131]

In Spain, according to the 1978 Constitution, the *comunidades autónomas* are represented in the Senado through the election of a minor quota of its members by the regional councils. Due to the limited powers granted to the Senado, the demands being made by the territorial autonomies are however much more vocal at the centre through the presence in the lower chamber (Congreso de los deputados) of regional parties whose support is often instrumental in forming majorities in support of the national government. In any case, bilateral negotiations between the national executive and regional governments remain crucial for the relationship between the central state and the system of autonomies.[132]

In Italy, the 1948 Constitution provides for the election of one of the two chambers, the Senato della Repubblica, on a 'regional basis'. This provision, however, has been implemented only in relation to the definition of the territorial constituencies for the election of the senators, without any direct connection between the Senate and the regional autonomies. In the absence of an upper house capable of territorial representation, the Constitution (article 126.1) provides for the institution of a bicameral committee charged with the task of maintaining stable relations with the system of autonomies. The 2001 constitutional reform that significantly increased the powers of territorial autonomies provided for the integration of the committee by representatives of regions and municipalities.[133] This provision has, however, not yet been implemented. In contrast, the relationships between the centre

[130] G Hooghe and L Marks, 'Unraveling the central state, but how? Types of multi-level governance' (2003) 97 *American Political Science Review* 239.

[131] See House of Commons Library, *The Sewel Convention*, Briefing Paper CBP-8883 May 2020, available at: researchbriefings.files.parliament.uk/documents/CBP-8883/CBP-8883.pdf.

[132] JM Castellà Andreu, *Estado autonómico: pluralismo e integración constitucional* (Madrid, Pons, Fundación Manuel Giménez Abad, 2018).

[133] M Cartabia and N Lupo, *The Constitution of Italy: A Contextual Analysis* (Oxford, Hart Publishing, 2022) 76.

and autonomies continue to be rather successfully managed in Italy through a system of conferences involving the representatives of national government and regional and municipal executives.

In conclusion, it seems that in both federal and in quasi-federal systems, legislatures find it difficult to play an effective role in the democratic coordination between the different levels of government. This role seems to be much more effective for executives, through negotiating and connecting forums that often avoid any form of publicity. This trend is detrimental to some fundamental requirements of transparency and democratic participation in decision-making processes that are becoming increasingly important in contemporary multilayered government systems. A proper parliamentarisation of such processes could, in principle, respond more comprehensively to these needs.

Some more promising results have been achieved by parliaments in relation to their relationship with supranational levels of government. The most remarkable example is offered by the European Union. Here, over the last two decades, parliaments have managed to 'fight back' against the possible de-parliamentarisation of the Union's crucial decision-making processes.[134] With the Lisbon Treaty, the European Parliament has acquired a full legislative co-decision power with the Council. The Treaty has also granted national parliaments new powers as 'watchdogs' of national competencies for the preventive control of the subsidiarity principle on the draft legislative acts issued by the Commission. I have already commented on the mixed results reached in the implementation of these provisions. More significant progress has been made in relation to the increasing role of national parliaments in controlling and directing the position of the executives within the Council. In this respect, principally by parliaments in some northern European countries, very advanced oversight procedures have been set up with binding effect on the national governments' decisions. But also in other countries such as Italy[135] and Germany,[136] the role of parliaments in European matters has significantly increased following the conclusion of the Maastricht Treaty.

These developments have contributed to the construction of a 'multilevel parliamentary field' in which both national parliaments and the European Parliament are both indispensable elements of the EU's democratic legitimacy. These two levels are linked through complex interactions that could not properly be compared either to those existing in a full federal polity or to a loose framework of interinstitutional relations.[137] In this unique democratic context, interparliamentary relationships are established along both horizontal (among national parliaments) and vertical (EP–national parliaments) lines. This complex institutional environment can best be described as a 'system' in which both the European Parliament and the national parliaments discharge a fundamental

[134] T Raunio and S Hix 'Backbenchers learn to fight back: European integration and parliamentary government' (2000) 23 *West European Politics* 142.

[135] For Italy see the essays collected in N Lupo and G Piccirilli (eds), *The Italian Parliament in the European Union* (Oxford, Hart Publishing, 2017).

[136] O Höing, 'With a Little Help of the Constitutional Court: The Bundestag on its Way to an Active Policy Shaper' in C Hefftler, C Neuhold, O Rozenberg and J Smith (eds), *The Palgrave Handbook of National Parliaments and the European Union* (London, Palgrave Macmillan, 2015).

[137] B Crum and JE Fossum, 'The Multilevel Parliamentary Field: A framework for theorizing representative democracy in the EU' (2009) 1 *European Political Science Review* 249.

democratic role: responding to the normative principle enshrined in Article 10 TEU according to which 'the functioning of the Union shall be founded on representative democracy'. This role is played first and foremost by enforcing the principle of political accountability of European and national executives.[138] This euro-national system extends the traditional limits of the parliamentary encyclopaedia well beyond state borders, without diminishing the salience of national constitutions. From this point of view, the European polity – even with its shortcomings and problematic aspects – remains an unparalleled democratic achievement from a comparative perspective.

[138] A Manzella, 'The European Parliament and National Parliaments as a System' in S Mangiameli (ed), *The Consequnces of the Crisis on European Integration and on Member States* (Cham, Springer, 2017).

Conclusions

The New Parliamentary Encyclopaedia: Combining Specialised Knowledge with Common Sense

I. Old and New Encyclopaedism

In this book, I have tried to draw a parallel between encyclopaedism and parliamentarism over the last three centuries. The two phenomena offer striking analogies as providers of common intellectual and political platforms for modern democracies. Between the eighteenth and nineteenth centuries, both encyclopaedism and parliamentarism developed as responses to the growing complexity inherent in knowledge and politics in modernity. Abandoning the pansophic ideals of the Middle Ages and the Renaissance, modern encyclopaedias supported a project of democratisation and free access to knowledge in line with the needs of the rising bourgeoisie as the social backbone of the new parliamentary regimes. Since the Renaissance, most of the great modern encyclopaedias have nevertheless retained the ambition of also being 'theatres', sites of comprehensive, public representation of the civilisations to which they belonged. In the nineteenth century, as cultural artefacts, they were intimately involved in the nation-building processes of several European states. In the twentieth century, encyclopaedias continued to satisfy the demand of an expanding public interested in gaining concise, comprehensive and accessible information in connection with the growing specialisation of knowledge and the emergence of new scientific disciplines. However, the relative importance of encyclopaedic works declined: all in all, they were assigned a minor, although significant, niche within the thriving publishing market. At the same time, they faced growing competition from the new electronic media as predominant disseminators of a new mass culture. At the turn of the century, traditional encyclopaedias were confronted with even more challenging developments. The advent of the internet imposed a new communicative paradigm, characterised by the free and easy access for everyone to any piece of information. The new platform embodied the promise of getting 'everything, everywhere all at once'. Very soon, however, the utopian perspective of removing any kind of mediation in the access to information proved unrealistic. This explains the emergence in the worldwide web of a new, impressive encyclopaedic project, like that promoted by *Wikipedia*. With its bottom-up structure, its openness and its multi-language versions, *Wikipedia* seems to resume the universalistic ideals of Enlightenment encyclopaedism. At a more fundamental level, the universal success of the internet as a global platform for the exchange of every possible piece of information could hardly be conceivable without the existence of powerful search engines which perform some of the traditional functions attributed to encyclopaedias. More recently, new, impressive AI applications have emerged, whose generative versions seem capable of providing a new kind of encyclopaedia, continuously recreating its entries to respond to the demands of users.

The history of modern parliamentarism has several analogies with these developments, especially if we consider the cognitive value implied in the representative function of legislatures. Parliaments were the great political encyclopaedias of the nineteenth century, in the sense that they gave an understandable and public form to the politics of their age. The majority–opposition cleavage, political parties, and the emergence of national political leaders were all phenomena made possible by the existence of parliaments. Legislatures acted as great political theatres, performing a crucial nation-building function. The very construction of a modern public sphere was made possible by parliamentarism in strong symbiosis with the dominant medium of the liberal age, the press. In the nineteenth century, the rise of parliamentary government reflected the changing power structures in European societies. Constitutional monarchies with their dual power structures established an equilibrium between the different components of the liberal political elites. From the mid-nineteenth century, however, the extension of the franchise and the emergence of mass parties transmitted new demands to the institutional system that the traditional parliamentary class was unable to meet. Mass democracy and the professionalisation of politics were translated in structural transformations of the legislative assemblies. They set up a double cognitive grid at the intersection between the new parliamentary groups and the standing committees with legislative capacity. This infrastructure proved so effective that, even today, it continues to constitute the core of the parliamentary encyclopaedia in most modern legislatures.

However, we have seen how this system is currently facing radical challenges. The historical role assumed by modern parliaments as providers of politically qualified knowledge is in question due to a multitude of different factors. Some of them affect the very core of democratic representation. The fragmentation of social pluralism in forms of extreme individualism calls into question the synthesis provided by the parliamentary political encyclopaedia. In the 'age of distrust', individuals seem to dismiss any instance of institutional representation and prefer self-representational practices. When collective political action is at stake, this often assumes the form of temporary and issue-oriented movements rather than initiatives taken by the political parties represented in parliaments. In contrast, contemporary public policies are increasingly developed at the supranational or sub-national level, questioning the cognitive horizon of national parliaments, traditionally focused on the national state as the main arena for political decision-making. As a consequence, parliaments are losing ground vis-a-vis the executives: the latter seem to be far better equipped to play their role in the complex environment of contemporary governance, thanks to their direct links with supranational authorities or with the system of territorial autonomies. Executives become predominant also as a consequence of the personalisation of political leadership and the presidentialisation even of parliamentary systems as a global trend.[1] A further element of crisis arises due to the decline of the agencies traditionally involved in mediating between the parliaments and the people. Nineteenth-century parliaments flourished by relying, on the one hand, on their strong connection with public opinion secured

[1] T Poguntke and P Webb (eds), *The Presidentialization of Politics in Democratic Societies: A Framework for Analysis* (Oxford, Oxford University Press, 2005); see also, P Rosanvallon, *Le bon gouvernement* (Paris, Seuil, 2015) 15 ff.

by the press and, on the other, on the personal ties of their members with their constituencies. Later, in the twentieth century, parliaments continued to enjoy social relevance thanks to the mediation of large organisations such as mass political parties. The decline of these structures risks leaving parliaments in a communicative vacuum that challenges their representative function.

Is the marginalisation of parliaments and of their political encyclopaedia inevitable due to these developments? This book attempts to argue that representative assemblies can still play a crucial encyclopaedic role in the democratic systems of the future.

Democracy cannot survive the dismantling of pluralism into social fragmentation. General, comprehensive representative institutions are as necessary as ever in order to provide democratic government in an era of social complexity. The marginalisation of parliamentary assemblies can hardly be compensated for with stronger forms of popular control over the executives.[2] The latter appear unfit to saturate the entire space of political representation, without fatally endangering the stability of democratic government as we know it. Both in parliamentary and in other democratic systems, even today parliamentary assemblies can act as *crucial catalysts for political representation*. The cognitive added value produced by parliamentary decision-making is today one of the most effective antidotes against the demagogy of misinformation.[3] The perpetuation (and also the resilience) of the parliamentary encyclopaedia in such an apparently highly anti-encyclopaedic era is therefore not only explained by the traditional conservative spirit of the parliamentary institutions. Rather, it appears to be linked to the fundamental function of representing pluralism in the context of the growing complexity of our societies. On the one hand, parliamentarism supports a democratic model that is exactly the opposite of that advocated by Carl Schmitt, who maintained that 'a democracy demonstrates its political power by knowing how to refuse or keep at bay something foreign and unequal that threatens its homogeneity'.[4] On the other hand, parliamentary representation rejects the idea of an inevitable, chaotic fragmentation of political demands, and incorporates the need for common and organised platforms where the key political choices can be adequately deliberated by the entire community. Even today, the principles of political accountability, of publicity and of debate inherent to parliamentarism are indispensable to securing the survival of democracies as 'governments of the people'. The alternative would be a slide down into the anonymity of unarticulated governance where, together with the principle of political accountability, the effective exercise of popular sovereignty guaranteed by the democratic constitutions will also cease to exist.[5] This envisages a post-democratic scenario in which 'politics and government are increasingly slipping back into the control of privileged elites

[2] This is instead the opinion of Pierre Rosanvallon, who thinks that the best remedy for the 'presidentialisation of democracies' should be found in stronger forms of popular participation according to a model of *démocratie d'appropriation* (see Rosanvallon, ibid, 187–214).

[3] A Manzella, *Elogio dell'Assemblea, tuttavia* (Modena, Mucchi, 2020) 47.

[4] C Schmitt, 'On the Contradiction between Parliamentarism and Democracy' in C Schmitt, *The Crisis of Parliamentary Democracy* (1st edn 1926) (Cambridge, MA, 1985), 9. The text appeared in (1926) 23 *Hochland* 257 and was republished as the preface to the second edition of *Die geisteschichtliche Lage des heutigen Parlamentarismus* (München-Leipzig, Duncker & Humblot, 1926).

[5] On these possible risks, see M Luciani, 'L'antisovrano e la crisi delle costituzioni' (1996) 1 *Rivista di diritto costituzionale* 124.

in the manner characteristic of pre-democratic times'.[6] Another alternative is the rise of authoritarian regimes in different forms, from technocratic to autocratic. Over the last two decades, such regimes have continued to extend their reach, not to mention the widespread diffusion of illiberal movements even within the most established democracies.[7]

Renovation of representative institutions can be an antidote against the hollowing-out of our democratic regimes.[8] Political and social forces opposing the post-democratic syndrome should find the proper strategies to re-empower political citizenship for our age. This goal has much to do with the need to find forms of democratic transition from the first phase of 'wild' globalisation to a new equilibrium between the national dimension and global interdependence. The reframing of the parliamentary encyclopaedia can be an important part of this programme. In the next sections I try to summarise some possible actions to be taken in this direction.

II. Building 'Wikipedian Parliaments'

The first step towards the innovation of the traditional representative institutions can arise from a radical renegotiation of their relationship with citizens. In order to remain the living encyclopaedia of democratic politics, parliaments' approach to knowledge should adopt some of the suggestions deriving from the 'Wikipedian' experience. Addressing the major political issues of our age implies the incorporation in public decisions of the best scientific and technical knowledge available at any given moment. This makes it as necessary as ever for parliaments to support their decision-making with solid evidence that can come from the executive, from independent agencies, from experts and scientists. But this is not enough. The acquisition of 'common knowledge' is also crucial for the enlargement of parliaments' cognitive basis. To achieve this result, legislatures should become 'listening institutions', introducing procedures that give citizens a say in parliamentary decision-making. Some public engagement tools have already been successfully experimented, as we have seen. Such innovative channels can be conducive to better and more legitimated decisions only if they are designed in a complementary rather than a competitive manner vis-a-vis representative institutions. They should therefore be clearly oriented from the outset to their successful inclusion within the complex parliamentary ecosystem. Poorly designed participative or deliberative experiments risk proving disruptive in this environment, resulting in further delegitimisation of representative institutions. Public engagement should be taken seriously. This requires a two-way responsible relationship. That is, from the parliaments towards the citizens, in order to establish at the outset the expected effects of public participation in parliamentary decision-making; and from the citizens towards the parliaments in the sense of requiring the participants' commitment to a constructive contribution to parliamentary work. Digitalisation of parliamentary procedures is crucial to achieving this new interactive relationship. Parliaments, however, should remain physical

[6] C Crouch, *Post-democracy* (Cambridge, Polity, 2004) 6.

[7] For some data on these trends, see Freedom House, *Freedom in the World 2022: The Global Expansion of Authoritarian Rule*, Freedom House, 2022, available at: freedomhouse.org/sites/default/files/2022-02/FIW_2022_PDF_Booklet_Digital_Final_Web.pdf.

[8] P Mair, *Ruling the Void: The Hollowing of Western Democracy* (London, Verso, 2013).

places for the in-person meeting of parliamentarians and citizens. The 'digital excarnation'[9] of parliaments would destroy their essence as assemblies, that is, places for the actual meeting of people debating the future of the political community.

III. Developing the 'Federalising Capacity' of Parliaments

Most contemporary democracies are based on a complex multilevel structure. Their poliarchical character is continuously expanding. This development appears crucial for the survival of democracy in ever more complex societies. On the one hand, the different forms of self-government prove more adaptable to responding to the growing diversification of citizens' political demands. On the other hand, multilateral coordination among national states or the intervention of supranational organisations like the European Union seem to represent the only way forward to tackle some of the most urgent political questions of our age. Nevertheless, strong national representative institutions seem to be as indispensable as ever for securing democratic government insofar as executives and parliamentary assemblies articulate *together* the principle of political accountability in our societies. As mentioned earlier, the former have apparently taken advantage of their position since they are better equipped to interact with supranational organisations and sub-national governments. Moreover, heads of government are more visible and effective in representing political leadership in our contemporary 'audience democracies'. Executives alone are, however, unable to respond to the surcharge of conflictual political demands coming from society. Both in parliamentary and presidential systems, elected assemblies can offer crucial contributions in transforming our fragmented polyarchies into pluralistic democracies. In this new context, national parliaments cannot claim to retain the monopoly of political representation, which today is inevitably much more diffused and dispersed than in the past. They can, however, offer a decisive contribution in governing the flourishing institutional pluralism of our age. They have the opportunity to play a crucial role in mediating between the supranational and local levels of contemporary democracies. On the one hand, federal arrangements have their drawbacks, including centrifugal pressures (with sometimes secessionist temptations); diseconomies of scale; incapacity to face systemic challenges (as those recently posed by the Covid pandemic); and growing territorial inequalities. On the other hand, supranational organisations often appear to be incapable of gaining full democratic legitimisation and, as a result, are often marked by a stigma of 'democratic disconnection' with the citizens. National parliaments can address at least some of these problems through different institutional arrangements. Particularly in federal systems, the bicameral structure of legislatures allows for the direct representation of local communities at the centre. In regional states, a variety of procedures has been introduced in order to facilitate stable forms of contact and consultation with the political institutions (executives and elected assemblies) of the other levels of government. At a supranational level, the European Union has adopted a very rich range of institutional arrangements through which national parliaments participate in the shaping of European policies. These examples illustrate how parliaments can expand their

[9] On the concept of 'digital excarnation' see R Kearney, *Touch: Recovering our Most Vital Sense* (New York, Columbia University Press, 2021) 113–32.

cognitive and political synapses beyond the borders of the national state. Their encyclopaedic nature should evolve in order to become a federalising factor for ever more complex and articulated democracies.

IV. Opening an Instituent Perspective in the Parliamentary Encyclopaedia

The construction of a new parliamentary encyclopaedia does not mean that legislatures should claim to offer a harmonious and all-embracing synthesis of the political knowledge of our age. If parliaments are traditionally the place of mediation and compromise, the very core of parliamentary democracy resides in controversy. The encyclopaedic patterns of parliamentarism are incompatible with an illusory depoliticisation of social conflict. On the contrary, the new parliamentary encyclopaedia should be conceived in order to elucidate the alternative political options deriving from such conflict. The conceptual framework for this political and intellectual achievement can be inspired by the political theory that assumes contention as the very core of institutional life, rather than as something that should be expelled from its context. From a constitutional theory perspective, this means that the endeavours to build new forms of parliamentarism should stick to a 'polemic' rather than 'irenic' interpretation of constitutionalism.[10] Parliaments as institutions are today asked to rediscover an 'instituent' approach to politics, capable of thinking about *order* through *conflict*,[11] 'provided that we do not think of the institution *statically* – in a conservative sense – but *dynamically*, as constant *instituting* in which conflict can become an instrument of a politics increasingly inspired by justice'.[12] From this point of view, parliaments can offer a political space through which democracy is 'kept alive by an institutionalised conflict that makes the place of power empty, that is to say always contestable'.[13] As Hegel pointed out, opposition is inherent to parliaments: without this fundamental divide, parliaments lose their institutional salience.[14] The encyclopaedic architecture of parliaments assumed

[10] M Luciani, 'Costituzionalismo irenico e costituzionalismo polemico' (2006) 4 *Giurisprudenza costituzionale* 1643.

[11] I make reference to Roberto Esposito's political theory that proposes an 'instituent' vision of politics that is neither negatively destituent (post-Heideggerian), nor affirmatively constituent (post-Deleuzian, post-Spinozian). This approach assumes conflict at the centre of institutional life: 'Instituting should therefore be conceived as producing innovation *not* starting from nothing (according to the political theology of *creatio ex nihilo*), but starting from an *already* established reality, where the past is the negative that must be integrated and radically renewed through ever new institutions': see R Esposito, *Pensiero istituente: Tre paradigmi di ontologia politica* (Torino, Einaudi 2020) and R Esposito, *Istituzione* (Bologna, il Mulino 2021). For an English translation of the recent developments of Esposito's thought, see R Esposito, *Politics and Negation: For an Affirmative Philosophy* (Cambridge, Polity, 2019).

[12] R Fulco, 'A political ontology for Europe: Roberto Esposito's instituent paradigm' (2021) 54 *Continental Philosophical Review* 367, available at: doi.org/10.1007/s11007-021-09542-z.

[13] Esposito, *Pensiero istituente* (n 11).

[14] 'By those who have reflected only a little on the nature of an assembly of states [Stände] and are familiar with the phenomena affecting them, it cannot be overlooked that, without opposition, such an assembly lacks vitality inside and outside, that an anti-thesis of this kind belongs to it precisely as its essence, as its justification, and that it can only be said to be properly constituted if it expresses an opposition; without opposition, his role is only that of a party, or even of a shapeless mass': GWF Hegel, 'Verhandlungen in der Versammlung der Landstände des Königsreichs Württemberg: Abteilungen I-XXXVIII (1815–1817)' in *Gesammelte Werke* (Hamburg, Meiner, 1990) Vol XV, *Schriften und Entwürfe* (author's translation).

this pattern at its core, not least through the oppositional setting of the members' benches in the British Parliament, or through the right–left spatial divide of the continental parliamentary hemicycles. This criterion became a fundamental cognitive category of modern politics. Today there is the need for a more comprehensive presentation of the multidimensional cleavages that affect our complex societies. From the perspective of parliaments, this implies openness to a degree of innovation capable of triggering those 'paradigm shifts' that have in the past characterised the history of modern political representation.

Such a radical innovation can hardly be conceived as deriving from within the parliamentary institutions themselves. The new forms of encyclopaedic parliamentarism will be made possible only if political parties, social movements, civil society organisations and individual citizens push towards this direction. Parliaments can provide political parties with critical support against the pervasive virtualisation of political debate, a spiral that is rapidly evading their control, to the advantage of other centres of power. Civic society organisations could also find more articulated channels to transmit their demands to representative institutions. Last but not least, citizens will also have the chance of rediscovering the essential meaning of the assembly for the purpose of escaping self-isolation and the decline of their political dimension.

V. Memory, Reason and Imagination for the New Parliamentary Encyclopaedia

Through these strategies, parliamentary encyclopaedism can play a crucial role in the pluralistic democracies of the future. This programme requires, however, a paradigm shift capable of advancing parliamentary democracy from modernity to contemporaneity. The alternative is the absorption of the glorious principles of parliamentarism in a post-modern narrative in which the great symbolic forms of the tradition survive as mere 'citations' of the past, deprived of any actual relevance.[15] In contrast, contemporaneity is 'a singular relationship with one's time, which adheres to it, and, at the same time, keeps a distance from it'; 'the contemporary is he who firmly holds his gaze on his own time so as to perceive not its light, but is darkness'.[16] In line with this perspective, parliaments should openly address the crisis that currently undermines the traditional forms of political representation.[17] The full adaptation of the parliamentary encyclopaedia to the contemporary 'infosphere' requires a quantum leap in terms of innovation to reinterpret the three great Baconian principles that inspired Diderot and D'Alambert's work: memory, reason and imagination.

Memory should remain a crucial dimension in the parliamentary encyclopaedia. As we have seen, parliaments have in the past operated as living custodians of the civic memory of their countries. The continuity of parliamentary institutions, regularly renovated through free elections, reflects the continuity of our constitutions. The central role of procedural

[15] On the concept of post-modern narrative, see JF Lyotard, *The Post-modern Condition: A Report on Knowledge* (1st edn 1979) (Manchester, Manchester University Press, 1984).

[16] G Agamben, 'What is the Contemporary?' in G Agamben, *'What is an Apparatus?' and Other Essays* (Stanford, CA, Stanford University Press, 2009).

[17] G Rizzoni, 'Il parlamento dal moderno al contemporaneo' (2021) 1 *Diritto Pubblico* 241, 257 ff.

precedents is but one aspect of the commitment to memory in parliamentary proceedings. Any event that occurs within the parliamentary premises is recorded, archived and made public, becoming a fragment of the political history of the nation. In the age of the 'cancel culture', the ongoing renovation of political memory assumes a central value for the future of contemporary democracies.[18] Parliaments can be the place where different political cultures build the shared civic memory of their community. Such a memory is intrinsically forward-looking, since it is interlinked with the political drama represented every day in the parliamentary assemblies.

The second component of the parliamentary encyclopaedia should continue to be reason. Contemporary parliamentary decision-making cannot be described according to the Hobbesian dictum '*Auctoritas, non veritas facit legem*'. On the contrary, parliamentary deliberation should simultaneously be rational and reasonable. Rational, because it must be evidence-based and bound to find the most suitable correspondence between the ends and the means chosen for political action. Reasonable, because it is expected to create an acceptable equilibrium between the different interests and values at stake in any decision. We have seen above how the categories of parliamentary rationality can be innovated and expanded: they can no longer be based on either the omniscient logos of the nineteenth-century liberal elite, or on the collective intelligence of twentieth-century political parties. The Wikipedian parliaments must identify new combinations between common knowledge and the most advanced findings of science and technology.

Parliamentary rationality remains essentially different from the constraints binding the actions of administrative authorities, since it is but the expression of the freedom of the political community. From this perspective, imagination is the most crucial component of the forthcoming parliamentary encyclopaedia. As Nadia Urbinati put it,

> the nature of representativity as reflective adhesion (of the representative to the represented) cannot be understood without contemplating the role of imagination because, … representativity does not pertain to an existential or factual presence to be replicated or mimicked, but to a presence through ideas and communication that the political actors (representatives and represented) create.[19]

Parliamentary encyclopaedia should therefore open an imaginative space for the political empowerment of the citizen. The challenge for contemporary parliaments centres on the problem of how to combine some of the inalienable principles of parliamentarism (free mandate, national representation, procedural autonomy) with the need to break the wall of separation from citizens. Such a move should be aimed at rendering the deliberative dimension of our democracies more inclusive and articulated. In this context, parliaments need to update their encyclopaedic patterns in order to intercept the new formats that are currently shaping public policies. This entails, for example, rethinking the system of parliamentary committees. A major step forward would be their radical reform on the basis of the new contemporary public policies emerging at the global level (including environmental sustainability, digitalisation, the fight against climate change, women's empowerment, etc). As we have seen, these are the categories used today by great supranational organisations

[18] M Luciani, 'Itinerari costituzionali della memoria' (2022) 4 *Rivista AIC* 84.

[19] N Urbinati, *Representative Democracy: Principles and Genealogy* (Chicago, IL, University of Chicago Press, 2006) 122.

to design the global policies of the future. All in all, parliaments need to update and extend their cognitive grid with a view to intercepting new and cross-cutting issues, those that express the great political cleavages of our age. Only in this way, can they make their contribution in construing the 'world encyclopaedia' imagined by HG Wells for the replacement of the old national encyclopaedias. Such a new form of encyclopaedia should not be intended to be a 'miscellany', but rather, 'a concentration, a clarification and a synthesis'.[20] Adapting this nascent world encyclopaedia to national contexts and needs may be the next mission of parliamentary assemblies.

[20] HG Wells, 'World Encyclopaedia. Lecture delivered at the weekly evening meeting of the Royal Institution of Great Britain, November 20th, 1936' in HG Wells, *World Brain* (North Haven, CT, Read Books, 2016) 29.

BIBLIOGRAPHY

Books

Allen, RC, *The British Industrial Revolution in Global Perspective* (Cambridge, Cambridge University Press, 2009).

Allgemeine Encyclopädie der Wissenschaften und Künste (Leipzig, Gleditisch and Brockhaus, 1818–89).

Alsted, JH, *Encyclopedia septem tomis distincta* (Herborn, 1630).

Amato, G and Clementi, F, *Forme di stato e forme di governo* (Bologna, il Mulino, 2012).

Ambrosini, G, *Partiti politici e gruppi parlamentari dopo la proporzionale* (Firenze, La Voce, 1921).

Anderson, B, *Imagined Communities: Reflections on the Origin and Spread of Nationalism*, 2nd edn (London, Verso, 1991).

Atienza, M, *Contribución a una teoria de la legislación* (Madrid, Civitas, 1997).

Bagehot, W, *Physics and Politics* (London, Henry S King & Co, 1872).

—— *The English Constitution* (1st edn 1867) (Oxford, Oxford University Press, 2009).

Baranger, D, *Parlamentarisme des origines: Essai sur les conditions de formations d'un exécutif responsable en Angleterre (des années 1740 au début de l'âge victorien)* (Paris, PUF, 1999).

—— *Penser la loi: Essai sur le législateur des temps modernes* (Paris, Gallimard, 2018).

Barthes, R, *La Préparation du roman* (Paris, Seuil, 2003).

Bastid, P, *Les Discours de Sieyès, dans les débats constitutionnels de l'an III (2 et 18 thermidor),* (Paris, 1939).

Bayle, P, *Dictionnaire historique et critique* (Rotterdam, P Leers, 1697).

Bentham, J, *Essay on Political Tactics* (1st edn 1791) (Oxford, Clarendon Press, 1999).

Berthélemy, J, *Essai sur le travail parlamentaire et le système des commissions* (Paris, Librairie Delagrave, 1934).

Beyme, K von, *Die parlamentarische Demokratie: Entstehung und Funktionsweise 1789–1999*, 4 Aufl (Wiesbaden, Springer, 2014).

Blair, AM, *Too Much to Know: Managing Scholarly Information before the Modern Age* (New Haven, CT, Yale University Press, 2010).

Blick, A, *Electrified Democracy, the Internet and the United Kingdom Parliament in History* (Cambridge, Cambridge University Press, 2021).

Bod, R, *A New History of the Humanities: The Search for Principles and Patterns from Antiquity to the Present* (Oxford, Oxford University Press, 2013).

Borges, JL, *A Universal History of Infamy* (London, Penguin Books, 1975).

Boston, J, *Governing for the Future: Designing Democratic Institutions for a Better Tomorrow* (Bingley, Emerald Publishing, 2017).

Boston J, Bagnall, J, Barry, A, Hellyer, G and Sharma, P, *Foresight, Insight and Oversight: Enhancing Long-term Governance through Better Parliamentary Scrutiny* (Institute for Governance and Policy Studies, Victoria University of Wellington, 2019).

Brand, J, *British Parliamentary Parties* (Oxford, Clarendon Press, 1992).

Briggs, A and Burke, P, *A Social History of the Media from Gutenberg to the Internet* (Cambridge, Polity Press, 2009).

Buchex, BJ and Roux, PC, *Histoire parlementaire de la révolution française, ou journal des assemblées nationales, depuis 1789 jusqu'en 1815* (Paris, Paulin Libraire, 1834).

Burke, P, *A Social History of Knowledge: From the Encyclopédie to Wikipedia* (Cambridge, Polity Press, 2012).

—— *What is the History of Knowledge?* (Cambridge, Polity Press, 2015).

Camby, J-P, *La loi* (Issy-les-Moulineaux, LGDJ, 2015).

Cammarano, F, *Storia politica dell'Italia liberale: L'età del liberalismo classico* (Roma-Bari, Laterza, 1999).

Carr, N, *The Shallows: What the Internet is Doing to Our Brains* (New York, Norton, 2011).

Carré de Malberg, R, *La Loi expression de la volonté générale: Etude sur le concept de la loi dans la Constitution de 1875* (Paris, Librairie du Recueil Sirey, 1931).

Carstairs, A, *A Short History of Electoral Systems in Western Europe* (London, George Allen, 1980).

Castellà Andreu, JM, *Estado autonómico: pluralismo e integración constitucional* (Madrid, Pons, Fundación Manuel Giménez Abad, 2018).
Cartabia, M and Lupo, N, *The Constitution of Italy: A Contextual Analysis* (Oxford, Hart Publishing, 2022).
Cedroni, C, *La rappresentanza politica: Teorie e modelli* (Milano, Franco Angeli, 2004).
Chambers, E, *Cyclopædia: or, An Universal Dictionary of Arts and Sciences*, 1st edn (London, James & John Knapton; John Darby; and others, 1728).
Coke, E, *The first part of the Institutes of the lawes of England, or a commentarie upon Littleton, not the name of a lawyer only, but of the law it selfe* (London, 1629).
Collison, R, *Encyclopaedias: Their History throughout the Ages* (New York, Hafner, 1966).
Compte, A, *Cours de Philosophie Positive* (Paris, Bachelier, 1830).
Connil, D, *Les groupes parlementaires en France* (Issy-les-Moulineaux, LGDJ, 2016).
Constant, B, *Cours de politique constitutionelle*, 3rd edn (Brussels, 1819).
Conti, G, *Parliament the Mirror of the Nation: Representation, Deliberation and Democracy in Victorian Britain* (Cambridge, Cambridge University Press, 2019).
Cooper, J, *The Origins of the Standing Committees and the Development of the Modern House* (Houston, TX, Rice University Studies, 1970).
Cox, GW and McCubbins, MD, *Legislative Leviathan: Party Government in the House* (Berkeley, CA, University of California Press, 1993).
Craveri, B, *La civiltà della conversazione* (Milano, Adelphi, 2001).
Croce, B, *Storia d'Italia dal 1871 al 1915* (Bari, Laterza, 1929).
Crouch, C, *Post-democracy* (Cambridge, Polity, 2004).
Cuomo, E, *Critica e crisi del parlamentarismo (1870–1900)* (Torino, Giappichelli, 1996).
Dalton, R and Wattenberg MP (eds), *Parties Without Partisans: Political Change in Advanced Industrial Democracies* (Oxford, Oxford University Press, 2002).
Darnton, R, *The Business of Enlightenment: A Publishing History of the Encyclopédie, 1775–1800* (Cambridge, MA, Harvard University Press, 1979).
—— *The Forbidden Best-Sellers of Pre-Revolutionary France* (New York, Norton, 1996).
De Benedetto, M, Lupo, N and Rangone, N (eds), *The Crisis of Confidence in Legislation* (Baden Baden, Nomos, 2020).
De Broglie, V, *Ecrits et discours* (Paris, 1863).
De Jouvenel, R, *La République des camarades* (Paris, Grasset, 1914).
De la Platière, J-M et al (eds), *Encyclopédie méthodique: Manufactures, arts et métiers* (Paris, 1785–1828).
Delia, L, *Droit et philosophie à la lumière de l'Encyclopédie* (Oxford, Voltaire Foundation, 2015).
Dobson, A, *Listening for Democracy: Recognition, Representation, Reconciliation* (Oxford, Oxford University Press, 2014).
Donolo, C, *L'intelligenza delle istituzioni* (Milano, Feltrinelli, 1997).
Douglas, M, *How Institutions Think* (Syracuse, NY, Syracuse University Press, 1986).
Dumont, E, *Souvenirs sur Mirabeau et sur les deux premières assemblées législatives* (Paris, PUF, 1932).
Domorenok, E, *Governing Sustainability in the EU: From Political Discourse to Policy Practices* (Abingdon, Routledge, 2019).
Duverger, M, *Political Parties: Their Organization and Activity in the Modern State* (1st edn 1951) (New York, Wiley, 1954).
—— *Janus: Les deux faces de l'Occident* (Paris, Fayard, 1979).
Enciclopedia italiana, 36 vols (Rome, Treccani, 1929–39).
Encyclopédie Méthodique, 200 vols (Paris, 1782–1832).
Encyclopaedia Metropolitana, 20 vols (London, Fellowes et al, 1817–45).
Encyclopédie Nouvelle, 8 vols (Paris, 1834–42).
Encyclopédie; ou Dictionnaire raisonné des sciences, des arts et des métiers, 28 vols (eds D Diderot and J le Rond D'Alambert) (Paris, Briasson et al, 1751–72).
Engelsing, R, *Der Buerger als Leser: Lesergeschichte in Deutschland 1500–1800* (Stuttgart, JB Metzlersche and AE Poeschel, 1974).
Epstein, SR, *Freedom and Growth* (London, Routledge, 2000).
Erskine May, T, *Treatise on the Law, Privileges, Proceedings and Usage of Parliament* (London, Knight, 1844).
[Espasa] *Enciclopedia Universal ilustrada Europeo-americana*, 72 vols (Madrid, Espasa et al, 1908–30).

Esposito, R, *Living Thought: The Origins and Actuality of Italian Philosophy* (Stanford, CA, Stanford University Press, 2012).

—— *Politics and Negation: For an Affirmative Philosophy* (Cambridge, Polity, 2019).

—— *Pensiero istituente: Tre paradigmi di ontologia politica* (Torino, Einaudi, 2020).

—— *Istituzione* (Bologna, il Mulino, 2021).

Fabbrini, S, *Compound Democracies: Why the United States and Europe Are Becoming Similar* (Oxford, Oxford University Press, 2007).

Farneti, P, *La classe politica italiana dal liberalismo alla democrazia* (Genova, ECIG, 1989).

Fasone, C, *Sistemi di commissioni parlamentari e forma di governo* (Padova, Cedam, 2012).

Favoreu, L, *La politique saisie par le droit* (Paris, Economica, 1988).

Ferguson A, *An Essay on the History of Civil Society* (Dublin, Boulter Grierson, 1767).

Ferraro, F, *Razionalità legislativa e motivazione delle leggi: Un'introduzione teorica* (Milano, Giuffré Francis Lefebvre, 2019).

Foord, AS, *His Majesty's Opposition 1714–1830* (Oxford, Clarendon Press, 1964).

Foucault, M, *The Order of Things* (1st edn 1966) (New York, Routledge, 2002).

Floridi, L, *The Fourth Revolution: How the Infosphere is Reshaping Human Reality* (Oxford, Oxford University Press, 2014).

Frye, N, *The Great code: the Bible and literature* (New York, Harcourt Brace Jovanovich, 1982).

Furetière, A and Basnage de Beuval, H, *Dictionnaire universel contenant généralement tous les mots françois tant vieux que modernes, et les termes des sciences et des arts* (Leers, The Hague, 1701).

Garrigues, J (ed), *Histoire du Parlement* (Paris, Colin, 2007).

Gauchet, M, *La crise du liberalisme 1880–1914* (Paris, Gallimard, 2007).

Gay, P, *Schnitzler's Century: The Making of Middle-Class Culture, 1815–1914* (New York, Norton, 2002).

Glasbergen, P, Biermann, F and Mol, A (eds), *Partnerships, Governance, and Sustainable Development* (Cheltenham, Edward Elgar, 2007).

Goodrum, CA and Dalrymple, HW, *The Library of Congress* (Boulder, CO,Westview, 1982).

Griglio, E, *Parliamentary Oversight of the Executives: Tools and Procedures in Europe* (Oxford, Hart Publishing, 2020).

Guerrieri, S, *Costituzioni allo specchio: la rinascita democratica in Francia ed in Italia dopo la liberazione* (Bologna, il Mulino, 2021).

Guizot, F, *Histoire des origines du gouvernement représentatif (Cours de 1820–1822)* (Paris, 1856).

Habermas, J, *The Structural Transformation of the Public Sphere: An Inquiry into a Category of Bourgeois Society* (1st edn 1962) (Cambridge, Polity, 1992).

Habermas, J, *Theorie des kommunikativen Handelns* (Frankfurt am Main, Suhrkamp, 1981).

Habermas, J, *Faktizität und Geltung: Beiträge zur Diskurstheorie des Rechts und des demokratischen Rechtsstaates* (Frankfurt am Main, Suhrkamp, 1992).

Han, Byung-Chul, *In the Swarm: Digital Prospects* (Cambridge, MA, MIT Press, 2017).

Hansard Society, *Survey of Political Engagement 15: The 2018 Report* (London, Hansard Society, 2018).

Harris, B, *The Origins of the British Welfare State: Social Welfare in England and Wales, 1800–1945* (Basingstoke, Palgrave Macmillan 2004).

Harris, J, *Lexicon Technicum; Or an Universal English Dictionary of Arts and Sciences*, 2 vols (London, Brown et al, 1704–10).

Hazard, P, *La crise de la conscience européenne* (1st edn 1935) (Paris, Le Livre de Poche, 1994).

Headrick, DR, *When Information Came of Age: Technologies of Knowledge in the Age of Reason and Revolution, 1700–1850* (Oxford, Oxford University Press, 2000).

Hegel GWF, *Grundlinien der Philosophie des Rechts* (Hamburg, Meiner, 2009–11).

—— *Encyclopedia of the Philosophical Sciences in Basic Outline* (1st edn, 1817) (Cambridge, Cambridge University Press, 2014).

Heurtin, J-P, *L'espace public parlementaire: Essai sur les raisons du législateur* (Paris, PUF, 1999).

Hislop, D, *Knowledge Management in Organizations: A Critical Introduction* (Oxford, Oxford University Press, 2009).

Hix, S, Noury, A and Roland, G (eds), *Democratic Politics in the European Parliament* (Cambridge, Cambridge University Press, 2007).

Hobsbawm, EJ, *The Age of Capital* (London, Weidenfeld & Nicolson, 1975).

—— *Nations and Nationalism Since 1780: Programme, Myth, Reality*, 2nd edn (Cambridge, Cambridge University Press, 1990).

Hofmann, H, *Repreaesentation: Studien zur Wort-und Begriffsgeschichte von der Antike bis ins 19 Jahrhundert*, 4.Aufl (Berlin, Duncker & Humblot, 2003).
Huber, JD, *Rationalizing Parliament: Legislative Institutions and Party Politics in France* (Cambridge, Cambridge University Press, 1996).
Humboldt, A von, *Kosmos – Entwurf einer physischen Weltbeschreibung* (Stuttgart, Cotta, 1845–62).
Hupka, W, *Wort und Bild: Die Illustrationen in Wörterbüchern und Enzyklopädien* (Tübingen, Max Niemeyer Verlag, 1989).
Irti, N, *L'età della decodificazione* (Milano, Giuffré, 1989).
Ismayr, W, *Der Deutsche Bundestag*, 3 Aufl (Wiesbaden, Springer, 2012).
Jardin, A and Tudesq, AJ, *La France des notables*, 2 vols (Paris, Seuil, 1973).
Jemielniak, D, *Common Knowledge? An Ethnography of Wikipedia* (Stanford, CA, Stanford University Press, 2014).
Joana, J, *Pratiques politiques des députés français au XIXe siècle: Du dilettante au spécialiste* (Paris, L'Harmattan, 1999).
Kafker, F, *Notable Encyclopedias of the Late Eighteenth Century: Eleven Successors of the Encyclopédie* (Oxford, Voltaire Foundation at the Taylor Institution, 1994).
Kahneman, D, Sibony, O and Sunstein, CR, *Noise: A Flaw in Human Judgment* (New York, Little, Brown Spark, 2021).
Kaul, I, Grunberg, I and Stern, MA (eds), *Global Public Goods: International Cooperation for the 21st Century* (New York, Oxford University Press, 1999).
Kearney, P, *Touch: Recovering our Most Vital Sense* (New York, Columbia University Press, 2021).
Keyes, P, *The Post-Truth Era: Dishonesty and Deception in Contemporary Life* (New York, St Martin's Press, 2004).
Kelsen, H, *The Essence and Value of Democracy* (1st edn 1929) (Lanham, MD, Rowman and Littlefield, 2013).
Kleineres Brockhaus'sches Conversations-Lexicon, 4 vols (Leipzig, Brockhaus, 1854).
Kogan, H, *The Great EB: The Story of the Encyclopaedia Britannica* (Chicago, IL, University of Chicago Press, 1958).
Koiré, A, *Du monde clos à l'univers infini* (Paris, Gallimard, 1993).
Koss, S, *The Rise and Fall of the Political Press in Britain* (Chapel Hill, NC, University of North Carolina Press, 1981).
Koß, M, *Parliaments in Time: The Evolution of Legislative Democracy in Western Europe, 1866–2015* (Oxford, Oxford University Press, 2018).
Krehbiel, K, *Information and Legislative Organization* (Ann Arbor, MI, University of Michigan Press, 1991).
Kreppel, A, *The European Parliament and Supranational Party System: A Study in Institutional Development* (Cambridge, Cambridge University Press, 2002).
Kuhn, T, *The Structure of Scientific Revolutions* (Chicago, IL, University of Chicago Press, 1962).
Kyle, CR, *Theater of State: Parliament and Political Culture in Early Stuart England* (Stanford, CA, Stanford University Press, 2012).
Leibholz, G, *Das Wesen der Repräsentation unter besonderer Berücksichtung der Repräsentativsystems: Ein Beitrag zur allgemeinen Staats- und Verfassungslehre* (Berlin, Walter de Gruyter, 1929).
Leopardi, G, *Zibaldone di pensieri* in *Opere Complete*, Vol II (Firenze, Sansoni, 1969).
Linnand, S and Sobolewski, F, *The German Bundestag: Functions and Procedures* (Rheinbreitbach, Neue Darmstadter Verlagsanstalt, 2015).
Leyland, P, *The Constitution of the United Kingdom: A Contextual Analysis* (Oxford, Hart Publishing, 2021).
Lih, A, *The Wikipedia Revolution: How a Bunch of Nobodies Created the World's Greatest Encyclopedia* (New York, Hyperion, 2009).
Loewenberg, G and Patterson, SC, *Comparing Legislatures* (Lanham, MD, University Press of America, 1979).
Lotman, J, *Culture and Explosion* (1st edn 1992) (Berlin, Mouton de Gruyter, 2009).
Loveland, J, *The European Encyclopedia: From 1650 to the Twenty-First Century* (Cambridge, Cambridge University Press, 2019).
Lowndes, V and Roberts, M, *Why Institutions Matter: The New Institutionalism in Political Science* (London, Palgrave Macmillan, 2013).
Luhmann, N, *Legitimation durch Verfahren* (Frankfurt am Main, Suhrkamp, 1983).
Lupo, N and Piccirilli, G (eds), *The Italian Parliament in the European Union* (Oxford, Hart Publishing, 2017).
Lyotard, JF, *The Post-modern Condition: A Report on Knowledge* (1st edn 1979) (Manchester, Manchester University Press, 1984).
Macpherson, CB, *The Political Theory of Possessive Individualism: Hobbes to Locke* (Oxford, Clarendon Press, 1962).

Magnusson, L, *Nation, State and the Industrial Revolution: The Visible Hand* (London, Routledge, 2009).

Mair, P, *Ruling the Void: The Hollowing of Western Democracy* (London, Verso, 2013).

Mancini, M and Galeotti U, *Norme ad usi del Parlamento italiano* (Roma, Tipografia della Camera dei deputati, 1887).

Manin, B, *The Principles of Representative Government* (Cambridge, Cambridge University Press, 1997).

Mann, T, *Betrachtungen eines Unpolitischen* (Berlin, S Fischer, 1918).

Manzella, A, *Il Parlamento* (Bologna, il Mulino, 2003).

—— *Elogio dell'Assemblea, tuttavia* (Modena, Mucchi, 2020).

Maranini, G, *Storia del potere in Italia* (Firenze, Vallecchi, 1983).

March, J and Olsen, J, *Rediscovering Institutions: The Organizational Basis of Politics* (New York, The Free Press, 1989).

Marchand, J, *La Bibliothèque de l'Assembleée Nationale* (Bordeaux, Societé des Bibliophiles de Guyenne, 1979).

Martuccelli, D, *La societé singulariste* (Paris, Colin, 2010).

Masserschmidt, K and Oliver-Lalana, D (eds), *Rational Lawmaking under Review: Legisprudence according to the German Constitutional Court* (Berlin, Springer, 2015).

Mathieu, B, *La loi* (Paris, Dalloz, 2010).

McKay, W and Johnson, CW, *Parliament and Congress: Representation and Scrutiny in the Twenty-First Century* (Oxford, Oxford University Press, 2010).

Menhennet, D, *The House of Commons Library: A History* (London, House of Commons Library, 2000).

Mertens B, *Gesetzgebungskunst im Zeitalter der Kodifikationen: Theorie und Praxis der Gesetzgebungstechnik aus historisch-vergleichender Sicht* (Tübingen, Mohr Siebeck, 2003).

Miceli, V, *Principi di diritto parlamentare* (Milano, Società Editrice Libraria, 1910).

Mirkine-Guetzévich, B, *Les nouvelles tendences du droit constitutionnel* (Paris, Marcel Giard, 1931).

Mohl, R von, *Politik (Staatsrecht, Völkerrecht und Politik: Monographien 2)*, 2 vols (Tübingen, 1862–69).

Monsaingeon, G, *Mappamundi: Art et Cartographie* (Marseille, Editions Parenthèses, 2013).

Montesquieu, C-L, '*Esprit des lois*' in *Œuvres Complétes*, vol II (Paris, Gallimard, 1951).

Moretti, F, *Modern Epic: The World System from Goethe to García Márquez* (New York, Verso, 2010).

—— *The Bourgeois: Between History and Literature* (London, Verso, 2013).

Morisi, M, *Le leggi del consenso: Partiti e interessi nei primi parlamenti della repubblica* (Soveria Mannelli Rubbettino, 1992).

Mosca, G, *Teorica dei governi e governo parlamentare* (1884) in *Scritti politici*, Vol I (Torino, UTET, 1982).

Musella, L, *Il trasformismo* (Bologna, il Mulino, 2003).

New Plenary Hall of the Chamber of Deputies on the 1918–2018 Centenary (Soveria Mannelli, Rubettino, 2018).

Nichols, T, *The Death of Expertise: The Campaign Against Established Knowledge and Why It Matters* (Oxford, Oxford University Press, 2017).

Norton, P, *The Voice of the Backbenchers: The 1922 Committee: The First 90 Years 1923–2013* (London, Conservative History Group, 2013).

Ober, J, *Democracy and Knowledge: Innovation and Learning in Classical Athens* (Princeton, NJ, Princeton University Press, 2008).

Oertzen, J von, *Das Expertenparlament: Abgeordetenrollen in den Fachstrukturen bundesdeutscher Parlamente* (Baden Baden, Nomos, 2006).

Ory, P, *Qu'est-ce qu'une nation? Une histoire mondiale* (Paris, Gallimard, 2020).

Ostrogorsky, M, *Democracy and the Organization of Political Parties*, Vols I–II (London, Macmillan, 1902).

Paine, T, *The Rights of Man* (1st edn 1791) (Mineola, NY, Dover Publications, 1999).

Palermo, F and Kössler, K, *Comparative Federalism: Constitutional Arrangements and Case Law* (Oxford, Hart Publishing, 2017).

Palonen, K, *The Politics of Parliamentary Procedure: The Formation of the Westminster Procedure as a Parliamentary Ideal Type* (Leverkusen-Opladen,Verlag Barbara Budrich, 2016).

—— *Parliamentary Thinking: Procedure, Rhetoric and Time* (Cham, Palgrave Macmillan, 2019).

Panebianco, A, *Modelli di partito. Organizzazione e potere nei partiti politici* (Bologna, il Mulino, 1982).

Pasquino, P, *Sieyès et l'invention de la Constitution en France* (Paris, Odile Jacob, 1998).

Penny Cyclopaedia of the Society for the Diffusion of Useful Knowledge, 27 vols (London, Knight, 1833–43).

Peters, BG, *Institutional Theory in Political Science: The 'New Institutionalism'* (London, Continuum, 2005).

Pettegree, A, *The Invention of News: How the World Came to Know Itself* (New Haven, CT, Yale University Press, 2014).

Pielke, R, *The Honest Broker: Making Sense of Science in Policy and Politics* (Cambridge, Cambridge University Press, 2007).
Piretti, MS, *La giustizia dei numeri: Il Proporzionalismo in Italia (1870–1923)* (Bologna, il Mulino, 1990).
Pitkin, HF, *The Concept of Representation* (Berkeley, CA, University of California Press, 1967).
Pivati, G, *Nuovo dizionario sceintifico e curioso sacro*-profano (Venezia, Milocco, 1746–51).
Pliny, *Natural History*, Vols I–X, Loeb Classical Library (Cambridge, MA, Harvard University Press, 1938–62).
Poguntke, T and Webb, P (eds), *The Presidentialization of Politics in Democratic Societies: A Framework for Analysis* (Oxford, Oxford University Press, 2005).
Posner, P, *The Politics of Unfunded Mandates* (Washington, DC, Georgetown University Press, 1998).
Poudra, J and Pierre, E, *Traité pratique de droit parlementaire* (Versailles, Cerf et fils; Paris, J Baudry, 1878).
Prins, A, *La démocratie et le régime parlementaire* (Bruxelles, Librairie Européenne Muquardt, 1884).
Profitt, M (ed), *Leveraging Wikipedia, Connecting Communities of Knowledge* (Chicago, IL, ALA, 2018).
Proust, J, *Diderot et l'Encyclopédie* (Paris, Albin Michel, 1962).
Quermonne, JL, *Le Gouvernement de la France sous la Ve République* (Paris, Dalloz, 1987).
Rabelais, F, *Complete Works* (Berkeley, CA, Berkeley University Press, 1991).
Reckwitz, A, *Die Gesellschaft der Singularitäten. Zum Strukturwandel der Moderne* (Berlin, Suhrkamp, 2017; English translation, *The Society of Singularities* (Cambridge, Polity Press, 2020).
Redlich, J, *Recht und Technik des Englischen Parlamentarismus: die Geschaftsordnung of Commons in ihrer geschichtlichen Entwicklung und gegenwartigen Gestalt* (Leipzig, Duncker & Humblot, 1905), English translation, *The Procedure of the House of Commons: A Study of its History and Present Form* (London, Constable, 1908).
Reiher, M, *Parlamentarier als Beruf: Rekrutierungswege und politische Karrieren am Beispiel des Deutschen Bundestages* (Baden Baden, Nomos, 2019).
Ridola, P, *Democrazia pluralistica e libertà associative* (Milano, Giuffré, 1987).
—— *Democrazia rappresentativa e parlamentarismo* (Torino, Giappichelli, 2014).
Riehm, U, Böhle, K and Lindner, R, *Elektronische Petitionssysteme: Analysen zur Modernisierung des parlamentarischen Petitionswesens in Deutschland und Europa* (Berlin, Edition Sigma, 2013).
Riescher, G, *Zeit und Politik: Zur institutionellen Bedeutung von Zeitstrukturen in parlamentarischen und praesidentiellen Regierungssystemen* (Baden Baden, Nomos, 1994).
Ripoll Servant, A, *The European Parliament* (London, Palgrave, 2018).
Rizzoni, G, *Opposizione parlamentare e democrazia deliberativa: Ordinamenti europei a confronto* (Bologna, il Mulino, 2012).
Rokkan, S, *State Formation, Nation-building, and Mass Politics in Europe* (Oxford, Oxford University Press, 1999).
Rogari, S, *Alle origini del trasformismo: Partiti e Sistema politico nell'Italia liberale, 1861–1914* (Roma-Bari, Laterza, 1998).
Romanelli, R, *Il comando impossibile: Stato e società nell'Italia liberale* (Bologna, il Mulino 1988).
Roncaglia, G, *L'età della frammentazione: Cultura del libro e scuola digitale* (Bari, Laterza, 2018).
Rosa, H and Trejo-Mathys J, *Social Acceleration: A New Theory of Modernity* (New York, Columbia University Press, 2013).
Rosanvallon, P, *Le peuple introuvable: Histoire de la représentation démocratique en France* (Paris, Gallimard, 1998).
—— *La démocratie inachevée: Histoire de la souveraineté du peuple en France* (Paris, Gallimard, 2000).
—— *La Societé des égaux* (Paris, Seuil, 2011).
—— *Le bon gouvernement* (Paris, Seuil, 2015).
—— *Le Parlement des invisibles: Déchiffrer la France* (éd augmentée et mise à jour, Paris, Seuil, 2020).
Rose, ME, *The Relief of Poverty 1834–1914* (Basingstoke, Palgrave Macmillan, 1986).
Rose, R, *Understanding Big Government: The Programme Approach* (Beverly Hills, CA, Sage, 1984).
Rousselier, N, *Le Parlement de l'éloquence: La souveraineté de la délibération au lendemain de la Grande Guerre* (Paris, Presses de Sciences Po, 1997).
Russell, M and Gover, D, *Legislation at Westminster: Parliamentary Actors and Influence in the Making of British Law* (Oxford, Oxford University Press, 2017).
Russell, M, Morris, B and Larkin, P, *Fitting the Bill: Bringing Commons Legislation Committees into Line with Best Practice* (London, The Constitutional Unit, 2013).
Sabbatucci, G, *Il trasformismo come sistema: Saggio sulla storia politica dell'Italia unita* (Roma-Bari, Laterza, 2003).
Salvemini, G, *Il ministro della malavita e altri scritti sull'Italia giolittiana* (Milano, Feltrinelli, 1962).
Saward, M, *The Representative Claim* (Oxford, Oxford University Press, 2010).
Scoppola, P, *La Repubblica dei partiti: Profilo storico della democrazia in Italia* (1945–1990) (Bologna, il Mulino, 1991).

Scheuerman, W, *Liberal Democracy and the Social Acceleration of Time* (Baltimore, MD, Johns Hopkins University Press, 2004).
Schmidt, VA, *Democracy in Europe: The EU and National Polities* (Oxford, Oxford University Press, 2006).
Schmitt, C, *The Crisis of Parliamentary Democracy* (1st edn 1926) (Cambridge, MA, MIT Press, 1985).
Schneider, J, *The Committee System in the US Congress* (Washington, DC, Congressional Research Service, 2009).
Schuettemeyer, SS, *Fraktionen im Deutschen Bundestag 1949–1997: Empirische Befunde und theoretische Folgerungen* (Opladen, Wiesbaden, Westdeutscher Verlag, 1998).
Schwartz, NL, *The Blue Guitar* (Chicago, IL, University of Chicago Press, 1988).
Selinger, W, *Parliamentarism: From Burke to Weber* (Cambridge, Cambridge University Press, 2019).
Sparrow, A, *Obscure Scribblers: A History of Parliamentary Reporting* (London, Politico's Publishing Ltd, 2003).
Spree, U, *Das Streben nach Wissen: Eine vergleichende Gattungsgeschichte der populären Enzyklopädie in Deutschland und Großbritannien im 19 Jahrhundert* (Berlin, de Gruyter, 2009).
Steffen, A, *Teilstudie 3: Befragung der Nutzer der Bundestags- Webseiten zu den öffentlichen Petitionen. Follow-up-Studie zu den Öffentlichen Petitionen des Deutschen Bundestags. Gutachten im Auftrag des Deutschen Bundestages vorgelegt dem Büro für Technikfolgen-Abschätzung beim Deutschen Bundestag (TAB)* (Berlin, Zebralog GmbH & Co, 2010).
Stone, L and Fawtier, J, *An Open Elite? England 1540–1880* (London, Oxford University Press, 1986).
Sunstein, C, *Republic Divided: Divided Democracy in an Age of Social Media* (Princeton, NJ, Princeton University Press, 2017).
Svenson, N, *The United Nations as a Knowledge System* (London, Routledge, 2016).
Tkacs, N, *Wikipedia and the Politics of Openness* (Chicago, IL, University of Chicago Press, 2014).
Triepel, H, *Die Staatsverfassung und die politischen Parteien* (Berlin, Liebmann, 1927).
Tsebelis, G and Money, J, *Bicameralism* (Cambridge, Cambridge University Press, 1997).
Turi, G, *Il fascismo e il consenso degli intellettuali* (Bologna, il Mulino, 1980).
Urbinati, N, *Representative Democracy: Principles and Genealogy* (Chicago, IL, University of Chicago Press, 2006).
—— *Democracy Disfigured: Opinion, Truth, and the People* (Cambridge, MA, Harvard University Press, 2014).
Vasoli, C, *L'enciclopedismo del seicento* (Napoli, Bibliopolis, 1978).
Venturi, R, *Le origini dell'Enciclopedia* (Roma, Edizioni U, 1946).
Venturini, V, *Libri, lettori e biblioteche a Montecitorio. Storia della Biblioteca della Camera dei deputati* (Milano, Wolters Kluwer, 2019).
Vico, GB, '*Scienza nuova*' in *Opere filosofiche* (Firenze, Sansoni, 1971).
Vincent de Bouvais, *Opus Preclarum Speculum Maius intitulatum in Speculum Naturale, Speculum Doctrinale, Speculum Morale et Speculum Historiale Quadripartitum Vincentii Presulis Inchoat numine felici* (Venezia, Liecthenstein, 1494).
Wahrman, D, *Imagining the Middle Class: The Political Representation of Class in Britain c 1780–1840* (Cambridge, Cambridge University Press, 1995).
West, WN, *Theatres and Encyclopedias in Early Western Europe* (Cambridge, Cambridge University Press, 2002).
XML, *Parliament* (Amsterdam, XML, 2016).
Yates, F, *The Art of Memory* (London, Routledge, 1966).
—— *Theatre of the World* (London, Routledge & Kegan Paul, 1966).
Yeo, R, *Encyclopaedic Visions: Scientific Dictionaries and Enlightenment Culture* (Cambridge, Cambridge University Press, 2010).
Yordanova, N, *Organising the European Parliament: The Role of Committees and their Legislative Influence* (Colchester, ECPR Press, 2013).
Wefing, H, *Parlamentsarchitektur: Zur Selbstdarstellung der Demokratie in ihren Bauwerken. Eine Untersuchung am Beispiel des Bonner Bundeshauses* (Berlin, Duncker & Humblot, 1995).
Weber, M, *Parliament and Government in Germany under a New Political Order* in M Weber, *Political Writings* (1st edn 1918) (Cambridge, Cambridge University Press, 1994).
—— *The Vocation Lectures: Science As a Vocation, Politics As a Vocation* (1st edn 1919) (Indianapolis, IN, Hackett Publishing, 2004).
—— *Economy and Society* (1st edn 1922) (Cambridge, MA Harvard University Press, 2019).
Westlake, M, *A Modern Guide to the European Parliament* (London, Pinter Publishers, 1994).
Wheare, KC, *Legislatures* (Oxford University Press, 1968).
Whitaker, R, *The European Parliament's Committees: National Party Influence and Legislative Empowerment* (London, Routledge, 2011).

Wilson, TW, *Congressional Government: A Study in American Politics* (1st edn 1885) (Cleveland, OH, The World Publishing Company, 1956).
Winkler, HA, *Weimar 1918–933: Die Geschichte der ersten deutschen Demokratie* (München, Beck, 1993).
Zielonka, J, *The Lost Future and How to Reclaim It* (London, Yale University Press, 2023).

Chapters in Edited Volumes

Abbatista, G, 'La 'Folie de la raison par alphabet': le origini settecentesche dell'Enciclopedia Britannica (1768–1701)' in G Abbatista (ed), *L'enciclopedismo in Italia nel XVIII secolo* (Napoli, Bibliopolis, 1996).
Agamben, G, 'What is the Contemporary?' in G Agamben, *'What is an Apparatus?' and Other Essays* (Stanford, CA, Stanford University Press, 2009).
Arendt, H, *Truth and Politics in Between Past and Future* (1968) (London, Penguin, 2006).
Astuti, G, 'Legge (diritto intermedio)' in *Enciclopedia del diritto* (Milano, Giuffrè, 1973) Vol XXIII.
Avril, P, 'Les commissions parlementaires, entre groupes politiques et gouvernement' in F Fraysse and F Hourquebie (eds), *Les Commissions parlementaires dans l'espace francophone* (Paris, Montchrestien, 2011).
Barberis, W, 'L'Enciclopedia einaudiana' in *Enciclopedismo antico e moderno* (Bari, Fondazione Gianfranco Diogaurdi, 2020).
Beddie, L, Macintosh, A and Malina, A, 'E-democracy and the Scottish Parliament' in B Schmid, BK Stanoevska-Slabeva and V Tschammer (eds), *Towards the E-Society* IFIP International Federation for Information Processing, Vol 74 (Boston, MA, Springer, 2001).
Benoit, C and Rozenberg, O, 'Introduction' in *Handbook of Parliamentary Studies: Interdisciplinary Approaches to Legislatures* (Cheltenham, Edward Elgar, 2020).
Benoit, C and Rozenberg, O, 'Les Legislatives Studies: de l'art de couper des bûches et de collectionner les barils de porc' in O Rozenberg and E Thiers (eds), *Traité d'études parlementaires* (Bruxelles, Bruylant, 2018).
—— 'Political Science Approaches to Legislatures' in C Benoit and O Rozenberg (eds), *Parliamentary Studies: Interdisciplinary Approaches to Legislatures* (Cheltenham, Edward Elgar, 2020).
Beyme, K von, 'Wandlungen des Parlamentarismus, von Weimar nach Bonn' in HP Schneider and W Zeh (eds), *Parlamentsrecht und Parlamentspraxis in Bundesrepublik Deutschland* (Berlin, De Gruyter, 1989).
Biefang, A, 'Visualisierungen des Parlamentarismus im 19 Jahrundert. Ein Problemaufriss in europaeischer Perspektive' in A Schulz and A Wirsching (eds), *Parlamentarische Kulturen in Europa. Das Parlament als Kommunikationsraum* (Duesseldorf, Droste Verlag, 2012).
Blumer, JG, 'In Praise of Holistic Empiricism' in K Brants and K Voltmer (eds), *Political Communication in Postmodern Democracy: Challenging the Primacy of Politics* (New York, Palgrave Macmillan, 2011) II.
Borchert, J and Golsch, L, 'Deutschland: von der 'Honorationenzukunft' zur politischen Klasse' in J Borchert (ed), *Politik als Beruf. Die politische Klasse in westlichen Demokratien* (Opladen, Leske+Budrich, 1999).
Bradley, AW and Pinelli, P, 'Parliamentarism' in M Rosenfeld and A Sajo (eds), *The Oxford Handbook of Comparative Constitutional Law* (Oxford, Oxford University Press, 2012).
Bray, M, 'Dall'Enciclopedia Italiana alla Enciclopedia Einaudiana' in *Enciclopedismo antico e moderno* (Bari, Fondazione Gianfranco Dioguardi, 2020).
Bressanelli, E, 'The Political Groups as Organisations: The Institutionalisation of Transnational Party Politics' in P Ahrens, A Elomaki and J Kantola (eds), *European Parliament's Political Groups in Turbulent Times* (Cham, Palgrave, 2022).
Burke, E, 'Speech to the Electors of Bristol' in *The Works of the Right Honourable Edmund Burke*, Volume I (London, Rivington, 1826).
Caney, S, 'Political Institutions for the Future: A Fivefold Package' in I González-Ricoy and A Gosseries (eds), *Institutions for Future Generations* (Oxford, Oxford University Press, 2016).
Carducci, G, 'Candidature' in *Edizione nazionale delle opere di Giosuè Carducci*, Vol XXV, *Confessioni e battaglie*, Serie seconda (Bologna, Zanichelli, 1938).
Cartier, E, 'Le Parlement et la durée' in G Toulemond and E Cartier (eds), *Le Parlement et le temps: Approche comparée* (Paris, Institut Universitaire Varenne, 2017).
Caygill, T and Griffiths, AM, 'Parliament and Petitions' in C Leston Bandeira and L Thompson (eds), *Exploring Parliament* (Oxford, Oxford University Press, 2018).

Cole, JY, 'The Congressional Research Service' in JY Cole and J Aikin (eds), *Encyclopaedia of the Library of the Congress: For Congress, the Nation and the World* (Washington, DC, The Library of the Congress, Bernan Press, 2004).

Cole JY and Aikin J, 'America's Library: A Brief History of the Library of the Congress' in JY Cole and J Aikin (eds), *Encyclopaedia of the Library of the Congress: For Congress, the Nation and the World* (Washington, DC, Library of the Congress, Bernan Press, 2004).

Cotta, M, 'The Rise and Fall of the "Centrality" of the Italian Parliament: Transformations of the Executive-Legislative Subsystem After the Second World War' in GW Copeland and SC Patterson (eds), *Parliaments in the Modern World: Changing Institutions* (Ann Arbor, MI, University of Michigan Press, 1994).

D'Alambert, JB, 'Discours Préliminaire' in D Diderot and J le Rond D'Alambert (eds), *Encyclopédie; ou Dictionnaire raisonné des sciences, des arts et des métiers*, 28 vols (Paris, Briasson et al, 1751–72) Vol I (1751).

Delon, M, 'L'Encyclopédie de Diderot et d'Alambert, totalisation et inachèvement' in *Enciclopedismo antico e moderno* (Bari, Fondazione Gianfranco Dioguardi, 2020).

De Spiegeleer, C, 'The nationalization and mediatization of European monarchies in times of sorrow: Royal deaths and funerals in the second half of the nineteenth century' in E Woodacre, LHS Dean, C Jones, RE Martin and ZE Rohr (eds), *The Routledge History of Monarchy* (London, Routledge, 2019).

Detienne, M, 'From Assembly Practices to Forms of Politics: A Comparative Approach' in M Detienne, *Comparing the Incomparable* (Stanford, CA, Stanford University Press, 2008).

Decaro, M, 'I bicameralismi nell'Unione europea' in M Decaro (ed), *Il bicameralismo in discussione. Regno Unito, Francia, Italia: Profili comparati* (Roma, Luiss University Press, 2008).

Diderot, D, 'Encyclopédie (Philosophie)' in D Diderot and J le Rond D'Alambert (eds), *Encyclopédie; ou Dictionnaire raisonné des sciences, des arts et des métiers*, 28 vols (Paris, Briasson et al, 1751–72) Vol VII (1755).

D'Onofrio, F, 'Committees in the Italian Parliament' in M Shaw and J Lees (eds), *Committees in Legislatures: A Comparative Analysis* (Durham, NC, Duke University Press, 1979).

Eco, U, 'Dall'albero al labirinto' in U Eco, *Dall'albero al labirinto: Studi storici sul segno e l'interpretazione* (Milano, La Nave di Teseo, 2017).

Ehrenberg, J, 'The History of Civil Society Ideas' in M Edwards (ed), *The Oxford Handbook of Civil Society* (Oxford, Oxford University Press, 2011).

Elia, L, 'Commissioni parlamentari' in *Enciclopedia del diritto*, Vol VII (Milano, Giuffré, 1960).

Evans, P, 'Introduction: The Growth of Many Centuries' in P Evans (ed), *Essays on the History of Parliamentary Procedure: In Honour of Thomas Erskine May* (Oxford, Hart Publishing, 2017).

Fasone, C, 'Parliaments in comparative and political analyses' in C Benoît and O Rozenberg (eds), *Parliamentary Studies: Interdisciplinary Approaches to Legislatures* (Cheltenham, Edward Elgar, 2020).

Fowler, R, 'Encyclopaedias: Definitions and Theoretical Problems' in P Binkley (ed), *Pre-Modern Encyclopaedic Texts* (Leiden, Brill, 1997).

Fromage, D, 'The *Spitzenkandidaten* procedure for the election of the European Commission President: A critical view' in T Marguery, S Platon and H van Eijken (eds), *Les élections européennes 40 ans après* (Bruxelles, Bruylant, 2020).

Frosini, TE, 'L'antiparlamentarismo e i suoi interpreti' in A Cerri, P Häberle, M Jarvad et al (eds), *Il diritto fra interpretazione e storia. Liber amicorum in onore di Angel Antonio Cervati*, Roma, Aracne, 2010).

Gauchet, M, 'La droite et la gauche' in P Nora (ed), *Les lieux de mémoire*, tome 3, *Les France. 1. Conflits et partages* (Paris, Gallimard, 1992).

Giuliani, F, 'Il discorso parlamentare' in L Violante (ed), *Storia d'Italia: Annali 17 Il Parlamento* (Torino, Einaudi, 2001).

Gicquel, J, 'La IV République: la République-Janus' in M Calamo Specchia (ed), *La Costituzione francese/La Constitution Française* (Torino, Giappichelli, 2009).

Gramsci, A, 'Quaderno 13. Noterelle sulla politica di Machiavelli' in *Quaderni del Carcere, a cura di V Gerratana* (Torino, Einaudi, 1977) Vol III.

Hegel, GWF, 'Verhandlungen in der Versammlung der Landstände des Königsreichs Württemberg. Abteilungen I-XXXVIII (1815–1817)' in *Gesammelte Werke* (Hamburg, Meiner, 1990) Vol XV, *Schriften und Entwürfe*.

Heidar, K and Koole, R, 'Parliamentary Party Groups Compared' in K Heidar and R Koole (eds), *Parliamentary Party Groups in European Democracies: Political Parties Behind Closed Doors* (London, Routledge, 2000).

—— 'Representative Democracy and Parliamentary Party Groups' in K Heidar and R Koole (eds), *Parliamentary Party Groups in European Democracies: Political Parties Behind Closed Doors* (London, Routledge, 2000).
Heurtin, J-P, 'The Circle of Discussion and the Semicircle of Criticism' in B Latour and P Weibel (eds), *Making Things Public: Atmospheres of Democracy* (Cambridge, MA, ZKM Karlsruhe, Mit Press, 2005).
Höing, O, 'With a Little Help of the Constitutional Court: The Bundestag on its Way to an Active Policy Shaper' in C Hefftler, C Neuhold, O Rozenberg and J Smith (eds), *The Palgrave Handbook of National Parliaments and the European Union* (London, Palgrave Macmillan, 2015).
Holbach, PH, 'Rèpresentants' in D Diderot and J le Rond D'Alambert (eds), Encyclopédie; ou Dictionnaire raisonné des sciences, des arts et des métiers (Paris, Briasson et al, 1751–72) Vol XIV (1765).
Humboldt, W von, 'Über die innere und äussere Organisation der höheren wissenschaftlichen Anstalten' (1st edn 1810) in *Werke in fünf Bänden*, Bd 4 (Darmstadt, Wissenschaftliche Buchgesellschaft, 2010).
Inglehart, B, 'The Changing Structure of Political Cleavages in Western Society' in RJ Dalton, PA Beck and C Flanagan (eds), *Electoral Change in Advanced Industrial Democracies: Realignment or Dealignement?* (Princeton, NJ, Princeton University Press, 1984).
Jekewitz, P, 'Politische Bedeutung, Rechtsstellung und Verfahren der Bundestagfraktionen' in HP Schneider and W Zeh (eds), *Parlamentsrecht und Parlamentspraxis in Bundesrepublik Deutschland* (Berlin, De Gruyter, 1989).
Johnson, N, 'Committees in the West German Bundestag' in J Lees and M Shaw (eds), *Committees in Legislatures: A Comparative Analysis* (Oxford, Martin Robertson, 1979).
Karpen, U, 'Gesetzgebung in Rechtsvergleich' in W Kluht and G Krings (eds), *Gesetzgebung: Rechtsetzung durch Parlamente und Verwaltungen sowie ihre gerichtliche Kontrolle* (Heidelberg, Müller, 2014).
Kelly, R, 'Select Committees: Powers and Functions' in A Horne, G Drewry and D Oliver (eds), *Parliament and the Law* (Oxford, Hart Publishing, 2014).
Klein, H, 'Art 21' in T Mauntz and G Düring (eds), *Grundgesetz Kommentar* (München, Beck, 2009).
Koenig, M, 'Knowledge Management: Where is it Going?' in S McCallum, L Bultrini, J Sempéré and W Newman (eds), *Knowledge Management in Libraries and Organizations* (Berlin, De Gruyter, 2016).
König, J and Woolf, G, 'Encyclopaedism in the Roman Empire' in J König and G Woolf (eds), *Encyclopaedism from Antiquity to the Renaissance* (Cambridge, Cambridge University Press, 2013).
—— 'Introduction' in J König and G Woolf (eds), *Encyclopaedism from Antiquity to the Renaissance* (Cambridge, Cambridge University Press, 2013).
Kluth W, 'Entwicklung und Perspektiven der Gesetzgebungswissenschaft' in W Kluth and G Krings (ed), *Gesetzgebung. Rechtsetzung durch Parlamente und Verwaltungen sowie ihre gerichtliche Kontrolle* (München, CF Müller, 2018).
Kocka, J, 'Bürgertum und bürgerliche Gesellschaft im 19 Jahrhundert: europäische Entwicklungen und deutsche Eigenarten' in J Kocka (ed), *Bürgertum im 19 Jahrhundert: Deutschland im europäischen Vergleich*, Band 1 (München, Deutscher Taschenbuch Verlag, 1988).
Kreppel, A, 'Legislatures' in D Caramani (ed), *Comparative Politics* (Oxford, Oxford University Press, 2020).
Krueper, J, 'Das Wissen des Parlament' in M Morlok, U Schliesky and D Wiefelspuetz (eds), *Parlamentsrecht: Praxishandbuch* (Baden Baden, Nomos, 2016).
Latour, B, 'From Realpolitik to Dingpolitik, or How to Make Things Public' in B Latour and P Weibel (eds), *Making Things Public: Atmospheres of Democracy* (Cambridge, MA, MIT Press, 2005).
Lees, JD, 'Committees in the United States Congress' in JD Lees and M Shaw (eds), *Committees in Legislatures: A Comparative Analysis* (Oxford, Martin Robertson, 1979).
Leston-Bandeira, C and Walker, A, 'Parliament and Public Engagement' in C Leston-Bandeira and C Thompson (eds), *Exploring Parliament* (Oxford, Oxford University Press, 2018).
Luciani, M, 'Il Parlamento negli anni Novanta' in L Violante (ed), *Storia d'Italia: Annali 17. Il Parlamento* (Torino, Einaudi, 2001).
Lupo, N, 'La continuità del diritto parlamentare: La riadozione del regolamento prefascista nella Camera dei deputati' in U De Siervo, S Guerrieri and A Varsori (eds), *La prima legislatura repubblicana : Continuità e discontinuità nell'azione delle istituzioni*, Vol II (Roma, Carocci, 2004).
—— 'Parliaments' in R Masterman and R Schuetze (eds), *The Cambridge Companion to Comparative Constitutional Law* (Cambridge, Cambridge University Press, 2019).
Lupo, N and Rizzoni, G, 'Foreign influences on (the procedure and content of) the Italian legislative process' in N Lupo and L Scaffardi (eds), *Comparative Law in Legislative Drafting: The Increasing Importance of Dialogue Amongst Parliaments* (The Hague, Eleven International Publishing, 2014).

Luther, J, 'The Search for a Constitutional Geography and Historiography of Second Chambers' in J Luther, P Passaglia and R Tarchi (eds), *A World of Second Chambers: Handbook for Constitutional Studies on Bicameralism* (Milano, Giuffré, 2006).

Manzella, A, 'The European Parliament and National Parliaments as a System' in S Mangiameli (ed), *The Consequnces of the Crisis on European Integration and on Member States* (Cham, Springer, 2017).

Mastropaolo, A, 'Notabili, clientelismo e trasformismo' in L Violante (ed), *Storia d'Italia: Il parlamento* (Torino, Einaudi, 1999).

Mill J, 'On Government' in *Essays on Government, Jurisprudence, Liberty of the Press, Prisons and Prison Discipline, Colonies, Law of Nations, Education* (London, Innes, 1823).

Mill, JS, 'Considerations on Representative Government' in JS Mill, *On Liberty and Other Essays* (1st edn 1861) (Oxford, Oxford University Press, 1998).

Mollier, J-Y, 'Les racines de l'antiparlementarisme au début de la troisième République (1870–1900)' in M Vovelle (ed), *Révolution et République: l'exception française* (Paris, Kimé, 1994).

Natzler, D, Bagnall, D, Brochu, J-P and Fowler, P, 'Controversy at the Antipodes (and Elsewhere). The International Cousins of the Treatise' in P Evans (ed), *Essays on the History of Parliamentary Procedure: In Honour of Thomas Erskine May* (Oxford, Hart Publishing, 2017).

Nelles, P, 'Libraries' in A Grafton, GW Most and S Settis (eds), *The Classical Tradition* (Cambridge, MA, The Belknap Press of Harvard University Press, 2010).

Neuhold, C and Settembri, P, 'The Role of the European Parliament Committees in the EU Decision-making Process' in T Christiansen and T Larsson (eds), *The Role of Committees in the Policy-Process of the European Union* (Cheltenham, Edward Elgar, 2007).

Nidermayer, O, 'Nach der Vereinigung. Der Trend zum Fluiden Fuenfparteisystem' in OW Gabriel, O Nidermayer and R Stoess (eds), *Parteidemokratie in Deutschland* (Wiesbaden, Westdeutscher Verlag, 2002).

Norton, P, 'The United Kingdom. Exerting influence from within' in K Heidar and R Koole (eds), *Parliamentary Party Groups in European Democracies: Political Parties Behind Closed Doors* (London, Routledge, 2000).

Ormières, JL, 'Les rouges et les blancs' in P Nora (ed), *Les lieux de mémoire*, tome 3, *Les France. 1. Conflits et partages* (Paris, Gallimard, 1992).

Orsina, G 'L'organizzazione politica nelle Camere della proporzionale (1920-1924)' in F Grassi Orsini and G Quagliariello (eds), *Il partito politico dalla grande guerra al fascismo: crisi della rappresentanza e riforma dello Stato nell'età dei sistemi politici di massa (1918–1925)* (Bologna, il Mulino, 1986).

Paguntke, T, 'Party Organizational Linkage: Parties without Firm Social Roots?' in KR Luther and F Mueller-Rommel (eds), *Political Parties in the New Europe: Political and Analytical Challenges* (Oxford, Oxford University Press, 2002).

Palanza, A, 'La perdita di confini: le nuove procedure interistituzionali nel Parlamento italiano' in L Violante (ed), *Storia d'Italia: Annali 17. Il Parlamento* (Torino, Einaudi, 2001).

Perticone, G, *Parlamentarismo e antiparlamentarismo nel post-Risorgimento* in G Perticone, *Scritti di storia e politica del post-Risorgimento* (Milano, A Giuffrè, 1969).

Peters, BG, 'The United States Congressional Administration' in T Christiansen, E Griglio and N Lupo (eds), *The Routledge Handbook of Parliamentary Administrations* (London, Routledge, 2023).

Poguntke, T, 'Parties in a Legalistic Culture: The Case of Germany' in RS Katz and P Mair, (eds), *How Parties Organize: Change and Adaptation in Party Organization in Western Democracies* (London, Sage Publications, 1994).

Polsby, NW, 'Legislatures' in F Greenstein and NW Polsby (eds), *Handbook of Political Science*, Vol 5 (Reading, MA, Addison-Wesley, 1975).

Raunio, T, 'Understanding the European Parliament's Party Groups' in K Heidar and R Koole (ed), *Parliamentary Party Groups in European Democracies: Political Parties Behind Closed Doors* (London, Routledge/ECPR, 2000).

Radaelli, CM, 'The Europeanization of Public Policies' in K Featherstone and CM Radaelli (eds), *The Politics of Europeanization* (Oxford, Oxford University Press, 2003).

Ridard, B, 'L'activité parlamentaire et l'instant' in G Toulemond and E Cartier (eds), *Le Parlement et le temps: Approche comparée* (Paris, Institut Universitaire Varenne, 2017).

Rioux, J-P, 'Le Palais-Bourbon' in P Nora (ed), *Le lieux de la mémoire*, II, *La Nation*, Vol 3 (Paris, Gallimard, 1986).

Rizzoni, G, 'Political Architecture and the Seduction of Space: The Form of Parliaments and European Identity' in L Rorato and A Saunders (eds), *The Essence and the Margin: National Identities and Collective Memories in Contemporary European Culture* (Amsterdam, Rodopi, 2009).

—— 'How Can Parliaments Improve Citizens' Confidence in Legislation?' in M De Benedetto, N Lupo and N Rangone (eds), *The Crisis of Confidence in Legislation* (Baden Baden, Nomos, 2020).

—— 'Parliamentary Administrations and the Provision of Scientific Expertise' in T Christiansen, E Griglio and N Lupo (eds), *The Routledge Handbook of Parliamentary Administrations* (London, Routledge, 2023).

Romanelli, R, 'Electoral Systems and Social Structures: A Comparative Perspective' in R Romanelli (ed), *How Did They Become Voters? The History of Franchise in Modern European Representation* (The Hague, Kluwer Law International, 1998).

Rozenberg, O, 'Comparer les parlements' in Y Doloye and JM Waele (eds), *Politique Comparée* (Brussels, Bruylant, 2018).

Russell, M, 'The British House of Lords: A tale of Adaptation and Resilience' in J Luther, P Passaglia and R Tarchi (eds), *A World of Second Chambers: Handbook for Constitutional Studies on Bicameralism* (Milano, Giuffré, 2006).

Saalfeld, T, 'Bureaucratisation, Coordination and Competition: Parliamentary Party Groups in the German Bundestag' in K Heidar and R Koole (eds), *Parliamentary Party Groups in European Democracies: Political Parties Behind Closed Doors* (London, Routledge, 2000).

Saiegh, SM, 'Lawmaking' in S Martin, T Saalfeld and KW Strom (eds), *The Oxford Handbook of Legislative Studies* (Oxford, Oxford University Press, 2014).

Santos, F and Saboia Vieira, F, 'Brazil's Parliamentary Administration' in T Christiansen, E Griglio and N Lupo (eds), *The Routledge Handbook of Parliamentary Administrations* (London, Routledge, 2023).

Schmitt, C, 'On the Contradiction between Parliamentarism and Democracy' in C Schmitt, *The Crisis of Parliamentary Democracy* (1st edn 1926) (Cambridge, MA, MIT Press, 1985).

Schulz, A and Wirsching, W, 'Introduction' in A Schulz and A Wirsching (eds), *Parlamentarische Kulturen in Europa. Das Parlament als Kommunikationsraum* (Duesseldorf, Droste Verlag, 2012).

Seaward, P, 'Parliamentary Law in the Eighteenth Century: From Commonplace to Treatise' in P Evans (ed), *Essays on the History of Parliamentary Procedure: In Honour of Thomas Erskine May* (Oxford, Hart Publishing, 2017).

Shaw M, 'Conclusion' in M Shaw and J Lees (eds), *Committees in Legislatures: A Comparative Analysis* (Durham, NC, Duke University Press, 1979).

Sieckmann, J, 'Legislation as Implementation of Constitutional Law: A Foundation for the Demand of Legislative Rationality' in LJ Wintgens and AD Oliver-Lalana (eds), *The Rationality and Justification of Legislation: Essays in Legisprudence* (Dordrecht, Springer, 2013).

Skorkiaer Binderkrantz, A, 'Legislatures, Lobbying, and Interest Groups' in S Martin, T Saalfeld and KW Strom (eds), *The Oxford Handbook of Legislative Studies* (Oxford, Oxford University Press, 2014).

Stabile, G, 'Camillo, Giulio, detto Delminio' in *Dizionario Biografico degli Italiani*, Vol 17 (Roma, Istituto dell'Enciclopedia italiana, 1974).

Tega, W, 'L'unità del sapere e l'ideale enciclopedico nel pensiero moderno' in W Tega (ed), *L'unità del sapere e l'ideale enciclopedico nel pensiero modern: Antologia* (Bologna, il Mulino, 1983).

Thaysen U, 'Fraktionenstaat: Oder was sonst?' in P Haungs and E Jesse (eds), *Parteien in Krise?* (Köln, Verlag Wissenschaft und Politik, 1987).

Thiébault, JL and Dolez, B, 'Parliamentary Parties in the French Fifth Republic' in K Heidar and R Koole (eds), *Parliamentary Party Groups in European Democracies: Political Parties Behind Closed Doors* (London, Routledge, 2000.

Trapp, H, 'Orte der Versammlung' in Oesterreichische Gesellschaft fuer Architektur (ed), *Umbau 27 – Plenum. Orte der Macht. Sonderausgabe Biennale Venedig 2014* (Basel, Birkhaeuser, 2014).

Türk, P, 'Les commissions parlementaires et le gouvernement' in F Fraysse and F Hourquebie (eds), *Les Commissions parlementaires dans l'espace francophone* (Paris, Montchrestien, 2011).

Vidal-Naquet, A, 'La revalorisation du Parlement et l'équilibre au sein de l'exécutif. Vers un rééquilibrage au sein de l'exécutif?' in X Magnon, R Chevontian and M Stéfani (eds), *Pouvoir exécutif et Parlement: de nouveaux équilibres? L'impact de la révision constitutionnelle du 23 juillet 2008 sur le rééquilibrage des institutions* (Aix-en-Provence, Presses Universitaires d'Aix-Marseille, 2012).

Wells, HG, 'The Brain Organization of the Modern World. Lecture delivered in America, October and November, 1937' in HG Wells, *World Brain* (1st edn 1938) (North Haven, CT, Read Books, 2016).

—— 'World Encyclopaedia. Lecture delivered at the weekly evening meeting of the Royal Institution of Great Britain, November 20th, 1936' in HG Wells, *World Brain* (1st edn 1938) (North Haven, CT, Read Books, 2016).

William, M, 'The European Parliament: Political Groups, Minority Rights and the "Rationalization" of Parliamentary Organization. A Research Note' in H Doering, (ed), *Parliaments and Minority Rule in Western Europe* (Frankfurt, Campus, 1995).

Journal Articles

Anderson, E, 'The Epistemology of Democracy' (2006) 3(1–2) *Episteme* 8.

Asher, M, Leston-Bandeira, C and Spaiser, V, 'Do Parliamentary Debates of e-Petitions Enhance Public Engagement with Parliament? An Analysis of Twitter Conversations' (2019) 11(2) *Policy & Internet* 149.

Auel, K and Christiansen, T (eds), 'After Lisbon: National Parliaments in the European Union (2015) 38 *West European Politics* 261.

Barberia, L, Plümper, T and Whitten, GD, 'The political science of Covid-19: An introduction' (2021) 102 *Social Science Quarterly* 2045.

Bellamy, R and Kröger, S, 'The politicization of European integration: National parliaments and the democratic disconnect' (2016) 14 *Comparative European Politics* 125.

Blais, A and Loewen, P, 'The French Electoral System and its Effects' (2009) 32 *West European Politics* 345.

Blanchard, G and Olsen, M, 'Le système de renvois dans l'Encyclopédie: Une cartographie des structures de connaissances au XVIIIe siècle' (2002) 31–32 *Recherches sur Diderot et sur l'Encyclopédie* 45.

Bochel, C, 'Petitions Systems: Outcomes, Success and Failure' (2020) 73(2) *Parliamentary Affairs* 250.

Bolstad, E and Pettersen, SA, 'How to Build an Encyclopedia for the 21st Century: Lessons Learned from The Great Norwegian Encyclopedia' (2019) 13 *Studia lexicographica* 153.

Brian, E, 'L'ancêtre de l'hypertexte' (1998) 47 *Les Cahiers de Science et Vie* 28.

Brunet, P, 'Que reste-t-il de la volonté générale?' (2005) 114 *Pouvoirs: La Loi* 5.

Cammarano, F, 'Le notable à l'époque libérale' (2002) 114 *Mélanges de l'école française de Rome* 673.

Carman, C, 'The Process is the Reality: Perceptions of Procedural Fairness and Participatory Democracy' (2010) 58 *Political Studies* 731.

Chiantera-Stutte, P, 'Fiducia, interesse e consenso: riflessioni sulla rappresentanza in Edmund Burke' (2015) 29(I) *Giornale di storia costituzionale* 115.

Conrad, T, 'Balzac, l'épique et l'encyclopédique' (2016) 2 *Romantisme* 35.

Crapez, M, 'De quand date le clivage gauche/droite en France?' (1998) 48(1) *Revue française de science politique* 42.

Crum, B and Fossum, JE, 'The Multilevel Parliamentary Field: A framework for theorizing representative democracy in the EU' (2009) 1 *European Political Science Review* 249.

Debré, M, 'Trois caractéristiques du système parlementaire français' (1955) 1 *Revue française de science politique* 21.

Donato, C, 'Eighteenth-century Encyclopedias and National Identity' (1993) 4–6 *History of European Ideas* 959.

Ganzevles, J, van Est, R and Nentwich, M, 'Embracing Variety: Introducing the inclusive modelling of (Parliamentary) technology assessment' (2019) 1(3) *Journal of Responsible Innovation* 292.

Goldberg, AC, 'The evolution of cleavage voting in four Western countries: Structural, behavioural or political dealignment?' (2020) 59 *European Journal of Political Research* 68.

Goodsell, CT, 'The Architecture of Parliaments: Legislative Houses and Political Culture' (1988) 18 *British Journal of Political Science* 287.

Greer, SL, King, EJ, da Fonseca, EM and Peralta-Santos, A, 'The Comparative Politics of COVID-19: The Need to Understand Government Responses' (2020) 15 *Global Public Health* 1413.

Habermas, J, 'Remarks on Dieter Grimm's: 'Does Europe need a Constitution?' (1995) 1 *European Law Journal* 303.

Harris, I, 'What Was Parliamentary Reporting? A Study of Aims and Results in the London Daily Newspapers, 1780–96' (2020) 39 *Parliamentary History* 255.

Holbraad, M and Lamrani M, 'Revolutionary circles. A morphology of radical politics' (2021) 91 *Focaal – Journal of Global and Historical Anthropology* 1.

Holst, C and Molander, A, 'Public Deliberation and the Fact of Expertise: Making Experts Accountable' (2017) 31 *Social Epistemology* 235.

Hontebeyre, P, 'La fixation de l'ordre du jour prioritaire un pouvoir sans contre-pouvoirs' (1984) 34 *Pouvoirs: L'Assemblée* 13.

Hooghe, G and Marks, L, 'Unraveling the central state, but how? Types of multi-level governance' (2003) 97 *American Political Science Review* 239.

Horton, R, 'Offline: Why the Sustainable Development Goals will Fail (2015) *Lancet* 383(9936).

Jaeger, WP, Lyons, J and Wolak, J, 'Political Knowledge and Policy Representation in the States' (2017) 45 *American Politics Research* 907.

Jeanneau, B, 'L'antiparlementarisme d'hier à aujourd'hui' (1993) 64 *Pouvoirs* 23.

Jennings, W, Stoker, G, Valgarðsson, V, Devine, D and Gaskell, J, 'How Trust, Mistrust and Distrust Shape the Governance of the COVID-19 Crisis' (2021) 28 *Journal of European Public Policy* 1174.

Joana, J, 'L'invention du député: Réunions parlementaires et spécialisation de l'activité politique au XIXe siècle' (1996) 35 *Politix. Revue des sciences sociales du politique* 23.

Johnson, N, 'Opposition in the British Political System' (1997) 32 *Government and Opposition* 489.

Kaase, M and Klingemann, H-D, 'Social structure, value-orientations and party system' (1982) 10 *European Journal of Party Research* 367.

Kirchheimer, O, 'The Waning of Opposition in Parliamentary Regimes' (1957) 24 *Social Research* 127.

Koskimaa, V and Raunio, T, 'Encouraging a longer time horizon: The Committee for the Future in the Finnish Eduskunta' (2020) 26 *Journal of Legislative Studies* 159.

Langley, V, 'CRS at 100 – Informing the Legislative Debate Since 1914' (2014) 3 *Library of Congress Magazine* 14.

Le Beguec, G, 'Naissance et développement des groupes parlementaires sous la IIIème République' [2003] *Parlement(s): Histoire et politique* 1.

Leston Bandeira, C, 'The Impact of the Internet on Parliaments: A Legislative Studies Framework' (2017) 60(4) *Parliamentary Affairs* 655.

—— 'Parliamentary petitions and public engagement: An empirical analysis of the role of e-petitions' (2019) 47 *Policy & Politics* 415.

Livingston, WA, 'A Note on the Nature of Federalism' (1952) 67 *Political Science Quarterly* 81.

Luciani, M, 'L'antisovrano e la crisi delle costituzioni' (1996) 1 *Rivista di diritto costituzionale* 124.

—— 'Costituzionalismo irenico e costituzionalismo polemico' (2006) 4 *Giurisprudenza costituzionale.*

—— 'Itinerari costituzionali della memoria' (2022) 4 *Rivista AIC* 84.

Lupo, N, 'I regolamenti parlamentari nella I legislatura repubblicana (1948–1953)' (2008) 15 *Giornale di storia costituzionale* 117.

—— 'Le metamorfosi del Parlamento' (2019) 1 *Rassegna di diritto pubblico europeo* 1.

Manheim, K and Kaplan, L, 'Artificial Intelligence: Risks to Privacy and Democracy' (2019) 21 *Yale Journal of Law and Technology* 106.

Marcilla Córdoba, G, 'Argumentación jurídica y racionalidad legislativa en el Estado Constitucional' [2004] *Anuario de filosofía del derecho* 337.

Matthews, F, 'The value of "between-election" political participation: Do parliamentary e-petitions matter to political elites?' (2021) 23 *British Journal of Politics and International Relations* 427.

Mazzoleni, G and Schulz, W, 'Mediatization of Politics: A Challenge for Democracy?' (1999) 16 *Political Communication* 247.

Mendelson, E, 'Encyclopedic Narrative: From Dante to Pynchon' (1976) 91 *Modern Language Notes* 1267.

Miller, B and Stecker, C, 'Consensus by Default? Interaction of Government and Opposition Parties in the Committees of the German Bundestag' (2008) 17 *German Politics* 305.

Mirkine-Guetzévich, B,'Le régime parlementaire dans les récentes Constitutions européennes' (1950) 2–4 *Revue internationale de droit comparé* 605.

Morris, C, 'On the History of the International Encyclopedia of Unified Science' (1960) 4 *Synthese* 517.

Norton, P, 'Nascent Institutionalisation: Committees in the British Parliament'1988) 4 *Journal of Legislative Studies* 143.

Nybom, T, 'The Humboldt Legacy: Reflections on the Past, Present, and Future of the European University' (2003) 16 *Higher Education Policy* 141.

Orsini, A, Le Prestre, P, Haas, PM, Brosig, M et al, 'Forum: Complex systems and international governance' (2020) 22(4) *International Studies Review* 1008.

Palonen, K, 'Max Weber, Parliamentarism and the Rhetorical Culture of Politics' (2004) 2 *Max Weber Studies* 273.

—— 'A comparison between three ideal types of parliamentary politics: representation, legislation and deliberation' (2018) 1 *Parliaments, Estates & Representation* 6.

Pattberg, P, Kaiser, C, Widerberg, O et al, '20 Years of global climate change governance research: Taking stock and moving forward' (2022) 22 *International Environmental Agreements* 295.

Pizzorno, 'Opposition in Italy' (1997) 4 *Government and Opposition* 61.

Plümper T, Neumayer, E and Pfaff, KG, 'The Strategy of Protest against Covid-19 Containment Policies in Germany' (2021) 102 *Social Science Quarterly* 2236.

Pontier, JM, 'Le rôle des intergroupes au Parlement français' (1982) 32 *Revue française de science politique* 810.

Puschmann, C, Bastos, M and Schmidt, JH, 'Birds of a feather petition together? Characterizing e-petitioning through the lens of platform data' (2017) 20(2) *Information, Communication & Society* 203.

Rauh, C and Wilde Pieter, P de, 'The opposition deficit in EU accountability: Evidence from over 20 years of plenary debate in four member states' (2017) 57 *European Journal of Political Research* 194.
Raunio, T and Hix S, 'Backbenchers learn to fight back: European integration and parliamentary government' (2000) 23 *West European Politics* 142.
Rizzoni, G, 'Il parlamento dal moderno al contemporaneo' (2021) 1 *Diritto Pubblico* 241.
Romano, S, 'Sulla natura dei Regolamenti delle Camere parlamentari' [1905] *Archivio giuridico* 75.
Russell, M, 'What Are Second Chambers For?' (2001) 54 *Parliamentary Affairs* 442.
Sarasin, P, 'Was ist Wissensgeschichte?' (2011) 36(1) *Internationales Archiv für Sozialgeschichte der deutschen Literatur* 159.
Sarasin, P, 'More Than Just Another Specialty: On the Prospects for the History of Knowledge' (2020) 1 *Journal for the History of Knowledge* 1.
Senigaglia, C, 'The debate on democratization and parliament in Germany from 1871 to 1918' (2020) 3 *Parliaments, Estates & Representation* 290.
Stafford-Smith, M, Griggs, D, Gaffney, O et al, 'Integration: The key to implementing the Sustainable Development Goals' (2017) 12 *Sustainable Science* 911.
Strøm, K, 'Parliamentary Committees in European Democracies' (1998) 14 *Journal of Legislative Studies* 64.
Suteu, S, 'Constitutional Conventions in the Digital Era: Lessons from Iceland and Ireland' (2015) 38(2) *Boston College International and Comparative Law Review* 251.
Taagepera, R, 'Seats and votes: A generalization of the cube law of elections' (1973) 2 *Social Science Research* 257.
Urvoas, J-J, 'La lente mais irrépressible renaissance des commissions parlementaires' (2013) 146b *Pouvoirs: Le renouveau du Parlement* 21.
Verzichelli, L, 'I gruppi parlamentari dopo il 1994. Fluidità e riaggregazioni' (1996) 2 *Rivista italiana di scienza politica* 391.
Yeo, R, 'A Solution to the Multitude of Books: Ephraim Chambers's Cyclopaedia (1728) as "the Best Book in the Universe"' (2003) 1 *Journal of the History of Ideas* 61.
Yoshinaka, A, MCelroy, G and Bowler, S, 'The Appointment of Rapporteurs in the European Parliament' (2010) 4 *Legislative Studies Quarterly* 457.

Electronic

Acosta, M, Nestore, M, Jarquín-Solís, ME and Doubleday, R, 'A typology of advisory bodies in legislatures and research perspectives' [2019] *Journal of Legislative Studies* 1, available at: doi.org/10.1080/13572334.2022.2070985.
Anderson, R, 'The "Idea of a University" Today' (2010) *History and Policy. Policy Papers*, available at: www.historyandpolicy.org/policy-papers/papers/the-idea-of-a-university-today.
Austermann, P 'Die Entwicklung der Entschädigung und der Reisebezogenen Ansprüche im Deutschen Abgeordnetenrecht' (2014) 2 *Zeitschrift Für Parlamentsfragen* 270, available at: www.jstor.org/stable/24243398.
Bade, JN, 'The Magic Mountain of Weimar Politics: The Impact of the Assassination of Walther Rathenau on Thomas Mann's "Der Zauberberg"' (2014) 106(1) *Monatshefte* 37, available at: www.jstor.org/stable/24549905.
Le Beguec, G, 'Naissance et développement des groupes parlementaires sous la IIIème République' (2003) *Parlement(s). Histoire et politique*, available at:www.parlements.org/parlements/num0_7_LeBeguec.pdf.
Brudnick, IA, *The Congressional Research Service and the American Legislative Process, CRS Report to the Congress*, March 2008, 5, available at: ecommons.cornell.edu/bitstream/handle/1813/77742/RL33471_20080319.pdf?sequence=1.
Cheng, X, Lin, X and Shen, XL et al, 'The dark sides of AI' (2022) 32 *Electronic Markets* 11, available at: link.springer.com/article/10.1007/s12525-022-00531-5.
Congressional Research Service, Organizational Structure, available at: www.loc.gov/crsinfo/about/structure.html.
Deutscher Bundestag Drucksache 20/2200, 20. Wahlperiode, Bericht des Petitionsausschusses (2. Ausschuss): Bitten und Beschwerden an den Deutschen Bundestag; Die Tätigkeit des Petitionsausschusses des Deutschen Bundestages im Jahr 2021 (22.06.2022) available at: dserver.bundestag.de/btd/20/022/2002200.pdf.

Eliassen, KA and Pedersen, MN, 'Professionalization of Legislatures: Long-Term Change in Political Recruitment in Denmark and Norway' (1978) 2 *Comparative Studies in Society and History* 286, available at: www.jstor.org/stable/178050.

Esmark, A 'The technocratic take-over of democracy: connectivity, reflexivity and accountability', paper prepared for ICPP 2017, Singapore, available at: www.ippapublicpolicy.org/file/paper/594bba371f736.pdf.

Freedom House, *Freedom in the World 2022: The Global Expansion of Authoritarian Rule* (Washington, Freedom House, 2022), available at: freedomhouse.org/sites/default/files/2022-02/FIW_2022_PDF_Booklet_Digital_Final_Web.pdf.

Fulco, R, 'A political ontology for Europe: Roberto Esposito's instituent paradigm' (2021) 54 *Continental Philosophical Review* 367, available at: doi.org/10.1007/s11007-021-09542-z.

Fumagalli, C, 'Time and Democratic Deliberation' in KH Goetz (ed), *The Oxford Handbook of Time and Politics*, online edn (Oxford Academic, 4 April 2019), available at: academic.oup.com/edited-volume/35419.

German Ministry of Interior and Community, available at: www.bmi.bund.de/EN/topics/constitution/electoral-law/voting-system/voting-system-node.html

Hamm, KE, Hedlund, RD and Post, SS, 'Committee Specialization in US State Legislatures during the 20th Century: Do legislatures tap the talents of their members?' (2011) 11 *State Politics and Policy Quarterly* 299, available at: eds.s.ebscohost.com/eds/pdfviewer/pdfviewer?vid=6&sid=83bbecc8-21ae-463e-9545-dbf65a930faf%40redis.

Harrison, M, 'ChatGPT's explosive popularity makes it the fastest-growing app in human history' (*The Byte*, 3 February 2023) 2, available at: futurism.com/the-byte/chatgpts-fastest-growing-app-human-history.

Heezen, J and Marzocchi, O, *Achievements of the committee on petitions during the 2014–2019 parliamentary term and challenges for the future* (European Parliament Policy Department for Citizens' Rights and Constitutional Affairs, Brussels, 2020).

Hicks, E, 'MPs pay: the never ending controversy' in historyofparliamentonline.org, available at: thehistoryofparliament.wordpress.com/2013/12/09/mps-pay-the-never-ending-controversy/.

Hube, C, 'Bias in Wikipedia' in *Proceedings of the 26th International Conference on World Wide Web Companion (WWW 17 Companion)* (Geneva, International World Wide Web Conferences Steering Committee, 2017), available at: doi.org/10.1145/3041021.3053375.

House of Commons Liaison Committee, *The effectiveness and influence of the select committee system, Fourth Report of Session* (HC 2017–19) 1860, available at: publications.parliament.uk/pa/cm201719/cmselect/cmliaisn/1860/1860.pdf, 53.

House of Commons Library, *E-Petitions in the UK*, July 2019, available at:researchbriefings.files.parliament.uk/documents/CBP-8620/CBP-8620.pdf.

——*The Sewel Convention*, Briefing Paper CBP-8883 May 2020, available at: researchbriefings.files.parliament.uk/documents/CBP-8883/CBP-8883.pdf.

Inter-Parliamentary Union (IPU), *Informing Democracy: Building Capacity to Meet Parliamentarians' Information and Knowledge Needs* (Geneva, IPU, 2008), available at: www.ipu.org/PDF/publications/inform_dem_en.pdf.

—— Brazil, *A Digitally Mature Parliament*, June 2022, available at: www.ipu.org/news/case-studies/2022-06/brazil-digitally-mature-parliament.

—— *The state of open data in parliaments in 2022*, available at: www.ipu.org/innovation-tracker/story/state-open-data-in-parliaments-in-2022.

—— *World e-Parliament Report 2022* (Geneva, IPU, 2022), available at: www.ipu.org/resources/publications/reports/2022-11/world-e-parliament-report-2022.

Inter-Parliamentary Union (IPU) and the International Federation of Library Associations and Institutions (IFLA), *Guidelines for parliamentary research services* (IPU, Geneva, 2015), available at: www.ifla.org/files/assets/services-for-parliaments/publications/guidelines-for-parliamentary-research-services-en.pdf.

Inter-Parliamentary Union (IPU) and United Nations Development Programme (UNDP), *Global Parliamentary Report 2022. Public engagement in the work of parliament* (Geneva, IPU, 2022).

Julie Carriat and Mariama Darame, 'A l'Assemblée nationale, la Nupes à l'épreuve de la lutte des places' *Le Monde* (30 June 2022), available at: www.lemonde.fr/politique/article/2022/06/30/a-l-assemblee-nationale-la-nupes-a-l-epreuve-de-la-lutte-des-places_6132633_823448.html.

Macintyre, C, 'Parliamentary Architecture and Political Culture', paper presented as a lecture in the Senate Occasional Lecture Series at Parliament House, Canberra, 9 May 2008, available at: www.aph.gov.au/~/~/link.aspx?_id=3AB8830A90D34C71AB5337BF650579F9#_ftn25.

Murugesan, S and Cherukuri, A, 'The Rise of Generative Artificial Intelligence and Its Impact on Education: The Promises and Perils' (2023) 56(5) *Computer* 116, available at: www.computer.org/csdl/magazine/co/2023/05/10109305/1MET4MpWNZS.
OECD, *Innovative Citizen Participation and New Democratic Institutions: Catching the Deliberative Wave* (OECD Publishing, Paris, 2020), available at: doi.org/10.1787/339306da-en.
Portinaro, PP, 'Tecnocrazia' in *Enciclopedia Treccani delle Scienze Sociali* (1998), available at: www.treccani.it/enciclopedia/tecnocrazia_%28Enciclopedia-delle-scienze-sociali%29/.
Preece, WE and Collison, RL 'Encyclopaedia' in *Encyclopaedia Britannica*, available at: www.britannica.com/topic/encyclopaedia.
Rizzoni, G, 'Un nuovo tentativo di "stabilizzazione dell'opposizione": lo statuto della coalizione parlamentare dell'Ulivo' (2003) Associazionedeicostituzionalisti.it, available at: www.associazionedeicostituzionalisti.it/old_sites/sito_AIC_2003-2010/dibattiti/partiti/rizzoni-20030207.html.
Roncaglia, G, 'Encyclopedias and encyclopedism in the era of the Web' (2021) 12 JLIS.it, *Italian Journal of Library and Information Science* 69, available at: doi.org/10.4403/jlis.it-12757.
Rubio, R and Vela, R, 'Open Parliaments around the World. Open Parliaments Tools in Comparative Perspective' (2019) 49 Luiss School of Government Working Papers, available at: sog.luiss.it/sites/sog.luiss.it/files/WP%2049%20Rubio-Vela.pdf.
Schäfer, A and Merkel, W, 'The Temporal Constitution of Democracies' in KH Goetz (ed), *The Oxford Handbook of Time and Politics*, online edn (Oxford Academic, 4 April 2019), available at: academic.oup.com/edited-volume/35419.
Schmidt, JH and Johnsen, K, 'On the Use of the E-Petition Platform of the German Bundestag' (2014) 3 HIIG Discussion Paper Series, available at: ssrn.com/abstract=2444672 or dx.doi.org/10.2139/ssrn.2444672.
Solia, G, 'Notabili' in *Enciclopedia Treccani delle scienze sociali* (Roma, Istituto dell'Enciclopedia italiana, 1996), available at: www.treccani.it/enciclopedia/notabili_%28Enciclopedia-delle-scienze-sociali%29/.
Tony Blair Institute for Global Change, *A New National Purpose: AI Promises a World-Leading Future of Britain* (June 2023), available at: www.institute.global/insights/politics-and-governance/new-national-purpose-ai-promises-world-leading-future-of-britain.
United Nations, Resolution adopted by the General Assembly on 25 September 2015. Transforming our world: the 2030 Agenda for Sustainable Development, available at: www.un.org/ga/search/view_doc.asp?symbol=A/RES/70/1&Lang=E.
Weber, KM, Gudowsky, N and Aichholzer, G, 'Foresight and technology assessment for the Austrian parliament – finding new ways of debating the future of industry 4.0' (2019) 109 *Futures* 240, available at: doi.org/10.1016/j.futures. 2018.06.018.
Wikipedia, sv, 'Wikipedia: Five pillars', available at: en.wikipedia.org/wiki/Wikipedia:Five_pillars.
—— 'Gender bias on Wikipedia', available at: en.wikipedia.org/wiki/Gender_bias_on_Wikipedia.

INDEX

accountability, principle of 142, 145, 147
administrative apparatus
  Big Government 74, 89
  research services 8, 102
adversarial systems
  British party system 48–50
Agenda for Sustainable Development 123–124
Alexander the Great 11
Alexandria, Library of 11
alphabetic organisation
  arbor scientiarum 14
  Chamber's *Cyclopedia* 16, 27
  dictionaries 14
  Diderot and D'Alambert's *Encyclopédie* 20, 27
  egalitarian nature 15
  expansive reading facilitated by 18
  generally 14–15, 112
  indexes 63
  predominance in European encyclopaedism 16
Alsted, JH
  Encyclopedia septem tomis distincta 14
amateur politicians 55, 56, 72, 74
Anderson, R 25
anticipatory governance 138–139
arbor scientiarum 14, 20, 27–28
Arendt, Hannah 3
Aristotelian corpus, influence 11
ars inveniendi 14
artificial intelligence 115–116, 136, 143–144
authoritarianism, defending against 146

Bacon, F 149
  arbor scientiarum 14, 20, 27–28
  ars reminiscendi 14
Bagehot, W 30–31, 44, 57, 71, 82–83
Balzac, H de
  Comédie humaine 27
Bandeira, CL 130
Baranger, D 66–67
Barry, C 60
Barthes, R 27
Basile, E 47
Bayle, P
  Dictionnaire historique et critique 15, 16, 17, 19
  Nouvelles de la République des Lettres 15
Beccaria, C 67
Bentham, J 67
  Essay on Political Tactics 42, 62, 65
Berthélemy, J 93
Bible, encyclopaedic nature 27
bicameralism 99–101, 109
  federal systems 139, 147
Big Government 74, 89
Bildung
  cultural unity of, preservation 8, 21, 25
Bismarck, O von 71
black swan events 137
Blair, Ann 13
books *See also* **libraries**
  changing reading styles 16–17, 18
  desacralisation 16
  printed 12, 36
  prohibited 35
Borges, JL
  On Exactitude in Science 112
bourgeoisie
  bourgeois public sphere 8, 30–31, 32–37, 45–47
  bourgeois reading style 16
  encyclopaedias and 16, 143
  nineteenth century 34–35, 45–47
  parliaments and 30–31, 32–37, 45–47, 70
Braunfels, S 48, 92
Brazil
  parliamentary research services 104
  public consultations 134
budget offices 8
Burke, E 40–41, 42, 43, 56–57

Cambridge University
  Chamber's *Cyclopedia* 18
Camus, A-A 60
Canadian Senate 100
capitalism
  centralization of political sovereignty 32
Carducci, G 52
Carnap, R 110
Cavour, CB di 52
Chambers, E
  Cyclopaedia 10, 16–18, 27
  The Literary Magazine 17
chatbots 116
ChatGPT 116
Christo and Jeanne-Claude 48
Churchill, W 49–50
Cicero 13
citizens' assemblies 134

classics 11, 12
classification systems *See also* **organisation**
  arbor scientiarum 14, 20, 27–28
  Comte's system 26
  generally 16, 18–19
  parliamentary research services 104
cognitive representation, parliamentary 7, 44, 48–53, 69, 72, 146–147
Coke, E 61
Coleridge, ST
  Encyclopaedia metropolitana 15
committee system
  Big Government and 89
  Britain 56, 84, 96–97, 101, 133
  committees of inquiry 6, 56
  European Parliament 97–99
  France 77, 79, 93–94
  generally 121
  Germany 77, 91–92
  institutionalisation generally 88–90, 106
  Italy 81, 94–96, 137
  late modern reforms 137–139
  legislative bargaining 105
  party system and 77, 79, 89–90, 109, 144
  permanent specialist committees 73, 74
  professionalisation of politics 89–90, 107–109, 144
  research services 102, 104, 108
  specialisation and information-gathering 91, 107–109
  United States 90–91
communication sphere
  communication revolution 36
  expansion 4
  globalisation 120
  personalisation of political leadership 119, 144
Comte, A
  Cours de philosophie positive 24, 26
Conference of the Parts 124
Constant, B 34–35
Constitutional Courts 105–106
copyright, English law of 17–18
Covid-19 pandemic 3–4, 125, 135, 147
Craveri, B 35
critical encyclopaedism 15, 19
Croce, B 52
cross-referencing
  Chamber's *Cyclopedia* 18, 27
  Diderot and D'Alambert's *Encyclopédie* 21, 27
cube law 85
culture *See also* **Western European culture**
  cultural unity, preservation 8, 21, 22
  encyclopaedic interpretations in literature 26–27
  general culture, encyclopaedism and 11–13, 27
  national encyclopaedias 8, 21–24, 27, 28, 143
  public service broadcasters 113
customary law 66, 67
  British common law 68

debate
  British 'conversational style' 46, 50
  declamatory style 46
  nineteenth century rhetoric 56–58
  parliamentary space, articulation 46–47, 49–50
  principle of 145
  rational 72
Debré, M 93
decentralisation tendency in late modernity 121
Delacroix, E 61
Delminio, GC
  L'Idea del Teatro 13
democracy *See also* **representative government; suffrage**
  anti-democratic forces 4
  Athenian 41
  audience democracies 119–120, 147
  compound 122–123
  Covid pandemic 3–4
  democratic legitimacy 122–123, 141–142, 147
  direct 38, 41
  knowledge, processing 2, 6
  large-scale polities 41–42
  parliamentarism and encyclopaedism 3
  party democracy 119
  political conflict, parliaments' role 4–5, 148–149
  populist rejection of epistocracy 5
  public engagement 128–135
  shared 'explanations of the world' 4
  social fragmentation and 145–146
  split-level 122
  technocratic take-over 43, 108
  unifying function 6–7
  Wikipedia, participatory democracy 114
De Pretis, A 52
Detienne, M 46, 135
dictionaries
  Chamber's *Cyclopedia* 16–18
  dictionaries of arts and sciences 15–16
  encyclopaedias distinguished 16n
  Furetière's *Dictionnaire universel* 14, 16
  Harris' *Lexicon Technicum* 16
  historical 16
  universal 16
Diderot, D and D'Alambert, J le R
  critical encyclopaedism 15, 36
  Encyclopédie 7–8, 10, 14, 18–22, 25, 27, 47, 59, 149
dispositio 57–58
Disraeli, D
  Coningsby 36–37
doctrinaires 35, 43–44

education
educational purpose of encyclopaedias 11, 18, 25–26
electronic media programming 113
Humboldtian model 25–26
pedagogic function of representative government 44, 58, 61, 70
elected representatives
accelerated turnover 103
amateurs 55, 56, 72, 74
British Reform Acts 68, 70
Burke's 'natural aristocracy' 40–41, 42, 43–44, 46
decline in voter trust 117–119, 144
egalitarian status 57
French revolutionary assemblies 71
generalists 8, 29, 56, 58, 88
lawyers 56
liberal parliaments 8, 55, 56–58, 69–72
notables 8, 55, 73
party system *See* party system
performative role 118
professionalisation of politics 74, 88–90, 109
remuneration 88–89
seniority, decline 103
elections 43, 53
British Reform Acts 68, 70
constituencies 70
cube law 85
electoral reforms 69–70
electoral systems 70
European Parliament 86
first past the post system 85
France 79
intergroup coalitions 126
Italy 80
party systems and 83, 85
proportional electoral systems 70, 80
electorate
changing value orientations 117–119
echo-chambers, creation 120
volatility 119
electronic media
accessibility 113, 143
artificial intelligence 115–116, 136, 143–144
British Broadcasting Company 113
challenge presented by 28, 143
chatbots 116
communication with the people 135–136
digital encyclopaedias 113–114, 143
e-petitions 129–132
global monopolies in information mediation 114
human cognition, impact on 116
interactive public engagement 134–136, 146–147
internet 7, 28, 113–116, 120, 136, 143
network organisational model 113–114
pedagogic programmes 113
printed encyclopaedias replaced by 113, 114
public consultative procedures 129–132, 133
public engagement via interactive media 134–135
public service broadcasters 113
search engines 114, 143
semantic web 115–116
social media 119, 120, 133, 136
voter mistrust 118–119
Wikipedia 111, 113, 114–115, 143
worldwide web 7, 113–116
Encarta 113
Enciclopedia del diritto 114
Enciclopedia Einaudi 112
Enciclopedia Espasa 24, 112
Enciclopedia italiana 24
Enciclopedia Treccani 114
Encyclopaedia Britannica 22, 23
globalised market 111–112
instalments, publication in 23
monographic treatises 23, 28
New Encyclopaedia Britannica 112
online version replacing printed 113, 114
organisation 23, 112
encyclopaedias
accessibility 23–24, 112, 113, 143
Alsted's *Encyclopedia septem tomis distincta* 14
Bacon 14, 20, 27–28, 149
bourgeoisie and 16, 143
Chamber's *Cyclopedia* 10, 16–18, 27
contents, generally 15–16
cultural unity, preservation 8, 21, 22, 143
dictionaries distinguished 16n
Diderot and D'Alambert's *Encyclopédie* 7–8, 14, 15, 18–22, 27, 36, 47, 59, 149
digital 113–114, 143
educational purpose 11, 18, 20, 25–26
Enlightenment 16–18, 20–21, 27, 143
financing 17
genres 15–16
globalised market 111–112
humanistic 12–14
illustrations, use of 20, 112
meaning 10, 11, 12
mirror of knowledge, as 12, 14
mirror of their age, as 27
national 8, 21–24, 27, 28, 143
nineteenth century 8, 21–28, 143
origins 10–16
Pliny the Elder's *Naturalis Historia* 11
pocket editions 112
Renaissance 12–15, 27, 143
Scalich's *Encyclopaedia* 11
seventeenth century 15
size 28

specialist contributors 20, 23
speculum, as 12–13
summary and compendium of other works 17–18
twentieth century 28, 110–142
universalistic approach 112
encyclopaedic pattern processing
assumptions made by 8
Bacon 14
circular structure 3, 8, 14, 21, 27
Diderot, D and D'Alambert, J le R 14, 18–21, 25
meaning 3
encyclopaedism
arbor scientiarum 14, 18, 20, 27
components 14, 20, 61, 67
crisis of encyclopaedic parliaments 69–71
critical 15, 19
Enlightenment concept of legislation 67–68
general culture, idea of 11–13, 27
libraries 11, 16–17
meaning 10
Middle Ages 12, 143
modernity and 10
origins 3, 7–8, 10–16
parliamentarism and 3, 6, 27–29, 44, 69–70, 116–142, 143, 144
pre-modern 11–16
public sphere and 27–29
representative government 44
Western European culture 10–16, 25–27
Encyclopédie Methodique 15
Encyclopédie nouvelle 24
Engelsing, R 16
enkuklios paideia 11, 27
Enlightenment
American Founding Fathers 58
Code Napoléon 67–68
Diderot and D'Alambert's *Encyclopédie* 7–8, 15, 18–22, 27, 36
encyclopaedias 16–18, 20–21, 27, 143
legislation, concept of 66–68
reading style 16–17, 18
Republic of Letters 17, 20, 21–22, 27
e-petitions 129–132
epistocracy, reaction against 5, 129
Epstein, S 32
Erskine May, T
Treatise 32, 61–62, 63–64
Esposito, R 5
European Centre for Parliamentary Research and Documentation 103
European Commission 98, 141
European Parliament
committee system 97–99
compound democracy 122–123
Conference of the Presidents 87, 97
democratic legitimacy 122–123, 141–142, 147
elections 86
e-petitions 131
EU enlargement 88
Europeanisation of domestic policies 121–122
intergroup coalitions 127
Lisbon Treaty 98, 123, 141
Maastricht Treaty 141
national parties and 85–86, 88
national political systems and 87, 122–123, 141–142, 147
Next Generation Strategy 122
party system 85–88, 107, 122
public policies 122–123
rapporteurs 98
Research Service 102
Spitzenkandidaten 86
split-level democracy 122
trilogues 98
European Union
democratic legitimacy 122–123, 141–142
subsidiarity principle 141
executive role 7, 8, 74, 89, 92, 102–103, 125, 141, 144, 145

federalism 139–141
bicameralism 139, 147
centrifugal pressures 147
developing federalising capacity 147–148
expansion 121
flexibility 139–140
Germany 99
United States 99
Filangieri, G 67
Finland, Committee for the Future 138
Foster, N 48
Framework Convention on Climate Change 124
France
1791 Constitution 39–40
Affaire Dreyfus 51
Algerian war 78
anti-parliamentarism 72
Bibliothéque du Corps législatif 60–61
birth of modern political representation 37–40, 45–46
Chamber of Deputies 51
Code Napoléon 67
committee system 77, 79, 93–94
Comte's *Cours de philosophie positive* 26
Conference of the Presidents 78, 79, 80
Constituent Assembly 36
Diderot and D'Alambert's *Encyclopédie* 7–8, 14, 15, 18–22, 25, 27, 36, 47
electoral system 71, 79
Encyclopédie Méthodique 22

Encyclopédie nouvelle 24
Estates General 37–38, 40, 45, 62, 69
fait majoritaire 79
Fifth Republic 79, 93
Fourth Republic 78
French Revolution 22, 30, 31, 36, 37–40, 50–51, 71
hemicycle parliamentary topography 8, 46, 48, 51, 69
intergroup coalitions 126, 127
Larousse 24, 112
National Assembly 31, 37–40, 45–46, 48, 50–51, 71, 77, 79
National Convention 46
nineteenth century bourgeoisie 34–36, 45–47
Palais Bourbon 46, 60–61
Paris salons 35
Parliamentary Assemblies 46
parliamentary library 60–61
parliamentary procedure 64, 80
party system 77–80, 106
President, election 79
public service broadcaster 113
republic of the parties 78
restoration and Orleanist monarchy 71
Right–Left orientation 50–52
saisine parlamentaire 79
Senate 100
suffrage 71
Tennis Court Oath 37–38
Third Estate 31, 37–40
Third Republic 71, 78
vote bloqué 79, 80
Whites and Reds 51
franchise *See* **suffrage**
freedom of speech 33, 57
free mandate doctrine 8, 30, 69, 73–74, 150
Furetière, A and Basnage de Beuval, B
Dictionnaire universel 14, 16

Gauchet, M 51, 71
Gaulle, C de 78–79
Gay, P 35
generalism
generalist elected representatives 8, 29, 56, 58, 88, 102
generalist parliaments 70
Gentile, G
Enciclopedia italiana 24
Germany
Allgemeine Encyclopädie der Wissenschaften und Künste 22
anti-parliamentarism 66
Bildung, Humboldtian model 25
Bismarck 71
committee system 77, 91–92
e-petitions 130
federal system 99, 140
Fraktionen 75–77
Frankfurt National Assembly 65
Humboldt's educational principles 25–26
Kleineres Brockhaus'sches Conversations-Lexicon 24, 112
Konversations-Lexicon 22–23, 112
nineteenth century bourgeoisie 34
Organstreitverfahren 76
parliamentary procedure 65–66
party system 75–77, 106
protected democracy 76
Reichstag building 47–48
research service 102
suffrage 71
Technische Hochschulen 26
Weimar Republic 75
Gisors, J-P 46
Gladstone, WE 59
globalisation
communication sphere 120
crisis of legislative rationality 125
designing global policies 150–151
market for encyclopaedias 111–112
monopolies in information mediation 114
public policy platforms 123–125
Goethe, JW von
Faust 26
Google 114
Great Britain *See* **United Kingdom**
Greek Parliament 102
Greek theatre 46
Guizot, F 43–44

Habermas, J 32, 87
Hammond, A
Treatise on the Practice and Proceedings in Parliament 63
Harris, J
Lexicon Technicum 16
Hatsell, J
Precedents of Proceedings … 62, 63
Hegel, GWF 148
Enzyklopädie der philosophischen Wissenschaften 24, 25
Hobbes, T 150
Holbach, PH D' 38–39
Hooker, J 44–45
humanism 12–14, 58
Humboldt, A von 25–26
Humboldt, W von 24, 25

Iceland 138
public participatory procedures 134
illustrations, use in encyclopaedias 20, 112

imagination
component of encyclopaedism 14, 20, 61, 67, 149, 150
knowledge and 20
political empowerment of citizenry 150–151
Indian Council of States 100
individualism
crisis of institutional representation and 117–119, 144
industrial revolution 32–33, 36
information processing *See also* **classification systems; encyclopaedic pattern processing; organisation**
artificial intelligence 115–116, 136, 143–144
by parliaments 3
global monopolies in information mediation 114
instalments, publication in 23, 24
institutions
nature of 1
relationship with knowledge 1–2
representative 1–2
International Encyclopaedia of Unified Sciences 110
International Federation of Library Associations and Institutions 103
internet *See* **electronic media**
Inter-Parliamentary Union 103
Ireland
public participatory procedures 134
Senate 100
Italy
anti-parliamentarism 72
Chamber of Deputies 47, 52, 80
cognitive map of national politics 52–53
committee system 81, 94–96, 137
connubio 52
constitutional monarchy 52
declaration of internet rights 134
Enciclopedia italiana 24
intergroup coalitions 127
legislative process 94–95
Library of the Chamber of Deputies 61
parliamentarism 31
parliamentary procedure 65, 81
'parliamentary revolution' 52
parliament for groups 82
party system 80–82, 106
public consultations 134
public service broadcaster 113
questione romana 52
research services 102
Right–Left orientation 52
Senate 100
suffrage 80
territorial autonomies 140–141

Jefferson, T 58, 59
A Manual of Parliamentary Practice … 62–63
Johnson, Ben 14
Johnson, Boris 84
Joly, J de 60–61
judicial review 105–106

Kleineres Brockhaus'sches Conversations-Lexicon 24, 112
knowledge
accessibility 18, 23–24, 26, 28, 113, 143
artificial intelligence 116, 136
classification *See* classification systems
cognitive representation 7, 48–53
collection 6
collective, sources of 5
communication sphere 4
critical encyclopaedism 15, 19
democratic institutions, aggregated by 6
Diderot and D'Alambert's *Encyclopédie* 18–21, 25, 27
digital infosphere 7, 113–114, 116, 143
electronic media *See* electronic media
encyclopaedic processing *See* encyclopaedic pattern processing; encyclopaedism
Enlightenment approach 18–19, 20–21
expansion 12–13, 28
external analytical capacity 138–139
fragmentation 4, 8, 9, 110–111, 112
general culture, idea of 11–13, 27
global monopolies in information mediation 114
humanistic approach 12–14
ideologies/collective intelligence 73
imagination and 20
implicit 19–20
institutionalisation 7
memory and 14, 20
nature of 1
open model 18
organisation *See* alphabetical organisation; organisation
pansophic approach 14, 18–19, 143
parliamentary functions and 2, 6
parliamentary libraries 11, 32, 58–61, 101–102, 103
parliamentary research services *See* research services
parliamentary ability to produce 2, 5–6, 69
political decision-making and 3–4
populist rejection of epistocracy 5
print reproduction systems 12, 36
processing 2
reason and 20
relationship with institutions 1–2
scenic representation 13–14
shared 'explanations of the world' 4

sources 17
specialisation 4, 8, 21, 23–24, 28, 89–90, 110, 112
visualisation 20
Kuhn, TS 110

Larousse 24, 112
legislation/legislative function
Britain 68
committee system 90
crisis of legislative rationality 125
customary law and 66, 67
drafting legislative texts 68
Enlightenment concept of legislation 66–68
independent regulatory authorities and 125
Italy 94–95
judicial review 105–106
legislative bargaining 105
legislative inflation 125
legislative rationality 32, 66–68, 105–106, 125, 150
nineteenth century 32, 68
party system and 105
pre-modern law-making 66
principles of encyclopaedism 67
rationality and systematicity 67
self-interested oligarchic groups 72
supranational authorities 123–125, 144, 147
United States 90
liberalism
generalist politicians 88
legislative function 66–68
liberal parliaments 5, 8, 30, 37, 55, 66–72, 88, 144
national encyclopaedias 22–23
nineteenth century rhetoric 56–57
notables 8, 55, 73
press 144
suffrage 35, 37, 43, 71–72
libraries
encyclopaedic ideal 11, 16–17
parliamentary 11, 32, 58–61, 101–102, 103
literature, encyclopaedic interpretations in 26–27
Lithuania 138
Loveland, J 15–16
Lullism 14

Machiavelli, N 58
Madison, J 43
magazines and periodicals
party system 33
press *See* press
prohibited 35
Republic of Letters 17
Mancini, M and Galeotti, U
Norme ed usi del Parlamento italiano 65
Manin, B 119–120
Manners-Sutton, C 59
March, J and Olsen, J 5
Mayer, J
Konversationlexicon 23
Melville, H
Moby Dick 26
memory
ars reminiscendi 14
component of encyclopaedism 14, 20, 61, 67, 149
knowledge and 14, 20
national political identity 47
parliaments as 'theatres of memory' 47–48, 149–150
treatises on parliamentary procedure 61–66
Mendelson, E 26
Miceli, V 65
Michels, R 108
militancy and the professionalisation of politics 72
Mill, J 34
Mill, JS 68, 71
mirror, concept of
encyclopaedias as 12, 14, 27
parliaments as 8, 70–71
modernity
birth of modern parliamentary representation 37–44
crisis of late modernity 116–142
encyclopaedia as invention of 10
individualism 32, 43, 117–119, 144
industrial revolution 32–33, 36
knowledge and political decision-making 3–4, 69
rise of modern state 32–33
Mohl, R von 65
monarchies, constitutional 40, 41, 52, 144
monocameralism 99
Montesquieu 41, 43, 101
Esprit des Lois 38
Moréri, L
Grand Dictionnaire Historique 15
Moretti, F 26
multilevel governance
centrifugal pressures 147
developing federalising capacity 147–148
European Union 87, 122–123, 141–142
federal systems 139–140, 141
flexibility 139–140
generally 144
Italy 140
Spain 140–141
UK devolved assemblies 140
Mussolini, B 24

national representation
modern parliamentarism 8, 30, 69, 150
nation-building
imagined community 31
national encyclopaedias 22, 28, 143

national political identity, parliaments and 47
parliamentary role 8, 28–29, 30–31, 44, 46, 69–70, 144
public service broadcasters 113
representative government 44
time, organisation 54

Neurath, O 110

Norway
Great Norwegian Encyclopedia 22

notables
liberal parliaments 8, 55, 73

organisation *See also* **classification systems**
alphabetic *See* alphabetic organisation
arbor scientiarum 14, 18, 20, 27–28
Chamber's *Cyclopedia* 18
Comte's system 26
cross-referencing 18, 20
Diderot and D'Alambert's *Encyclopédie* 20–21, 25
digital infosphere 7
Encyclopaedia Britannica 23
esprit de système, rejection 8, 19, 20
Hegel's *Enzyklopädie der philosophischen Wissenschaften* 25
hierarchical 20
illustrations, use of 20, 112
interdisciplinary 112
maps of knowledge 112
monographic treatises 22, 23, 28, 112
national encyclopaedias 28
network model 7, 113–114
search engines 114, 143
subject matter, by 14–15
unifying function 14–15

Ory, P 30

Ostrogorsky, M 84, 108

Paine, T 41–42

Palonen, K 157

Paraguay 138

Paris Agreement 124

parliamentarism
basic principles 8
encyclopaedic 3, 6, 27–32, 37, 143, 144
legislative rationality, concept of 32, 66–68, 105–106, 125, 150
modern 3, 5, 30–31, 37–44
rationalised 79
shifts in representation 3

parliamentary documentation
accessibility 135–136

parliaments
administrative apparatus 74, 89, 102
analytical capacity, enlarging 138–139
anti-parliamentarianism 66, 72
architecture 8, 45–50
bicameralism 99–101, 109, 147
bourgeois public sphere 30–31, 32–37, 45–47
Britain 33–34, 36–37, 38, 39–45, 48–50, 56
Burke's concept of 40–41, 56–57
chamber size 49–50
cognitive representation 7, 44, 48–53, 69, 72, 146–147
collection of knowledge by 6
communication with the people 42, 135–136
composition 30
contemporary democracies 2
crisis of institutional representation 117–119
deliberative machine, as 41
encyclopaedic 3, 6, 27–29, 37, 69–70, 116–142
expert 8
explanatory function 4
France 34–36
generalist 70
information, processing 2–3
knowledge, importance for 2, 6
knowledge produced by 2, 5–6
legislative function *See* legislation/legislative function
liberal 5, 8, 30, 37, 55, 66–72, 88, 144
libraries attached to 11, 32, 58–61, 101–102, 103
members *See* elected representatives
mirror of the Nation, as 8, 70–71
modern 30–31, 32, 37–44, 69
monuments, as 47–48
nation-building role 8, 28–29, 30–31, 44, 46, 69–70, 144
nineteenth century 30–37, 45–47, 55–72, 75, 144–145
oversight function 2
party/group system *See* party/group system
physical form 8
'political encyclopaedias', as 28, 30–32, 36
political pluralism 4–5, 6
political theatre, as 14, 31, 44–48, 56, 69
pre-modern parliamentary assemblies 30, 69
press, symbiosis with 33, 36–37, 70, 144, 145
procedural autonomy 30, 33, 150
publicness and separateness 28, 33, 37–46
representative role 28
responsive representation 7
space and topography 8, 45–46, 48–53, 74, 149
Speaker's position 46, 48–49
specialisation 56, 73
suffrage *See* representative government; suffrage
symbolic function 45–53, 69
technical support bodies 8
'theatres of memory', as 47–48
twentieth century 73–109
United States Constitution 41–43

party/group system
affiliated organisations 88, 108
bicameralism 100–101
Britain 33, 46, 49–50, 71, 82–85, 106, 126
changing value orientations and 117–119, 121
committee system and 77, 79, 89–90, 109, 144
continental model 85–88, 126
development 144
electoral systems and 83, 85
European Parliament 85–88, 107, 122
extra-parliamentary parties 78, 81, 82, 84–85
financing channels 72
fragmentation 5, 117–119, 145
France 77–80, 106
Germany 75–77, 106
ideologies/collective intelligence 73
institutionalisation 75, 77, 80–81, 85–86, 105, 106–107
intergroup coalitions 126–127
intermediary role of parties 107
Italy 80–82, 106
legislative bargaining 105
majority-opposition divide 4, 7, 33, 46, 49–51, 83, 90, 122, 126, 144
mandatory party membership 74
mass suffrage and 74, 75, 83–84, 144
nineteenth century 75, 144
ordering function 107
party democracy 119
party discipline 73, 83, 84
party functionaries 102, 108
party parliaments 5, 8, 33, 46, 49–50, 71, 72, 73–90, 106, 144
power to ban parties 75–76
press and 88, 108
professionalisation of politics 8, 55, 72, 74, 88–90, 107–109, 144
republic of the parties 78, 81–82
research and knowledge-processing structures 104, 107
specialisation and information-gathering 107
territorial roots 73, 85, 117
threshold requirements 76, 81, 84, 85
voter mistrust 117–119, 144
Peel, R 59
Penny Cyclopaedia 23–24
personalisation of political leadership 119, 144
petitions 129–132
Philippines 138
Pliny the Elder
Naturalis Historia 11
political conflict, role of parliament 4–5
political decision-making
knowledge and 3–4
science and 3–4
political elites
notables 8, 55, 73
structuration 55
political identity, sources of 5
political knowledge, production 69
political pluralism 4–5, 6
political theatre, parliaments as 14, 31, 44–48, 56, 69
populism
disintermediation of social demands 6–7
rejection of epistocracy 5
Portalis, J-E-M 67
post-truth strategies 4
Poudra, J and Pierre, E
Traité pratique de droit parlementaire 64
presidential systems
parliamentary research services 102–103
separation of powers doctrine 102–103
press
Britain 33, 36–37
party system and 88, 108
rise of parliamentarism and 33, 36–37
symbiosis with parliaments 54, 70, 144, 145
principle of difference 42–43
print reproduction systems 58
accessibility of knowledge 12, 36
parliamentary documentation 135
replacement by digital media 113, 114
procedural autonomy doctrine 30, 33, 150
procedure, parliamentary 57–58
dispositio 57–58
French reforms 80
Italian reforms 81
treatises on 61–66
professionalisation of politics
committee systems 107–109, 144
nineteenth century 56
party system 8, 55, 72, 74, 88–90, 107–109, 144
specialisation 88–90
twentieth century 73–109
proportionality, judicial review of 105–106
protest movements 118
Ptolemy II Philadelphus 11
public engagement
audience democracies 119–120, 147
citizens' assemblies 134
consultative and deliberative procedures 132–134
conventions and focus groups 134
digital interactive media 134–136, 146–147
enhancing 149
enlarging parliaments' cognitive basis 146–147
e-petitions 129–132
interactive relationships 128, 146–147
public policies
anticipatory governance 138–139
European Parliament 122–123

external analytical capacity 138–139
fragmentation 125
global organisations 123–125
global policies 150–151
new formats in late modernity 121–125, 137–139
scientific evidence shaping 125
self-organizing adaptive behaviour 125
short-termism 137–138
public sphere
audience democracy 119–120
bourgeois 8, 30–31, 32–37, 45–47
disintermediation 6–7, 9
encyclopaedism and 27–29
fragmentation 5, 6–7, 9, 117–119, 144, 145
late modern transformations 119–120
national encyclopaedias 8, 21–24, 27, 28
new forms of relationship with 135–136
parliamentary architecture 8, 45–50
parliaments' role 28, 32, 44–45, 144
political theatre 14, 31, 44–48, 143
press 33, 36–37, 54
Pugin, A 60

quadrivium 12

Rabelais, F
Gargantua 13
Rattazzi, U 52
reason
Code Napoléon 67
component of encyclopaedism 14, 20, 61, 67, 149, 150
Enlightenment concept of legislation 67–68
knowledge and 20
legislative rationality 32, 66–68, 105–106, 125, 150
rational debate 72
Redlich, J 56, 65–66
regionalism 121
regulatory authorities, independent 125
Regulatory Impact Analysis 132
representative government *See also* **elected representatives; parliaments; suffrage**
adaptation and innovation 126–128
birth of modern 37–41
Burke's 'natural aristocracy' 40–41, 42, 43–44, 46
closed representative paradigm 129
cognitive value 7, 44, 69, 144, 145, 146–147
communication with the people 42, 135–136
composition of liberal parliaments 8, 55, 56–58
crisis of 117–119
elections 43, 53, 68
encyclopaedic interpretation 44
Enlightenment concept of legislation 66
free mandate doctrine 8, 30, 69, 73–74, 150
individualism 32, 39, 43, 117–119
intergroup coalitions 126–127
legitimisation crisis 128
majority–opposition divide 4, 7, 33, 46, 49–51, 83, 90, 122, 126, 144
national representation principle 8, 30, 69, 150
nation-building 44, 46
party/group system *See* party/group system
pedagogic function 44, 58, 61, 70
performative aspect 118
political competence of representatives 43–44
principle of difference 42–43
public engagement 128–135
social fragmentation and 145–146
social pluralism and 116, 125, 126–128, 145
unifying function 6–7
voter mistrust 117–119, 144
Republic of Letters 17, 20, 21–22, 27
research services
classification of information 104
committee system 102, 104, 108
generally 8, 102
Germany 102
Greece 102
international 103
Italy 102
parliamentary committees 102, 104
partisan sources 104
presidential systems 102–103
public accessibility 104
separation of powers doctrine 102–103
United States 102
Right–Left orientation 50–52, 149
Roman libraries 11
Romano, S 65
Romilly, S
Reglemens observés dans la Chambre des Communes … 62
Rousselier, N 46
Royer-Collard, P-P 35

Salvemini, G 52
Sarkozy, N 79–80, 93
Sarsfield, Comte de 62
Saward, M 118, 127–128
Scalich, P
Encyclopaedia 11
Schmitt, C 68, 145
science and politics, conflict 3–4
sectarian governments 83
separation of powers doctrine 91, 102
Shakespeare, W 14, 58
short-termism 137–138
Sieyès, E-J 38, 39–40, 43
Smellie, W
Encyclopaedia Britannica 23

social pluralism, political representation and 116, 125, 126–128, 145
space, parliamentary
architecture 8, 45–50
British Parliamentary topography 46, 48–50, 83, 149
cognitive maps, as 48–53, 69, 72
European Parliament seating organisation 85
fixed disposition of seats 51, 52
hemicycle 8, 46, 48, 51, 69, 74
Italian Chamber of Deputies 52
party systems 8, 45–46, 48–53, 74, 85
political theatre, as 14, 31, 44–48, 56, 69
Right–Left orientation 50–52, 149
symbolism 45–53, 69, 143
'theatres of memory', as 47–48, 149–150
verbal exchange, effecting 46–47, 49–50
Spain
comunidades autonómas 140
Enciclopedia Espasa 24, 112
specialisation
committee system 91, 107–109
fragmentation of knowledge 110–111, 112
parliamentary committees 73, 74, 89–90
party system and 107
professionalisation of politics 88–90
specialist knowledge 4, 8, 21, 23–24, 28
speculum
encyclopaedia as 12–13
suffrage 35, 37, 43, 55, 144
British Reform Acts 68, 70, 83
France 71
Italy 80
liberal bourgeoisie 70–71
party system and 74, 75, 83–84, 144
political expectations and 71–72
restrictions 37, 39, 43, 70–71
universal 71
support staff
United States 91

technical support bodies 8
Tennis Court Oath 37–38
territorial representation
party system 73, 85
second chambers 99–100
Thiers, A 61
time, organisation
cyclicity 53–54
division of powers and 54–55
elections 43, 53
nation state, formation 54
pre-modern parliaments 53
synchronicity 53, 54
Tolstoy, L
War and Peace 26
trivium 12
Türk, P 94

Ukraine, war in 125
United Kingdom
1922 Committee 84
backbenchers 83
birth of representative government 32–33, 36–37, 38, 40–42
British Broadcasting Company 113
Cabinet 84
Chamber's *Cyclopedia* 10, 16–18, 27
Chartist movement 130
committee system 56, 84, 96–97, 101, 133
common law 68
confidentiality of parliamentary proceedings 45
copyright law 17–18
devolved assemblies 130, 134, 140
electoral system 83
Encyclopaedia Britannica 22, 23, 112
e-petitions 131–132
Erskine May 32, 61–62, 63–64
executive accountability 83
frontbenchers 49, 83
Glorious Revolution 40
government and Parliament, fusion of powers 49–50
House of Commons, cognitive map 48–50
House of Commons Library 59–60, 104
House of Lords 99, 100, 101
individualism 32, 39, 43
industrial revolution 32–33, 36
influence of British Parliament 56
legislation 68
monarchy and Parliament 40, 41
Nationalist parties 85
opposition parties 46, 49–51, 83
Parliament 33–34, 36–37, 38, 39–41, 44–45, 46
parliamentary procedure 32, 61–64
Parliamentary topography 46, 48–50, 149
party system 33, 46, 49–50, 71, 82–85, 106, 126
party whips 83, 84
Penny Cyclopaedia 23–24
petitions 129–130
press 33, 36–37
Prime Minister 49
public consultations 133
Reform Acts 68, 70, 83
rise of modern state 32–33
St Stephen chapel 48–49
Sewel Convention 140

Speaker 48
suffrage 68, 70, 83
United Nations 123–124
United States
American Constitution 41–43
committee system 90–91
Congressional Research Service 102–103
Connecticut compromise 99
federal system 99, 140
Founding Fathers 42, 58
Jefferson's *Manual* 62–63
Legislative Reference Service 102
Library of Congress 11, 58–59, 102
partisan information sources 104
presidential form of government 91
Senate 100
separation of powers doctrine 102–103
universities
Chamber's *Cyclopedia* 18
Humboldtian model 25–26
Urbinati, N 150
Uruguay 138
verbal exchange *See* **debate**
Vico, GB 114
Vienna Circle 110

Weber, M 3, 55, 66, 88, 89
Wells, HG 110–111, 151
West, W 14
Western European culture *See also* **culture**
Bildung 25–26
changing value orientations and 117–119
cultural unity, preservation 8, 21
early modern 12–14
encyclopaedic interpretations in literature 26–27
encyclopaedism 10–16, 25–27
scenic representation 13–14
Wikipedia 111, 113, 114–115, 143
accurateness 115
continuous updating 114–115
contributors and sources 114
neutral point of view 115
Wilson, W 90
World Bank 123

www.ingramcontent.com/pod-product-compliance
Ingram Content Group UK Ltd.
Pitfield, Milton Keynes, MK11 3LW, UK
UKHW050944290926
15470UKWH00005B/1629

9 781509 963911